CHICAGO PUBLIC LIBRARY
HAROLD WASHINGTON LIBRARY CENTER
030859968

D1000533

FORM 125 M

The Chicago Public Library

Received July 3, 1972

Errata

In the illustration insert following page 160, on pages eight, eleven, and twelve, "Mrs. Abingdon" should read "Mrs. Abington."

THE DRAMATIC COBBLER

THE DRAMATIC COBBLER

The Life and Works

of

Isaac Bickerstaff

Peter A. Tasch

Lewisburg
BUCKNELL UNIVERSITY PRESS

© 1971 by Associated University Presses, Inc.
Library of Congress Catalogue Card Number: 77-159838

Ref
PR3318
B4
Z9

Associated University Presses, Inc.
Cranbury, New Jersey 08512

R 822
B472Yt
Cop. 1

30859968

ISBN: 0-8387-7937-9
Printed in the United States of America

THE CHICAGO PUBLIC LIBRARY
JUL - 3 1972 B

To
MILDRED A. MARTIN
The Best of Teachers

CONTENTS

FOREWORD

By

Geo. Winchester Stone, Jr.

The modern heyday of scholarly research and publication on the London stage of the eighteenth century continues. To the useful and entertaining volumes we now have on audiences, records of performances, texts, genres, acting, architectural structures, lighting, heating, costume, finance and actor biography comes Mr. Peter A. Tasch's thorough and well-documented book on one of the most successful of play-doctors of the period. One seldom gets such a full and detailed view of the art of fitting plays for the theatre or for the early popularization of English theatrical musicals. The title *Dramatic Cobbler* is aptly taken from Francis Gentleman's characterization of Bickerstaff's essential work.

As a mender of plays, or one who helped fit or renew them for the stage, Bickerstaff had to possess a quick understanding of public taste, and this he could not get from reading the critics alone. Somehow he felt the pulse of the theatre-going public with remarkable accuracy. Mr. Tasch discusses in packed, but readable detail some 22 productions by Bickerstaff—his sources, his competition, his successes and his few failures. The range of his discussion carries him in the history of performances well down into the nineteenth century, and across the water to the Americas, as well as across genres. One is glad to have not only the account of Bickerstaff's major successes in such works as the musicals *Love in a Village, The Maid of the Mill,* and *The Pad-*

lock, but also the history of his treatment of *The Plain Dealer, The Hypocrite,* and *The Recruiting Serjeant.*

One is here constantly kept in the presence of the work-a-day theatre, as well as of some of the almost anonymous forces that made it work. And the major anonymity is probably Bickerstaff himself, so little is known about him. One feels, however, that Mr. Tasch has assembled, analyzed, and assimilated all that is to be known about this successful "cobbler" and tragic individual. In doing both tasks Mr. Tasch has set forth clearly the operating procedures of a man alert to the demands of the theatre's patrons in what Matthew Arnold called the "elegant and indispensable eighteenth century."

PREFACE

Although music has always been present on the British stage, its presence has frequently been begrudged by suspicious critics on the watch for possible immorality, or its close kin, mere frivolity. The importation of Italian opera at the beginning of the eighteenth century, popular as it was, rarely pleased its critics, who believed that it confirmed their distrust: they found it at best ridiculous and at worst downright vicious. Thus, when *The Beggar's Opera* championed home-grown melodies and burlesqued the imports, critics applauded, but only until they scented immorality behind the tunes. Ballad opera, because of its inevitable satiric content, and because of its dependence on an already established body of music, flourished for not more than a generation. In contrast, Italian opera at the King's Theatre outlived its carping critics. Occasional musical afterpieces and operatic versions of plays by Shakespeare, as well as *The Beggar's Opera,* were produced at the two legitimate theatres during the 1740s and 50s, but neither manager encouraged the writing of new English operas. This situation drastically and permanently changed in the decade 1760–1770, and the man primarily responsible for the dramatic revolution was Isaac Bickerstaff.

To the disgust of the critics and the applause of the audiences, he proved that English lyrics could be wedded to Italian-inspired music to create the first successful English comic operas. At first Bickerstaff doubted that English words suited Italian music, but his own successes persuaded him otherwise. Covent Garden, willingly, and Drury Lane, belatedly and reluctantly, produced his musicals at the expense of tragedies and comedies. Later writers were to maintain the form and content Bickerstaff's comic operas had established until the time of Gilbert and Sullivan. Bickerstaff was discouraged from attempting innovations in content by conservative audiences on whom he depended for his livelihood, and changes in form were thwarted when Bickerstaff's career unexpectedly ended in 1772. At that time he was experimenting with short operas, but rumors of his homosexuality forced him to flee the country.

In addition to his comic operas, Bickerstaff adapted Restoration and other comedies at Garrick's request, and worked as his general assistant at Drury Lane. Though he helped found a short-lived journal, and was at work on a subscription edition of fables when he fled, Bickerstaff's importance is as the introducer and popularizer of comic opera on the English stage. Until now there has been no study of his career.

My interest in Isaac Bickerstaff began simply enough because of his name. The DNB assured me that he was not a descendant of *The Tatler,* and my own confidence beguiled me into believing that I could learn about him during one summer. At that time I was a Harvard Junior Fellow, and the treasures of Widener and Houghton libraries were open to me. There is probably a point where research becomes compulsive rather than scholarly; if so, I passed it unknowingly and found myself unable to stop work on Bickerstaff. No lead was too small to hunt down; no scholar too august to beseech for information. The Society of Fellows enabled me to travel to England and then to France.

I suppose that from a practical point of view I should have worked on a "major figure," but by the time I realized that, I was hooked. I wish that I could write that in this book the reader will find the complete life and death of Bickerstaff, or even enough material to know what he was like as a human being. Considering how many people have so generously aided me, I find the results disappointing; but my disappointment is outweighed by my gratitude to those who put aside their own problems to help me with mine. I mention some of them in appropriate footnotes, but I wish to thank the following here: The Society of Fellows, Harvard University; my wife, Alison, who cannot type, but who did everything else; Barry L. Hillman, who unselfishly stopped work on his biography of Bickerstaff and sent me his findings; Helen D. Willard, Curator, Theatre Collection, Harvard College Library, who proves that a collection is only as good as its curator, thus making the Harvard collection one of the best; Harry R. Beard; George Winchester Stone, Jr.; Dorothy E. Mason of the Folger Shakespeare Library; Brinley Rhys; James L. Clifford; George J. McFadden, who read an early draft and whose advice led to revision; Arthur H. Scouten, whose careful reading and advice prevented many mistakes, no matter how many of mine still remain. To librarians who helped me, especially when all too often the desired material did not exist, my deepest appreciation; to the Public Records Office (London), the Irish Genealogical Society, The Society for Theatre Research, and the Garrick Club, my thanks for material I could not otherwise have found.

ACKNOWLEDGMENTS

Part of Chapter 6 first appeared in different form as "Bickerstaff, Colman and the Bourgeois Audience," RECTR, 9 (May 1970), 44–51. Material on *The Sultan* (Chapter 13) appeared as "Garrick's Revisions of Bickerstaff's *The Sultan*," *PQ*, 50 (January 1971), 141-149.

Illustrations are reprinted by permission of the Harvard Theatre Collection, Harvard University.

THE DRAMATIC COBBLER

1

IS THERE A MR. BICKERSTAFF?

In a story by Hugh Walpole a critic visits a small island off the Cornwall coast to meet a man named Bickerstaffe, but when he reaches what he thinks is the right house and asks for him, he is told, "There isn't any Mr. Bickerstaffe."

The answer appears to apply also to the two most famous Bickerstaffs of the eighteenth century, but for different reasons. The Isaac Bickerstaff who bested the astrologer Partridge was a fiction created by Swift, Congreve and Steele; but the real Isaac Bickerstaff (1733–1808?), who wrote some of the most popular plays of the century, eventually did his best to disappear—and succeeded. He, who fled from England and changed his name, would have been content to say, "There isn't any Mr. Bickerstaff."

For an author who proudly added "Esquire" after his name, who associated with most of the leading London artists of the 1760s, and who established comic opera in England, Isaac Bickerstaff gives his critics very little autobiographical data. If the playwright suffered from jokes about his name, he did it quietly; nor did any of the jibes at him after he fled associate him with his "namesake." In an age when almost every other playwright, poetaster, author, politician, and gentleman sat for a portrait, there is not even a caricature to show that Bickerstaff existed. During a time when the private lives of writers were bruited about in the monthly journals, and "Green-Room" gossipmongers publicized the careers of the performers at Drury Lane and

Covent Garden, when one man's affair was another man's anecdote, and ladies paid to have their memoirs included in novels, the lack of gossip about Bickerstaff is astounding. His self-effacement was so complete that until now less has been known about him than, say, his fellow Irish dramatist, the eccentric Paul Hifferman who never revealed where in London he lived.

Bickerstaff's comic operas were good theatre rather than great literature, but their effect on the London stages of the 1760s was revolutionary. When Bickerstaff arrived in London in 1755 the theatres were showing nothing that a playgoer absent for twenty or more years would find strange. Thanks to its actor-manager, David Garrick, the playgoer would have seen a new kind of acting at Drury Lane; but he would have encountered nothing new at Covent Garden, where John Rich was still producing pantomimes—old, new and "revised." Neither manager successfully encouraged departures from successful forms, and in Garrick's case shrewd commercial conservatism and superb acting combined to discourage experimentation by the dramatists. Although each of the patent theatres "brought new sets of dancers from abroad, increased the singing and music, and put on new attractions,"[1] in 1755 what was new was not innovative. John Brown's *Barbarossa* was Drury Lane's most ambitious serious play, while at Covent Garden, John Rich revived "some twenty-one older plays" (Stone, 436). Although *The Beggar's Opera* continued to be performed at both theatres, the vogue for ballad operas had peaked twenty years before.

Ten years after Bickerstaff arrived, the state of the theatres was remarkably different. At Drury Lane three of the four new mainpieces were operas, and at Covent Garden the two new mainpieces were both comic operas. Of these five operas, only Bickerstaff's *The Maid of the Mill,* which was performed twenty-nine times during its first season, was successful. The conclusions are twofold: comic opera had become fashionable, but only Bickerstaff could successfully fashion it. He had imitators during the 1760s—Cumberland's *The Summer's Tale* played five nights in December 1765—but none of their works was as popular as his. Nothing better illustrates Bickerstaff's effect on the London stage than to see what kinds of plays were being produced at Covent Garden in 1755, and what it was presenting in 1765 after Bickerstaff had written *Thomas and Sally* (an afterpiece), *Love in a Village,* and *The Maid of the Mill* for that theatre:

	January–December, 1755	January–December, 1765
Tragedies (including Shakespeare):	75 nights	32 nights
Shakespeare's Histories:	9 nights	5 nights
Comedies (including Shakespeare):	85 nights	71 nights
Musical mainpieces (including operas and oratorios):	15 nights	81 nights
	(184 nights)	(189 nights)

Of the 81 nights devoted to musical mainpieces during 1765, 48 were productions of Bickerstaff's comic operas. He was so successful that Drury Lane, unable to compete with him, hired him away from Covent Garden.

Between 1760 and 1772, Bickerstaff suffered only one operatic failure (*Love in the City*), but his successes were played at both London patent theatres, summer houses, throughout the provinces, and in Scotland, Ireland and the colonies. London's pleasure gardens, for example Vauxhall, Marylebone and Ranelagh, produced his "entertainments," popular singers were delighted to perform his songs, and music anthologies printed them. In addition to his comic operas, Bickerstaff successfully revised two once-popular comedies, Wycherley's *The Plain Dealer* and Cibber's *The Non-Juror*. (For dates and casts of first-night and other performances, see Appendix A.)

The London stage was a small world during the time Bickerstaff wrote for it. The patentees and their companies, the dramatists and the critics who published in the London newspapers and journals, or in pamphlets of their own devising, frequently jostled one another as they changed roles. For instance, the dramatist Hugh Kelly was also the critic-author of *Thespis,* a poetic accounting of performers and writers at both houses, and an editor of *The Public Ledger*. Garrick wrote, acted, and directed plays for Drury Lane, the theatre which he owned in partnership. Players turned memoirists retailed green-room gossip, and reviewers hacked for newspapers in which theatre managers held stock. Few of those involved in the London theatres played only one role.

Critiques of plays and performances were therefore often nothing more than free advertisements, or condemnations of a rival's work. Above the puffs and spiteful attacks, however, there was a considerable amount of criticism which took its task seriously. Critics—anonymous, pseudonymous, or by name—who attempted to deal with plays as literature inevitably rested their judgments on three bases: morality, pragmatism, snobbery. The kind of morality respected was of the conventional variety, which condemned socially unequal marriages, elopements, sexual innuendoes. Conventional too was the base of pragmatism: there was a very unwilling suspension of disbelief when it came to operas. Finally, no critic found anything funny in anything *low*. The servant-filled gallery might like it, but not so anyone with *taste*. The critic was the arch-Tory of the theatrical world, and with few exceptions (notably, William Hazlitt) the critic was equally Victorian whether he was writing in the 1760s or the 1860s. He saw his responsibility as that of improving the taste of the audience while correcting the improprieties of the dramatist. The criticisms that encumbered Bickerstaff's plays throughout their careers will be seen to adhere to these three criteria.

It was not as though Bickerstaff had set out to turn eighteenth-century critical precepts upside-down. His plots were conventional and borrowed, and his characters were familiar. Despite the novelty of comic opera, and its attendant unacceptability to critics as dramatic literature, Bickerstaff saw himself less as an innovator than as a domesticator: he was taming a continental genre to domestic tastes. His music was Italian, and whenever possible he attacked his audience's preference for simply arranged English and Scottish melodies. His argument was snobbery—home-grown music was "low." But here, however, patriotic snobbery defeated Bickerstaff's cultural snobbery. As for those critics who saw Bickerstaff's comic operas inculcating immorality among the unwary, nothing but a closed theatre could satisfy them. Instead, Bickerstaff depended upon his best critics, his audiences, to guide him. To the despair of the critics who were trying to educate them, Bickerstaff continued to entertain them. Only when he satirized his audience (in *Love in the City*), or when he tried to educate them about music—in short, when he was a critic—did he lose them. He regained his audiences by giving them the conventional, sentimental stories they enjoyed, and relegating his lectures to Prefaces and other publications.

Bickerstaff's major comic operas (*Love in a Village, Maid of the Mill, Love in the City, Lionel and Clarissa*) are variations on standard comedy situations. There is the war between generations: the sons and daughters insist upon choosing their marriage partners despite the wishes of their parents. Disguises: handsome young men in the houses where pretty young girls live invariably turn out to be suitors rather than what they pretend to be. Elopements: One of the two couples in each play either plans to or does elope. Old Maids or crotchety mothers: every play has one or the other, and she is always shown up, usually by the younger generation. Bickerstaff could work with stock situations and characters (fops, witty servants, old bachelors and the like) with competent professionalism, and though he upset critics by presenting elopements onstage or suggesting economic miscegenation, there is little in his comic operas—*Love in the City* excepted—which makes them outstandingly comic. It is the opera part of comic opera that raises Bickerstaff's plays above the average. Not a composer himself, he had the talent to write words for already composed music, and the taste to select which music would be most appropriate for his plays. His songs were carefully integrated into the plays, and before later prima-donnas and composers added songs at whim, the music and the dialogue were carefully balanced.

But Bickerstaff's twelve-year reign in the London theatres ended abruptly when he fled the country. The reason for his flight was simple: homosexuality was an offense punishable by death. Afraid that he was to be publicly labeled a homosexual, and unwilling to risk arrest and conviction, Bickerstaff fled to France in 1772 and thus lost all chance to defend himself. The accusation was made, the proof was offered, and for all practical purposes, Bickerstaff was no more.

The typical attitude toward the exiled Bickerstaff was expressed in the *Biographia Dramatica* of 1782 which also formed the basis for all subsequent accounts of his life:

> A native of Ireland, and for some time one of the most successful writers for the stage. He was probably born about the year 1735, having been appointed one of the pages to Lord Chesterfield, when he was Lord Lieutenant of Ireland, in 1746. He was once an officer of marines, but left the service with circumstances which do not reflect credit on him as a man. He is said to be still living at some place abroad, to which *a deed without a name* has banished him, and where he exists poor and despised by all orders of people.[2]

When the *Biographia Dramatica* of 1812 was published, it simply reprinted the information, and its concluding sentence has been taken to mean that Bickerstaff was alive in 1812. However, there is no definite death date, and accounts of his death began in 1772 and continued to 1816. His birth date, though, and some additional background have been found.

Isaac John Bickerstaff was born on 26 September 1733, probably in Dublin.[3] His father, John, was the Deputy to the Groom Porter, Sackville Bale.[4] The office had been established by Charles II in 1674, and the Porter had "full power and authority to assign, nominate, appoint, and license such persons as he should think good, to have, maintain, and keep bowling alleys, bowling greens, tennis courts, or any other games hereafter to be invented in such places within the city of Dublin, and elsewhere in the kingdom of Ireland, where the same might be most conveniently kept and used, for the honest and reasonable recreation of good and civil people . . . and to have the care and oversight that no dice-maker should make or sell any false dice, nor suffer any to be sold nor used in gaming in the said places tolerated, nor elsewhere in Ireland."[5] When the Earl of Chesterfield, then Lord Lieutenant of Ireland, suppressed the office in 1745, John Bickerstaff received a pension, and his son Isaac became one of Lord Chesterfield's pages.

Dublin, in Bickerstaff's youth, was a singing city, and his preference for Italian music was formed then. Musicians such as the Italian composer Geminiani and his pupil the English violinist Matthew Dubourg both played there, and Dubourg gave private lessons from 1737 to 1741. Handel lived there during 1741–1742, and as a result of Handel's visit,

> . . . the musical activities of Dublin were increased a hundredfold. . . . For a time Italian music was all the rage in Dublin. Castrucci, who had acted as conductor of Handel's band in England, came over to Ireland in 1750. He gave concerts at the Rotunda, and must have been very popular with his Irish audiences, for his funeral, which took place in Dublin in 1752, was attended by such crowds that the parish beadle of St. Mary's, where he was buried, was crushed to death.[6]

Thomas Arne and his wife Cecilia Young lived in Dublin from 1742 until the autumn of 1744, and again from October, 1755 to 1756;[7] and his brother-in-law, John Lampe, composed for Thomas Sheridan, the manager of the Capel-Street Theatre, during the late forties.

The two theatres of Dublin staged the popular London plays, which were often speedily pirated to Ireland. Popular London actors and actresses—Theophilus Cibber, West Digges and Henry Mossop among them—appeared on Dublin stages. And there were music halls on Crow Street and Fishamble Street, with the proceeds from concerts performed there going to charity. In short, Dublin was much less the provincial city it later became.

It was the Dublin of the 1730s and 40s that formed Bickerstaff's tastes, and as one of Lord Chesterfield's pages he had the opportunity to mingle with Dublin's fashionable society. When he was twelve years old, Bickerstaff gained a commission in the Fifth Regiment of Foot, the Northumberland Fusiliers, from Chesterfield who was leaving Ireland. On 29 October 1745, Bickerstaff was listed as an ensign in the regiment then commanded by Major-General Alexander Irwin.[8] Twelve was not an uncommonly young age, considering that Irwin's own son was made an ensign at the age of eight and was a full lieutenant by nine. Then too, "The appointment of officers to regiments on the Irish Establishment" at this time "was practically in the hands of the Lord Lieutenant. Unless the Sovereign or the Minister in power had any candidate the recommendation of the Irish Viceroy was accepted."[9] Bickerstaff was promoted to second lieutenant in 1746. While he remained in the Fifth Regiment, he enjoyed noble protection. In December, 1750, Chesterfield wrote to the Duke of Dorset, Cranfield Sackville, "Isaac Bickerstaff, whose family was known to your Grace at Dublin, and particularly to Mr. Bayle [Sackville Bale, the Groom Porter?], was my fourth page. He is now a second lieutenant, and I beg leave only to recommend him to your general protection."[10]

During the ten years in which Bickerstaff served as second lieutenant, the Fifth Regiment remained at Kinsale, Ireland. But in 1755 the regiment shipped to England, landing at Bristol in March of that year. And Bickerstaff came into some money: before leaving Ireland, he sold his share in a Trust begun by his father, to his sister Catherine for £200.[11] On 23 August 1755 Bickerstaff resigned his lieutenancy and went on ensign's half-pay.[12] Half-pay amounted to £1 12s 6d per week, no inducement for early retirement; but with £200, and this small pension, Bickerstaff moved to London with the idea of becoming a writer.

His first work, *Leucothoë,* a dramatic poem, was published but never performed, and by 1758 Bickerstaff was sufficiently broke to join the marines as a second lieutenant in the 91st Company, Plymouth Marine Corps, on 26 March 1758. Socially as well as financially this was a step downward from his lieutenancy in the army. Marines in the literature of this period are always shown as dividing their time between gluttony and sleep. Few marines could rise above the rank of captain, which was equal to lieutenant in the Navy, and none above the rank of major. They were seldom men of either birth or talent. Bickerstaff served from 26 March 1758 to 1 May 1763 when, with the proclamation of peace after the Seven Years' War, the Corps was reduced from 135 companies to 70. Plymouth Orders of 1 May 1763 state:

> The following Officers are to be placed on half-pay at once—22 Captains, 54 First Lieutenants and 60 Second Lieutenants, the juniors of each ranks being placed on the half-pay list.[13]

Bickerstaff, who was in France on 1 May 1763,[14] was one of those officers so placed. Had he left the marines in any way other than honorably he would not have received his pension, a pension which he continued to receive for the next 45 years.

While he was in the marines, he wrote the short comic opera *Thomas and Sally,* with music by Thomas Arne, and the oratorio *Judith* with the music again by Arne. Their success as collaborators and the popularity of *Thomas and Sally* encouraged them to create the most successful comic opera of the century, *Love in a Village*. Although Bickerstaff was never solvent for long, with the success of *Love in a Village* in 1762 he no longer had to consider the armed services as a possible career. He spent his time and his money until 1772 in London and France, often borrowing £50 and more from Garrick toward the end of his career. Apparently he was sufficiently in debt when he fled the country for it to be thought that he went over the water to escape creditors.[15]

Although two new works by Bickerstaff were produced at Drury Lane after 1772, his flight effectively prevented him from realizing any profit from them, and for all practical purposes, his career ended when he fled. Before he died—perhaps as late as 1816—Bickerstaff was reported to be living in France, Italy, and finally back in London; but always in poverty.

2
"A USEFUL LESSON TO THE FAIR SEX": *LEUCOTHOË, THOMAS AND SALLY*

With Dublin and the army behind him, Isaac Bickerstaff found himself in London in 1755; and in the best of tradition, he was young, alone, and ambitious to be a writer: within a year he was to have his first work published, critically acclaimed, and commonly ignored. *Leucothoë* indicates that he was hopeful of being more than a grub-street author, for almost any other genre, a town eclogue for instance, or a novel, would have been more profitable than this pastoral opera or "Dramatic Poem," as he termed it in his Preface. And instead of writing a panegyric to the esteemed David Garrick, he went out of his way to war with him.

Garrick had produced *The Fairies,* an operatic mishmash of *A Midsummer Night's Dream*—with songs from Shakespeare, Milton, Waller, Dryden, Lansdown, and Hammond, and music by John Christopher Smith—on 3 February 1755.[1] Bickerstaff probably arrived in London after the last spring performance on 10 March, but the opera was revived on 7 November 1755, and of course was published. Bickerstaff was furious at the idea of turning Shakespeare's plays into operas, and when Garrick produced an operatic version of *The Tempest* on 11 February 1756, he attacked such "barbarity" in his Preface to *Leucothoë.* Whatever were the faults of his work, Bickerstaff said it was "under-taken and pursued with a laudable design."

The ridiculousness [Bickerstaff wrote], not to say barbarity, of turning

SHAKESPEAR'S plays into operas, and larding them with songs from quite different authors, as hath been lately practised upon our most justly approved theatre, is, I apprehend, of so glaring a nature, that every one, who is endued with the smallest spark of taste, must immediately be struck with it. It is indeed the same thing, as if any person should take it into his head to reduce one of our antient Gothick cathedrals to a modern summer-house, and ornament it with designs from Halfpenny's Chinese architecture! Such is the devastation and overturning! Such are the breaks and patches![2]

From architecture Bickerstaff turned to the dining-room table.

There is no man in England . . . who has greater respect for a piece of beef ["A thing to which Shakespear has been more than once compared," he explained in a footnote.] than I have; but should I therefore like it cut into mince meat, and mixed with my custard and apple-pie? Certainly, no: the impropriety of the olio would then disgust me. So do the vigorous lines of SHAKESPEAR, when I meet them hashed up, with Waller and Cowley, in the luscious compositions of a musical entertainment. (vi-vii)

Having disposed of any attempts to adapt Shakespeare for English opera, Bickerstaff asked, ". . . what occasion is there that we should have English operas at all?"

Let any common lover of musick go but once to the King's theatre in the Haymarket, and he will easily perceive, that the Italian composition does, and must, with all its inconsistencies, for ever excel any thing we can produce of the like nature; and this, not for want of abilities in our composers, but thro' the insuperable disadvantages of our language. Had I seen any of their musical dramas before I undertook this, LEUCOTHOË should never have been written. . . . (vii)

Before Bickerstaff's career was abruptly ended, he was to write in a Preface to a collection of music by Italian and French composers the opposite of the foregoing paragraph:

It has often been said indeed, that our Language is too hard, and rough, to admit of a Union with those graceful and delicate Sounds; but this is a meer Common-place Observation, without any Ground in Reason or Fact; which some late Attempts, to apply English Words to Italian Music on the Stage, have sufficiently destroyed; and the Editor makes no Doubt, the present Work will further prove the Futility of.[3]

Leucothoë was never set to music, and Bickerstaff had the poem published without "the graces of that harmony for which it was originally intended" (vii). He was concerned in his

Preface about what to call his poem. He lacked confidence to call it a *"Tragedie."*

> Opera he must not call it [Bickerstaff explained], because it should then end happily, which the disposition of his fable would not admit of: he therefore lets it go under the denomination of a DRAMATIC POEM. But because it is, save in that once instance of its catastrophe, an opera, he begs leave to subjoin what one of the first English poets hath written of that species of the drama . . . . (viii)

The Preface concludes with a lengthy excerpt from Dryden's Preface to *Albion and Albanius.*

Significantly, for musical precedent Bickerstaff went to Dryden for literary respectability, rather than to Handel or to Dryden's contemporary Purcell. For almost all of his dramas, he began from a literary basis, and added music; he was knowledgeable about music without being a composer.

Perhaps *Leucothoë* would have succeeded as an opera, but no composer was willing to take the chance. Dodsley published it in May 1756 for 1s 6d, but with two exceptions the poem went unnoticed by critics. The two who reviewed it praised it. The editor of the *Monthly Review, or Literary Journal,* Ralph Griffiths, wrote the longest review of a work by Bickerstaff ever to be published in that magazine.[4] The second notice appeared in the *Journal Encyclopédique,* 15 October 1756.

In nine pages, Griffiths wrote a careful explication of *Leucothoë,* concentrating on the propriety of specific passages, commenting on the beauties and blemishes as he came to them, and suggesting changes which Bickerstaff should have made. For instance, Griffiths wrote, "As the laws of the Opera require a happy ending, and admit of the marvellous, we could rather have wished that Apollo had brought *Leucothoë* to life [instead of changing her into a tree]; the one was as easy as the other." Griffiths had "perused [the poem] with some satisfaction . . . it is certainly more of a piece, than most of the motley Operas which of late have been represented on our theatres . . ." (p. 153).

> The Poem [Griffiths continued] under our consideration, has in a great measure answered our idea; the numbers are, in general, not only smooth, with the addition of rhyme, and happily varied to express the different passions, but nature, in describing those passions, is not violated, and the sentiments generally rise from the subject. (p. 153)

The French reviewer for the *Journal Encyclopédique* noted in his two-page article that although the poem had not been produced, it deserved that honor: *"L'Auteur a tiré un très-bon parti de ce suject qui étoit destiné a être mis en musique."* He might have agreed with Griffiths about the passions, but he phrased it differently: *"Les scènes d'amour entre Apollon & Leucothoë, sont très bien ménagées, & peut-être un peu trop naturelles. . . ."* He found Apollo lacking certain qualities which an urbane lover—let alone a God—should possess: "*. . . ensuite il est au-dessous du petit maître qui ne garde aucune bienséance*" (p. 115). Shrugging his shoulders at the end of Bickerstaff's poem, when Leucothoë became a tree and Clytie a stone statue, he asked, *"lequel des deux étoit le plus aise?"* (p. 116).[5]

The two reviews reveal more about their countries than about *Leucothoë,* but they were the only ones the poem received. David Baker in his *Biographia Dramatica* (1782) wrote, "The poetry of this little piece is pleasing, and the conduct of it ingenious" (II, 188), and that was its last notice. If Bickerstaff had hoped that publication of *Leucothoë* would bring him a composer-partner, he was disappointed. It did not even bring him much attention, and assuredly very little money. Two years after it was published, Bickerstaff joined the Marines.

Whatever else he did in the service, he found time to write the short comic opera *Thomas and Sally,* with music by Thomas Arne. When Bickerstaff and Arne collaborated, Arne had been writing theatre music for at least as long as Bickerstaff had been living; he had composed the overture and one song for Fielding's *Tom Thumb* in 1733. He left Drury Lane in 1759 to go to Covent Garden because Garrick had refused to hire one of his pupils, Charlotte Brent. When *Thomas and Sally* was first performed in 1760 at Covent Garden, Charlotte Brent played Sally. But how did Arne and Bickerstaff come to work together?

In retrospect, only the "why" of their joining forces is explicable. Unlike Arne, Bickerstaff could write a good libretto, something that Arne never learned to do. It must have galled Arne to have Garrick—no judge of music—tell him that:

> I have read y^r^ play & rode your horse, and I dont approve of Either—they both want that particular Spirit which alone can give pleasure to ye Reader & the Rider—When the one wants Wit, & ye Other ye Spur, they jog on very heavily—I must keep ye horse, but I have return'd you ye Play—I pretend to some little knowledge of the last, but as I am no Jocky, they cannot say that a Knowing one is taken in.[6]

Garrick endorsed the letter, "Designed for Dr. Arne who sold me a Horse, a very dull one, & sent me a Comic Opera ditto" (*Letters,* p. 1266). Perhaps armed with *Leucothoë,* a letter of introduction from a mutual friend in Dublin, and a certain amount of self-confidence, Bickerstaff met Arne and convinced him that they should work together. Conceivably, Bickerstaff wrote the play without even consulting Dr. Arne, submitted it to Covent Garden, and hoped for a composer. From his Preface to *Thomas and Sally* the collaboration might just have been that casual:

> He [Bickerstaff] wrote it merely to comply with the request of a theatrical person, whom he had an inclination to oblige; it was designed and finished in somewhat less than a fortnight; and his excuse for now suffering it to appear in print (and he really thinks such an excuse necessary) must be the nature of a musical entertainment, which requires, that the words should be put into the hands of the audience, who would otherwise find it impossible to accompany the performers in what they sing upon the stage. (pp. i-ii)

The story of *Thomas and Sally* marks no revolutionary departure in either theme or plot; rather it is conventionally sentimental. Sally is a pure young country lass who loves a patriotic, robust sailor, Thomas. While he is at sea, the villainous 'squire tries to seduce Sally, but despite the encouragement of a wicked old woman, Sally's virtue and the timely return of Thomas thwart him. Thomas and Sally go off to marry and—subject to the navy's ordering him back to sea—they will live pastorally ever after.

Thomas Arne's biographer has written that *Thomas and Sally*

> sounds very simple and ingenuous, but actually there is a great deal more in it than that, for in the hands of Isaac Bickerstaff, the characters and sentiments they express are delightfully exaggerated; Sally's virtue and Thomas's nautical and patriotic fervour are most amusingly overdrawn; and the words of the recitatives are ridiculous enough, which if sung in the proper spirit can produce a most ludicrous effect. (Langley, p. 68)

But this is a modern reaction, for one looks in vain for eighteenth-century critics who noticed the ludicrous effect. *The London Magazine,* for instance, thought the work, "Pretty and characteristical: But the merit of these little pieces rests on the musick and performance, which we do not doubt gave great pleasure."[7] For the critics, the main asset (setting aside the music) of *Thomas and Sally* was its didacticism:

> This piece being professedly written for music, has but little merit as a drama, except, that the virtue of *Sally* is proof against the offers of the *Squire,* who in point of fortune is her superior, which circumstance affords a very useful lesson to the female sex. It is set to music by Dr. *Arne*, with that taste and delicacy of expression so peculiarly natural to this great master.[8]

Three years later, the same writer, or an imitator, was still lecturing the "female sex":

> The Plot is extremely simple, and the Conduct of the Piece has little to recommend it, except in the instance of *Sally's* integrity to *Thomas*, who, though in an humble situation in life, rejects every tempting solicitation from the *Squire*, notwithstanding his importance and superiority; a circumstance, that affords a very useful lesson to the Fair Sex.[9]

Finally, if anyone needed to know exactly what that useful lesson was:

> The Incident, of *Sally's* withstanding the tempting solicitations of the *Squire*, and preserving her integrity to her absent lover, affords this very useful Lesson to the Female Sex, viz. that, plighted Faith should ever be preserved inviolate, and that Virtue in an humble station, is more noble and exalted, than Vice in the palaces of the rich and opulent.[10]

Despite these reviews, *Thomas and Sally* survived, and continued to be enjoyed in London and in the provinces. From its opening night, 28 November 1760, it was successful at Covent Garden where it was performed 25 times before the Spring 1761 season ended in April. After its first performance at Drury Lane on 9 April 1763 in a slightly altered form, it became part of the repertory at both houses. It was successfully performed in Dublin for the first time on 27 April 1761, and in Edinburgh on 19 January 1765.[11] Up to the Victorian era in Dublin, it was performed 104 times.[12] *Thomas and Sally* was the first of Bickerstaff's works to be performed in America, at the Southwark Theatre, Philadelphia, 14 November 1766.[13] On 2 October 1779 it was first produced in Kingston, Jamaica, by the American Company of Comedians who also performed it on 13 April 1784 at Montego Bay.[14] The printed version went through several editions and was anthologized.

In the twentieth century, *Thomas and Sally* was revived at the Lyric Theatre, Hammersmith, on 10 April 1926, and at other theatres both in London and New York during the 1930s. It became part of the Intimate Opera Company's repertory

(*Annals,* col. 249), and it has been recorded by that group.

When *Thomas and Sally* was first published, there was some difficulty in deciding what it was. It was registered at Stationer's Hall on 25 November 1760 by the publisher, George Kearsly, as "A Musical Entertainment as it is Performed at Theatre Royal in Covent Garden," and the same description follows the title in the printed edition. But Arne's copy of the music, which was registered on 31 January 1761, was called a "Dramatic Pastoral." When a stage historian who called himself a friend of Bickerstaff reviewed the play, he termed it a "Ballad Farce."[15] In this century, Langley referred to it as a "light opera" (p. 66), and suggested that in 1760 this kind of work was a novelty: "It was a real opera with the action carried on in recitative in the place of spoken dialogue. Since Purcell's DIDO AND AENEAS there had only been one attempt at grand opera in English; this was Galliard's *Calypso and Telemachus* produced in 1712. It failed . . . [because] the average Englishman . . . can only tolerate opera in comic form" (p. 69).

If the success of *Thomas and Sally* had depended on Bickerstaff's Preface to it, then the opera would not have lasted until the author's first night. He began his Preface to this, his first produced work, by writing:

> The public has made so little difficulty hitherto, in swallowing nauseous, or, at best, insipid verses, when they have been wrapped up in agreeable music; that to offer a word, either by way of defence, or apology, for the following trifle, seems altogether unnecessary.
>
> . . . .
>
> He [Bickerstaff] is no stranger to the whimsical prejudice, which inclines most people to measure the worth of dramatic pieces by their length; and because a musical entertainment is unavoidably the shortest of any, makes them, for that reason, deny its being capable of any degree of merit at all. (pp. i-ii)

Still, though his work is "neither a Tragedy, a Comedy, or even so much as a Comedy of two acts; he flatters himself, there are some few, who will not condemn it, merely because it is not, what it was not designed for. . ." (pp. ii-iii). After the first edition, Bickerstaff changed *Thomas and Sally* into a "Comedy of two acts" by dividing the work into acts instead of the original "Parts."

Bickerstaff's Preface was a mixture of bravado and diffidence —with very little of the latter. If critics insisted upon attacking his work, then, as he admitted in the Preface, "there are some as bad lines in it, as the worst dabblers in sing-song ever were guilty of; but he thought it needless to correct them, as everything of this kind must be castrated, in order to make it perfectly musical; and stretched and altered, to fit the shape of the stage" (p. iii).

"Thus far by way of Preface," which, Bickerstaff assured his readers, he had written only to please those who wanted their money's worth in a book. As for a Dedication:

> . . . in this place he would be understood to inscribe the following rhimes to those vagrant choristers, who, like the bards of old, sing verses about the public streets; and if, when they have thought proper to advance his ballads to a place in the *Chimney-sweeper's Garland,* the *Sweetheart's Delight*, or any other of their ingenious collections they should . . . be the means of rendering more reasonable in their demands those grinders of the muses, who have the conscience to expect six and thirty pretty songs in one book for a half-penny; he shall think the time and pains they cost him in composing, very well bestowed. (pp. iv–v)

Belatedly recognizing that he was not writing from a position of strength, Bickerstaff concluded by praising the music and the performance of his piece, and pleading to the critics that they "will suffer the insignificancy of this piece, to screen it from their cognizance; and that they will not attempt to break a butterfly upon a wheel" (pp. vi-vii).

On the opening night, 28 November 1760, the Covent Garden cast for *Thomas and Sally* (two tenors and two sopranos) was

The 'Squire	Mattocks
Thomas	Beard
Sally	Charlotte Brent
Dorcas	Mrs Vernon (the former Jane Poitier)

Beard and Mattocks probably changed roles because a 23 April 1761 playbill listed the 'Squire to be sung by Mattocks, and Thomas by Beard—for the first time.[16]

One performer who was not listed was Charles Dibdin, who joined Covent Garden as a singer and dancer in 1760. Dibdin acted in and also wrote much of the music for some of Bickerstaff's best plays. In various memoirs he also recorded his comments about Bickerstaff and his works. For instance, in his *A Complete History of the Stage* he wrote, "Some of the poetry is neat and lyric [in *Thomas and Sally*], for this author knew the art of writing for music; but whatever there is technical in it is completely false. I heard a sailor say, when he heard the expression, 'tack about and bear away,' 'why that's go out of the door, and go up the chimney' " (V, 259).

On the same night that Dibdin was receiving £1 10s for singing five nights in *Thomas and Sally,* Bickerstaff was awarded £85 6s in ready money and £12 18s from the sale of tickets given him by the theatre, £98 4s in all on the seventh night's performance (Stone, 828-829). As an apprentice author, in contrast, Bickerstaff made only about £25 for letting Kearsly publish the opera.

The publication and production of *Thomas and Sally* did not prevent Bickerstaff from continuing to tinker with the work. Between the first (1761) and third (1765) editions there are considerable additions, deletions and shiftings about of numbers for so short a work. Still further changes occur between the third and "A New Edition" printed shortly after 1767.[17]

As it was performed until after 1765, *Thomas and Sally* opened with the 'Squire and Huntsmen ready to hunt foxes. The 'Squire sang:

The ecchoing horn calls the sportsmen abroad,
  To horse, my brave boys, and away;
The morning is up, and the cry of the hounds,
  Upbraids our too tedious delay. (etc. p. 1)

In the "New Edition" the opera began more sentimentally with "Sally discovered spinning at the Door" of her cottage, singing:

My time how happy once, and gay!
  Oh! blithe I was as blithe could be:
But now I'm sad, ah, well-a-day!
  For my true love is gone to sea. (etc. p. 1)

In the earlier editions Sally's song appeared in Act I, scene ii and was preceded with Recitative:

In vain I strive my sorrows to amuse;
Stubborn they are, and all relief refuse:
What med'cine shall I fly to, or what art!
Is there no cure for a distemper'd heart? (I, ii, 2)

Both the original score and the first edition of the play gave the 'Squire another *carpe diem* air which followed Dorcas's attempt to persuade Sally to listen to the 'Squire:

Life's a garden, rich in treasure
  Bury'd like the seeds in earth;
There lie joy, contentment, pleasure,
  But 'tis love must give them birth.

That warm sun its aid denying,
  We no happiness can taste;
But in cold obstruction lying,
  Life is all one barren waste. (I, iv, 8)

In subsequent editions this song was omitted and replaced by the 'Squire's hunting song which originally opened the opera.

Act II always began with a patriotic song sung by sailor Tom; but in the two early editions, Thomas referred to the French with whom Britain was then at war:

From ploughing the ocean, and thrashing Mounseer,
  In old England we're landed once more;
Your hands, my brave comrades, hallo boys, what cheer!
  For a sailor that's just come a-shore?

Those hectoring blades thought to scare us, no doubt,
  And to cut us, and slash us—Morbleu!
But hold there, avast, they were plaguily out,
  We have slic'd them, and pepper'd them too. (Etc. II, i, 14)

The song ended patriotically with an optimistic view of the ship of state:

No quicksands endanger, no storms overwhelm,
  Steady, steady, and safe may she sail;
No ignorant pilots e'er sit at her helm,
  Or her anchor of liberty fail.

After the Seven Years' War Thomas's patriotism became more generalized and his song concluded with this pious stanza:

Then bless the king, and bless the state,
  And bless our captains all;
And ne'er may chance unfortunate,
  The British fleet befal;
But prosp'rous gales, where'er she sails;
  And ever may she ride,
Of sea and shore, till time's no more,
  The terror and the pride. ("New Edition," II, i, 11)

Bickerstaff and Arne were as uncertain about how to end their opera as they were how to open it. Both the first and the later editions ended with Sally and Thomas singing what the third edition numbered as the fourteenth air. It ended with the following admonition to British youths:

> Ye *British* youths, be brave, you'll find,
> The *British* virgins will be kind;
> Protect their beauty from alarms,
> And they'll repay you with its charms.

But this ending did not always satisfy, for in the first edition of the music, and with a slight difference, in the third edition of the play a brief scene was added between the 'Squire and Dorcas for the sake of a joke. "Scene VIII. The 'Squire in a Passion, Dorcas following":

> 'Squire: Pr'ythee, Dorcas, forbear;
> Dorcas: Pr'ythee, 'Squire, but hear,
> Nor make for a girl such a pother.
> 'Squire: But just in the nick,
> To be play'd such a trick,
> Say, what shall I do?—
> Dorcas: —Get another.
> 'Squire: Get another—But where
> Shall I find one so fair?
> Dorcas: In the next—tho' with this you miscarry'd;
> Leave your rival to grieve,
> Whom no change can relieve.
> 'Squire: What change can he wish for?
> Dorcas —He's marry'd. (3d edition [1765], pp. 21–22)

In the music, the last two lines read, "True, that change may be wished for / He's married." The opera then concluded with "a spirited country dance."

For those people who were unable to attend a performance of *Thomas and Sally* in London or elsewhere, the newspapers and monthly magazines printed liberal selections of the songs. And, as Bickerstaff scoffed in his Preface, there were numerous "ingenious collections" of music. In these anthologies, the songs varied from insipid pastorals to bawdy glees; with the increased number of comic operas produced after Bickerstaff's early successes, the books often included the favorite songs from them as well as from Vauxhall, Ranelagh, and the other pleasure gardens. Not everyone was pleased, however, for even as Bickerstaff railed against the English predilection for traditional ballads, others rebelled against the "modish insipidity of the age." John Aikin, for instance, haughtily dismissed comic opera, "that vile mongrel of the drama," and was contemptuous of its "mushroom growth."[18]

> We were concerned to find [Aikin wrote] that the more modern any collection was, it was remarkably the more deficient in poetical merit; so that a total decay of all taste for genuine poetry, in this pleasing branch of it, was to be apprehended. This we in great measure attributed to the fashionable rage for music, which had encouraged such a mushroom growth of *comic operas,* that vile mongrel of the drama, where the most enchanting tunes are suited with the most flat and wretched combinations of words that ever disgraced the genius of a nation; and where the miserable versifier only appears as the hired underling of a musical composer. (p. iv)

There would be no newly-popular songs in Aikin's anthology:

> The soft warbler, who fills up a vacancy of thought with a tune, in which the succession of words gives no idea but that of a succession of sounds, will here be much disappointed in meeting with the names of *Prior, Congreve* and *Landsdown,* instead of *Arne, Brent* and *Tenducci.* (p. ix)

Ten years later, an editor included songs by Bickerstaff in his collection along with songs by Aikin and his daughter, Mrs. Barbauld, which Aikin had first published anonymously. "A Collection of Songs, Chiefly such as are Eminent for Poetical Merit" (1782) followed the custom of dividing the songs into several categories: "Elegiac and Pastoral, Passionate and Descriptive, Comic and Humorous, and Anacreontic and Jovial." Four songs by Bickerstaff, three from *Thomas and Sally,* were included. The fourth song was one which Thomas might have sung:

Jolly true blues of the main,
  Well skilled in heaving the log,
Attend to a sailor's rough strain,
  Who sings of your favourite grog,
[Refrain] For grog is the liquor of life
  The delight of each true British tar;
It banishes sorrow and strife,
  And softens the hardship of war.

His vineyards the monsieurs may boast,
  And delight in the soup of a frog;
But too soon he shall find to his cost,
  That claret must yield to good grog.
    For grog is the, &c.

Each Saturday night that revolves,
  My messmate he gives me a jog;
The wife or the sweetheart he loves,
  He takes off a can of good grog;
    For grog is the, &c.

If Jove should as whilom descend,
  Of some female mortal a-gog,
His nectar he surely would mend,
  By mixing his liquor with grog.
    For grog is the, &c.

I heard an Hibernian declare,
  By Saint Patrick, tho' born in a bog,
That while he could see with an ear,
  No wine he would drink except grog.
    For grog, &c.

No danger our hearts can dismay,
  No terror we feel from a flog;
For what is a dozen a-day,
  To a double allowance of grog?
    For grog, &c.

Now war is declar'd, let's advance;
  May the flincher be hang'd like a dog;
Who strikes to Spain, Holland, or France,
  Is a stranger to freedom and grog.
    For grog is the, &c. (pp. 336–337)

Neither in *Thomas and Sally,* nor in any of the other comic operas by Bickerstaff, did it seem that he was the "hired underling of a musical composer," as Aikin wrote. On the contrary, even in this first opera where he was writing with the best composer of the period, Bickerstaff proved his ability as a song writer. Although he consistently complained of the difficulty of fitting English words to continental tunes in his other operas, eighteenth-century critics usually accepted the results with only perfunctory grumbling: they knew less about music than he did and contented themselves with appeals to authority and occasional mutterings to the effect that the roast beef of old England was good enough for them.

The boundaries of Bickerstaff's taste in music can be seen in Appendix *C* where all the composers whose music he used, the number of tunes (where known) of each, and the operas in which he put them, are listed. Bickerstaff's predilection for Italian music will be apparent.

Having written a dramatic poem and a short comic opera, Bickerstaff next collaborated with Thomas Arne on the oratorio *Judith,* which was produced on Friday, 27 February 1761 at Drury Lane. Musically Arne thought highly of *Judith,* for on the last page of his manuscript, now in the British Museum, he wrote "Laus Deo." The choruses of *Judith,* wrote Langley, "are . . . not only the most important part of the oratorio but the greatest music that ever came from [Arne's] pen. It is doubtful whether any other English composer ever wrote more grandly or more vigorously . . ." (p. 88). On the British Museum manuscript, Charles Dibdin wrote, "*Judith* is one of the noblest compositions that ever stampt fame on a musician."

Judith was performed twice more in 1761, on 4 and 5 March at Drury Lane. In 1762 it was sung on Friday, 2 April. On 29 February 1764 it was performed at the Chapel of the Lock Hospital in Grosvenor Place for the Benefit for a Public Charity. One of those who saw the performance was John Wesley who recorded his impression in his Journal for Wednesday, 29 February:

> I heard *Judith,* an oratorio, performed at the Lock. Some parts of it were exceeding fine; but there are two things in all modern pieces of music, which I could never reconcile to common sense. One is, singing the same words ten times over; the other, singing different words by different persons, at one and the same time. And this, in the most solemn addresses to God, whether by way of prayer or of thanksgiving. This can never be defended by all the musicians in Europe, till reason is quite out of date.[19]

At the King's Theatre on Friday, 15 March 1765, *Judith* was performed again. In addition to these performances, individual songs were sung at Covent Garden, usually during a Benefit: for instance, at Miss Brickler's Benefit on 16 May 1767, she sang "a favourite song from *Judith* accompanied by Dibdin, on a new instrument call'd Piano Forte" (Stone, 1247). This was the first public appearance in England for this instrument.[20]

For no reason very relevant to the occasion *Judith* was chosen by Garrick to be performed on Wednesday morning, 6 September 1769, the first day of his Shakespeare Jubilee at Stratford-on-Avon. *The London Chronicle* of Saturday, 2 September to Tuesday, 5 September 1769 printed a long excerpt from the oratorio in anticipation of the Jubilee, and named Bickerstaff as the librettist.

For the 1764 production, and subsequent ones, Bickerstaff provided a final chorus differing from the original. There are other changes; for instance, perhaps as a matter of decorum, the following speech by Judith was omitted in the 1764 edition:

When we were left together in the Tent,
There *Holofernes* lay, stupid with Wine:
Then came the Spirit of the Lord upon me,
And drawing from his Sheath his shining Faulchion
I smote him twice, and strook away his Head,
Which when my faithful *Abra* had received,
We pass'd unquestioned 'till we reach'd *Bithulia.* (p. 17)

The most thorough revision occurred at the end of the oratorio. As it was first written, the final Chorus dissatisfied Arne and Bickerstaff enough for them to drop it and incorporate Judith's final speech into a new Chorus. Originally the following speech and chorus formed the last scene:

Judith: Here, O ye Sons of *Jacob,* let us rest!
Yet since God heard you, when in sore Affliction
Ye sung a Hymn in Honour to his Name,
Joyful repeat it now; for to his Ear
Such Songs of Praise and Piety are sweet,
In grateful Clouds to Heaven they ascend
And fall again in Blessings on Mankind.
Chorus of Israelites.
Hear, Angels hear! celestial Choirs,
In Raptures catch your golden Lyres,
With us your Voices raise;
To him the first and last be given,
In lowest Earth, in highest Heav'n,
All Glory, Pray'r and Praise. (p. 22)

Without changing the thought of the final scene, Arne and Bickerstaff tinkered with it to increase the stature of the final "Grand Chorus":

Here, Sons of Jacob! let us rest;
And pour out from the pious breast
A hymn to reach th' Almighty's throne,
And draw his choicest blessings down.

O Lord our God, whose mighty Arm
Cou'd all thy heathen foes disarm;
With fell destruction driv'n:
To thee our grateful song we raise,

To thee our everlasting praise
In earth as 'tis in heav'n. (1764 edition, p. 16)

Since its first performance, *Judith* has excited little comment. Until Langley's biography of Arne, most musicologists—if they mentioned *Judith* at all—dismissed the oratorio as a post-Handel failure. Burney wrote that Arne's oratorios "were so unfortunate, that he was always a loser whenever they were performed." He did allow some praise in the form of a double negative:

> And yet it would be unjust to say that they did not merit a better fate; for though the choruses were much inferior in force to those of Handel, yet the airs were frequently admirable. But besides the great reputation of Handel with whom he had to contend, Arne never was able to have his Music so well performed. . . .[21]

George Hogarth quoted Burney and added that Arne's oratorios were unsuccessful. In this century there has been no great reevaluation of *Judith* except by Langley, who, agreeing with Dibdin, wrote that because of *Judith,* Arne deserves "a place among the hierarchy of great choral writers" (p. 88). Even this challenging statement has been ignored by a reviewer for *The Musical Times,* who, while writing of his enjoyment of *Thomas and Sally,* added that in *Judith,* Arne's "solos too often fall into a basic hymn-tuney style and his choruses are trite."[22] He also called Arne a "musical journalist," a term more polite than the one which Arne and his contemporaries, less concerned with euphemisms, employed: "crotchet-monger."[23]

It was as hack and crotchet-monger that Bickerstaff and Arne were to be most popular. Together they created the most successful comic opera of the century: *Love in a Village.*

3

"A TUNEFUL *CROTCHET*-LOVING AGE!": *LOVE IN A VILLAGE*

The two most important influences on the course of English light musical drama were *The Beggar's Opera* and *Love in a Village.* Gay's opera encouraged other English writers to look to their own country's musical resources rather than to imitate continental operatic models. At the same time, however, it allowed the playwright to dominate the composer; for if *The Beggar's Opera* parodied conventions of Italian operas, it also, by relying on traditional or previously written music, inhibited English composers from writing original music for their operas. The authors of ballad operas who followed Gay were men like Fielding, Lillo, Cibber, Charles Johnson, Coffey, and Henry Brooke —men who took advantage of a newly popular kind of drama, but who, like Gay, were not primarily musicians or composers. Composers were relegated to the role of "compiler" if they were employed by the authors of ballad operas or pasticcios.

By recent critical consent, *Love in a Village* has been accepted as the first comic opera, but in the eighteenth century the term was not often distinguished from ballad opera. For instance, John Burgoyne in the Preface to his comic opera, *The Lord of the Manor,* wrote

> I cannot easily bring myself to allow the higher branch of our Comic Opera, to be of foreign extraction. From the time the Beggar's Opera appeared, we find pieces in prose, with songs interspersed, so approaching to regular comedy in plot, incident and preservation of character, as to

> make them a distinct species from any thing we find abroad—and is it too much to add that the sense, wit, and humour to be found in some of them are sterling English marks by which we may claim the species as our own . . . ?[1]

He insisted that "the French have nothing upon their musical comic stage to compare as resembling comedy, with *Love in a Village,* or [Bickerstaff's] *Maid of the Mill* . . ." (Preface).

Charles Dibdin was another author who considered *The Beggar's Opera* and *Love in a Village* together because of the relationship of the music to the dialogue. "Those are ballad operas," he wrote, "and therefore the airs ought to come in as breaks to the dialogue." What determined the difference between ballad and comic opera was the quality and positioning of the songs rather than their origin:

> . . . in pieces constructed like [Bickerstaff's] *Maid of the Mill,* the songs are or ought to be of weight and consequence, and therefore the attention of the audience should be judiciously diverted by interesting and measured dialogue, in order to prepare for the effect of that song which is intended to wind it up, and at the end of which the performer, if possible, should always go off the stage.[2]

By the twentieth century, critics separated ballad from comic operas, usually commenting that the later form owed a large debt to the earlier, and also usually disagreeing about whether a particular opera was in fact ballad or comic. One critic whose word has been accepted is William J. Lawrence:

> Comic opera had its origin at Covent Garden in December 1762 with Bickerstaff's *Love in a Village,* which, in spite of the fact that it presented a patchwork plot set to patchwork music, attained a success and a long-sustained popularity unequalled save by *The Beggar's Opera.*[3]

The difference between ballad and comic opera is in the relation between the words and the music. In ballad operas, the familiar music was a vehicle for the lyrics, which frequently were satirical. All of the songs in ballad operas, no matter what were their lyrics, owed some part of their effectiveness to the surprise the audience must have experienced at hearing new words set to the old airs. The authors of these words used the music as a means to other than musical ends. The performers were not necessarily singers but actors who could manage a song with simply arranged lyrics.

Comic operas were written by authors and composers who

emphasized the music; the important roles were performed by singers who could be persuaded to act. More consistently than in ballad operas, the music in comic operas was utilized to illustrate character or help forward the story. Whether it was adapted or composed for the opera, the music rather than the words was the primary concern of the librettist and composer. Lawrence found the same points when he wrote:

> Though the prime differentiation of the early comic opera lay in the use of concerted music to carry on the business of the scene, the distinction between it and ballad opera was not so much one of form as of method. Ballad opera was designed for the player who could sing, comic opera for the singer who could make some attempt at acting. The latter demanded for its adequate representation some extension of the personnel of the theatre, practically an extra vocal staff. Outside London this proved a check to its immediate popularity and tended to prolong the life of ballad opera.[4]

Love in a Village represented the ABCs of comic opera for London in the early 1760s. It was written by Arne and Bickerstaff, produced by John Beard, who also sang in it along with Charlotte Brent, and performed at Covent Garden. This combination was too strong for its critics, and it overwhelmed the competition at Drury Lane, which was ill-prepared and unwilling to stage a full-length comic opera. As opposed to Covent Garden, which in 1762 employed fourteen singers, Drury Lane had only four.

Of the 42 songs in *Love in a Village,* Arne wrote five specifically for the opera ("Well Come Let Us Hear," though not marked, is his); Samuel Howard (1710-1782) contributed two. Music for the remaining songs was compiled by Edward Toms (according to Joseph Reed),[5] a musician who performed at Vauxhall, from previously written works by fourteen composers including Arne.[6]

Love in a Village was produced 37 times between its first performance on 8 December 1762 and 28 May 1763, the last performance by the Covent Garden company for the spring season. Bickerstaff received two Benefits in December, and in 1763 alone, the printed edition went through eight authorized editions and a pirated one.

In the treatment of *Love in a Village* by the press, Bickerstaff's luck was good—up to a point. As in his Preface to *Thomas and Sally,* Bickerstaff combined self-deprecation with arrogance. The newspapers accepted his low opinion of the opera "as a piece of

Dramatic writing," and usually followed his suggestion that they praise the music. But the point at which his luck turned bad was the Advertisement Bickerstaff added to his Prefatory remarks:

> It may not be improper to observe, that there is an Incident or two in this Opera, which bear some Resemblance to what may be found in a Piece called the *Village Opera,* written in the Year 1729, by *C. Johnson.*[7]

No one really minded plagiarism: the French had been plundered for years, and earlier English plays often reappeared in different guises. The charge of plagiarism was raised only when the critic had a personal animus against the plagiarist. It was Bickerstaff's minimizing the amount of plagiarism which antagonized his critics, not the thievery itself; most critics and writers took the attitude that success was its own excuse. As Dibdin wrote, "Every author has a right to imitate whatever he is capable of improving."[8] Bickerstaff's tactless understatement forced his readers to compare the two plays and to discover how much more than a "Resemblance" his opera bore to Johnson's. No one cared about his borrowing from Wycherley—from *The Gentleman Dancing Master* he took the idea of Lucinda's passing off Eustacc as a music master—but Bickerstaff was never allowed to forget his indebtedness to Johnson.

He might have arrived at Johnson's *Village Opera* by way of an adaptation of Dancourt's *Le Galant Jardinier.*[9] Dancourt's play was adapted by James Wilder and produced at Smock-Alley as *The Gentleman Gardener,* a ballad opera, around 1751. According to Kinne, "Wilder's piece . . . has more in common with *The Village Opera*" than with *Le Galant Jardinier.* For both Johnson and Bickerstaff, the ultimate source was *As You Like It,* with Rosalind being the ancestor for Rosella and Rossetta.

Bickerstaff's indebtedness to *The Village Opera* is difficult to exaggerate. The critic in *The Theatrical Review,* 1763, wrote, "Mr. Bickerstaff has borrowed (to give it no harsher appellation) his whole plot from The Village Opera . . . he has made equally free with the sentiments and language of that piece. . . ."[10] There are differences, of course, between the two operas, but there are far more similarities. In the songs and dialogue of *Love in a Village* Johnson's opera is once again performed. The opening song, a duet sung by Rossetta and Lucinda—and consistently praised throughout the comic opera's career—was adapted ("to give it no harsher appellation") from Johnson's fifth air sung by Freeman:

Rossetta

Hope! thou nurse of young desire,
["desires" in 2nd ed.]
Fairy promiser of joy,
Painted vapour, glow-worm fire
Temp'rate sweet, that ne'er can cloy:

Lucinda

Hope! thou earnest of delight,
Softest soother of the mind;
Balmy cordial, prospect bright,
Surest friend the wretched find:

Both

Kind deceiver, flatter still,
Deal out pleasures unpossest
With thy dreams my fancy fill,
And in wishes make me blest.
(Air I. I, i, 1)

Freeman

Hope, thou Nurse of young Desire
Fairy Promiser of Joy,
Beauteous Prospect, Glow-worm Fire
Delighting, never known to cloy.

Kind Deceiver, flatter still
Let me be in Wishes blest;
My Breast with fancy'd Pleasures fill
And Raptures, tho' in Dreams possess'd.[11]

In an unusual case of the mock-pastoral anticipating the model, Johnson's Lucas and Bickerstaff's Hawthorn both sing of their unrequited love:

Hawthorn

My Dolly was the fairest thing!
Her breath disclos'd the sweets of spring;
And if for summer you wou'd seek,
'Twas painted in her eye, her cheek.

Lucas

My Dolly was the Snow-drop fair,
Curling Endive was her Hair;
The Fragrant Jessamine, her Breath;
White Kidney-Beans, her even Teeth.

Her swelling bosom, tempting ripe,	Two Daisies were her Eyes;
Of fruitful autumn was the type:	Her Breasts in swelling Mushrooms rise;
But, when my tender tale I told	Her Waist, the straight and upright Fir;
I found her heart was winter cold.	But all her Heart was Cucumber.
(Air XXVI. II, ix, 43)	(*Village Opera,* p. 2)

Not only did Bickerstaff take over some of Johnson's lyrics, he also appropriated speeches. Young Freeman soliloquized in the garden about his love for Betty in the *Village Opera:*

> Let me examine myself—Wou'd I marry this Girl? No. Wou'd I make a Mistress of her? No. Two Things called Reason and Honour forbid them both. What do I then pursue? A Shadow: When I have her in my Possession, as I hope I shall soon, how am I to behave? My Blood rebels at the Question. There she is, and Rosella with her, on the Terrace—Oh my Heart! how it dances at the Sight. (p. 26)

Young Meadows also soliloquizes about his love:

> Well, would I marry her? would I make a mistress of her if I could? Two things, called prudence and honour, forbid either. What am I pursuing, then? a shadow. Sure my evil genius laid this snare in my way [Etc.]. (*Love in a Village,* I, iv, 9)

Sir Nicholas Wiseacre describes the effect Betty has on the country folk:

> She has bewitch'd all the Parish; every Tree in my Park has a Sonnet in Praise of her fix'd upon it, and her Name is graven by your Bone and Buck-handle Knives on every Bark; and those who cannot write, set their Marks there; so that my Trees are like to be stripp'd stark naked by these Lovers in Dowlas. (*Village Opera,* II, ii, 31)

Justice Woodcock speaks directly to Rossetta: "Have you a hankering after some lover in dowlas, who spoils my trees by engraving true lovers knots on them, with your horn, and buck-handled knives?" (II, viii, p. 40).

Beard himself, who played Hawthorn, and to whom Bickerstaff dedicated *Love in a Village,* must have been aware of the plagiarism as soon as he saw the opera in rehearsal, if not before, because in 1756 he had appeared in *The Villagers,* a farce afterpiece adaptation of *The Village Opera.* (It was a failure.) Despite the borrowings, Beard liked *Love in a Village* well enough to choose it for the opera in which he made his final appearance, 23 May 1767. If Beard overlooked the resemblances, certainly the critics did not.

The first attack on Bickerstaff's borrowing came in *The Theatrical Review* (1 January 1763). The critic agreed with Bickerstaff, who in his Prefatory address to Beard had remarked, "If this Opera is considered merely as a piece of Dramatic writing, it will certainly be found to have very little merit." The reviewer noted that "The author has prevented any criticism that could be made upon its merit . . . which, however it may be recommended for its modesty, is not less remarkable for being just" (p. 26).

The reviewer's irony was merely beginning:

> We could have wished, that Mr. *Bickerstaff* had dealt with equal candour in another place, where he informs the reader, 'That there is an incident or two in this opera, which bear some resemblance to what may be found in . . . The *Village Opera*. . . .' There is indeed a resemblance, and that with a witness, between the two pieces—*Mr. Bickerstaff's* is barely an alteration, and sorry are we to say it, an alteration very much for the worse from the *Village Opera*. (pp. 26–27)

For the remaining ten pages of the article, the writer exposed the wholesale borrowing from Johnson's work.

> Having been thus tediously exact in our comparison . . . we shall upon the whole observe, that Mr. *Bickerstaff* has not shewn all that candour in his acknowledgement to Mr. *Johnson,* which he would be thought to possess, and possibly so illiberal a freedom as he hath taken with the *Village Opera,* would not be suffered by an English audience, was it not that the injustice of the proceeding is hidden by the uncommon merit of the performers. (p. 36)

Despite these accusations of plagiarism, however, the incontestable fact remains that *The Village Opera* failed and *Love in a Village* succeeded. Johnson's opera was not even revived to take advantage of the popularity of Bickerstaff's play. Bickerstaff's work succeeded because it was better operatically, structurally and "sentimentally."

It was the music which kept *Love in a Village* in the repertory, sometimes to the despair of both theatre critics and critics of the theatre. When *Love in a Village* and *Maid of the Mill* were constantly being performed, the evangelist George Whitfield asked, "Why should the devil's house have all the good tunes?"[12]

Not only the audiences, but also the performers wanted *Love in a Village:* throughout the last part of the eighteenth century and the early decades of the nineteenth, singers chose this opera in which to make their debut:

> It would be a shame indeed to be supposed necessary to add [Tate Wilkinson wrote], that when the English nightingale, Mrs. Crouch, made her first entrance on the York Theatre [during the 1787 season], in the character of Rossetta . . . that she was admired and followed. Why ladies are so generally attached to that worn out opera, I have not yet been able to account for, but Rossetta is the rage of all the opera ladies. (III, 49)

Among the actress-singers who chose Rossetta for their first appearance were Mrs. Bannister (Miss Harper), Mrs. Billington (Miss Weichsell), and Mrs. Martyr (Miss Thorton). Even the great tragic actress Sarah Siddons sang Rossetta in 1773 at Wolverhampton. Male singers sometimes chose Young Meadows as their first role, and Incledon sang Hawthorn at his Farewell Benefit at the King's Theatre, Haymarket, on 24 March 1817.[13]

The most famous song in *Love in a Village* is "There was a Jolly Miller Once" (I, v, Air VIII). With this song Hawthorn makes his initial appearance. No composer was listed for this song in any of the eighteenth-century editions examined. As early as 1771, a newspaper correspondent wrote to the *St. James Chronicle:*

> I shall be much obliged to any of your Correspondents, who will inform me if the song in Love in a Village, which begins, "There was a jolly Miller once," is wrote by the Author of that Opera, or whether it is only the Beginning of an old Song, and where the Remainder may be got, if in Print? [signed] Cantator Jocusus.[14]

No one replied to Cantator. The tune was used for "The Budgeon It is a Delicate Trade"[15] which had been printed in *The Triumph of Wit, or Ingenuity Displayed,* and in *A New Canting Dictionary,* &c., "With a complete collection of Songs in the canting dialect [1725]" (Chappell, II, 667). At least three ballad operas had utilized the tune: *The Quaker's Opera,* 1728; *The Devil to Pay,* 1731; and *The Fashionable Lady, or Harlequin's Opera,* 1730. The tune also was the bearer of a harvest-supper song, "Here's a health unto our Master." As for the words to

"The Jolly Miller," they may well have originated with Bickerstaff whose version appears in I, vi, Air VIII:

> There was a jolly miller once,
> Liv'd on the river Dee;
> He work'd and sung, from morn 'till night,
> No lark more blyth than he.
> And this the burthen of his song,
> For ever us'd to be,
> I care for nobody, no not I,
> If no one cares for me.

However much Bickerstaff might have aligned himself with opera music rather than with "common ballads," as he termed them in his Dedication, his words to several of his songs belong to folk tradition; and some of the tunes themselves, "The Jolly Miller," "Larry Grogan," and "St. Patrick's Day," for instance, were traditional or ballad in origin. Margery's Air, "How happy were my days till now," is a "betrayed maid" lament, especially in its last stanza:

> Oh the fool, the silly, silly fool,
> Who trusts what man may be;
> I wish I was a maid again,
> And in my own country (I, ix, Air XIII, 19)

The only song Justice Woodcock sings, "When I followed a lass that was forward and shy," was alleged by him to have been popular "in London, about thirty years ago. . . . I dare swear you have heard it often" (II, iii, 30). It is a simply scored Air in 6/4 time ending with lines that out of context sound Blakean:

> Green was her gown upon the grass;
> Oh! such were the joys of our dancing days. (II, iii, Air XVIII, 30)

In fact they are Cibberian. Colley Cibber wrote the words to the tune of "Joan's Placket is Torn," a melody which was mentioned by Pepys on 22 June 1667.

Among the maudlin songs which Lucinda must sing, she has one comic number which is based on a well-known traditional belief:

> Believe me, dear aunt,
> If you rave thus, and rant,
> You'll never a lover persuade;
> The men will all fly,

And leave you to die,
Oh, terrible chance! an old maid—
How happy the lass,
Must she come to this pass,
Who antient virginity 'scapes:
'Twere better on earth
Have five brats at a birth
Than in hell be a leader of apes. (II, ii, Air XVII, 29)

"We must blame Lucinda," Francis Gentleman declared, "for mentioning *five brats* at a birth . . . it is not within the pale of decency."[16] Arne composed the music for this song especially for the opera, and no one else seemed to object to the words.

Bickerstaff proved his versatility with the trio which ends Act II. In it Hawthorn, Lucinda and Rossetta alternate between the humorous and sentimental when Hawthorn invites Lucinda

Well, come, let us hear, what the swain must possess
Who may hope at your feet to implore with success?
Lucinda: {He must be first of all,
Rossetta: {Straight, comely and tall:

Lucinda: Neither aukward,
Rossetta: Nor foolish;
Lucinda: Nor apish,
Rossetta: Nor mulish:

Lucinda: {
Rossetta: {Nor yet shou'd his fortune be small.

Hawthorn: What think'st of a captain?
Lucinda: All bluster and wounds!

Hawthorn: What think'st of a squire
Rossetta: To be left for his hounds,

Lucinda: {The youth that is form'd to my mind,
{Must be gentle, obliging, and kind;
{Of all things in Nature love me,
Rossetta: {Have sense both to speak, and to see,
{Yet sometimes be silent and blind.

Hawthorn: 'Fore George a most rare matrimonial receipt,

Rossetta: {Observe it ye fair in the choice of a mate;
Lucinda: {Remember 'tis wedlock determines your fate.
(II, xiv, Air XXI, 51)

Although many of the lyrics dealt directly with the actions of the characters, there were other songs with sentiments more general, such as the following which was sung by Hawthorn in Act III, scene i:

> The world is a well furnish'd table,
> Where guests are promisc'ously set;
> We all fare as well as we're able,
> And scramble for what we can get.
>
> My simile holds to a tittle,
> Some gorge, while some scarce have a taste;
> But if I am content with a little,
> Enough is as good as a feast. (Air XXXII, p. 54)

Rossetta sighs in song (*poco largo*) with this reflection:

> When we see a lover languish,
> And his truth and honour prove,
> Ah! how sweet to heal his anguish,
> And repay him love for love. (III, viii, Air XXXVIII, 65)

A sad far cry from Congreve's "If there's delight in love, 'tis when I see / That heart, which others bleed for, bleed for me."

Under Arne's professional guidance, *Love in a Village* proved a better opera than Johnson's, and Bickerstaff constructed a better play. Whereas Johnson only alluded to Heartwell, the second suitor, Bickerstaff recognized the value of symmetry and brought Lucinda's lover Eustace onto the stage. Admittedly, once he got there he added little except in the scene, borrowed from Wycherley, in which Lucinda passes him off to her aunt as a music master. As "The Dramatic Censor" put it, Eustace is "more a cypher" than Young Meadows—and he is "a mere loving milksop" (Gentleman, I, 167).

Lucas in *The Village Opera* sang the already quoted "My Dolly was the Snow-drop fair," but he is an unrealized character. When Bickerstaff created Hawthorn for Beard, he paired the character with Woodcock and gave him several agreeable songs. Hawthorn, as his neighboring squire, is a balance to Woodcock.

Throughout *Love in a Village,* however much the characters are leveled into mediocrity, they are fitted together more persuasively than were the succession of characters in the *Village Opera,* where in some scenes the secondary roles existed only to continue the social satire begun in *The Beggar's Opera.* Instead of using them a mere vignette of country life as in Johnson's opera, Bickerstaff balances Hodge and Margery against romanticized love. Hodge's rejection of Margery and her decision to go to London as a Fanny Hill are the only realistic parts of this bucolic comedy.

The third reason for the success of this opera was its sentimentality. The progress of sentimentalism from *The Village Opera* to *Love in a Village* reveals itself in the treatment of two aspects of an important eighteenth-century social issue: the degree of parental authority, especially in parents choosing marriage partners for their children, and the permissibility of two socially unequal partners marrying. These problems are mooted —not seriously—in both operas. In the *Village Opera* they are resolved by an action of the hero; Young Freeman actually asserts himself to prevent a fraudulent marriage, and announces his intention to marry the supposed maid Betty. In *Love in a Village* the fathers make the necessary decisions. Sir William unites his son and Rossetta before Young Meadows even can reveal his true identity. As for Eustace, the plans for the elopement discovered, Justice Woodcock reluctantly gives him to Lucinda as a present. Thus neither of the two sets of lovers does more than hope and talk in *Love in a Village*. Their passivity is characteristic of the sentimental character whose strong suit is virtue not action.

The song to Dolly sung by Lucas and Hawthorn also epitomizes the rise of sentimentality upon which Bickerstaff capitalized and aided. Gone are the "low" images of kidney-bean teeth and mushroom breasts. In their place are the bland abstractions of the four seasons. A trademark of sentimentality is the blurred image.

In print the eighteenth-century theatre critic was in favor of virtue and the preservation of the social order. The following quotations may help explain why *Love in a Village* was acceptable to its early audiences in terms of morality; they come from an essay entitled, "Reflexions of the Drama, and the Stage proved to have risen in good sense and decency, however it has of late years declined in the brilliancy of Wit or the sparkle of Imagination."[17] According to its author, Hugh Kelly, Restoration writers like Wycherley, Congreve and Vanbrugh, with a "culpable degree of levity were endeavouring to say brilliant things rather than just ones" (p. 23). Wit is secondary to judgment in the dramatic poet. Wycherley, Congreve and Vanbrugh are to be scorned "for perverting the original end of the stage. . . ." Modern writers sensibly recollect that the sole end of the stage is to blend amusement with instruction; and therefore never neglect the heart, through a view of bawding to the imagination;—hence, instead of finding them eternally on the scent for snip-snap and repartee, we see them studious in the discovery of manly sentiments and laudable reflexions. . . . (p. 26)

For those who were indifferent to "manly sentiments and laudable reflexions," *Love in a Village* successfully offered good music; and as Hazlitt wrote, "To enter into good acting, requires an effort; but to hear soft music is a pleasure without any trouble."[18]

The first reviews of *Love in a Village* were favorable and concentrated on the performance. The critic of the *St. James Chronicle* attributed the opera to the author of *Thomas and Sally:*

The author himself speaks so modestly of his piece as a dramatick performance that it would be cruel to enter too critically into an examination of its merit, or to shew how much it is in every particular inferior to the Beggar's Opera, the great prototype of all these ballad dramas. Suffice it then to say that it is on the whole, no unpleasing performance. That there is just as much fable, as the author might think it safe to put into an opera; that the dialogue is at least natural; and that in two or three of the parts there are even some strokes of character. The songs, says the author, are some of them tolerable: To which we reply, in the words of Tester, *very tolerable:* Nay, some of them more than tolerable.[19]

After discussing the music and the performers, the review reproved the first-night audience for its political fervor: "We are sorry to see the spirit of party run so high, as to produce very loud applause in the theatre, on Miss Brent's [Rossetta's] delivering the following words—'When princes are oppressive in their government, subjects have a right to assert their liberty' " (p. 674). Rossetta—with a nod to Wilkes—was objecting to her father's authoritarian manners.

In *Lloyd's Evening Post,* the writer praised Miss Brent and Miss Hallam for their opening duet ("Hope! thou earnest of delight"), and included in the critique a sentiment soon to become all too familiar in reviews of operas: "It is not to be expected that Operas, in which the action is interrupted by musick, should have complicated plots; simplicity and nature are most pleasing in this."

Unlike later reviews, this one asserted, "The dialogues of this piece rise much above mediocrity, and the Airs are truly poetic and pleasing, and, what more, the words of them are perfectly well adapted to the characters." The writer hoped that "as we have now a power of representing English Operas to advantage . . . the Italian pieces may soon be exploded." He concluded by wishing that Bickerstaff "may meet with all the future encouragement such a genius ought to expect from a sensible and polite nation."[20] For the moment, Bickerstaff was indeed receiving encouragement. The first edition of *Love in a Village* was published on 9 December; by 13 December, the *Public Advertiser* was advertising that the edition had been sold out. To prevent a pirated edition from being sold, the shareholders of the comic opera went to court. They won the case in 1768 when the Master of the Rolls granted a perpetual injunction against the printer and obliged him to account with the booksellers for the profits of the whole number printed, published, and sold by him,[21] although the Opera was not, till after the printing of the pirated edition, entered at Stationer's Hall (16 February 1763, just over two months after the opera was first performed and printed). The four shareholders, each of whom owned a quarter of the play, were the booksellers William Griffin (who became a friend of Bickerstaff during the 1760s and printed many of his works), John Newbery, George Kearsly, and William Nicoll.[22]

The English reviewers immediately recognized Bickerstaff's debt to Johnson, but they were not concerned with his French borrowings. On the other side of the channel, the French might not have known about Johnson, but they knew their Marivaux. In a favorable review published in the *Journal Encyclopédique,* the critic noted a resemblance between Bickerstaff's opera and *Le Jeu de l'Amour et du hazard,* and to a number of other unspecified works. Besides the inevitable close summary of the opera, the French critic wrote the following:

> *A Londres, comme en France, les Spectateurs n'exigent dans un Opéra comique que de l'esprit & beaucoup de gaieté: l'Auteur a parfaitement rempli ces deux objets: peut-être même que s'il eût voulu donner plus de vraisemblance à cette pièce, il eut été force de sacrifier l'enjouëment à la régularité. D'ailleurs, doit-on juger d'après les règles les ouvrages d'un genre qui est lui-même hors des règles, & qui cependant plait beaucoup depuis plusieurs années? nous craignons seulement qu'il ne plaise un peu trop, & qu'a force d'amuser, il n'élève a la fin le goût de la frivolité sur l'amour du beau, du bon & de l'utile. (pp. 106–107)*

The writer concluded with general praise for the opera, and

high hopes for the author's future works, not however, without a touch of chauvinism.

> *On doit regarder cet ouvrage comme un heureux présage du succès des pièces que l'Auteur donnera dans un autre genre de Comique. Il est jeune, & veut se livrer tout entier à la carrière du théâtre; & pour s'y former, il s'est rendu à Paris, où il étudie les bons modèles du Théâtre François, non seulement en les lisant, mais encore en les voyant représenter. Au reste nous l'avons entendu chanter les arriettes de sa pièce qui ont fait le plus de plaisir à Londres; mais quelle différence d'avec celles qui sont le succès de nos pièces modernes en ce genre? (p. 113)*[23]

Aside from the writer's comments on the opera, this review is important because it places Bickerstaff in France by 1 May 1763 when this issue of the *Journal* was published. He can be traced to Chaillot, because in John Baker's diary entry for 24 May 1763, Baker wrote that he went to "Chaillot to see Mr. Bickerstaff, author of Love in a Village."[24]

The longest criticism of the opera was written by Francis Gentleman in his *The Dramatic Censor,* 1770. Like most theatre critics, he shared with Addison the hearty English opinion that operas were nonsensical and out of nature. And like most critics he realized that the opera was part of English theatre repertory whether or not he ignored it.

> Though as advocates for nature, we have declared critical war against operatical compositions in general—an instance of dangerous resolution at present—we only mean to try such pieces as they appear, considering the songs as part of the dialogue. . . . (p. 156)

Gentleman was the first critic to defend Bickerstaff's plagiarisms. He first intimated that the charge against *Love in a Village* was perhaps exaggerated, and then in Bickerstaff's defense he told the following anecdote:

> . . . a young clergyman . . . who being reproached with preaching one of Tillotson's sermons, replied,—"Sir, if you know this matter, not one in a hundred of my congregation does; I am certain, it is much better than any thing my own head could produce; and I hope you will allow I do my flock more justice by borrowing elsewhere, than palming my own stuff upon them." Far be it from us to suppose this absolutely our author's case, we only mention the matter in a friendly way to shew that if it really was, he has a very *modest* and good defence to offer. (I, 156)

Gentleman worried about propriety: the proper use of images

in various songs, and the appropriate use of language by each of the characters. He worried about the indecency of Rossetta and Lucinda discussing the latter's father, accusing him of being libidinous, and implying that he had been a rake in his time. "I am sorry our bard slipped by decency to make two well-bred young ladies speak [that way]," Gentleman declared (I, 157). For the sake of propriety it would have been better had Margery and Hodge been less intimate; nor was Gentleman happy with Rossetta's understanding of Justice Woodcock's amorous innuendoes toward her. Of that scene (II, iv), Gentleman wrote, "though arch, [it] has much too strong a taint of indelicacy. . ." (I, 161-162).

He found that the songs contained "the most trite, hackneyed sentiments [and] awkward versification . . . and not a shadow of genius; as to the essence of dramatic merit, a moral, there is no trace of it to be discovered. . ." (I, 167).[25] On the contrary, Gentleman believed that the two romantic couples illustrated "a notable breach of filial duty." Even though "there are no very pernicious inferences arising from these incidents, yet they recommend indiscretion, and are void of any useful tendency; and brings them at best under the insipped denomination of merely inoffensive" (I, 167). "Inoffensive," in fact was Gentleman's conclusion about the play, and "with some spirit, an agreeable share of ease and regularity."

It was Gentleman who called Bickerstaff a "dramatic cobler" (II, 470), an apt description. Another critic decided that he was a tailor. Bickerstaff, so the *Theatrical Review* in 1771 reported,

> has discovered a very happy Talent, in altering the Works of other Dramatic Authors, and fitting them for the Stage in more advantageous lights, than when they first appeared: So that, this Gentleman, may be compared to a Taylor, who, though not able to make a complete new Suit of Cloaths himself, has an admirable hand at altering and amending an old one.

The reviewer compared the performances at Covent Garden and Drury Lane (where it had first been performed on 3 April 1769): "Take the whole together, we think the two Theatres are upon an equal footing with respect to the Performing of this Opera" (I, 52-55).

Despite reviewers who insisted that the opera was a product of plagiarism, that the plot, dialogue and music were all or in part insipid, and that opera in general was beneath notice; despite all the unenthusiastic criticism, *Love in a Village* continued to be successfully performed wherever it was produced.

It reached Boston on 19 June 1766 where it was performed at the Academy, "*alias* the Assembly Room in Lodge Alley. . . ."[26] Plays and operas were not then officially acted, but "read." In the case of operas, it was advertised, "all the songs will be sung accompanied by instrumental music" (Sonneck, p. 34). When *Love in a Village* opened in Boston, it was announced as a "moral lecture" to evade the law against theatrical performances.[27]

The first critical notice printed in America of an opera appeared in the *Pennsylvania Gazette* for January, 1767 after *Love in a Village* had been produced at the Southwark Theatre in Philadelphia.

> I must beg leave to inform the public that the pleasing "Love in a Village" is done here beyond expectation, and must give real delight to every person void of ill-nature. . . . I could wish to see the house better filled whenever this justly applauded entertainment is exhibited. (Sonneck, p. 38)

The opera was performed 81 times in the United States, the last performance in the nineteenth century being at Burton's Theatre, New York, on 12 November 1849 (Macmillan, p. 63). Since then, however, it has received at least one more performance: in 1954 it was produced at Sewanee University with some alterations.

"Inoffensive" as *Love in a Village* was to some critics, the opera's moral utility—or its lack—was commented upon in this country as well as in Britain. The December 1794 *New York Magazine* found that in general "we have been pleased; but we find a difficulty in determining with what in particular. . . ."

> This praise cannot be extended to all parts of the play. The two best drawn characters (Hodge and Madge) are a disgustful exhibition of folly and vice; and what adds to their impropriety is the imperfect conclusion of the plot, which might have been rendered eminently moral and important. (Sonneck, pp. 101–103)

The first performance of *Love in a Village* in Dublin was on July 1763 (Loewenberg, cols. 266-267).

> In the infancy as I may stile it, of the English vocal drama [Hitchcock wrote], the appearance of this beautiful opera attracted the attention,

> not only of the musical cognoscenti, but also of all ranks and degrees. It made an impression, unknown since the days of Gay, and the *Beggar's Opera,* which till then had stood unrivalled, but was now obliged to behold a very formidable competitor. (II, 112)

The two Dublin theatres were fiercely competitive; in 1764 they fought for customers when each of them produced *The Beggar's Opera.* Crow-Street produced *Love in a Village* alternately with Gay's opera in its effort to fill the house. In all, *Love in a Village* was performed 415 times in Dublin between 1763 and 1836.[28]

It was popular enough in Ireland for it to serve as a model for a political satire in 1789. The satire, probably by Henry Grattan, was directed against the Irish government. In its printed form the satire was titled, "The Songs of 'Love in a Village,' With Additional Songs; As they Were Performed at the Fancy Ball in the Castle of Dublin, on St. Patrick's Night, by a Select Group. 1789."[29] Bickerstaff's opening air, "Hope! thou nurse of young desire," became

> Hope! the courtier's first desire,—
> Airy promiser of place!
> Dreams of future wealth inspire
> Softest soother of disgrace.

"There was a Jolly Miller" became

> There was a mulish Marquess once [Marquess of Buckingham,
> Lived in the castle yard, Lord Lieutenant of Ireland]
> He jobb'd and scraped, from morn till night,
> No scriv'ner work'd so hard;
> Yet this the burden of his song
> For ever now must be,—
> "I care for nobody, no, not I,
> For nobody cares for me!"

Elsewhere the opera was popular. In Edinburgh it was first performed in 1765, and remained in the Edinburgh repertory at least until 1834. In St. Petersburg the *Théâtre Anglais* performed *Love in a Village* on 28 April 1772;[30] on 24 February 1791 it played in Calcutta.

As early in the nineteenth century as 1811, *The Dramatic Censor,* in reviewing a Covent Garden performance on 22 November, could refer to *Love in a Village* as "That old favourite, domestic opera. . . ." An opera which has "remained as a stock opera of primary importance." Still fighting the battle against the patent absurdity of operas, the writer admitted that the war had been lost: "we became reconciled at last, not only to tolerate the folly, but to enjoy it" (p. 453).[31] In support of the good old cause against opera, he expended a few charges of anti-opera ammunition before settling down to the previous night's performance. It was not as good as it used to be.

"By the bye," observed *The Dramatic Censor,* "we do not approve of the inroad that is made upon morals and humanity, by the dramatist suffering *Hodge* to go off in triumph, after his brutal treatment of *Madge.* In poetical justice, he should have been compelled to marry the simple victim of his sensuality, and not to insult her with impunity. Such a procedure is not proper in a theatrical Author, whose duty it is to make Vice and Folly bow down, in contrition, before the altars of Equity and Virtue" (p. 454).

By 1811, *Love in a Village* was being performed in a heavy-handed fashion. Its original "becoming simplicity . . . its pastoral features are all changed, and it is no more like what it was (when it was most attractive) than a *polisson* of Saint Giles's is similar to an Arcadian Shepherd!" The characters were coarsened, the performers were more florid than had been their counterparts in the good old days. Rossetta "is no longer *piquante* and alluring, like a gentlewoman in masquerade, but sings and flirts like a shameless wench who roars ballads at the corner of Cranbourn-alley" (pp. 454-455).

The charge of degeneracy from a pristine, simple state was not merely nostalgia and old age: the theatres were larger, and intimacy was lost in the crowd. Other operas of Bickerstaff were produced at this time, and they also were compared unfavorably with their initial runs. Latter-day composers added more Italianate music to the operas, and the vogue for *bravura* singing reached even Bickerstaff's pastel efforts. Prima-donnas, never easy to direct, took advantage of their fame to elaborate their parts. On 2 November 1824 at Drury Lane, for instance, Mrs. Bedford "sang with considerable feeling and delicacy one of Moore's melodies, 'The harp that once through Tarah's halls.' But what connexion this beautiful Irish lament has with the situation of the gay Rossetta, we leave it to those at whose request it was introduced to explain. A more inappropriate air could not, we think, have been selected."[32] But this practice of adding airs plagued operas throughout the eighteenth century. As early as 1736, Colley Cibber was complaining in his Preface to his masque, *Venus and Adonis,* "Songs are so often turn'd out of their Places, to introduce some favourite Air of the Singer, that in a few Days the first Book you have bought, is reduc'd to little more than the Title Page of what it pretends to. . . ."[33]

Audiences, like prima-donnas, were always a nuisance. *The Dramatic Censor* in 1811 complained that where once "Rank and Beauty formerly sat, exhibiting to the humbler occupants of the pit and galleries, succeeding and successful examples of pure politeness, and rigorous propriety . . . we have coarse loungers, who squat themselves down, with their bodies on one bench and their soiled boots on another, with their hats nailed on their heads, like so many tipsy graziers reposing in a Smithfield tavern . . ." (p. 456). *The Dramatic Censor* notwithstanding, theatre audiences were never as good as they used to be.

The professional critic was not the only one to cry *ubi sunt.* An irate, anonymous correspondent wrote to one of the London newspapers about Miss Keppel's first performance as Rossetta on 19 October 1816 at Drury Lane. Instead of hearing, "Hope! thou nurse of young desire," he heard:

> "*Ope,* thou nur-ur-ur-se—of young *desire!*" Instead of an invocation to Hope, first giving her simple name, and then calling her by her office, as "Hope!—thou nurse of young desire," the intention of the composer and poet, Miss Keppel gave an imperious command to some old wrinkled beldame, who was performing the office of pap making &c. to a brat in swaddling clothes to *open* something—I hope not to open *her* mouth!—she might at least have bid the poor woman "hope." When she came to the word *young,* I imagined the *playfulness of her fancy,* (for she seems a playful lady,) might have made her indeavour to *imitate the child;* for being any thing but the real note, I do not know what else she could mean. In short, my hope was over, and I was doomed to listen to vulgar pronunciation. "Moy," "toyrant," &c. notes seldom in tune, ill-executed, and misplaced cadences and false emphasies, till I expected to see the enraged ghosts of Bickerstaff and Arne, rise on the stage to rescue from the merciless hands of the young murdress, their lovely *Rosetta!*[34]

The poignancy of this opening duet may not be felt in print, but when Miss Hallam, the first Lucinda, sang the second stanza, "she could not suppress her emotion, but burst into a flood of unfeigned sorrow."[35] The scene in which Rossetta and Lucinda are discovered at work, seated upon two garden chairs, always moved Hazlitt, a critic not usually sentimental. The scene opens "with those two young beauties sitting in a bower of roses like a flower stuck in the stomacher of beauty, and where that unconscious siren [Miss Stephens as Rossetta] 'warbles her native wood-notes wild' with such simplicity and sweetness. . . ."[36]

By 1820, Hazlitt was nostalgically recalling Miss Stephens's first performances: "Those were happy days when first Miss Stephens began to sing. When she came out in . . . Rossetta in *Love in a Village*! She came upon us by surprise, but it was to delight and charm us."

> There was a new sound in the air, like the voice of Sprnig; it was as if Music had become young again, and was resolved to try the power of her softest, simplest, sweetest notes. Love and Hope listened, as her clear, liquid throat poured its delicious warblings on the ear. . . . They were the sweetest notes we ever heard, and almost the last we ever heard with pleasure! (XVIII, 342–343. *The Examiner,* 25 June 1820)

For Hazlitt, *Love in a Village* and Miss Stephens came to be inseparable. His description of the opera in *The Comic Writers of the Last Century* (1819) anticipated his praise of Miss Stephens: *Love in a Village* is "one of the most delightful comic operas on the stage. It is truly pastoral; and the sense of music hovers over the very scene like the breath of morning."[37]

Critics like Hazlitt are rare in any age, however, and during the 1760s Bickerstaff and his works were likely to be handled by poetasters such as Cuthbert Shaw, who had never recovered from reading *The Dunciad.* Shaw included Bickerstaff among the host of poets in his *The Race* (1764). Shaw let such writers as Johnson, Archibald Campbell, Cleland, Murphy, Kenrick, Arne, Woty, and Churchill race for the favor of *Fame.* Critics and playwrights, as well as non-dramatic poets, were included in the contest, but surprisingly Garrick was absent. Appropriately, Samuel Derrick of Bath fame acted as flag-waver to begin the race.

> . . . then Bickerstaff advanc'd,
> His Sing-Song-Muse, by vast success enhanc'd;
> Who, when fair Wright, destroying reason's sense,
> Inveigles our applause in spite of sense,
> With Syren-voice our juster rage confounds,
> And clothes sweet nonsense in delusive sounds,
> Pertly commends the judgment of the town,
> And arrogates the merit as his own,
> Talks of his taste! how well each air was hit!
> While *Printers* and their *Devils* praise his wit;

And wrap'd in warm surtout of self-conceit
Defies the critic's cold, and poet's heat.

He eye'd the rabble round, and thus began:
"Goddess, I wonder at the pride of man;
"Fellows, whose accents never yet have hung
"On skilful *Beard's* or *Brent's* harmonious tongue,
"Dare here approach, **who chatter like a parrot,*
[Shaw's footnote, "*See *Love in a Village, an Opera."*]
"*But hardly know a sheep's head from a carrot.
"Whose tasteless lines ne'er grac'd a royal stage
"Nor charm'd a tuneful *crotchet*-loving age!
"Prove then, oh! Goddess, to my labors kind,
"And let these sons of *Dullness* lag behind,
"Whilst **hoity toity, whisky frisky,* I
[Shaw's footnote, "*See *Love in a Village."*]
"On ballad-wings spring forth to victory."
So sure!—but justice stops thee in thy flight,
And damns thy labours to eternal night.
Brands that success which boasts no just pretence
To genius, judgment, wit or common sense;
But who for taste shall dare prescribe the laws,
Or stop the torrent of the mob's applause?[38]

While Covent Garden was profiting from the combination of Arne, Bickerstaff, Beard, and Brent, Drury Lane was suffering. It was indeed a "*crotchet*-loving age," one which was encouraged by Beard who had the talent to produce musical works from burlettas like *Midas* to serious operas like *Artaxerxes*. With Charlotte Brent as Beard's "Most powerful engine to demolish the success and humble the pride of Drury-Lane,"[39] Garrick's acting was in vain. "That bewitching Syren charmed all the world; and, like another Orpheus, drew crowds perpetually after her" (II, 65). "In short, the people were allured by nothing but the power of song and sing-song; Shakespeare and Garrick were obliged to quit the field to Beard and Brent" (II, 66). Davies asserted that Covent Garden operas were responsible for Garrick's taking a vacation on the continent in 1763. Before he left, Garrick recommended that some musical pieces be performed to compete with Beard, but as Davies put it, "three English operas, were played in succession, with little or no profit to the manager, the poet, or the musician."[40] Unable to compete with Covent Garden, Lacy (Garrick's partner) decided to ridicule the new taste in music with a "rehearsal" play which he hoped to produce on 29 March 1764.[41]

"Music Alamode; or, Bays in Chromatics: A Burlesque Entertainment" was the instrument with which Lacy thought he could pry some of the audience away from Covent Garden. "Music Alamode" presented the author—"Doctor Crotchet"—on stage discussing with a player—Drury Lane's John Packer—the play which was about to be rehearsed, a pastoral, "Damon and Daphne." Dr. Crotchet was a caricature of Dr. Arne, and "Damon and Daphne" a combination of *Thomas and Sally* and *Love in a Village,* with a deft allusion to Arne's borrowing from Handel added for good measure. The farce would have been worth producing, but "Music Alamode" was never performed.

The success of *Love in a Village,* despite the charges of plagiarism, immorality and insipidity, inhibited as well as inspired later opera writers. At the same time that it encouraged them to allow original music to help forward the plot, its success discouraged most writers from carrying the process any further. In addition, the simple story of *Love in a Village* was no incentive to complicate later operas. Thus, by its continued popularity, Bickerstaff's opera weaned authors from their dependence on ballads and folk music, and encouraged them to compose original, operatic airs; but for the same reason, it froze English comic opera in its own form. With few exceptions, comic operas and the expectations of audiences from Bickerstaff until Gilbert and Sullivan can be summarized by quoting John Bannister:

> An English opera is, properly, a comedy enlivened by music. A plot, diversified characters, and interesting occurrences are expected; and these; to be relished, must be understood. Such are the principles on which the operas which have longest retained their reputation (as those of Bickerstaff, Sheridan and O'Keefe,) are formed; but where the business and passion of whole scenes, or sometimes of whole acts are consigned to recitative and song, it is much to be feared that fashion, rather than feeling, causes the piece to be endured; and that, a few *cognoscenti* excepted, the audience in general keep their places chiefly that they may not be singular in society, by acknowledging their ignorance of performances and performers which so many exult in having seen.[42]

4

PAMELA REVISITED: *THE MAID OF THE MILL*

The success of *Love in a Village* encouraged Bickerstaff to write the same comic opera again: this time he called it *The Maid of the Mill.*[1] For seven of the ten parts Beard cast performers who had played comparable roles in the earlier work. One name was conspicuously absent: Thomas Arne. In his place was the 24-year-old Samuel Arnold. One new name was conspicuously present, and would remain so for the rest of Bickerstaff's career: Charles Dibdin.

The music for *The Maid of the Mill* was composed and compiled by Samuel Arnold, despite the notice on the title page which gave Bickerstaff the credit. Arnold "consented to accept of the managers only the sum of £12 rather than resign the opportunity of bringing his talents before the public."[2] Having been a student of Bernard Gates at the Chapel Royal, like Beard before him, Arnold was hired to be the composer for Covent Garden in 1761; the comic opera would be his first major assignment. He and Bickerstaff drew their music from 21 composers; in addition, Arnold contributed the Quartetto "Lye still my Heart," which concluded Act One; the Air "When a Maid," and the concluding Quintetto of Act Two. The most curious thing about the list of composers whose names were published[3] with the score was the absence of Thomas Arne, who never collaborated again with Bickerstaff after *Love in a Village.* Neither man publicly explained why.

Charles Dibdin joined Covent Garden as a singer and dancer in 1760 at the age of fifteen. On the same night that he received £1 10s for having sung for five nights in *Thomas and Sally* ("and 1 night in *Romeo*"), Bickerstaff was awarded £85 6s in ready money and £12 18s from the sale of tickets given him by the theatre, £98 4s. in all (Stone, 828-829). Although he did nothing for *Love in a Village,* by the time Beard came to cast *The Maid of the Mill,* Dibdin was hustling a supporting role for himself. The part of Ralph had been tentatively assigned to John Dunstall, who had played a good Hodge in *Love in a Village;* but Dibdin declared that "Nothing could be so ridiculous, for he was pretty well advanced in life, and totally incapable of singing any one of the songs; and, in every other respect, completely unfit for the character."[4]

> It is inconceivable [Dibdin continued] the murmurs that were raised against me. The author was told I should damn his piece, and nothing was unattempted to prevent me from appearing in it. I enjoyed all this, and no persuasion could induce me to rehearse it in earnest; for, so contemptible was their spite, that I would rather have lost fifty parts than have undeceived them. (*Life,* I, 47)
>
> . . . .
>
> I came out in the character. I was encored in all the songs; and, what further happened, it is not becoming in me to declare; nor, indeed, in some sense, very flattering: for, if Ralph-handkerchiefs were then worn, so are Belcher's now. (p. 47)

Dibdin won "universal and repeated applause" throughout the run of the opera (*Life,* I, 49). On the other hand, rumor suggested that the character of Ralph "had been refused by every other comedian, and offered to Dibdin as a last resort" (Wyndham, I, 156). Nor were all of Dibdin's contemporaries enchanted by his Ralph: "Mr. Dibdin," wrote Francis Gentleman, "certainly has not the shadow of any merit in acting . . . the young miller could scarce have fallen into worse hands" (II, 117).

Despite Bickerstaff's initial reluctance to see Dibdin as Ralph, and despite Dibdin's rather abrasive character, the two became friends and collaborators until Bickerstaff fled the country. Thereafter, Dibdin did his best to disassociate himself from his tainted colleague, but to his discomfiture, rarely succeeded.

Confidence in the success of *The Maid of the Mill* was tangibly demonstrated when the bookseller T. Lowndes paid £23 10s. for a *one-eighth* share of the copyright on 16 October 1764, over three months before it was produced.[5] In contrast, Bickerstaff was paid only about £25 for letting Kearsly publish *Thomas and Sally*. Lowndes rid himself of his share, presumably at a profit, on 16 November 1764, so that when the opera was registered at Stationer's Hall on 31 January 1765, the shares were distributed in the following manner:

Isaac Bickerstaff	1/4
J. Newberry [sic]	3/16
Wm. Nicoll	3/16
Wm. Griffin	3/16
R. Baldwin	1/16
T. Caslon	1/16
T. Becket	1/16

Remembering the pirate printer of *Love in a Village*, the booksellers posted a no-trespassing sign on the page following Bickerstaff's Preface:

This Opera is entered at STATIONERS HALL, and whoever presumes to Print the Songs, or any Part of them, will be prosecuted by the PROPRIETORS.

Bickerstaff and thc proprictors were justified in their confidence in *The Maid of the Mill*. *Love in a Village* was going through its tenth edition when this opera was published, and *Thomas and Sally* was enjoying its third. Within ten years after publication, 20,000 copies of *The Maid of the Mill* were sold:

> Conservative figuring estimates that . . . shareholders would have to sell upwards of five thousand copies at the theatre price of one shilling each, in order to break even on their investment, and could begin to count profits only from then on. Over a period of about ten years, during which the play was performed 113 times, the potential buying public amounted to twenty thousand people. (Stone, xxvii, cci)

Bickerstaff dedicated his comic opera to William, Duke of Gloucester. In his Dedication, he included a short defense of the genre:

> How far the Comic Opera, under proper regulations, has a right to be acknowledged for a junior offspring of the Drama, and as such become a candidate for a share of public encouragement, I shall not pretend to determine; but if it can be rendered an agreeable amusement, the English Theatre has never scrupled to adopt what was capable of pleasing there; and though as a work of genius, it is by no means to be set in competition with good Tragedies and Comedies, it may, I apprehend, be permitted as

an occasional relief to them, without bringing either our taste or understanding into question. (pp. i–ii)

He then upheld France as a country in which comic opera prospered, an observation he made from first-hand experience. In his Preface, Bickerstaff acknowledged *Pamela* as his source for the plot. "Not only the general subject is drawn from *Pamela*," he explained, "but almost every circumstance in it."

> The reader will immediately recollect—the courtship of Parson Williams—the Squire's jealousy and behaviour in consequence of it, and the difficulty he had to prevail with himself to marry the girl, notwithstanding his passion for her—the miller is a close copy of Goodman Andrews—Ralph is imagined, from the wild son which he is mentioned to have had—Theodosia, from the young lady of quality, with whom Mr. B. through his sister's persuasion, is said to have been in treaty before his marriage with Pamela—even the gipsies, are borrowed from a trifling incident in the latter part of the work. (Preface, pp. i–ii)

For the sake of accuracy, Bickerstaff should have written in his Preface that his opera owed its origin to Fletcher and Rowley's comedy, *The Maid in the Mill.* Even if the reader allows with Bickerstaff that "the general subject is drawn" from Richardson's novel, he cannot help but feel that Bickerstaff was avoiding mention of the older comedy when he wrote that "almost every circumstance" of his opera could be found in *Pamela.*

Genest was the first to point out that Bickerstaff's Miller Fairfield, his son Ralph, and daughter Patty correspond to Fletcher's Miller Franio, his son Bustofa, and his supposed daughter Florimel. But Genest underestimated Bickerstaff's indebtedness when he wrote simply that the latter "seems to have had his eye on the characters of Franio, Florimel, and Bustofa" (V. 73-74). In *The Maid in the Mill,*[6] there are two plots; the one Bickerstaff utilized concerned the miller and his family, and Count Otrante's lust for Florimel. As late as 1750 Fletcher's play had been altered into a farce afterpiece and performed at Covent Garden (Stone, I, 189, 5 April 1750); although the farce was not published, it is unlikely that the serious plot of *The Maid in the Mill* was used. The portrayals of Otrante and Richardson's Squire B—— reveal a marked change in the taste of the English. Pamela's virginity protects her from Squire B—— (that and his own ineptitude); while Florimel's pretended sluttishness saves her from Count Otrante.

Bickerstaff's Lord Aimworth, who loves Patty = Pamela =

Florimel, has attained the epitome of English sensibility: not only is rape out of the question, but also he promises £1000 as a gift if she marries Giles, his tenant-farmer. The problems of social inequality face the lovers in all three works, but Pamela and Patty are ennobled with spiritual qualities, while Florimel is found to have a count for a father.

The Maid in the Mill has some fine bawdy scenes and rough-house humor. It would have been as impossible to transplant it unchanged to Bickerstaff's theatre as to have performed his kind of opera in 1623. Bickerstaff's *Maid* is filled with sentimental speeches and decorous longings; it lacks the vitality, slapstick comedy and theatricality of Fletcher's comedy; his characters exist in a pastel countryside.

The miller's son in Fletcher's hands was part of the dramatic tradition of the witty fool (or servant or clown). He puns in English and Latin, is rebellious to authority, is eager to take money for mental—if not physical—labor, and enjoys joking about sex even at his own expense. Bickerstaff's Ralph is surly and rebellious, but he lacks wit and humor. He was, as one contemporary reviewer called him, a "dissolute blockhead"[7] who would feel more at home with Watt Cockney in Bickerstaff's *Love in the City* than with Bustofa. Ralph's and Bustofa's fathers, Fairfield and Franio, have only their profession in common. In this instance, Bickerstaff was more indebted to Richardson than to Fletcher. For the sake of comparison, Franio is descended from Chaucer's miller, while Fairfield must make do with Goodman Andrews.

Without losing her attractiveness, Florimel holds off her would-be ravisher, who has kidnapped her, by a simple psychological trick. Realising that Count Otrante wants her maidenhead, she pretends to have lost it. The idea occurs to her after the Count has played a trick of his own. He has let his servants treat Florimel as a slut to show her that her reputation could be ruined even if she were not. As with Pamela, of course, later Florimel immediately accepts her lover's offer of marriage even after her mistreatment. There is not even a hint of Lord Aimworth's mistreating Patty; by 1765 audiences expected instances of sensibility. Aware of the disparity in social standing between Lord Aimworth and Patty, they would expect the miller to protest; he does:

> But good noble sir, pray consider; don't go to put upon a silly old man;

my daughter is unworthy—Patty child, why don't you speak? (III, x, 70)

But when Florimel and Otrante are to be wed, her father, who also is aware of the honor, says:

I'll sell my mill;
I'll pay some too; I'll pay the fiddlers,
And we'll have all i' the country at this wedding.
Pray, let me give her too. [The King had asked for this honor.] Here, my lord, take her,
Take her with all my heart, and kiss her freely;
Would I could give you all this hand has stoln too,
In portion with her! (V, ii, 283)

The enlightened Lord Aimworth promises to forsake all those who will not acknowledge Patty; but once Count Otrante has agreed to marry Florimel, he has nothing to say about social inequality—a subject they had threshed out earlier when he was hoping for a simple rape (III, iii, 250-251). It is left to the King to make the appropriate remarks when Count Otrante and Florimel enter to be married:

Here comes the brightest glory of the day;
Love yok'd with love, the best equality,
Without the level of estate or person. (V, ii, 293)

Remarks less effective for having been uttered after the King knew that Florimel's real father was also a Count.

The question of rank bothered still another author who wrote about socially mixed marriages. When Goldoni adapted *Pamela* as *La Buona Figliuola,* he wrote in his Preface, "The Reward of Virtue . . . was the Object of the English Author; a Design I was much pleased with; but I would not have the Honour of a Family sacrificed to the Merit of Virtue. . . ."[8]

A comparison between the two *Maids* is but one more proof that English tastes became increasingly finicky between 1623 and 1765. Bickerstaff wrote for an audience which, contrasted with its Jacobean ancestors, was more prudish, fastidious, conservative, and delicate. It also shows that Bickerstaff preferred to credit as his source a popular novel rather than an unfashionable play whose title would arouse little interest in the public.

If a comparison between the two *Maids* shows that Fletcher's version is written with more humor, and more vitality, it also shows that Bickerstaff knew how to work effectively with the kinds of characters and plot that his audience desired. He might be blamed for not writing a Jacobean comedy, but he must be credited with a successful eighteenth-century comic opera.

Reviewers for the contemporary newspapers and magazines were careful to watch for, and quick to point out, any lapses from eighteenth-century decorum. While critics were unhappy with Bickerstaff's lyrics because some of them were awkwardly fitted to already written music, they nevertheless complimented the music because it had been composed by acknowledged masters —not because they knew anything about it. As was the wont of reviewers, the critic for *The London Chronicle* discussed the opera under such heads as "Fable," "Sentiment," "Diction," and "Ballads," asserting that "Mr. Bickerstaff," probably

> from the necessity he was under of writing to particular airs, has shewn nothing of that agreeable facility of language, and aptness of figure, which are to be met with in some of his other performances. *Airs.* As the music is composed of favourite Airs from different masters, there is no necessity of saying any thing on this head.[9]

Under "Sentiment," neither *The London Chronicle* nor *Lloyd's Evening Post* found anything "new or extraordinary," though the latter's critic found the "sentiments . . . generally just."[10] The *Chronicle* reviewer, however, was impressed by one line:

> a single line in the character of Ralph; who, while his father and sister, lost in gratitude and wonder, at Lord *Aimworth*'s taking the latter for a wife, says,
>
> *"Down upon your knees and fall a crying."*
>
> How this passage may affect others I know not; but for my own part, I never met any thing fraught with more nature since I first commenced an acquaintance with the alphabet. (pp. 116–117)

At least one other reviewer was affected by this line:

> . . . we venture to affirm, that what Ralph says upon his sister's wanting a proper acknowledgement [of Aimworth's proposal], is as natural, comprehensive, and fine an effusion of simplicity, as ever fell from any author's pen, "Down on your knees, and fall a crying."[11]

The stage directions do not reveal how the line affected Patty and the other characters; perhaps she was remembering Rosalind's command to Phebe in *As You Like It:* "Down on your knees, / And thank heaven, fasting, for a good man's love" (III, v. 57-58). Apparently she ignored her brother, for after his command she speaks haltingly to Lord Aimworth, who after replying joins her in a duet "in the bill-and-coo strain" (Gentleman, II, 114).

As for Bickerstaff's "Diction," *The London Chronicle* wrote that

> he is not . . . so happy in this dialogue of his polished characters, as he has been in the more subaltern ones; in the first he is easy, natural and happy; in the latter, rather still, aukward, and affected. But this is a fault that will lessen in proportion, as he chuses to enlarge the circle of his politer acquaintances.

No dramatic piece in the eighteenth century was too innocuous to be inspected for possible immorality, and every work was expected to provide a moral. *The London Chronicle* chose for the appropriate moral "an expression from the *Fair Penitent: To be good is to be happy.*" *The St. James Chronicle,* however, scented the same odor of immorality which spoiled *Love in a Village:*

> We have . . . two small Objections to the Tendency of the Fable: . . . it seems to be an Encouragement to disproportionate Marriages; such as that mentioned by Sir Harry Sycamore of a Gentleman to his cookmaid. . . . Our second Objection . . . lies against the Character of Theodosia: Dossy, it must be owned, is a very forward Gal and, as she says herself *very willing to go off.* Elopement is a Lesson, which young Ladies are very apt to learn without teaching, and whenever it is introduced on the Stage, we think it ought to be exposed, or attended with such palliating Circumstances, and so much Distress on the Part of her, who is driven to so violent a Measure, as may make it in some sort excusable.[12]

On 7 May 1765, "A Friend to Merit Wherever he Meets it" puffed mightily for *The Maid of the Mill* and made one request:

> Mr. Woodfall [he wrote]: On Saturday last I was at the Comic Opera, *The Maid of the Mill,* for the Twelfth Time, and I am not ashamed to own that my Liking was increased at every Representation. Yes, Mr. Woodfall, your Criticks, these Gentlemen of *vast Taste and Abilities* may cry *Sing Song* as long and loud as they please; but I maintain that *The Maid of the Mill,* whether we consider it with regard to Plot, Character, Dialogue, Humour, or Sentiment, is the best Dramatic Piece that has appeared on the English Stage for Twenty Years. But I want to say a Word or two to the Author, with regard to his Music. I love fine Compositions as well as any Man, and I think that *The Maid of the Mill* is infinitely superior to any we have yet had on our Stage. In a word, its Fault is that it is *too good.* Now, if this

agreeable Author ever favours us with another Piece of the same Kind, suppose that he was not intirely to reject the higher Stile of Music, but here and there to throw in a few of our more familiar Airs; which would, I apprehend, season it better to the Taste of a *London* audience. I only mention this as wishing him to succeed as much as possible; for if a Comic Opera is really in itself so absurd, puerile, and contemptible an Entertainment as they would represent it, the greater his Merit, who has contrived to render it not only charming, but respectable.[13]

Whoever the author of the letter was, a kindred spirit was writing fifty years later to the *Morning Herald:*

I am an old fellow from the country, and have not much money to spend upon mere amusement; but, as I am fond of our national music . . . I was tempted . . . to Drury Lane Theatre, to enjoy the performance of my favourite comic opera of *The Maid of the Mill.*[14]

As did DeFoe's "True-Born Englishman," the music of *The Maid of the Mill* had settled down in England and become native. Twenty continental composers could find their music in this opera, while the Earl of Kellie (or Kelly) contributed the overture; but the letter-writer felt that *The Maid of the Mill* contained "our national music." In the 1815 performance, the Earl's overture was gone, and in its place, the writer complained, were

. . . four or five bold tunes without meaning, grace or character. . . . In short, Mr. Editor, I took notice, that out of *thirty-six* pieces of music in the original opera, there were *eleven* only retained. . . .

Now, Sir, is this wrong, or is it not? and if it be wrong, with whom lies the blame? I am a plain English country Gentleman, whose taste is unsophisticated, and cannot therefore admit that it is fair dealing towards me, and many honest men in the same predicament, who come up to London, to advertise an old Opera with additions . . . without telling us . . . what Songs &c. have been *omitted!* [The actress who played Patty] would have touched the heart more powerfully . . . by adhering to the original melodies, so chastely elegant and graceful as they are, than by embarking on the ocean of flourishes and cadences . . . these double-refined vocal clap-traps. . . .

It seems that the "Italian thrill and warble [*Lloyd's Evening Post*]" of 1765 had been replaced by Italian "flourishes and cadences," and at neither time were the critics happy at hearing them. The writer in 1815 left Drury Lane thoroughly disgruntled when he "found that a British audience could relish such a hodgepodge." He thought that the Drury Lane management might have staged *The Maid of the Mill* to promote a new singer's career; that every advantage should be accorded to her was to be expected, but not at the cost of the original music: "consistency is violated and propriety abused when a sacrifice is to be made of some of the sweetest music that ever did honour to our country."

The monthly journals in 1765 reviewed *The Maid of the Mill* with no new objections. *The Gentleman's Magazine*, which usually ignored new plays, published a favorable review even to the extent of claiming originality for Bickerstaff: ". . . tho' the circumstances or incidents of his piece may have been suggested by those of *Pamela*, they are . . . very different, and upon the whole it seems to have as good a claim to originality as most other performances of the kind even where no imitation is acknowledged." The reviewer found the play comic, the characters "well drawn and admirably sustained. . . . The songs are well adapted to their purpose. . . ."

> . . . the piece has great merit, at least in the opinion of the writer of this account, who speaks from his feeling, for when he read it alone in his study, having never seen the exhibition, it made him both laugh and cry.[15]

The Universal Museum's critic held back his tears while extending his praise. He noted that at Covent Garden (as opposed to Drury Lane), the operas "are in some measure united with taste and good sense." Bickerstaff's works were "equally calculated to feast the sense and please the ear." His earlier works "have gained universal applause,"

> yet his last production seems in a peculiar manner the favourite of the town; and he by this has shewn the connoisseurs of this kind of writing, that his former works are capable of being out-done; yet that none but himself is equal to the task. In fact, there is in this new opera so much nature, sentiment, and what is still more necessary, so happy an adaptation of the words to the music, that none but critics by profession can be displeased. To please such is not, perhaps, any judicious dramatist's aim, as the phlegm of precept almost universally destroys the fire of genius.[16]

With some additions, this same review was combined with that from *The Gentleman's Magazine* and published in the February 1765 *Gentleman's and London Magazine* of Dublin. The writer, whose review thus made the rounds of at least three monthly magazines, was one of the few to hold back the phlegm of precept and to fan the fire of genius by praising Bickerstaff's adaptation of the words to the music.

The French reviewed *The Maid of the Mill, "C'est-à-dire, la Fille Meunière,"* in the *Journal Encyclopédique:*

> *Une intrigue commune excessivement usée, mais toujours agréable quand elle est conduite avec art, des scènes ingénieusement dialoguées, des vers bien faits, et une très-bonne musique, ont fait le succès de cette piece sur le théâtre de l'Opéra Comique, tout aussi frequenté á Londres depuis quelques années, que le même théâtre est goûté a Paris. Qui a lu* Pamela, *connoit a peu près cette pièce dont voici le précis.*

After the customary summary, the critic continued:

> *L'opera finit, a la gran-satisfaction des Spectateurs qui ont beaucoup applaudi au Poète et au Musicien, c'est-a-dire, au même Auteur, comme le titre l'annonce.*[17]

In England, one of Bickerstaff's friends, Benjamin Victor, found the work "agreeable," exaggerated its initial run from twenty-nine to "thirty-five" nights, and believed that the music came "chiefly from *Italian* Burlettas."[18]

Another friend of Bickerstaff, Hugh Kelly, following Charles Churchill's *Rosciad,* published *Thespis* (Book the Second) in 1767. In general he praised *The Maid of the Mill,* complimented the author, applauded the performers, and misinterpreted one of the characters:

> Mark where that happy BICKERSTAFF has drest
> A GILES all rustic with a generous breast;
> Drawn with a master's highly finish'd art
> A rough coarse mansion round a princely heart;
> There, quite at ease, unmanacled by fears,
> BEARD a true son of comedy appears. . . . (p. 24)

Perhaps on stage Beard transformed Giles into a rustic prince, but in print he is a lout.

Giles might not have been nature's nobleman, but Lord Aimworth, to read Francis Gentleman's *The Dramatic Censor,* was "what every nobleman should be, and what we fear very few are, humane, generous, virtuous and disinterested; possessing too much delicacy of sentiment to approach the object of his love upon unworthy terms. . . ." Patty was drawn "with so many amiable qualities, that even pride must allow Lord Aimworth justifiable, in descending so much below his rank to secure happiness." For once, Gentleman withheld moral disapprobation and concluded, "we think the *Maid of the Mill* possesses such charms, such a chaste, pleasing simplicity, that both in representation and perusal, she must have many admirers" (II, 115, 118, 119).

One who did not admire her was the critic who wrote the *Theatrical Review* for 1771. He thought the production of 22 October 1771 at Drury Lane was "much the best Performance of any of Mr. *Bickerstaff's* Pieces," but thereafter, any praise was only reluctantly given by the writer who felt that the success of this opera was "far beyond what it merits."

> We do not mean to level our censure against this Piece in particular, but against *operatical Compositions* in general; for though these absurd and unnatural Performances may please the unthinking and injudicious, surely, all who wish well to the credit of the *British* Theatre, must behold with concern, their unjust usurpation of the throne of public Taste; and as this grievance may in a great measure be laid to Mr. *Bickerstaff's* Charge (he having of late years been almost the only Projector of these water-gruel Performances) we hope the Champions for the Rights and Privileges of the Comic and Tragic Muse will punish this bold Invader with unremitting severity, and hence stop the propagation of these illegitimate Bantlings of the Drama, or banish them and their crack-brained Author to those distant regions, where gloomy Superstition checks the daring flights of true Genius, and Dullness with her leaden sceptre irresistibly closes the piercing eyes of Criticism.[19]

Having exhausted his rhetoric, the reviewer stolidly paced on ward: "With respect to the Piece before us, the best encomium it merits is, that it is very inoffensive, as to its tendency." He found the plot simple, the scenes regular, but "from first to last, we meet with little that is interesting." The "versification of the songs . . . is wretched beyond conception; and it seems to be very evident that the Words were written to the Music. . . . It contains neither Wit, nor Satire, but we now and then meet with attempts at humour, which are generally very indifferently executed."

At the same time that the writer for *The General Evening Post* (1772) admitted that *The Maid of the Mill* was "one of the most agreeable musical pieces in our language," he thought that several of the characters were unnecessary. He objected to Patty's readiness to marry anyone whom Lord Aimworth's generosity prompted. And finally, in a splendid bit of rigoristic thinking, the reviewer discovered "nothing very generous in a man's promoting his own happiness."

> He is in love with Patty; he is miserable without her, and therefore

> resolves to marry her: where is the generosity of all this? Had he indeed beheld her without any degree of passion, and married her because he believed *her* happiness was at stake, then we might have called him a generous man; as things are however he has no title to the character, and may as well be called generous for eating, drinking, or gratifying any other of the appetites.[20]

Dibdin wrote about *The Maid of the Mill* in three different publications. In his *Life,* Dibdin gave his version of how he won the part of Ralph; in 1790, in his own periodical, *The By-Stander,* he gave his most extended criticism of the opera; and in his *History of the English Stage,* he judged the work briefly.

The By-Stander was published weekly by Dibdin with the aid of a few of his friends. According to him, he "wrote the whole of the prose, except some articles towards the end, and also some of the poetry . . ." (*Life,* III, 7-8). Anticipating an altered version of *The Maid of the Mill* by John O'Keeffe for Mrs. Billington, Dibdin upheld the original first act as "perhaps more perfect in all its requisites than any thing on the English Stage. What it will be when it is brought out with alterations . . . I will not pretend to say."[21]

In writing about the songs of Patty, Dibdin claimed "They were composed at a period when the character of the Italian music was nature, and therefore were capable of giving force and expression to the words of any language" (p. 302). "The very best song [John Christian] BACH ever composed was in the Part of Patty," Dibdin asserted. "He took great pains with it, out of compliment to the queen, at whose request the air was made." The song occurred in Act II:

> Trust me, would you taste true pleasure,
> Without mixture, without measure,
> No where shall you find the treasure
> Sure as in the sylvan scene:
>
> Blest, who, no false glare requiring,
> Nature's rural sweets admiring,
> Can, from grosser joys retiring,
> Seek the simple and serene.[22] (II, v, 33)

Surveying the other songs, Dibdin wrote:

> One of the most admirable of all PERGOLESE's comic songs was also alloted for [Patty]; the bravura song in the first act had ever been a remarkable favourite, and the song at the end of the second act was

GIARDINI'S *chef d'oeuvre.* The first and second songs were also charming, and throughout the whole part there was but one song against which the smallest objection could be made.

Dibdin neglected to name the unlucky song, but he challenged the new songs in the *Maid* to stand against Bickerstaff's:

I defy any one to put English words to any Italian song composed within these last fifteen years, and produce the same effect; and this is an incontrovertible proof that Italian compositions have degenerated; and, to prove the truth of this assertion, I need only appeal to any lover of music whether the substituted songs are equal to those which the Maid of the Mill has lost.

Although he refused to mention Bickerstaff by name, Dibdin upheld him against those who would alter the opera:

In fact, no man could be capable of altering the Maid of the Mill to advantage who is not capable of writing as good a piece himself, and even then it is very unlikely he should be able to select music half so well as the author of that opera. . . . (pp. 301–302)

Most of *The By-Stander* was devoted to attacking and counterattacking London newspapers, and lauding the good old days of the 1760s at the expense of 1789 and 1790. His praise of Bickerstaff, though not by name, was the most lavish of any of his printed references to his old colleague. In fact, it was probably due in part to Dibdin's *By-Stander* that London gossip-mongers continually accused Dibdin in the early 1790s of plagiarizing the words of his songs from a hidden Bickerstaff.

As Dibdin the stage historian, he was more judicious in his opinions about *The Maid of the Mill,* although he did maintain his opinion about the first act:

The Maid of the Mill, 1765, is much better written than *Love in a Village,* the first act is perhaps as perfect as any thing on the stage. It however anticipates the denouement, and every thing afterward declines. The fault of this author was that he was bigotted to Italian music, and French dialogue, and therefore the music in this opera is fine, and the dialogue dull, *Ralph* and *Fanny* are the best characters in the piece, but they are only an improvement on *Hodge* and *Madge.* (*History,* V, 260)

During the 1790s some reviewers worried about the opera's possible ill-effects on the unwary. In the *Anthologia Hibernica,* for instance, the critic seems to have been writing with the French Revolution at his door. He believed that *The Maid of the Mill* "is one of those delusions which frequently destroy the proper subordinations of society. The village beauty, whose simplicity and innocence are her native charms, smitten with the reveries of rank and splendor, becomes affected and retired, disdaining her situation and every one about her. So much for the tendency of such pieces." This Irish reviewer trembled at the thought of a drama being seen by "the artless rustic."

> I know no surer steps to corrupt the primitive simplicity of a village remote from the capital [he wrote for his cosmopolitan Irish audience], than to introduce a theatrical company—Romance among unfurnished heads, makes dreadful havock indeed.

As for *The Maid of the Mill:*

> The literary merit of this piece (if it have any) is like that of the novel from which it sprung. For laughter it has no food.—Sentiment, insipid sentiment, gives it what colouring it has. As a dramatic exhibition, the pleasure produced must be from its music.[23]

England had its Reverend James Plumptre who recommended that *The Maid of the Mill* be reserved, "rather for the higher classes than the lower . . . because the play might tempt country lasses into emulating Pamela with disastrous results"; Bickerstaff's comic operas were "contaminated by indecency and that of a gross kind . . ." (III, 8).

Despite the gloom of the *Anthologia Hibernica* and Reverend Plumptre, *The Maid of the Mill* survived several decades of tinkering until at least the 1830s. As Dibdin noted, O'Keeffe altered the opera for Mrs. Billington during the 1789-1790 season. It was reduced to two acts on 20 October 1797, and again refurbished with music by Bishop and others at Covent Garden on 18 October 1814 (Loewenberg, cols. 280-281). On 23 July 1828 it was presented at the Surry Theatre, and was announced for a further night "amid cheering approbation."[24] In cities other than London, *The Maid of the Mill* proved durably popular.

In Dublin, it was a great success in 1765—in two versions. The two theatres at that time were the Crow-Street, run by Barry, and Smock-Alley under Mossop's management. "Both managers," wrote Hitchcock, "thought [the comic opera] an object worth their utmost attention. The words of the opera were published, and equally free for both. But the music was in manuscript, and the sole property of the Covent-Garden manager. From him Mr. Barry purchased it, and consequently imagined, he had in this instance, securely triumphed over his antagonist."[25]

> In this dilemma, Mr. Mossop found an unexpected resource, in the great abilities of Signior Giordani. It is a fact well established, that though the parts were writing [sic] out in Dublin for Mr. Barry, yet did Signior Giordani sit down, and new compose the entire opera of the Maid of the Mill, in full score, with all the accompaniments, in less than a fortnight: and it was written out, studied, the scenes painted, and the opera brought out, two nights before they were able to accomplish it at Crow-street. (Hitchcock, II, 137)

Loewenberg (cols. 280-281) dated the opening performances as 25 March 1765 at Crow Street, and the next night (not two nights before) for Smock Alley. With the music written by one composer for the words—rather than the other way round—the Tommaso Giordani version of *The Maid of the Mill* might well have been superior to the original, notwithstanding his haste in composing it. "The opera pleased much," Hitchcock wrote. "The music did infinite credit to the genius of Signior Giordani. It was considered . . . as a wonderful effort of the human mind: and to it were applied Pope's words, 'The sound becomes an echo to the sense' " (II, 137). At Smock Alley, *"The Maid of the Mill,* ran nine nights, besides benefits. At Crow-Street, they gave up the contest after the fifth time" (Hitchcock, II, 137-183). In all, according to Hughes, the comic opera was performed 190 times in Dublin until the beginning of Victoria's reign (p. 136).

Among the other cities in which *The Maid of the Mill* was presented, were Brighton on 31 July 1770—the first opera produced there—and St. Petersburg on 5 May 1772, and possibly again on 16 May 1772. The American Company of Comedians presented it at Kingston, Jamaica, on 13 November 1779.[26]

In the United States, *The Maid of the Mill* remained in the repertory until 3 October 1818, when, according to Macmillan, it was presented for the last time at the Park Theatre, New York. Before then, it had been given 33 times since its first appearance on 1 May 1769 at the John Street Theatre. A performance at the Southwark Theatre, Philadelphia, on 14 November 1792, was seen by George Washington. *The Federal Gazette* for 17 November described the President's reactions as though either the reporter or Washington had just stepped out of *The Man of Feeling:*

When Mr. Hodgkinson as Lord Aimworth exhibited nobleness of mind in his generosity to the humble miller and his daughter Patty; when he found her blest with all the qualities that captivate and endear life, and knew that she was capable of adorning a higher sphere; when he had interviews with her upon the subject on which was painted the amiableness of an honorable passion; and when he bestowed his benefactions on the relatives, etc., of the old miller, the great and good Washington manifested his approbation of this interesting part of the opera by the tribute of a tear. (Macmillan, p. 62)

Washington's tear seems to have been the climax of *The Maid of the Mill's* career in America.

For all of the stupidity in the *Anthologia Hibernica's* review, the writer saw that sentiment—or more accurately, "sentimentality"—predominated in *The Maid of the Mill.* The opera depended mainly on two things for its success: the music and its attendant visual treat, and the recognition of the goodness of the human heart. No one was ever held spellbound by this play as he waited eagerly to see and hear what would happen next. Indeed, Bickerstaff depended on his audience's familiarity with the story from *Pamela,* and concentrated on presenting a pleasant, musical variation of it.

Bickerstaff himself, when he later wrote a comedy of intrigue, reflected on what he had accomplished in *The Maid of the Mill:* "It has been of late years the fashion for comedy to address herself rather to the heart and understanding than the fancy," he wrote, adding in a footnote:

This sort of comedy, if pleasantry be not intirely excluded, is certainly the most commendable of all; and the author begs leave to observe, that the *Maid of the Mill,* a piece written by himself, however trifling in other circumstances, was the first sentimental drama that had appeared on the English stage for near forty years.[27]

However deficient was Bickerstaff's theatre history, he knew enough to recognize when his audiences wanted sentimentality, and when they wished intrigue. But when an audience prefers the latter, *The Maid of the Mill* has nothing but the former to offer. Part of the appeal of the opera is that it is a Cinderella dream which most people share and occasionally enjoy seeing acted out. Tastes in expression might have changed from the time of Fletcher's *The Maid in the Mill* to Bickerstaff's *The Maid of the Mill,* but the wish to see the poor but honest girl make good remained constant.

As long as critics worried about the utility of drama and the sanctity of the social class system, they would disapprove of fairy-tale operas like *The Maid of the Mill.* Despite the critics, audiences enjoyed the opera for about 65 years, leaving theatres with a sense of well-being at having seen an idealized England in which a lord and a miller's daughter, a runaway couple, country bumpkins, and gentry all come together at the finale for a vaudeville of contentment. Only a few old Tories worried about possible injuries to the interest of society and the danger to class structure.

As a result of the success of *The Maid of the Mill,* articles of agreement between "Pricilla Rich widow and John Beard Gent: Manager of Theatre Royal in parish of St. Pauls Covent Garden Middlesex in behalf of themselves & such other persons as under the will of John Rich Esq. deceased shall hereafter become managers of said Theatre—and Isaac Bickerstaff of Lyons Inn in Parish of St. Clement Danes and said Bickerstaff for himself and executors" were drawn up and signed on 4 May 1765 by Priscilla Rich, John Beard, and Isaac Bickerstaff.[28] The agreement stated that Bickerstaff would supply Beard, Rich, "their Successors &c." with three new comic operas:

> That he will on or before 1st day of September 1766 deliver to them to be publickly exhibited at said Theatre Royal compleat copy of a new comic opera a dramatic performance written by him and called Love in the City or by whatsoever other Title together with the score of the music properly adapted thereto and therewith to be performed at the said Theatre and also before 1 September 1768 another new comic opera and score of the music &c. &c., and before 1 September 1770 another opera and new score &c. &c.

In addition to delivering three comic operas, "the said Isaac Bickerstaff shall and will attend all Rehearsals or practice of said operas and assist in properly preparing the same for the first publick representation on the stage of the said Theatre." This was an important article, for most playwrights were "gentlemen" who expected the theatre managers to stage their comedies or tragedies without help from them. It was also important because Colman, Beard's successor, had little practical staging experience; in addition, Bickerstaff would be doubly useful to Garrick when he moved to Drury Lane—as a writer and as an assistant.

The next article prevented Bickerstaff from free-lancing until 1770:

Said I. Bickerstaff shall not within said 5 years from 1 September next Introduce produce or deliver directly or indirectly any play, opera or other dramatic piece or performance or of any part thereof he is or shall be the compiler of or to any person concerned in the direction or management of any other theatre; or cause any of them to be publickly exhibited or represented at any other theatre except as hereafter mentioned without license in writing first obtained.

A "license in writing" must have been easy to obtain, for by 1765, Bickerstaff's *Daphne and Amintor* and his adaptation of *The Plain Dealer* were both being "publickly exhibited" at Drury Lane.

As payment for his plays, Bickerstaff was to receive the profits of the third, sixth, and ninth nights "of publick representation of such of them as shall have a run or continue to be performed for nine nights . . . after the usual charges are deducted."

The remaining two articles set forth when and where Bickerstaff could have his works performed:

Should the managers reject or decline performing any comic opera &c. by said I. Bickerstaff it shall be lawfull for him to get the same represented at any other theatre in Great Britain or Ireland—when any of the said opera have been represented nine nights it shall be lawfull for said Isaac Bickerstaff to get them acted in any theatre in the Kingdom of Ireland only on the penalty of £1,000.

The "nine nights" clause affected only *Lionel and Clarissa,* which was successfully staged at Covent Garden in 1768. By 1770, when the third of the three comic operas contracted for was due, Bickerstaff was at Drury Lane.

5

STEWED VENISON AND TAINTED BEAUTY: *DAPHNE AND AMINTOR, THE PLAIN DEALER*

Mrs. Cibber. They have been mostly amused with comic Operas, consisting of very indifferent poetry put to old tunes, without character, and scarcely any sentiment.
Mrs. Woffington. Astonishing!
Mrs. Cibber. And more so, when you consider that these harmonious pieces would fill houses, when Garrick and myself, in Shakespeare's best plays, could scarce pay expenses—this indeed was the principal reason of the manager's going abroad, and I think he would not have done wrong, if he had never acted till the vicious taste of the town had been entirely corrected.[1]

Garrick's return to Drury Lane from France brought no great change to the repertories of either theatre during September 1765. For the third year in succession, Drury Lane opened with *The Beggar's Opera.* The first comic opera of the season at Covent Garden was *Love in a Village* on 4 October. If Garrick had returned to sweep musical pieces from the London stages by his acting, or with an exciting schedule of new and old tragedies and comedies, he began very cautiously.[2]

Garrick's first new musical piece was Bickerstaff's *Daphne and Amintor* (8 October).[3] Why this work was not brought out by Covent Garden, or how it reached Garrick is not known.

Although *Daphne and Amintor* is a short comic opera, its stage directions call for a stately production. The opera begins with "The Prospect of a Garden belonging to Mindora's Palace, ornamented with Vases and Flower-pots. Four white Marble Statues, representing two Men and two Women, the former with Flutes, the latter with Guittars, appear at opposite sides" (p. 1). To prove that two love birds that Daphne saw were but "mere machines," Mindora "strikes the Statues with her Wand, who descend and dance; the Women first, and afterwards the Men. They seem to play to each other" (Stage directions, I, iii, 7). At the end of the opera, Mindora waves her Wand: "The Garden is instantly changed into a magnificent Palace, discovering a Number of Singers and Dancers. A rich Throne is on one Side, where she places *Daphne and Amintor,* seating herself between them: after which, the Whole concludes with a Dance proper to the Subject" (I, xi, 23).

Thus, with its elaborate setting, the production of *Daphne and Amintor* must have been somewhat of a gamble for Garrick, despite its brevity. Bickerstaff acknowledged Garrick's help in his Preface:

> . . . it would be very ungrateful in me not to acknowledge my obligations to Mr. Garrick for the great pains he has taken in preparing it for representation: if it succeeds, to him, indeed, it must be chiefly attributed; who . . . thinks nothing, however trifling, below his attention, that may prove an entertainment to the Public. (p. iii)

Bickerstaff probably adapted Saint-Foix's *L'Oracle* because he "saw it lately on the *French* Stage, and was charm'd with it there" (Victor, III, 70-71). When he published *Daphne and Amintor,* he gave full credit to the original French version. Unlike his *faux-pas* with Johnson's *The Village Opera,* there was no avoiding the indebtedness to other works. He mentioned both an anonymous translation and Mrs. Cibber's adaptation of 1753, *The Oracle,* explaining that he did not use the former because it was a literal translation, "and, for that reason, very indifferent." As for Mrs. Cibber's *Oracle:*

> I should certainly have made use of [it] upon this occasion; but I found, in consequence of my plan, such curtailing and so many alterations necessary, that, in the end, I thought it would be juster to give a more faulty paraphrase of my own. (p. ii)

Her translation was excellent, Bickerstaff believed, and her performance in it incomparable. "But, I imagine, the character of the Fairy, a legendary being, very different in England from what it is in France, threw upon it an air of childishness" (p. i). Therefore he transformed his Mindora into a magician. Because operas were currently popular, "the present taste of the town favouring the attempt; I thought, by the addition of music . . . I might be able to render the whole a toy, very capable of affording an hour's amusement" (p. ii).

Bickerstaff followed Saint-Foix's text closely with but modest changes. Saint-Foix called his lovers Lucinde and Alcindor; the fairy was simply La Fée.[4] The change in names (and the status of La Fée) was Bickerstaff's most radical departure from the original—not counting the addition of songs, of course; his "faulty paraphrase" was simply an adaptation or discreet translation.

The French were not amused. *"Cet Opera est une tres-foible traduction d'une des plus ingénieuses pièces du théâtre françois, de L'Oracle de M. de Sainfoix,"* an anonymous reviewer for the *Journal Encyclopédique* complained:

> *L'Auteur, pour mieux déguiser ce drame, y a fait quelques augmentations très mauvaises and quelques ariettes insoutenables. Les Anglois ont une predilection marquée pour* L'Oracle: *mais comme les grâces de l'expression et la délicatesse des sentiments ne peuvent guere passer d'une langue à une autre, toutes les traductions de cette pièce, qu'on a faites en Anglois, sont tres inférieures a l'original.*
>
> . . . .
>
> *Voici la troisième de ces traductions, aussi inférieure aux deux autres, que celles-là le sont a* l'Oracle *François.*[5]

Not all of the English were impressed either. "This is the third time that *The Oracle* . . . has been cooked up for the palates of English readers and English audiences," began an anonymous notice in *The Monthly Review:*

> Mr. Isaac Bickerstaff . . . hath taken up this pretty trifle, made some alterations in the plan, and added to it several poor and preposterous songs, unworthy of himself, by whom they were written, unworthy of Mr. Garrick, by whom this mess was suffered to be served up for the public entertainment, and unworthy of the toleration the piece met with from a *good natured,* shall we say? or a *tasteless* audience! (XXXIII, October 1765, 326–327)

From its opening night to the end of the Spring 1766 season, it suited the tastes of audiences thirty times. A great deal of the opera's success has been ascribed to the singing of Elizabeth Wright as Daphne; one reviewer in 1765 went so far as to write, "*Daphne and Amintor* . . . seems to be written entirely for the purpose of introducing Miss Wright on the stage in a new department [she had formerly appeared as only an actress] with some degree of éclat. . . . The music is entirely Italian, and being selected by so good a judge of harmony, cannot fail to please. . . ."[6]

The Italian composers who contributed to the opera included Mattia Vento and Giocchino Cocchi, both of whom composed operas for the King's Theatre in the Haymarket; and Pierre Monsigny and Niccolo Piccini. Some music by Baldassare Galuppi, who composed operas at the King's Theatre during the 1740s, was said by Dibdin to have been delightful. Dibdin also asserted that "a good overture and a pleasing duett" was composed by "Chalons," who, according to him, was the compiler, although an advertisement in *Lloyd's Evening Post* for 9 December 1765 indicated that the music was "compiled and the Words written"[7] by Bickerstaff. Sonneck named one "Shalon" as one of the contributing composers.[8] Nothing more is given about Shalon by Sonneck, nor is he mentioned in the *Quellen-Lexikon der Musiker und Musikgelehrten.* There is, however, a Jan Chalon, an Amsterdam organ master who composed; he died in London on 11 June 1765.[9]

In later editions of the comic opera, music by James Hook has been added. The first edition contained eleven songs, and opportunity for at least two dances.

Bickerstaff immediately ran into trouble over the Italian music. Instead of ending his Preface with graceful acknowledgements to Mrs. Cibber and Garrick, he again returned to his favorite theme of the superiority of continental music over native ballads:

> With regard to the music [Bickerstaff wrote], I apprehend it must please; as it has been selected with the greatest attention, both to the beauty of the airs, and its effect upon the theatre. There are, indeed, some people, who may possibly be of opinion, that I ought to have chosen old English and Scotch ballads; or got music composed in the same taste. But, in fact, such sort of compositions scarce deserve the name of music at all; at least, they can have little or no merit on the stage; where every thing ought to be supported by a degree of action and character. (p. ii)

The Monthly Review barely credited its eyes at the sight of this passage. In the same review, part of which has already been quoted, the writer apostrophied:

> Yes, gentle Reader, thou mayest well stare! but, distrust not us. It is

really in the book, and we have faithfully transcribed the passage, in which Mr. B. hath asserted that the music of the old English and Scotch ballads scarce deserves *the name of music at all!*—To think of refuting such a declaration as this, would be almost as absurd as the declaration itself.—There is such a piece as *The Beggar's Opera!* turn to that justly admired performance, Mr. B. then turn to thy own *Daphne and Amintor,*—and be dumb for ever! (pp. 326–327)

Unfortunately for its rhetoric, a footnote was added to the review so that its writer could strike a blow for morality:

We intend this epithet [in reference to *The Beggar's Opera*] only for the ballads: for as to this celebrated burlesque opera, considered as a dramatic composition, we do not think it entitled to any commendation: its very plan having an immoral tendency.

Another critic took to verse to show his dislike for Bickerstaff's taste in music. He took his theme from the Prologue to *Daphne and Amintor* which began:

A skilful cook, this useful art we'll boast,
To hash and mince as well as boil and roast;
Our cook tonight, has, for your fare, made bold,
To hash a piece of Ven'son, that was cold;
With fresh ingredients seasons high the stew,
And hopes the guests will heartily fall to. (Etc.)[10]

To this Prologue, which was dropped on 22 October, the critic replied in the *Poet's Corner* of the *St. James Chronicle* that he wanted no more

. . . foreign Mixtures, ragout Meat,
But with nutritious Viands treat
And we will often come and eat.
[Signed] Yours, Lovers of Surloin.[11]

An echo of the lament by the "Lovers of Surloin" appeared in Mrs. Brooke's novel, *The Excursion,* 1777. She satirized Garrick's supposed way of rejecting new plays, and at one point she had him say:

"But these authors—and after all, what do they do? They bring the meat indeed, but who instructs them how to cook it? Who points out the proper seasoning for the dramatic ragout? Who furnishes the savoury ingredients to make the dish palatable? Who brings the Cayenne pepper?— the— the— a— 'Tis amazing the pains I am forced to take with these people, in order to give relish to their insipid productions."[12]

In *Lloyd's Evening Post* there appeared a puffing letter from "Harmonicus," which was republished as a straight review in *The Public Ledger;* the writer reported that "Bickerstaff's new piece . . . was performed with universal satisfaction to a most crowded and polite audience. . . ." Before praising the music, "Harmonicus" wrote the familiar-sounding criticism of theatrical entertainment:

> The tendency of this little performance is entirely entertainment; the nature of the subject admitting no opportunity for the more serious business, Instruction.—The execution however, if any thing can compensate in theatrical exhibitions for a want of moral, atones for the unavoidable neglect of this circumstance. The Language is the last degree easy; the Ballads uncommonly elegant; and the Music such as must always give the highest satisfaction to an Audience of Taste. . . .[13]

The most unusually written notice of *Daphne and Amintor* appeared in *The London Chronicle,* Thursday, 24 October 1765; although a puff, it takes the reader some moments to realise what side the writer was on. The following is copied exactly as it was printed:

> Two the Pryntur.
> Sur
> I am a grate Lovier of the Dramma, and I thinks its a burnin Sheme for the Mangurs to debese the Stege by Singg-Songg as they dwo. I likes a Harleking Inturtenement wel enuff, there's sum Sens in that; but I Kant bare Operos whyle I thinks off the divine Shakesper. Daphne and Amintor has no Sens in it at all; its translated from the French, and the French has no good Plase; and the Mewsik is Italiun; and what's Italiun Mewsik goode for. I spakes my thots upon this Mater; the Inglish loves Bise and no Kikshas.
> [signed] Your's, &c. *Kritticus.*
> PS. As for Miss Wright, I dont think no-thing at all of hur.[14]

Bickerstaff's plays were embarrassing to critics who assumed that entertainment without instruction was immoral. Whatever the private views of an eighteenth-century gentleman were, he officially was in favor of public edification; therefore, to win his praise, a drama had to inculcate its audience with moral lessons. At the same time, whatever the official stand of an eighteenth-century gentleman was, no play would succeed without its being entertaining. Judging from the popularity of Bickerstaff's operas, the practice seems to have been that the gentleman damned the play as he bought the ticket. As long as Bickerstaff continued to write operas which merely entertained, critics yearned for the good old days when Jeremy Collier put an end to that sort of nonsense. One of the most morally outraged critics of Bickerstaff employed *Daphne and Amintor* as his whipping boy in his long letter to *The Public Ledger,* Friday, 8 November 1765.

> Theatrical Entertainments [wrote "Veritas"] were originally introduced, at least encouraged, to represent the actions of human life; to instruct the mind, purify the affections, purge the passions, and to strike home in live portraits, of vice and folly, virtue and wisdom, with delicacy and wit and genius, energy and excellence of language. These ought to be the exhibition of our Theatre. . . . But, Oh! Mr. Printer, what a falling off there is now. . . . Surely genius is become degenerated . . . hardly any thing appears, but patch work performances, transcribed at second hand from French authors, dullified with Lullabies, and little Italian effeminate squawlings. Dignity, sense, and wit, are entirely sacrificed to thin sounds and faint colours; as for example, what a mere nothing is the Opera of Daphne and Amintor! It is a piece of inconsistency, without any touch of verisimility. Nature is supposed most unnaturally to make an effort, under the management and direction of the stale obsolete magic art. Nay, it is wrote repugnant even to its own plan, since (in the sixth, eighth, and ninth pages) Daphne, who is taught to believe every thing insensible and lifeless, seems to penetrate beyond herself, into the looks of little birds, and talks of blood-shed and mortals alive. What an insult must this be to a sensible audience? Has not the force of nature been ever in our existence instilled by the great Creator of the world, to preserve and propagate our species? . . . Is there not again, something remarkable rude and daring in the preface, notwithstanding it has been brushed over with the fox's tail, and the plan so elaborated by the great man, who has a genius for every thing, by saying, Such sort of compositions, alluding to the English and Scotch, scarce deserves the name of music. I should be glad to know then, what music is? What composition? Does the author assume supreme judgment? Is his opinion the standard? What, must the Beggar's Opera which has so long out-lived its cotemporary, the Village Opera, that soon died in Drury Lane, now revived by the help of Silvia[?] and others into Love in a Village, together with the Chaplet, Eliza, Artaxerxes, and other inimitable pieces, which [has] more music and composition in each single song than all this author's patched collections put together, be antiquated, or to make way for his taste, be new set to be made relishing? If this is to be taken well, and indulged by Britons, then effeminacy must prevail. . . . My intention is in behalf of the public, to drive at the root of the evil, and to insist that the present management of the stage is a grievance to the sensible part, at least, of the public. . . .[15]

From the length and tone of this letter (only an excerpt has been copied), it should be obvious that "Veritas" saw *Daphne and Amintor* as a symptom of a general degeneracy of the stage.

Few theatre critics took as much trouble as "Veritas" either to praise or attack *Daphne and Amintor*. But in general, reviewers who disliked the opera, or any of Bickerstaff's works, disapproved because it succeeded despite its being *only* entertainment. In effect, when the critic condemned the opera for its amorality, he was also chiding the audience for supporting an unedifying drama; in the same way, some reviews which praised *Daphne and Amintor* also complimented the audience for its good taste in music. Typical of the notices which disparaged Bickerstaff's works was one in *The Theatrical Campaign, for 1766 and 1767,* which summarized the state of the theatre for 1767. It considered the works of Colman, Murphy and Bickerstaff, and found them all lacking. About Bickerstaff, it was written:

> Mr. Bickerstaff had met with the most unexpected success in three productions, *Thomas and Sally, Love in a Village,* and *The Maid of the Mill;* nor was his *Daphne and Amyntor* without many advocates. To criticise upon the musical part of these performances is out of our province; and, indeed, he secured himself from any attacks upon that head, at least in the three latter, by adopting old tunes, and adapting new words to them. With respect to the poetry and conduct of the pieces, as they have stood the test of criticism, and are still well received, it would be presumptuous in us, at this time of day, to attempt pointing out any defects that may have escaped the cursory eye which viewed them through the false medium of popular applause, whilst driven by the torrent of prejudice. We shall therefore only say, that he had raised the expectations of the town to their greatest zenith, and every one was impatiently waiting for the harmonious phoenix, the offspring of his brain.
>
> These [Colman, Murphy and Bickerstaff] were the bards, upon whom the theatrical world had founded all their expectations for the aera of genius, 1767.[16]

Bickerstaff's comic opera served as an excuse for critics in the 1760s to attack opera in general, but it hardly merited the attention on its own account. It was designed as a pleasant afterpiece, and as such it succeeded with its audiences.

Up to 1765 Bickerstaff wrote only operas and an oratorio, but his second work for Garrick was a revision of Wycherley's *The Plain Dealer*. There was no great demand for a comedy by Wycherley or for Restoration comedies at this time, although at the end of the spring 1765 season, Wycherley's *The Country Wife* had been cut down to a two-act farce by John Lee for his benefit at Drury Lane, and it ran for six nights. Still, plays were always being revised for Drury Lane productions, and Garrick himself had altered James Miller's tragedy of *Mahomet,* which was performed on 25 November 1765. Commenting on the custom, Arthur Murphy—who had adapted *The Country Wife* only to be anticipated by Garrick's version (*The Country Girl*)—

> remarked, that authors at this period were no longer content to revive good old plays with some necessary alterations: they went a step further: their ambition aspired so high, that numbers thought their genius would be better employed in raising a new superstructure on the foundation of a good old Comedy, than in submitting to exercise their diligence in retouching the works of their predecessors in order to make them fit for representation. This rage grew into fashion. . . .[17]

The impetus for revision came from Garrick, rather than from the demands of Drury Lane audiences. Encouraged by the popularity of *The Alchemist* in its revised form, he encouraged playwrights to refurbish once-popular plays. As Mrs. Brooke made Garrick say in her novel,

> Ah! we have no writers now—there was a time—your Shakespeares and old Bens—If your friend would call on me, I could propose a piece for him to *alter,* which perhaps— (*The Excursion,* II, 25)

In tailoring *The Plain Dealer* for Garrick's audiences, Bickerstaff measured out the comedy to the same symmetrical pattern he used for his comic operas. He adhered to Wycherley's plot, but changed or left out several incidents which he assumed would offend the public. He was anxious to play down the sexuality of the Olivia-Manly-Fidelia triangle, and of the scene between Fidelia and Vernish when the latter learns that Fidelia is not a man, but a woman disguised as one. Wycherley had allowed Vernish to discover Fidelia's sex simply by feeling her breasts. Plainly, all of the sexual by-play occasioned by the disguise and by Vernish's discovery could not be allowed. While Bickerstaff managed the discovery scene blandly enough,[18] he did not improve Manly's character in his alteration.

In addition to altering incidents, Bickerstaff combined many of Wycherley's "Lawyers, Knights of the Post, Bailiffs and Aldermen," into "Counsellor Quillit." He also merged two of Wycherley's sailors into "Oakam." The changes reduced the number of performers without materially damaging the plot, but much of the querulous law humor in the original is missing in Counsellor Quillit. By the time he completed his revamping, about half of the new *Plain Dealer's* dialogue was Bickerstaff's, and Wycherley's half was thoroughly subdued. Bickerstaff set off his lines with quotation marks when the comedy was printed, so that Wycherley's "reputation may suffer as little as possible, by a mixture, which, I hope, will be considered at worst as an alloy, without which, according to the rules of modern refinement, his more valuable materials could never have been wrought up" (Preface, vi-vii).

Bickerstaff explained in his Preface why he altered "one of the most celebrated productions of the last century." It had not been played,

> to the honour of the present age, because it was immoral and indecent. The licentiousness of Mr. Wycherly's Muse, rendered her shocking to us, with all her charms: or, in other words, we could allow no charms in a tainted beauty, who brought contagion along with her.

The comedy suffered from "enormous length, and excessive obscenity. . . ."

> I thought I met several things which called very much for correction; a want of symmetry might, I apprehended, be sometimes mistaken for strength. The character of Manly was rough, even to outrageous brutality; and inconsistent, in his friendship for Freeman, whom he knew to be guilty of the actions of a thief and a rascal. . . . Lord Plausible, and Novel, did not seem to me so well contrasted as they might be, while the other comic personages degenerated sometimes into very low farce; neither did I think the part of Fidelia so amiable, or the situations arising from her disguise, quite so amusing, as they were capable of being rendered by a little retouching.

In these passages from his Preface, Bickerstaff proved himself to be as orthodox in his beliefs about the stage as any of the critics who attacked his works. Morally, he was in agreement with those critics like Francis Gentleman who professed to be shocked at the "licentiousness of Mr. Wycherly's Muse." Structurally, he adhered to one of the underlying principles of Restoration and eighteenth-century drama: symmetry. Symmetry, as Johnson defined it, and which Bickerstaff asserted the comedy lacked, was the "Adaptation of parts to each other; proportion; harmony; agreement of one part to another."[19] For eighteenth-century dramatists, proportion, harmony, agreement, correspondence, were qualities of their heroes and heroines; symmetry required the action to rise, climax and fall at regular intervals; it was also necessary that for each serious couple there was a gay pair. Symmetry meant also guaranteeing a *balance of quality*. At the same time as the physical movement through a play followed a geometric pattern, a balance of quality insured just punishments and rewards: "poetic justice."

As a principle of social behavior, symmetry implied the maintenance of a class structure; hence, Bickerstaff's critics attacked him for allowing a country lass in *The Maid of the Mill* to marry a landed lord, even though, in the balance of quality, Patty and Lord Aimworth were equal. Symmetry precluded a dramatist from creating grotesques in his plays—Dryden "regularized" Caliban and found him a mate. And—since eccentricity is asymmetrical—Bickerstaff rounded off Manly. He also improved the contrast between Lord Plausible and Novel, and removed the "low farce" that threw Wycherley's comedy off balance. In short, the extremes were drawn in.

At its best, symmetry produced charming comedies with the grace of a formal dance, such as *She Stoops to Conquer* or *School for Scandal;* at its worst, Cordelia marries at the end of *King Lear*.

For the sake of symmetry, Bickerstaff sacrificed much of the wit in the lengthy byplays of Novel, Plausible, and Manly; they became short pieces, carefully marked by Bickerstaff as individual scenes à la comic opera. At the same time, he reduced the physical action of Wycherley's last scene to a minimum to let each character have his or her brief, neat exit speech. His awareness of symmetry was heightened by his familiarity with continental opera, which was as exactly proportioned as drama could be. As Dibdin wrote about Bickerstaff's method of writing, he "measured his scenes as an engraver squares a picture, and thus, though correct, by being always regular, they were always cold."[20] Bickerstaff succeeded in adapting *The Plain Dealer* into five balanced acts, but he emasculated the comedy.

The play was produced on 7 December; during its first month it was performed nine times. On 16 December, Bickerstaff enjoyed a Benefit—*Thomas and Sally* was the afterpiece, with Miss Wright singing the part of Sally. From January to 21 April 1766 the comedy was performed another eight times. The afterpiece on 21 April was *The Country Wife* as altered by Lee, who played Vernish in *The Plain Dealer*. Bickerstaff profited not only from the benefit night, but also from the sale of the printed edition to the booksellers. Although he had to go to court to collect, Bickerstaff received 100 guineas for the work. "At the sittings at Guildhall, before Lord Mansfield," wrote Arthur Murphy, "Mr. Bickerstaff (the author of *Love in a Village* and other Operas) recovered one hundred guineas for making a few alterations in Wycherley's Play of *The Plain Dealer*."[21]

Bickerstaff dedicated his comedy to Garrick: "The Greatest Ornament The Theatre Ever Had to Boast. In Gratitude for his Judicious Correction of these Alterations; and his Just and Lively Instructions, which have so greatly assisted them in Representation: and as a Tribute of Affection and Esteem, for his many shining and amiable Qualities, this attempt to Restore to the Stage one of the fathers of our English Comedy, is inscribed, by his most obliged and Obedient Servant, The Editor." After Bickerstaff fled the country, his expression, "as a tribute of affection and esteem for [Garrick's] many shining and amiable qualities," was pounced upon by his leading attacker William Kenrick in *Love in the Suds;* Kenrick italicized "affection" and "amiable" in a footnote.[22] The irony perceived by Kenrick of a sodomite correcting Wycherley was passed on to the public in his *Love in the Suds* when he allowed "Roscius" to lament:

> Who now correct, for modest Drury-lane,
> Loose Wycherly's or Congreve's looser vein?
> With nice decorum shunning naughty jokes,
> Exhibit none but decent, dainty folks?*
> Ah me! how wanton wit will shame the stage,
> And shock this delicate, this virtuous age!
> How will *Plain-dealers** triumph, to my sorrow!
> And PAPHOS rise o'er SODOM and GOMORRAH! (24–25)

The two footnotes contained excerpts from Bickerstaff's Preface, and from Wycherley's *Plain Dealer*. Referring in his first footnote to Bickerstaff's avowal that he had marked the passages which differed from the original—("a mixture which, I hope, will be considered at worst as an alloy, without which, according to the rules of modern refinement, [Wycherley's] valuable materials would never have been wrought up")—Kenrick rhetorically raised his eyes toward heaven:

> What a champion for decency and delicacy, morality and humanity! What improvement may not sterling wit receive from the mixture of such alloy! What an idea may we not hence acquire of modern refinement!

Kenrick was the only critic to attack Bickerstaff's attempt to "correct these, perhaps imaginary faults of the poet" (Preface, vi); others quarreled with the results, but they all felt that the attempt was justified. For a reason different from Kenrick's, Mrs. Clive seems to have been annoyed at Bickerstaff's Preface, specifically his last paragraph:

> I have nothing farther to add [Bickerstaff had written], but my thanks to the public, for their kind reception of this piece; and to acknowledge my obligation to the performers: Mr. Holland, and Mrs. Yates, have gained great reputation in two very difficult characters; but it might seem partial to dwell upon their particular merit, where every individual has a right to the highest applause. (Preface, p. vii)

Apparently Kitty Clive felt left out, because in a London newspaper for 27 December 1765, Bickerstaff wrote (or had written for him):

> Mr. B—k–er—ffe's compliments to the widow Blackacre; begs leave to assure her that it was with great concern he found himself under the necessity of omitting her name in his preface to the new edition of the Plain Dealer; desires her in his behalf to consider, that if strict justice was done to the *merit each individual performer, and to the author of that play,* there would be but little credit due to the *editor*.[23]

The best comment appeared shortly after the comedy was performed as a poem in the *St. James Chronicle,* Tuesday, 10 December, "On Seeing the Plain Dealer":

> Let the *Plain Dealer* run—and Hand and Heart
> Applaud each Actor as he plays his Part.
> Let Fiddlers for a while no Catches play
> And *Comic Opera* have a Holiday;
> And yet confess, that *much* we owe our Laugh
> To Wycherly, and *some* to Bickerstaff.
> [signed] *You may say that.*

Garrick's friend, John Hoadly, praised the comedy in a letter to Garrick, 4 December 1766: "You have done the stage great service by restoring Wycherley to it. I never read the plays till now. They will certainly be both stock plays [*The Plain Dealer* and Garrick's *The Country Girl*]: The Plain Dealer excellent. The reformer could go no farther, there was no castrating of Manly."[24]

In his *The Dramatic Censor* the comedy was subjected to seventeen pages of summary and criticism by Francis Gentleman, who worried about its "very vague" moral, and wondered whether plain dealing was enough? It "may be a jewel, yet in such a latitude as the Captain uses it, social communication becomes hurt by unnecessary, illtimed truths . . . as fools are most apt to give their opinion, the restraint of custom and civility becomes essential" (II, 255-256). Commenting on England of the 1760s, he observed without perceptible irony, "our public taste being moralized [,] though private vices are as enormous as ever, the dramatists of our day make an adherence to decency apologize for all the other essentials" (II, 241).

Gentleman echoed Bickerstaff's metaphor about ores and alloys, and added one of his own: the revising of the old comedies by omitting their smuttiness "is like recovering a picture highly finished from obscuring filth" (II, 241); unfortunately, Bickerstaff was not an expert restorer.

Not only Gentleman, but the *Theatrical Review* (London, 1772)[25] and Arthur Murphy compared revising an old play to restoring a great picture; they all agreed that Bickerstaff was not the artist for the job. Murphy took both Bickerstaff and Garrick to task for the unsatisfactory restoration: "Mr. Garrick ought to have told him, that a picture, drawn and coloured by the hand of a great master, ought not to be touched by a vain pretender to the art. *Manum de Tabula* would have been the proper advice." Bickerstaff, decided Murphy, who was a rival restorer, should have concerned himself with expunging the "lascivious wit, and the indecencies"; when he altered the comedy, "he was guilty of bold and rash presumption."[26]

Bickerstaff's *The Plain Dealer* remained on the London stage until 1796 when it suffered an alteration in its turn, this time by John Kemble[27] who played Manly. Kemble's version kept Counsellor Quillit and Oakam, but added a "Serjeant Ploddon," and emphasized Manly's role. Kemble depended on Bickerstaff's plotting, and employed more of his dialogue than Wycherley's. In the 31 years between Bickerstaff's and Kemble's versions, stage ranting had maintained its popularity with audiences. Whereas Wycherley had been content to give Olivia the following final exit speech, "And I my revenge" (V, iv), Kemble copied Bickerstaff's operatic rendition:

> My breast burns with fury, indignation, disdain, and must have vent. Coxcomb, idiot, brute! But think not long to triumph, for I go to have

such vengeance on ye,——. (Bickerstaff, V, xii, 99. Kemble, V, iv, 82)

Although Kemble, less influenced by opera than Bickerstaff, reduced the number of scenes Bickerstaff had created, he still depended on the adaptation rather than returning to the original comedy.

On the day before *The Plain Dealer* opened at Garrick's Drury Lane, Covent Garden produced a "musical comedy" by Richard Cumberland, *The Summer's Tale*.[28] To take advantage of the town's enthusiasm for comic operas, Cumberland, who was the most prolific writer for the stage in the eighteenth century, had been persuaded by some of his friends "to attempt a drama of that sort."[29] Even though Bickerstaff had temporarily transferred to Drury Lane with *Daphne and Amintor* and *The Plain Dealer,* he still considered Covent Garden his home, and comic opera his property. Even as fellow dramatists, it would be unlikely for Bickerstaff and Cumberland to be friendly—both were too prickly; as competing dramatists they warred even when they both later worked for Garrick.

Cumberland's *The West-Indian* and *The Fashionable Lover* were rightfully popular comedies, but he wrote over fifty other comedies and tragedies; it was his misfortune to go through life believing that his works were better than the reviews they received. His reputation was not improved by Sheridan, whose Sir Fretful Plagiary in *The Critic* was partially based on Cumberland. But his own worst enemy was the Cumberland who wrote his *Memoirs* in 1806 and 1807. In them the reader learns that Cumberland was a gentleman descended from gentlemen, and a scholar descended from scholars. If he were not always right, he was never wrong, and his unselfish humility assaults the reader from practically every page.

Unfortunately for Cumberland, he became saddled with Bickerstaff in contemporary satires of the drama; though he wanted nothing to do with him, for about twelve years their names were paired or juxtaposed in jingling satires. The two first met when Bickerstaff learned that *The Summer's Tale,* in rehearsal at Covent Garden, was by Cumberland:

> Bickerstaff [so Cumberland wrote in his *Memoirs*] . . . seemed to consider me as an intruder upon his province, with whom he was to keep no terms, and he set all engines of abuse to work upon me and my poor drama, whilst it was yet in rehearsal, not repressing his acrimony till it had been before the public; when to have discussed it in the spirit of fair

criticism might have afforded him full matter of triumph, without convicting him of any previous malice or personality against an unoffending author. (pp. 187–188)

In an effort to make amends, Cumberland wrote to Bickerstaff. If the letter still existed, Cumberland explained in his *Memoirs,* "it would be in proof to show that my disposition to live in harmony with my contemporaries was, at the very outset as a writer for the stage, what it had uniformly been to the present hour. . ." (p. 188). Bickerstaff's attack "was one of the most virulent and unfair ever made" upon Cumberland, yet he met it with becoming meekness:

. . . if his contempt of my performance was really what he professed it to be [Cumberland told Bickerstaff], he had no need to fear me as a rival, and might relax from his intemperance; on the contrary, if alarm for his own interest had any share in the motives for his animosity, I was perfectly ready to purchase his peace of mind and good will by the sacrifice of those emoluments, which might eventually accrue from my nights, in any such way as might relieve his anxiety, and convince him of my entire disinterestedness in commencing author; adding in conclusion, that he might assure himself he would never hear of me again as a writer of operas. (p. 188)

Whether or not Bickerstaff accepted Cumberland's generous offer, Cumberland did donate the £74 profit from his second Author's Night on 29 January 1766 to the Covent Garden Theatrical Fund (Stone, p. 1150).

The letter to Bickerstaff, which Cumberland recalled in his *Memoirs,* was sent after Bickerstaff allegedly apologized for his hostility. Cumberland "entirely ascribed his hostility to his alarm on the score of interest, and not to the evil temper of his mind" (p. 188), an ambiguous turn of phrase in view of the later scandal about Bickerstaff. Whatever the nature of Bickerstaff's mind, Cumberland explained that he had written to allay Bickerstaff's economic fears:

I understood he was wholly dependant on the stage, and that the necessity of his circumstances made him bitter against any one, who stept forward to divide the favour of the public with him. To insult his poverty, or presume on my advantage over him in respect of circumstances, was a thought, that never found admission to my heart, nor did Bickerstaff himself so construe my letter, or suspect me of such baseness; for Mr. Garrick afterwards informed me that Bickerstaff showed this letter to him as an appeal to his feelings of such a nature, as ought to put him to silence; and when Mr. Garrick represented to him, that he also saw it in that light, he did not scruple to confess that his attack had been unfair, and that he should never repeat it against me or my productions. (p. 189)

Cumberland's *The Summer's Tale* received generally unfavorable reviews, one of which in *The Universal Museum and Complete Magazine* (December 1765) went out of its way to compare Cumberland's opera to its detriment with *Love in a Village,* that "justly admired piece." Cumberland's imitation of Bickerstaff's characters was but "paltry"; in contrast, the "celebrated" Bickerstaff's adaptation of *The Plain Dealer* was "frequently played with universal applause to crouded audiences" (p. 616).

With no love lost between Cumberland and Bickerstaff, there would be no reason to expect to see their names linked; but mediocrity is a great coupler. In 1772, for instance, Sir Nicholas Nipclose (Francis Gentleman) rhymed in his "Poetical Dissection" *The Theatres,* addressing himself to Garrick:

The want of leisure, pitiful pretence,
Apologizes for rejected sense;
Previous engagements too are made a plea,
Engagements known full well to you and me;
Such as to name would make a cynic laugh,
Perhaps to CUMBERLAND OF BICKERSTAFF.
Oh had kind fortune of my father made
An Irish bishop, or as good a trade;*
Had she, when at my mother's breast I hung
With thriving Blarney* tipp'd my supple tongue;
Then of thy smiles secure I might have shone,
As many equal simpletons have done.[30]

Sir Nicholas made two footnotes: after "trade": "Mr. Cumberland's father is in that station. . . ." After "Blarney": "A phrase in Ireland for gross, ignorant, sycophantic flattery." In rhyming about excuses "for rejected sense," Nipclose was only anticipating Cumberland—and most authors of the time. Cumberland explained in his *Memoirs* how he wrote his first comedy, *The Brothers* (Covent Garden, 2 December 1769): "I had written this play, after my desultory manner, at such short periods of time and leisure, as I could snatch from business or the society of my family, and sometimes even in the midst of both. . ." (p. 196).

The two playwrights were again juxtaposed, this time by

William Combe in his *Sanitas, Daughter of Aesculapius,* in 1772. As part of a prayer to Apollo were the following lines:

> Thy vot'ry teach, great God of day!
> "Like CUMBERLAND, to Write a play:
> "Like BICKERSTAFF, My soul inspire,
> "To strike the operatic lyre!" (p. 12)

Cumberland must have been galled to discover that William Kenrick had linked him and Bickerstaff in *Love in the Suds* as henchmen of Garrick who kept away other writers:

> While puff and pantomime will gull the town,
> 'Tis good to keep o'erweening merit down;
> With BICKERSTAFF and CUMBERLAND go shares,
> And grind the poets as I [Roscius] grind the players. (pp. 21–22)

In his own warped way, Kenrick was often accurate about the information he included in his satires. Cumberland was hired by Garrick to read plays for him,[31] and Bickerstaff worked for Drury Lane presumably on a fee basis.[32] Cumberland's and Bickerstaff's activities at Drury Lane did not pass unnoticed by the anonymous wits who supplied London newspapers with tattle and epigrams, and one rhyming allusion was reprinted in 1776 in *The Spleen: or, The Offspring of Folly,* by "John Rubric" (the ubiquitous William Kenrick), and dedicated to George Colman. In Canto III occurs the following passage and its footnote:

> How loud and long the town's horse-laugh
> With *Kelly, Foote* and *Bickerstaff*
> At a *Joe Miller's* Jest
> How readily excus'd the fault!
> "Old songs and jokes are best." (Canto III, xiii, p. 21)
> Nay so it is, tho past belief,
> False to themselves, the rogues rob thief.*

Perhaps Cumberland had this episode in mind, when he wrote

*Like thieves too they 'peach each other; as appears from the following epigram: *On Bickerstaff's being employed by Garrick to detect the plagiarisms of Cumberland.*

> If foul the work, as fair the play,
> The bard shou'd peach, who robs his brother.
> Blind Fielding, as the wisest way,
> Thus sets on thief to catch another (pp. 21–22)

in his *Memoirs* how Garrick teased him about the reception of *The West Indian:*

> One morning when I called upon Mr. Garrick I found him with the St. James evening paper in his hand, which he began to read with a voice and action of surprise, most admirably counterfeited, as if he had discovered a mine under my feet, and a train to blow me up to destruction—"Here, here," he cried, "if your skin is less thick than a rhinoceros's hide, egad, here is that will cut you to the bone. This is a terrible fellow; I wonder who it can be."—He began to sing out his libel in a high declamatory tone . . . and began to comment upon the cruelty of newspapers, and moan over me with a great deal of malicious fun and good humour—"Confound these fellows, they spare nobody, I dare say this is Bickerstaff again; but you don't mind him; no, no, I see you don't mind him; a little galled, but not much hurt: you may stop his mouth with a golden gag, but we'll see how he goes on." (pp. 220–221)

Was Garrick seriously implying that Bickerstaff had been bribed to stop attacking Cumberland, perhaps about *The Summer's Tale*? In any event, the anecdote is another indication that Bickerstaff wrote not only for the stage but for the newspapers as well.

Cumberland was not a man to forget—let alone forgive—an enemy, even if, as in this case, his opponent had fled the country; for in 1774, Cumberland could still refer to the "ill natured Invective principally collected from the Strictures of Mr. Bickerstaff," in a letter which Cumberland wrote to Garrick. The letter, probably written on Monday, 14 March 1774, dates Goldsmith's reading of *Retaliation* to the Literary Club. At the meeting which Garrick missed, Cumberland heard Caleb Whitefoord read two satirical epitaphs. They "did me the honor," Cumberland wrote, "and by implication yourself, as the turn of both was a mock lamentation over me from you with a most severe and ill natured Invective principally collected from the Strictures of Mr. Bickerstaff and thrown upon me with a Dung-fork." Cumberland retaliated by cutting his name "out of the Wine Merchant's [Whitefoord's] ledger." The two epitaphs survive in manuscript, among the many papers of Caleb Whitefoord in the British Museum. In all his papers, however, there seems to be no reference to Bickerstaff; though as an acquaintance of Garrick in London, and the son of one of Bickerstaff's former commanding officers in the army, Whitefoord probably knew him. Cumberland would have agreed with the opening lines of another poem by Whitefoord had he ever seen them: "Alas poor Cumberland, thy dot is hard!—So oft the subject of some waggish Ditty—"[33]

Whatever Bickerstaff said about Cumberland, or whatever Cumberland thought that Bickerstaff had said about him, Cumberland was still remembering it in December 1774 when *The Choleric Man* was performed. He dedicated his Preface "To Detraction" and concluded it and his replies to Bickerstaff by writing:

> And now, sir, having addressed you under your general title; do not believe that I mean to mark you out by any particular one: your correspondence with me, you well know, has always been *anonymous*—except in the case of one unhappy gentleman, and he has fled the country. As for you, sir, wherever you inhabit, and whatever is your fortune, I bear you no ill-will; my character will keep out of your reach; and for my writings I shall not much differ in opinion from you about them: if you pursue the same studies with me, good luck attend you—give your works a good word, and be silent about mine. . . .[34]

Wondering whom Cumberland meant by the "unhappy gentleman," George Steevens wrote to Garrick who punningly replied on 13 January 1775: "The *Unhappy Gentleman* was that Wretch Bickerstaff, who, [Cumberland] says, was Ever *attacking* him, in the Papers I mean—"[35]

6
"BRANDY WON'T SAVE IT": *LOVE IN THE CITY*

In the spring of 1766, the 32-year-old Bickerstaff was prospering. From being a marine second lieutenant, he had become—by way of *Thomas and Sally, Love in a Village, Maid of the Mill* and *Daphne and Amintor*—the major writer of a new corps of musical dramas, to the despair of London critics and the delight of London audiences. His agreement with Covent Garden called for two more comic operas, and already he had successfully revised one comedy, *The Plain Dealer,* for the rival theatre. Having learned first-hand about French comic opera during the 1761-1762 season when he lived at Chaillot, Bickerstaff was now ready again to set off for Paris to collect music for his next opera, *Love in the City,* which, according to his agreement with Beard, was due by 1 September 1766.

Bickerstaff left for Paris on 15 May 1766 carrying a letter from Garrick to Marie Riccoboni as an introduction:

> The Bearer of this is a Gentleman who has written with great Success for the Stage—He will tell you all about Me, & can give You the best information about our theatrical affairs—His merit, as a writer, You are acquainted with, for, if I mistake not, I sent you, his *Love in a Village,* & *Maid of Ye Mill*—he has likewise given a piece to our theatre this Last Winter which I have sent you. . . . (*Letters,* II, 402, 512)

Once in Paris, Bickerstaff was able to gossip about Drury Lane to others besides Madame Riccoboni: "I have had a letter from

Bickerstaff," Garrick wrote to George Colman in Paris on 30 June 1766; "he is at Paris, & is going to give some Account of our Theatre in the *Journal Encyclopiq:* You will see it I suppose."[1]

After spending the summer in France, Bickerstaff returned to London, anticipated by the following newspaper puff:

> Mr. Bickerstaff is every moment expected from Paris, where he has been some time writing an Opera called Love in the City, which is to be represented early at Covent-Garden Theatre.[2]

Realizing that he was trying something new—a satire against the very people who were going to see his comic opera—Bickerstaff took more care with *Love in the City* than with his earlier comic operas: at least his Preface was written in the querulous tone of one who had worked long on something he was not altogether sure anyone else was going to appreciate. His certainty that whether or not his audience savored his Opera it nevertheless deserved praise led him to dictate taste in his Preface:

> To those who find fault with an opera [Bickerstaff began], merely for being such, it will be in vain to say any thing in defence of this: indeed the absurdity attach'd to the musical drama is so glaring, that there seems no great penetration necessary to discover it; and consequently any one who will cry out sing-song or tweedle-dee is capable of turning it into ridicule. Yet it should be considered, that its absurdity, gross as it is, constitutes, in a great measure, its power of pleasing; and however preposterous it may appear for people to carry on their most serious affairs in a song, we find the mind accommodate itself to those sort of illusions on the Theatre, with so much ease, that it is little better than impertinence and pedantry to enquire into their propriety. (pp. i–ii)

Having told his readers to accept the fact that they swallow the preposterous with ease, Bickerstaff then defended his choice of subject-matter which he wished to present through an absurd medium.

> . . . the admirers of lords and ladies, and fine sentiments will, probably, quarrel with [this Opera] for being LOW; but my endeavour has been, thro' the whole, to make my audience laugh; and however respectfully we may consider illustrious personages, I will venture to say they are the last company into which any one would think of going in order to be merry. (p. ii)

To an audience which enjoyed the sententious in sentimental

comedy, and applauded Whitehead's *School for Lovers,* Bickerstaff wrote:

> With regard to what is called sentiment, it is not because I dislike it in its place that I have neglected it; nor because there was any great difficulty to succeed in the pursuit; I could have got together, not only all the moral, but all the cardinal virtues, and half an hour's reading in the Oeconomy of Human Life, would have enabled me to ring the changes on them through my three acts, but I have deferred this to a better opportunity (p. ii)

Continuing his lecture, Bickerstaff next informed his audience what to expect from the music.

> The music of this piece is almost totally comic, and generally characteristic; I would therefore advise those of my auditors, who do not taste it at the first hearing, to give it a second, nay a third or a fourth; and after that, should they never desire to hear it again, I can only tell them they happen to dislike what has been repeatedly approved by all the polite nations of Europe.
>
> The songs are not offered as poetical ones, for most of them have had the disadvantage of being written to their several airs, in which I was always confin'd to a particular measure, often to a word, and not infrequently to a letter: indeed, though I may have employed very little wit and humour in the construction of this piece; labour and time it has cost me a great deal.

After all this bullying, Bickerstaff concluded by assuring his audience, in a sentence of last-minute humility, that what they were to see or read was not much of a play at all.

> If any one should be maliciously inclined to apply this hackney'd quotation of the Mountain's in labour, and brings forth a Mouse; let it be remembered, that I do not want to pass my Mouse for a Lion; I give it for what it is, a little squeaking thing, that has been produced with greater pains than it seems to require; certainly with more than it deserves.[3]

Even without a Preface to antagonize them, audiences were unlikely to enjoy *Love in the City,* which was probably the first full-scale satire against the middle-class "Cit" since Ravenscroft's *The London Cuckolds,* because "the merchants, clerks, and professional men . . . made up most of the pit audience."[4] Reviewers during Bickerstaff's time knew to whom to appeal even if he did not, and many of them spent almost as much space in their critiques soothing the indignation of the "spirited citizens" as they did damning the comedy. Although Bickerstaff probably won the favor of the gallery through the buffoonery of Shuter the comedian, as it turned out, the comedy was damned almost solely for being "low" and anti-bourgeois. On the same night that *Love in the City* opened at Covent Garden (21 February 1767), George Colman's comedy, *The English Merchant,* began its successful career at Drury Lane. This comedy, as one critic wrote, "may owe its success in a great measure . . . to the direct tendency of the title, and compliment thereby conveyed in opposition to *Love in the City,* which made Mr. Cockney appear so ridiculous, if not contemptible."[5]

The English Merchant was a sentimental comedy, which was performed fifteen times during the spring of 1767 at Drury Lane. At its climax, the noble father of Amelia, the heroine, falls in gratitude at the feet of the English Merchant, Freeport. This was an action that the audience could appreciate. Colman's comedy played against *Love in the City* for four nights, until Bickerstaff's opera died. The fate of both plays can be seen from the theatre account books.

Covent Garden: *Love in the City*		Drury Lane: *The English Merchant*
Saturday, 21 Feb:	£245. 14s	£235. 3s
Monday, 23 Feb:	£197. 5s	£193. 17s 6d
Tuesday, 24 Feb:	£136. 1s	£161. 9s 6d
Wednesday, 25 Feb:	£115. 13s 6d	£150. 14s 6d

(Stone, II, 1222–24)

On Thursday, 26 February, Covent Garden withdrew *Love in the City* and instead played *A Bold Stroke for a Wife*: it drew £220. 16s. At Drury Lane *The English Merchant* grossed £230. 9s 6d. (Stone, II, 1225).

From the Prologue of *The English Merchant,* it is evident that, like Bickerstaff, Colman had returned from France with a play.

> Our bard too made a trip; and, sland'rers say,
> Brought home, among some more run-goods, a play. . . .[6]

He dedicated it to Voltaire, and indeed, the comedy is taken from Voltaire's *L'Ecossaise.* The merchant Freeport is generous and unselfish; a man whose "business-like" manners hide a heart of easily-panned gold. The villain is Spatter, a Grub-Street journalist, for whom, it was rumored, the model had been William Kenrick. At any rate, a year after the success of the comedy, when Colman and the other Covent Garden managers fell out,

Kenrick wrote a vicious attack upon him. There is no satire in *The English Merchant* against the middle class, but through Freeport there is much praise.

Despite its failure, *Love in the City* is well-written and delightful. Its music came from seven continental composers, and from Charles Dibdin who composed "the overture, the first chorus, the finales of the first and second acts, and three songs."[7] Only an incomplete vocal score remains, however, with but one song of Dibdin's. The music which still exists is from Italian opera successes by Barthelemon, Jommelli, Galuppi, Cochi, Vento, Pergolesi, and Piccinni.

Before *Love in the City* opened, there were problems to be resolved. "Simpson, the hautboy-player, and some other persons, persuaded Beard, that [Dibdin's] music . . . would discredit his theatre; and, that, in particular, the overture, and a song beginning, 'Ah! why, my dear,' were written contrary to the rules of harmony" (Dibdin, *Life,* I, 53-54). Dibdin recalled that "the expression used was, that they were not grammatical. . . . Dr. Arne . . . having looked carefully over the scores, pronounced that there was nothing against the rules of harmony. . ." (*Life,* I, 56).

In addition to musicians who worried over Dibdin's grammatical ability, that other inevitable problem, the disgruntled actor, appeared in the form of Ned Shuter. He was to play "Wagg," a part subsequently omitted from the abridged version, *The Romp.* Shuter's role was made as much by him as for him; but according to Dibdin, who called Wagg "an unprofitable part," Shuter "was not very alert in assisting [the Opera's] success, which, by the bye, was a little ungrateful, for the part was almost dictated by himself; and, therefore, perhaps, contained all that reprehensible, indecent stuff which worthily caused the disapprobation of the audience" (*Life,* I, 57). As Wagg, Shuter assumed an Irish accent, sang a mildly bawdy song, mugged outrageously in some farcical scenes, declaimed, and concluded the comedy with a song.

Dibdin claimed that Shuter had no regard for Bickerstaff as an author, either because of or despite his appearances in *Love in a Village* and *Maid of the Mill;* in fact, he "would not allow this author to be more than a good cook. . . ." At the final performance of *Love in the City,* when Shuter "came off, at the end of the first scene, he was asked how the piece was going on, 'Going on!' said he, 'brandy won't save it.'"[8]

Despite Shuter's backstage grumblings, and Dibdin's memory of his performance, the first accounts allowed that "The actors in general did great justice to their characters. Mrs. Mattocks [Priscilla Tomboy] was inimitable; Mr. Mattocks and Mr. Dunstall remarkably excellent: nor can we forget the performance of Penelope, who notwithstanding all the terrors of a first appearance [Miss Brickler], discovered much taste and sensibility."[9]

Praising the actors was as far as most reviewers were willing to go, although one of the earliest notices, "From the Rosciad," also approved of the music.

> If unnatural and exaggerated characters, low ribaldry, instead of true wit and humour, inconsistency and absurdity, in the whole conduct of the drama, can intitle a piece to public favor, *Love in the City* will undoubtedly stand foremost in the list of fame.
>
> This piece received every possible advantage from the Performers, by a spirited exertion of their particular powers. The Overture is truly comic, and many of the airs pleasing. It is hardly to be doubted, but the Spirited Citizens, who are the true friends and principal support of all places of public entertainment will resent, with strict justice, the indignities cast upon them in this piece, by treating it with that contempt which it deserves.[10]

As an afterthought the reviewer added in brackets, "[It has since undergone some alterations.]" *The St. James Chronicle* reviewed—"defended" would be more accurate—*Love in the City* on Tuesday, 24 February.

> *Love in the City* . . . afforded Abundance of Conversation, without Loss of Time, or Hindrance of Business, on the other Side of Temple-Bar. It was low—It was indelicate—It affronted the Lord Mayor, the Aldermen, and the whole Court of Common-Council. So they said, who had not seen it. However, on *St. Monday,* the Obstacles to its Success (which were pointed out at the first Representation of it) were removed; and the Piece much mended in Point of Delicacy at least.
>
> To find Sense, and Sound into the Bargain, requires perhaps more than a common Fidler's or a common Scribbler's Industry and Skill. Mr. Bickerstaff has endeavoured at both; and, we may fairly say, he has succeeded. . . . A Dramatic Writer, who tacks *sing-song* Numbers to his Prose, labours under a peculiar Disadvantage: He must necessarily sometimes weaken the one to give force to the other. A remarkable Proof of this Observation may be brought from the humourous Circumstance in the Opera-Play now acting here, of *Barnacle's* singing an *Advertisement for a Wife.*
>
> . . . .
>
> The greatest Objection, we must ingenuously own, which can be

brought against the Plan of this Piece, is, that the Author has been contented with the stale Supposition, that a *Cit* must jump at an Alliance with a *Lord*. Even on his own Plan we cannot suppose that a prudent old *Cit* would at least have been convinced of his Lordship's identity.

However, if at either House (and why not?) the Entertainments are to be diversified, by the no very unnatural intermixture of Sound and Sense, Mr. Bickerstaff stands foremost in this Province. Whoever excells him (take these both together) *Erit mihi Magnus Apollo.*

Two of the monthly literary magazines both disapproved of the comic opera:

The city has long been the favourite scene of comedy [began *The Critical Review*'s writer]. Shakespeare has inspired us with a kind of veneration for the very name of *East-cheap,* and Ben Jonson has immortalized *Moor-fields* and *Coleman-Street.* Our present musical dramatist has, however, wooed the coy muses with most success by making *Love in a Village.* With his innocent *Maid of the Mill,* he was successful; but in *the City,* like true town coquettes, they have jilted him. We would advise him, therefore, to follow the example of Sir Francis Wronghead; and having made an unsuccessful journey to London, to take a journey into the country *again.*[11]

In *The Monthly Review,* John Langhorne[12] dismissed Bickerstaff's effort:

Of the music and scenery of this piece [he wrote], two of the essential constituents of musical dramas, it is not, perhaps, our province to speak. The subject is trite, and but indifferently handled; the characters, except that of the Creolian Girl, are not new; the airs are avowedly unpoetical; and the diction, as the Author intended it, *LOW.* On the whole, we cannot help subscribing to the general opinion, that this opera is every way much inferior to the former productions of this author.[13]

In Paris, the review in the *Journal Encyclopédique* was short and damning:

"The Love in the City, *&c. c'-est-à-dire, l'Amour à la Ville, Opéra Comique représenté sur le théâtre Royal, Covent Garden, par l'Auteur de l'Amour au Village. . . . L'Amour au Village est une assez mauvaise pièce dont nous avons rendu compte; mais encore est-elle fort audessus de l'Amour à La Ville; aussi le public lui a t'il rendu toute justice qu'elle meritoit.*"[14]

Bickerstaff's comic opera inspired two other writers, one against, and one for it, to write long reviews. The writer who disliked *Love in the City* ridiculed Bickerstaff's preface, and held up one song as proof that indeed the opera was "LOW":

> Success seems to have turned this poor author's brains [began the author of *The Theatrical Campaign*], or at least made him fancy, that he might write and say what he pleased with impunity. Nat. Lee, as great a candidate for Bedlam as he was, would certainly never have insulted his audience with such a preface. . . . As to the city, he has very modestly estimated its characteristic probity, by accusing an opulent trader with defrauding his customers of seventy-five per cent. in the smallest articles. . . .
>
> Indeed, Mr. B———, after this, it would not have been surprising, if you had personally told the audience, they were all a parcel of fools, and were condemning what they did not understand.
>
> . . . .
>
> [Bickerstaff] has considered the audience as so many cats, who were to be diverted with his mouse; and they have retaliated the compliment, by hunting his little squeaking thing into a hole, from whence it will never again make its appearance. . . .
>
> In whatever light we consider this production, it is equally contemptible. Whether we examine the sentiments, the characters, the fable, or the poetry, we must acknowledge . . . them . . . LOW. The song which he puts into Shuter's mouth, is said to be the best in it. . . .

Quoting the song, which was slightly bawdy, the reviewer found everything wrong with it including the "musical beauties of the air . . . but that is not the poet's legal property, as he smuggled it from France in his last voyage."

> As you are very fond, Mr. B———, of advice, will you give me leave to offer you a bit in return? In the next production with which you propose amusing the town, do not be so much afraid of throwing in a little sentiment, a little wit, and a little sense: believe me, it need not be quite so LOW; and you may, without any danger, write what your audience are capable of understanding; neither is it absolutely necessary, that they should be quite so much insulted. . . . (pp. 33–37)

This review, of which about half has been quoted, was concerned for the most part with Bickerstaff's Preface; about the play itself, the writer was relatively unconcerned: the play was "Low" and there was an end to it. On the other hand, Archibald Campbell defended *Love in the City* by making fun of the "public-spirited Citizens" who had attacked it. In his *The Sale of Authors,* "In Imitation of Lucian's Sale of Philosophers," Campbell approved of Bickerstaff's effort, while a grab-bag of writers including Samuel Johnson (whom he had previously satirized in *Lexiphanes*), Arthur Murphy, MacPherson (whom

Campbell accused of writing *Ossian* to make money), Garrick, Wilkes, Churchill, and the author of the review in *Lloyd's Evening Post* which has already been quoted, were attacked. Campbell defended Bickerstaff against the charge of the play being "Low" in Lucianic dialogue:

Mercury: . . . bring out, Mr. B——ff.
Citizens: SSS. SSSS. Off . . . Off . . . Away, away with him.
Mercury: O heavens! What's here to do? Misfortune upon misfortune! Why Gentlemen, don't you know, that this is the Author of your favourite pieces; *Love in a Village,* and the *Maid of the Mill*?
Author of the *Rosciad* [in *Lloyd's Evening Post*]: Ay, but he is likewise Author of *Love in the City;* and I hope that the Spirited Citizens, the true friends and principal support of all the places of public entertainment, will resent, with strict justice, the indignities cast upon them in this piece, and treat it with the contempt it deserves. I hope all their sentimental feelings and powers of indignation will be rouzed.
Citizens: Sssss. Sssss. Off, Off.

. . . .

Author of the *Rosciad:* Bravo, Bravo. Well done my warm friends to the Theatre, my public-spirited Citizens, who are so grossly and publicly abused, abused by being scandalously ridiculed in the most flagrant and contemptible manner. It calls aloud for your general condemnation. I shall condemn it for you to the utmost exertion of my powers in the Rosciad.*

Campbell footnoted, "The two speeches, put in the mouth of the Author, are almost word for word his own."

Mercury: So, it seems, this genius is the author of the Theatrical Register, whom I ordered out to be sold in lieu of his resemblance and Architype Doctor J——n. Waiter, lay hold of that fellow, and shut him up again with his Terrifications, Floscular Elegancies, and Sentimental Feelings.—Pray gentlemen of the City, if Mr. B——ff has ventured to ridicule you for your fondness of marrying your daughters among the Nobility, have not the nobility been also ridiculed for marrying their sons among you, in order to pay off mortgages on their estates contracted by debts at play, and keeping extravagant mistresses. And have you not laughed at such characters?
Citizens: Sssss. Off, Off.

. . . .

Mercury: Well, it seems the City must be sacred henceforth from ridicule, especially on the stage, and a Livery-man, or Common-Councilman, even a Grocer or Haberdasher is no more to be produced and exposed there than a Clergyman. But gentlemen, as you will not bear to be laughed at, I hope you do not deserve it. . . .

. . . .

Mercury: You see Mr. B——ff, there is no talking to these publick-spirited Citizens. You must do something to regain their favour tho', but for heaven's sake, let the scene of your Opera lie to the westward of Temple Bar. Can't you write *Love at Court,* where you may give the cits their revenge, and pay off the nobility and gentry; you may represent them as all very deep in the Citizen's books, and never paying their debts; but do not mention a word of their lying with their wives. You will then have reason to hope, that these true friends, and principal supports of all public entertainments, will themselves leave their Counters, and come with their wives and their children, their prentices and journeymen, to clap you and bear you out against the anger of the Boxes.[15]

Two eighteenth-century stage historians commented briefly. Victor said simply that *Love in the City* "met with an unfavourable reception. The Audience expected better Entertainment from the Author of the *Maid of the Mill*" (III, 79). Baker was not sure "Whether this opera was disliked on account of its supposed insufficiency in dramatic and musical merit, or whether it was condemned by a party of Cheapside wits, who thought themselves reflected on its title. . . ." In either case, Baker continued, the opera "in spite of its faults, was too good for their entertainment, and contains one character that recommends itself by unusual warmth of colouring, we mean *Priscilla Tomboy,* an unmanageable Creole wench, brought to London, and placed in a Grocer's family, for education."[16]

The play closest in time to Bickerstaff's comedy from which he might have borrowed some of his plot—and to which he did respond in his Preface—is *The Clandestine Marriage,* by Colman and Garrick (Drury Lane, 20 February 1766).[17] Bickerstaff was accused by Dibdin of borrowing part of the plot: "that author had complained that *The Clandestine Marriage* had anticipated *Love in the City,* though he himself had stolen the hint" (*History,* V. 261). Admittedly *The Clandestine Marriage* satirized the merchant, nouveau-riche class in the persons of the rich widowed Mrs. Heidelberg, her brother the merchant Sterling, and his older daughter; but the bent of the comedy is in a different direction. Still, in it there are two speeches which summarize what *Love in the City* is all about; the first is by Lovewell the romantic lead:

—But you know your father's temper.—Money is the spring of all his actions, which nothing but the idea of acquiring nobility or magnificence can ever make him forego—and these he thinks his money will purchase. —You know too your aunt's, Mrs. Heidelberg's, notions of the splendor of high life, her contempt for every thing that does not relish of what she calls Quality, and that . . . she absolutely governs Mr. Sterling and the whole family. . . . (I, i, 5)

The second speech is by Mr. Sterling to Lovewell:

> You're not rich enough to think of a wife yet. A man of business shou'd mind nothing but his business. . . . Get an estate, and a wife will follow of course.—Ah! Lovewell! an English merchant is the most respectable character in the universe. 'Slife, man, a rich English merchant may make himself a match for the daughter of a Nabob. (I, i, pp. 9–10)[18]

Despite Dibdin's assertion, however, and the two quoted speeches, since *Love in the City* was contracted for by name when Bickerstaff signed his articles in May 1765 (the year before *The Clandestine Marriage* was produced), Bickerstaff's complaint that Colman's comedy "anticipated *Love in the City*" may be valid.

The Epilogue (by Garrick) to *The Clandestine Marriage,* an amusing comic opera in miniature which satirized the vogue of musical comedies, caused Bickerstaff to defend that genre in his Preface to *Love in the City*. Garrick's skit concluded with a Recitative, *duetto, Trio,* and "full-mouth'd Chorus" in quick succession to "drive all Tragedy and Comedy before us!" The stage directions call for the "Company to rise, and advance to the Front of the Stage" for the final Air:

> Colonel Trill. Would you ever go to see a Tragedy?
> Miss Crotchet. Never, never.
> Colonel Trill. A comedy?
> Lord Minum. Never, never,
> Live for ever!
> Tweedle-dum and tweedle-dee!
> Colonel Trill, Lord Minum, and Miss Crochet. Live for ever!
> Tweedle-dum and tweedle-dee!
> CHORUS. Would you ever go to see, &c.[19]

Bickerstaff wrote in his Preface that anyone could find "fault with an opera, merely for being such . . . indeed the absurdity attach'd to the musical drama is so glaring, that there seems no great penetration necessary to discover it; and consequently any one who will cry out sing-song or tweedle-dee, is capable of turning it into ridicule" (p. i).

Although Bickerstaff worked with a plot which resembled those of Restoration intrigue comedies, and with characters similar to standard comic Restoration figures, the spirit of the comedy resembles early Dickens and nineteenth-century amiable caricature rather than a work by Crowne or Wycherley. The world pictured by Restoration wits was a much harsher one than the London scene presented by Bickerstaff where Wagg, masquerading as a Colonel, waits in Old Cockney's shop "eating almonds and raisins." Bickerstaff's characters look and sound as though Cruikshank were about to draw them. Barnacle, as an avuncular guardian who bestowed rewards and punishments at the final curtain, gained some particularization at Bickerstaff's hands because he is a comic figure in his own right. Like Congreve's Old Batchelor, Barnacle is at first an object of laughter; he is too eccentric in his merchant-like ways to be a touchstone for behavior; but his good sense is allowed to outlast his eccentricity. His ferocity lets him take command of any scene he is in, and he has several good songs, notably his "Advertisement for a Wife" in Act II, scene ix:

> This to give notice, that a man about fifty,
> Healthy and vigor'us, and of humor thrifty;
> Longing to taste of virt'ous fruition
> Wishes to change, out of hand, his condition:
>
> Beauty and youth little stress will be laid on;
> But, if he could, he would marry a maiden;
> So, to prevent any fruitless vexation,
> Widows are pray'd not to make application.
>
> Cash there must be, in hand or annuity;
> For which a jointure in case of viduity.
> From principals—letters post paid—as directed:
> Honour and secrecy may be expected. (p. 41)

The two sets of lovers are the traditional romantic couple (Spruce and Penelope); and in this case, the impetuous (Sightly and Priscilla). Although Spruce was left out of the farcical abridgement, and Penelope's importance minimized, Bickerstaff provided them both with good romantic songs, and gave them a fine scene when Spruce and then Penelope play at being in high society.

> Penelope: Pray, my lord, is a woman of fashion permitted to love her husband?
> Spruce:—I think it's rather against the rules . . . I suspect you have got some ungenteel prejudice . . . let us hear how you would like to live with your husband.

Penelope: . . . I would do every thing to please him with joy, and if ever he did any thing to displease me, I would bear it with patience.
Spruce: Oh, gad, Madam, this will never do—it smells so strong of Cheapside and the Poultry—it is overcoming—
Molly:—cousin Penny, how can you expose yourself—
Penelope: . . . if I must be a woman of fashion, you shall find I can stare, and laugh, and prate . . . and be as impertinent, idle, and good for nothing, as the best of them.

Bright in gold, in jewels blazing,
  Like a comet see me go;
Scatt'ring terror, and amazing
  All the little world below.

With a look their freedom awing
  How the Cits will hang their ears,
Gaping, staring, humming, hawing,
  When her ladyship appears. (II, vi, 33–34)

Miss Molly Cockney is in the main tradition of Old Maids with pretensions; playwrights had as much sympathy with them as they did with evil witches, and like all disappointed Old Maids or exposed witches, on the stage at least, she is driven from polite society.

Watt Cockney is an urban version of Bickerstaff's Ralph in *The Maid of the Mill* and anticipates the more unpleasant aspects of Goldsmith's Tony Lumpkin. As for the rest of the characters, Priscilla will be mentioned later, but Miss La Blond deserves notice because of her make-believe mad scene. Having been slighted by Watt, she pretends madness in an unsuccessful attempt to win him back. Her mad scene is a parody of all mad heroines in opera and tragedy—and Bickerstaff's *Leucothoë:*

I was in love once—but my love was false, false, false. Yonder is a butter-fly, let me catch it—softly, softly—It's a wasp, it is a wasp, it is a wasp.

. . . .

Four aldermen in a coach; ha! ha! ha!—And yet I cannot help crying when I think of the poor horses.

. . . .

Farewell, farewell, all hopes of ease,
The flames upon my vitals seize!
  What strange variety of pain!
  Cold, cold, as ice;
  And in a trice,
Now, now, I burn again.

But soft! who there in ambush lies?
  'Tis Cupid I know,

By his wings and his bow,
And the bandage he wears on his eyes!
Ah, urchin, your smiling
Is false and beguiling
A shaft from his quiver he drew;
He levels—see, see,
He shoots—and—ah me!
The traitor has shot me quite thro'. (III, vi, 58–59)

In *Love in the City,* Bickerstaff presented Covent Garden performers a very "actable" play; no one is in it merely for exposition or because of exigencies of plot. Each character has his or her own moment on the stage; even Old Cockney, who does not sing, has the following pleasantries in Act II, scene vii. He has just admitted to having a country home.

Old Cockney: . . . it's well enough for a mouthful of air of a Sunday—but London for my money—I see nothing in Europe like it.
Spruce: Then you have been abroad Sir?
Old Cockney: About two and twenty years ago, my lord, I was as far as Birmingham—My first wife, poor woman, she died of a dropsy! made it her request to be buried in the churchyard, with her father and mother; and as it was summer time, I thought it would be a pleasant journey. (p. 36)

The characters and their dialogues are rooted in the City. Bickerstaff might have written his opera in France, but he was careful to let his people allude to *Lloyd's Evening Post* and *Charles Say's Journal.* Barnacle spoke for many merchants when, in Act II, scene viii, he looks carefully at Spruce's clothing:

Let me see—is that Lyons or Spittle-fields? French—French!—Starving the poor weavers and their wifes—a pack of damn'd—
Old Cockney: Dear Brother! (p. 38)

The plight of the weavers of Spital fields was noted as well by Colman in his Prologue to *The English Merchant:*

Is there a *weaver* here from Spitalfields?
To his award our author fairly yields.
The *pattern,* he allows, is not quite new,
And he imports the *raw materials* too.
Come whence they will, from Lyons, Genoa, Rome,
'Tis English silk when wrought in English loom.

. . . .

So it have leave to rank in any class,
Pronounce it *English Stuff,* and let it pass!

The silk weavers had rioted in 1765 against the government failure to discontinue importing foreign weaves; in 1768 they were to riot again because of a reduction in wages. The English stage was not yet ready for dramas of social protest, but it stood four-square for "the roast-beef of old England" (including everything English-made) if the competitor was France.

In *Love in the City* the prose and the songs are more expertly integrated than in any of Bickerstaff's earlier comic operas. He was justified in writing in his Preface, "labour and time it has cost me a great deal"; for not only do the songs fit neatly into the action—forwarding it, not impeding it—but they also belong to the characters who sing them. What is immediately evident in most of the 32 numbers, be they duets, the quintetto, or the final vaudeville, is their theatrical energy. "The songs," as Bickerstaff wrote in his Preface, "are not offered as poetical ones." For instance, in a fight between Watt Cockney and Priscilla, she has called him a "paltry, dirty grocer." "Ah, spite!" Watt retorts:

Young Cockney: Furious still like a cat,
Squaling, biting, scratching;
Or yet what's worse than that,
A serpent mischief hatching.
Priscilla: What you say to me, Sir,
Is not worth remarking;
For every little cur,
We know will be barking.
Y. Cock.: There's a lady—Oh la,
Priscilla: You'd be glad to trap her;
Y. Cock.: Who I?
Pris.: Yes, you.
Y. Cock.: Nya, Nya.
Pris.: Conceited whipper-snapper.
Both: Say your worst,
Fret till you burst,
Only try,
Which you or I
Will be tired first. (III, ix, p. 63)

Despite its failure, *Love in the City* is Bickerstaff's best full-length comic opera. More than just the failure of one opera, its demise turned Bickerstaff away from further experiments, and encouraged by the successes of *Love in a Village* and *Maid of the Mill,* he reverted to harmless country tales and adaptations. Its failure offered no encouragement to other dramatists, and comic opera settled into a sentimental, pastoral mold until well into the nineteenth century.

From the wreck of *Love in the City,* Priscilla Tomboy emerged to sail across British, Irish, and American stages in *The Romp* for the next seventy years. Gone was Bickerstaff's satire, and four of his characters: Spruce, Wagg, Miss La Blond, and Old Molly Cockney. There were at least two abridgements, one made in 1767,[20] and the one in which Dorothy Jordan starred. The first version was a three-act abridgement with the subtitle *A Cure for the Spleen;* it was performed successfully between 1767 and 1778 in Ireland and then England. But by the time *The Romp* reached Covent Garden on 28 March 1778 it had lost its subtitle and one of its acts. The early permutations and peregrinations of the first *Romp* are difficult to follow because of the scarcity of notices, misinformation and lack of text; besides, it is Mrs. Jordan's version that counts. She acted Priscilla Tomboy in Dublin sometime between 1780 and 1782, at which time she arrived in England. Once in England her performance as the "Romp" was largely responsible for her quick success; by 1785 a lovely picture of her in character was printed by J. Cary in London, and in 1786 an anonymous author wrote *An Essay on the Pre-Eminence of Comic Genius: with Observations on the Several Characters Mrs. Jordan has appeared in.* "In the *Romp,* poor as it is," the author observed, "Mrs. Jordan displays a matchless power of enchaining attention and commanding applause" (London, 1786, pp. 14-15). Two years later, Fanny Burney commented on Mrs. Jordan:

> During the evening, in talking over plays and players . . . when Mrs. Jordan was named, Mr. Fairly and myself were to make the best of her. Observing the silence of Colonel Welbred, we called upon him to explain it.
>
> "I have seen her . . . but in one part. . . . And so well [done] that it seemed to be her real character; and I disliked her for that very reason, for it was a character that off the stage or on, is equally distasteful to me—a hoyden."[21]

When *The Romp* was published in 1786, its anonymous editor dedicated the play to Mrs. Jordan:

> You have made the piece peculiarly your own, by your happy conception and admirable representation of its principal character, and have raised this bagatelle to an importance, which the most sanguine partiality of its author could never have hoped for—You have rescued it from ob-

livion, and fostered it with the exertion of your splendid talents, and it is now respectfully offered to your acceptance.[22]

Despite bad notices for the play itself, young actresses continued to play Priscilla into the nineteenth century even after it was cut down to become an interlude. No doubt the play was altered at various times to fit different needs of provincial theatres. For instance, the playbill for the 22 April 1801 performance at the Theatre in Kighley gave as a sub-title for *The Romp,* "The Macaroni Grocer"; and four of the roles were acted by a theatrical family who might have been the original Crummles:

Miss Tomboy	Miss Goldfinch
Watty	Mr. Goldfinch
Quasheba	Master Goldfinch
Penelope	Mrs. Goldfinch

When Mr. Goldfinch was not acting, he was managing the company.

In America, *The Romp* proved a success even without Mrs. Jordan; between 28 October 1792, and 6 May 1837, it was performed at least 68 times (Macmillan, p. 63).

The performance of Mrs. Jordan as Priscilla Tomboy might have endeared her to her followers, and certainly the Romp was given good songs; but she herself is a hoyden with few charming qualities. At the risk of sounding like Fanny Burney's Colonel Welbred, this Tomboy is an unloveable spoiled child. Her speech to Penelope in front of her negro servant, Quasheba (I, ii), has been quoted approvingly by Wylie Sypher as being part of the anti-slavery literature of the eighteenth century, but she is still a hoyden for all that (Priscilla has threatened to horsewhip Quasheba):

Penelope: Oh, poor creature!
Priscilla: Psha,—what is she but a Neger? If she was at home at our plantation, she would find the difference; we make no account of them there at all: if I had a fancy for one of their skins I should not think much of taking it.
Penelope: I suppose then you imagine they have no feeling?
Priscilla: Oh! we never consider that there—(I, ii, 5)[23]

When Priscilla pretends to Young Cockney that she wishes to elope to Jamaica with him, she says that she will undertake to "raise the Negers—it's only giving them a few yams, and licking them, and they'll do anything you bid them" (II, iv, p. 31). If

Bickerstaff helped the anti-slavery movement with Priscilla, the contribution was accidental because the audiences always sided with the tomboy. Cary's print of Mrs. Jordan as Priscilla makes the viewer forgive her anything, and Hazlitt's remarks indicate what a good actress could do with the part:

In all the mischievousness, vivacity, and vulgarity of the part, Mrs. Alsop [Mrs. Jordan's daughter] was eminently successful: it was only in the rich, genial, vinous spirit which her mother threw over it, and made this and all her characters so delightful, that Mrs. Alsop failed, if it could be considered as a failure in any one merely not to do what Mrs. Jordan did.[24]

A disappointed author finds it easy to blame his play's failure on the cast or the audience; it seems this time, however, that it *was* the middle-class audience who was responsible for the flop of *Love in the City*. Bickerstaff was one of the first to discover that Britain was an audience of shopkeepers. The verses which appeared in the *Public Ledger* (5 March 1767), addressed to the "Author of *Love in the City*" contained advice which Bickerstaff heeded:

If e'er again the Muse engage
To laugh at Folly on the Stage,
Let Cockneys 'scape the stroke
Since 'tis with Men of Sense a Rule
That of all Fools, the Bo-Bell Fool
Can least endure a joke.

Even in failure, *Love in the City* netted its author £68. 18s at his Benefit on 24 February 1767; but it was not enough to keep him out of debt, for Bickerstaff borrowed about £100 from Beard during the spring of 1767.

With Beard's retirement in the same spring, Bickerstaff hoped to go to Drury Lane even though his operas (excluding *Love in the City*) were still popular at Covent Garden. Garrick would have been delighted. He might ridicule comic opera in his Epilogue to *The English Merchant,* but he was astute enough to give the audiences what they wanted.[25] All that prevented Bickerstaff from leaving Covent Garden was his contract.

Beard sold the patent on 1 July for £60,000 to George Colman, Rutherford, Powell, and Harris. In July Bickerstaff made tentative plans with Garrick, showing him two plays which he hoped would please the Drury Lane manager. But embarrassingly enough, neither Bickerstaff nor Garrick thought that Colman might want to keep him at Covent Garden. An account of Bickerstaff's falling between the two playhouses was printed in the November, 1767 issue of *The Universal, and Complete Magazine,* under the by-line of "The Theatrical Inspector. #1."

> . . . our modern *Roscius* was not idle; for knowing well of what consequence Mr. B. . .ff is to the other house as a writer, he deemed him an acquisition worthy of some pains. That gentleman was pleased with the prospect of a connection with Garrick, and therefore indulged him with a little piece he had prepared for this season, called *Incle and Yarico*. The musick was frequently played over at Hampton [Garrick's house], and the latter part of the summer was passed in *billing* and *cooing* between these two geniuses. In short, matters were settled as far as lay in Mr. B. . .ff's power. He wished it, but was unfortunately under articles to Mr. Beard, &c., for a certain term of years, to supply so many pieces every season. However, he thought, as the management of the house had got into other hands, he might be free; but, alas! he had *pawned his brains,* if I may so call it, with Mr. Beard, for something under an hundred pounds, i.e. Mr. B. . .ff had received so much in advance. To obviate this evil, Mr. Garrick lent him the money, which he carried to Mr. Beard; but had the mortification to be told, that he must tender it to the new managers, for that, together with the patent, he and his partners had disposed of all the articles, debts, &c. so that he had now nothing to do with it. He then waited upon Mr. Colman, who, instead of receiving the cash, signified an intention of keeping him strictly to his articles. This negociation took some time, during which Mr. B. . .ff had occasion to use the money; so that Mr. Garrick, for the present, has lost his money, without gaining the author; and dear *Incle and Yarico* is in imminent danger.[26]

Two letters written by Bickerstaff in July 1767, testify that he intended to work for Garrick. On 14 July he wrote:

> In consequence of Mr. George Garrick's desire I came to Town today [Bickerstaff was living across the Thames in Battersea] to meet you [David Garrick] but am so unfortunately circumstanced that I can't stay in town all night. Only set your day on a bit of paper and send it to Griffin's Shop and you may be sure of me. In the mean time, my piece ["Incle and Yarico"?] is ready, only to be copied out, but I don't think Mr. Carver will have any opportunity of displaying his art in the scenes which in my opinion need not cost you five pounds, the only thing pinches me a little is that Mr. Messink tells me, he has a design for a Rainbow in his Pantomime; now a Rainbow in my piece will have a beautiful effect being the consequence of a Storm and the decorations otherwise will be nothing, however, Sir you are to fix the Bow in whose Heaven you think proper. The Hypocrite I think I have made quite according to your plan; you will remember that I intend to present you

and Mr. Lacy with a very much improved copy of Love in a Village. If I have not waited upon you, attribute it to my unwillingness to be troublesome; on the other side you will see the plan of my scenes which are but two, and the part I would choose to compile myself from what you have in the house.[27]

Two weeks later, 27 July 1767, Bickerstaff was writing Garrick to refute a rumor that he had refused to break with Colman. He began with a reference to *The Hypocrite.*

I have put into your brother's hand with this letter the alteration of "The Nonjuror," and I flatter myself it is not ill done, because I have adhered as strictly as possible to your idea of what it should be; and with the assistance of Moliere, I think I have made it a clean, laughable, and (what in my opinion is no small excellence in one) not too long a comedy; though I must observe to you, that you will find many faults from my amanuensis, but I chose to let them remain rather than deface the copy.

I was very much hurt by a report which your brother mentioned to me, that Mr. Colman offered me my articles, and that I refused to accept them; I assure you, it is diametrically opposite to truth. When we met, he talked to me as supposing them valid and in full force, and in consequence of it, desired to know what I would give them next winter. I told him that I had been with you, having determined with myself to get rid of the articles, but that you had absolutely refused to hear of any thing of mine, or the music of a piece which I had ready and desired your opinion of, while I was under contract with them; and that at the same time you told me you did not think it would be just or honourable in me to break my articles with them, though they might not be strictly binding. I said this, because I found Mr. Colman entertained some little jealousies of you, which I know to be totally groundless, if I may judge by the manner in which I have always heard you talk of him; but I dare swear you will be able to judge of this matter yourself. I dare say I shall be able to give you "Inkle and Yarico," if you think proper to accept it, and "The Hypocrite" out of dispute. . . . I shall not hesitate to give it under my hand, that of all mankind, my inclination leads me to be employed by Mr. Garrick. . . . (Boaden, I, 267)

When Bickerstaff did leave Covent Garden for Drury Lane, *Incle and Yarico* disappeared. Perhaps Colman the Younger incorporated it in his comic opera of the same title when he as manager of Covent Garden produced it there in 1787.

During the spring of 1767, after Garrick's production of Colman's *The English Merchant,* Colman and Garrick's friendship cooled. Although Colman had signed an agreement with William Powell, John Rutherford, and Thomas Harris to purchase the patent of Covent Garden on 31 March 1767, he did not tell Garrick until 2 May (*Letters,* #458, p. 571). Colman's reticence—however justified—and Garrick's knowledge that Colman and others were trying to raise the money to buy the patent, prevented the two men from maintaining a formerly close friendship. Even after the purchase was officially announced, rumor and counter-rumor of actors leaving one house for the other kept Garrick and Colman from more than a formal reconciliation. Thus, when Bickerstaff was discovered planning to work for Garrick, Colman could not have been less sympathetic. Once Colman refused to release Bickerstaff, any chance for agreeable working conditions between them was destroyed. Bickerstaff was to assert that he was working against his will for Covent Garden, and that Colman as manager produced his comic operas in slipshod fashion. By the same token, Colman was to employ Bickerstaff as a buffer between Covent Garden and at least one author of an unwanted comic opera without in the least encouraging Bickerstaff.

Joseph Reed, formerly a rope maker, but in the 1760s a writer of the tragedy *Dido,* the farce *The Register Office,* and a comic opera, *Tom Jones,* had great difficulty—but showed even greater persistence—in peddling his opera. He unsuccessfully offered *Tom Jones* to Garrick and then tried Colman. But during the summer of 1767, Bickerstaff, who actively worried about anyone else writing a comic opera, was supposedly hurrying to complete his own version of Fielding's novel. Hearing of this from Bickerstaff's friend Hugh Kelly, Reed told Kelly that this action was "very disingenuous . . . as [Bickerstaff] could be no stranger to my having finish'd one on that plan, which had been accepted by Mr. Garrick."[28] Reed claimed that he had unsuccessfully submitted it to Covent Garden in July 1765; therefore, Bickerstaff must have known of it, no matter what he told Kelly.

> Mr. Bickerstaff still insisted on his right of producing an Opera on the subject at Covent-Garden the ensuing [Winter 1767]. I therefore waited on Mr. Colman . . . and desir'd him to prevent Mr. Bickerstaff from carrying so disingenuous a design into execution. Mr. Colman replied, "if he offer an Opera on that plan, we cannot refuse it. The circumstance is indeed very disingenuous, but we are oblig'd, in consequence of articles enter'd into by the late Managers & Mr. Bickerstaff to receive such Operas as he shall offer us, if it have sufficient merit for the stage."
>
> . . . .
>
> The dispute between Mr. Bickerstaff and me ran so high, that I threaten'd to make it public; however thro' the interposition of Mr.

> Kelly, it was at last so far compromised, that Mr. Bickerstaff agreed not to produce any Opera on the story of Tom Jones in the two ensuing seasons. (Reed, pp. 63–71)

Reed approached Garrick in mid-October, 1767 because "some hints were given me that Mr. Garrick possibly might not play my Opera agreeable to his promise, as there was so great an intimacy between him & Mr. Bickerstaff." He gave Garrick a letter which Bickerstaff had written to Reed in July or earlier, "wherein he avowed his right of founding an Opera on the story of Tom Jones."

> As Mr. Garrick perus'd the letter he cried, "very true—right—undoubtedly"—by which I understood he suppos'd Mr. Bickerstaff justifiable in his attempt to anticipate my opera. . . . I said, "Sir, it is in your power to prevent Mr. Bickerstaff's anticipation by giving me your honor that my piece shall be perform'd the next season." "No," replies he. . . . (Reed, p. 71)

Determined to have *Tom Jones* produced, Reed returned to Covent Garden and won the composer Arnold to his side. Arnold went to Colman and was told that "it would not be in their power to produce it that season, as they had two musical pieces, namely, the *Royal Merchant* [by Hull], & an Opera of Mr. Bickerstaff's [*Lionel and Clarissa*] to come out" (p. 72). *Tom Jones* finally did come out at Covent Garden on Saturday, 14 January 1769, where it had a successful run. By then Bickerstaff was working for Garrick.

The only trace of an adaptation of *Tom Jones* by Bickerstaff is in *Lionel and Clarissa,* in the characters of Colonel Oldboy and Diana. The colonel has vague kinship with Squire Western; and Diana, his daughter, might be compared with Sophia. From Reed's account it seems that neither Garrick nor Colman wanted any part of *Tom Jones,* and both managers were happy to use Bickerstaff as a convenient excuse to rid themselves of Reed.

Even though Bickerstaff was unable to work for Drury Lane during the autumn of 1767, he helped Garrick in his relations with two other playwrights, Hugh Kelly and Arthur Murphy, and indirectly with Oliver Goldsmith.

Kelly, the son of a Dublin tavernkeeper, arrived in London in 1760, where he worked as a staymaker and hack writer. In the spring of 1767 he had sufficiently interested Garrick in his first play to cause him to write to his brother George, "Have you seen *Kelly* yet?—do you know anything of his play?" (*Letters,*

#450, 562). By 27 June, Kelly had finished his comedy, which he was tentatively entitling "Fortune with Eyes." He wrote to Garrick that, having altered the first act, he was about to send him the play (Boaden, I, 264-265). Sometime during the summer Bickerstaff spoke to Garrick about the play, and on 1 September 1767 Kelly was writing Garrick, "My worthy friend Bickerstaff . . ." (Boaden, I, 268). Ultimately the comedy was called *False Delicacy* and was produced at Drury Lane on 23 January 1768 with great success. At the same time that Kelly was humbly submitting manuscripts of his sentimental comedy, Goldsmith was expecting Garrick to produce and act in his *The Good-Natured Man.* But after a long delay, Garrick rejected the comedy, and Colman produced it on Friday, 29 January 1768. Because sentimentality was in vogue, Garrick was reluctant to stage Goldsmith's "laughing comedy"; and, in fact, *False Delicacy* enjoyed a longer run than did *The Good-Natured Man.* As long as there were two theatres and only two new plays among Goldsmith, Kelly, and Bickerstaff, the three Irishmen could remain friends; but three plays and two theatres was another matter, and Bickerstaff had hoped that his comic opera, *Lionel and Clarissa,* would be produced in January 1768. Bickerstaff worried about Goldsmith's comedy crowding out his own opera, and Goldsmith had no love for *False Delicacy* because Garrick chose it over *his* comedy for Drury Lane. According to one account, neither Bickerstaff nor Goldsmith considered Kelly much of a playwright, and he apparently said little about his comedy to them. After *False Delicacy* had been playing for some time, Kelly revealed his authorship of it to Goldsmith and Bickerstaff, "who praised it before his face in the highest strains of panegyric; but no sooner turned down the Author's staircase, than he abused it to a common friend in the grossest terms, and 'talked of his [Kelly's] arrogance in thinking of *comedy,* when his highest feather was that of paragraph or Newspaper Essay writing.' Goldsmith kept back and was silent, but as it afterwards appeared, from the same principle of envy."[29]

The character of Bickerstaff that emerges, however sketchily, is not particularly appealing: he was terribly possessive about the dramatic territory which he had staked out for himself, and he warned off claim-jumpers like Richard Cumberland and Joseph Reed with an insistence that only financial insecurity could produce. But within this context, even Oliver Goldsmith shows the rough edges that competitiveness reveals; for the credit of Bickerstaff's character, however, there are not enough counterpointed anecdotes. For all the "prettiness" of Bickerstaff's comic operas, there was no relation between it and the London theatre world, which was a standard example of a buyer's market—the managers always had more plays than they needed. In this world, the sellers—professional dramatists—hustled their plays as determinedly as any other hucksters and with as little compassion for their rivals.

Perhaps an exception occurred when Bickerstaff helped to reconcile Garrick and Arthur Murphy—for a short time. The playwright with whom Garrick had the most trouble for the longest time, Murphy (1727-1805), another Irishman, was a journalist, barrister, biographer, anthologizer, translator, actor, and critic as well as being one of the best writers for the stage during Garrick's reign. He was also a trial of Garrick's patience. As a matter of fact, the opposite was equally true. In 1761 the two men quarrelled violently enough for Murphy to quit writing for Drury Lane. When Garrick heard of Murphy's resolve he wrote to a friend, "Wish Me Joy . . ." (*Letters,* #280, 349). In 1767, however, the two men were temporarily friends again, this time through the help of Bickerstaff. In his role of peacemaker, Bickerstaff acted as letter-carrier between the two men, and finally sometime in November, over a dinner at his house which Samuel Johnson attended, he brought Murphy and Garrick together—for a time.

> I closed with the offer of Mr. Garrick's friendship, and dined with him and Dr. Johnson at Bickerstaff's house. After dinner the plays were mentioned. "Prithee," says Dr. Johnson, "don't talk of plays;[30] if you do, you will quarrel again." He was a true prophet. (Murphy to Garrick, 13 January 1773; Boaden, I, 519–521.)

For Bickerstaff's efforts at reconciliation, Garrick called him "a good Christian" (*Letters,* II, #479, 587-588), but there was more than altruism prompting Bickerstaff. First of all, he owed Garrick £100, the amount which he had borrowed in an unsuccessful attempt to pay back Beard and leave Covent Garden; having failed to settle his debt at the theatre, he spent the money instead of returning it to Garrick. In the second place, Garrick did Bickerstaff a favor in August 1767, which put the latter under a great obligation, as can be seen in the following letter.

> My Dear Sir [wrote Bickerstaff], Did I conceive it possible for words

to convey my sense of your goodness to me, I would not only fill this sheet of paper, but half a score more with thanks and acknowledgements. However, Sir, give me leave to assure you that I will do my endeavours to prevent your ever having cause to repent, your kindness to me; a return the more Acceptable, as perhaps it is not what you have Always met with.

The post I want for my Brother is Gentleman at large, the Nature of which I have already Explained to you. I shall have the honour to kiss your hands next Thursday Morning Early, & I hope you did not forget you have promised to Dine at Battersea. But that shall be what day you please, and just as it suits your Convenience. I am with the Most perfect Gratitude Dear Sir your obliged & ever faithfully Devoted Ser^t I. Bickerstaff.[31]

Even for Bickerstaff the closing flourishes are more elaborate than usual; if only his explanations were as stately. There was no such office as "Gentleman at Large," and Bickerstaff's brother Robert died before 1755. Presumably Bickerstaff was referring to his brother-in-law Edward Brereton (who was actually his cousin as well). Brereton was a Lieutenant in the 22nd Regiment of Foot then in America; he was promoted to Captain in 1769. At the risk of complicating the issue, Bickerstaff had another cousin, William Brereton, who called himself a major. This Brereton, who seems like a character from a Thackeray novel, would have made an ideal Gentleman at Large, which, although it was not an official position, adequately described "a gentleman attached to the court but having no special duties assigned to him."[32]

Whatever Bickerstaff meant by "Gentleman at large," Garrick was prepared to get it for whomever Bickerstaff meant by his brother. For this reason, and the £100 that he owed Garrick, as well as for future favors that Garrick might do for him—and because they were friends—Bickerstaff was eager to be of service: "I should be extremely glad to be an humble instrument in bringing two such men [Garrick and Murphy] again together" (Boaden, I, 273-274).

Murphy was grateful for Bickerstaff's efforts: "I only regret that nobody but yourself has had the Christian benevolence to attempt what you have so handsomely accomplished" (Boaden, I, 229-230). But the reconciliation was temporary, and when Murphy wrote Garrick's biography he limited his praise to Garrick as an actor. As for Bickerstaff, Murphy invariably dismissed him with scorn.

7

"*SCRAPED, SQUALLED* AND *CLAPPED*": *LIONEL AND CLARISSA, THE ABSENT MAN*

Unsuccessful in his attempt to work for David Garrick during the summer of 1767, Bickerstaff had little wish to remain at Covent Garden, but no choice. As for Colman, he was determined to keep him as long as he was articled to the theatre and his comic operas were profitable, but he preferred legitimate drama, and his relationship with Bickerstaff was nowhere near the easy converse that Bickerstaff and Beard had enjoyed. Within the year, however, Colman and his fellow theatre managers were viciously feuding, and Bickerstaff made his escape. In the meantime, since for the playwright it was a matter of no play, no money, he worked on a comic opera which he was to call *Lionel and Clarissa.*

By 29 October, he had completed enough to write for an advance:

> Sir, I did not intend to trouble you till the Translation of Clarissa was compleat, but as I have done five Sheets of it and Mr. Griffin [William Griffin, the bookseller] tells me you had no objection to pay fifteen Guineas when part of the work was done, I shall be Obliged to you for answering my draft to the bearer for Ten, & am Sir, your humble Servt.[1]

Sometime during the autumn of 1767, a quarrel with Colman resulted in the following letter from Bickerstaff:

Sir. You represent the affair of my coming to you at the playhouse exactly as it happened. if my behaviour there seemed inconclusive, [?] it was because I was in some little hurry of spirits: I did not expect you would have sent for me into your Box to talk upon Business before friends whom I had not the honour of knowing, but I am not surprised at your seeming to think me reprehensible in this instance. I am told you represent my behaviour at your own house, as that of a ruffian or a mad man, though one expression excepted which was spoke with the utmost calmness, there was not on my part, the least incivility, or warmth.

I always have had for you, Sir, as a man of genius, the greatest respect, and have lately more than once joined with others in the praises of your apparent candour, and other good qualities; but I did not do this because you were become a manager; and I now tell you that as such I have no respect for you at all; for in your new capacity you have treated me as one Man of letters should not treat another without any consideration of circumstances; with Haughtiness, and oppression; when by a small, a reasonable relaxation of a power which nothing but my own folly has given you, and Law and Equity would deny you, you might have made me a grateful and acknowledging friend.

You desire to know what you are to expect from me this winter. The opera I had the honour to talk to you about called Lionel and Clarissa you shall have it complete in the latter end of November to be played immediately after Xmass, or sooner if it can be got up, but give me leave to say, my poverty but not my will consents [*Romeo and Juliet,* V, ii, l. 75]. I am sir, your humble Sv^{t}. . . .[2]

In his effort to complete *Lionel and Clarissa* by the end of November, Bickerstaff had "a great deal of scribbling on [his] hands," as he wrote to Arthur Murphy on 11 November; too much scribbling, for on 30 November he explained to Colman:

I should have sent you my Opera this day, but for an accident that happen'd [to] the Copy which obliges me to get a new one made & I should now be rather glad to read it to you myself than send it to you which I suppose will be the same thing to you & on Saturday if it be agreeable I will meet you and Mr. Powell where and at what hour you please for that purpose. I have had a Copy of the Music made in parts and should you approve the piece, you may hear the songs in your Orchestra on Monday or Tuesday at which time they may also be put into the hands of the Singers.[3]

Colman huffed:

I cannot suppose we can have the least objection to produce whatever you may (in consequence of our Article) think fit to offer the Public but I should rather wish to read the Opera myself than have it read to me.

Nine days later, very much concerned about rumors which

had reached him, Bickerstaff wrote to the chief prompter at Covent Garden, Joseph Younger.

> Dear Younger, I am Extremely uneasy by reports circulated with great Industry in the Purlieus of your playhouse that my Opera is not to be perform'd this Season because I did not deliver it in at a certain day. I do not know that any day was mention'd Except what I fixed myself and if there is any such design form'd against me I will venture to say there never was any more cruel or unjust. The music is compleat & the Opera transcribing as fast as possible. The first Act of which being finish'd I send it to you & the others will follow as speedily as the man can dispatch them. You may give this to Mr. Colman or keep it yourself till you get the rest.[4]

Younger reassured him:

> Mr. Colman is out of Town when he returns tomorrow [I] will show him your Ltr. In the meantime [I] beg you will not suffer prejudice or reports to induce you to entertain the most distant doubt of his Candour or his Honour as I am well assur'd you will never have occasion to complain of them.

Unable to give Covent Garden a fair and complete copy in time, Bickerstaff saw Christmas go by without a performance of *Lionel and Clarissa.* While he worried through his comic opera, Hugh Kelly's *False Delicacy* was being readied at Drury Lane, and Goldsmith's *Good Natured Man* was stealing a march at Covent Garden. Forgetting that he had told Colman that he expected *Lionel and Clarissa* to be staged immediately after Christmas, Bickerstaff complained to the manager on 26 January 1768:

> When I talked with you last summer . . . I told you that it would be impossible to have my opera ready till after Christmas; and named about the 20th of January. You received this with great goodness, said you were glad of it, because it would be the best time of the year for me, and then told me that Mr. Goldsmith's play should come out before Christmas; and this you repeated, and assur'd me of, more than once, in subsequent meetings. . . . The fact is, you broke your word with me, in ordering the representation of the "Good-Natur'd Man" in such a manner that it must unavoidably interfere with my opera. . . . At the reading it was said the "Good-Natur'd Man" should appear the Wednesday after; but at the same time it was whispered to me that it was privately determined not to bring it out till the Saturday fortnight, and that there was even a promise given to Mr. Kelly that it should not appear till after his nights were over.[5]

While *The Good-Natured Man* played ten nights through 9

February, and *False Delicacy* continued for fifteen nights through 23 February, Bickerstaff continued to have trouble with *Lionel and Clarissa.* He confessed himself unable to bring either the play or the players into line:

> As my opera is suffering extremely by the immeasurable length of it [he wrote to Colman in February, 1768], I am obliged to apply to you, as I find I have not sufficient Power myself to bring it into compass. I therefore entreat the favour of you, to order Mr. Younger to call it tomorrow, & that if possible (for otherwise it will be a useless meeting) you will be at the play house for a quarter of an hour yourself, to insist on the performers leaving out such songs and scenes as I think necessary to retrench.[6]

Finally, on Thursday, 25 February, *Lionel and Clarissa* was produced at Covent Garden. It was a noisy audience composed of friends of Bickerstaff, and of those people who had not forgiven him *Love in the City:*

> We were *scraped, squalled* and *clapped,* out of our senses at Covent Garden on Thursday; it was thought there were no less than 500 orders in the house. O shameful! Why are not a generous audience left to judge of a piece, without this forced imposition? If a thing has merit, they would undoubtedly encourage it, if not condemn it; was this as it ought to be, the invariable rule of both managers and authors, 'tis my opinion they would fare better.[7]

How *Lionel and Clarissa* fared was probably the least of Colman's worries during the autumn and winter of 1767; he wanted to compete with Drury Lane by "building up the company and by concentrating his attention upon the production of a greater variety of standard drama."[8] And comic operas were not part of standard drama. Even Bickerstaff had admitted that in his Dedication to *The Maid of the Mill;* comic operas were to "be permitted as an occasional relief to [Tragedies and Comedies], without bringing either our taste or understanding into question" (p. ii). But in attempting to strengthen Covent Garden, Colman fell out with his partners. At the same time that he was reluctantly readying *Lionel and Clarissa,* he was trying to keep Harris and Rutherford from undermining his authority. Eventually the feud reached the public by way of pamphlets, newspaper articles, blasts and counterblasts, tort and retort. By the spring of 1770 the managers had gone to court, and in July, hearings were begun in Chancery.[9] Colman's ally, Powell, was dead; but his widow became co-defendant. Rutherford had sold his share to Dagge and Leake for a profit, and these two men with Harris were plaintiffs. At the hearings, which began on 16 July, Bickerstaff and Dibdin testified that Colman's indifference to comic opera hurt *Lionel and Clarissa,* and that his mismanagement discouraged them from working at Covent Garden.[10]

Their testimony about Colman's inadequacy as a manager was precisely what Harris's attorneys hoped for; as they noted in their brief, "The Grand Object" in bringing Colman to court was to insure that "Mr. Colman shall not lay out or squander his Partners' money without their consent!" Thus they had to prove Colman guilty of mismanagement.

The burden of Bickerstaff's testimony was that by Colman's poor management of his operas, Covent Garden had lost considerable income—as well as a first-rate author and a promising composer. In addition, with their loss to Covent Garden, the theatre stood to continue losing money while Drury Lane reaped the profits from new and ever-better comic operas. Bickerstaff was supported on the question of poor management by Henry Woodward, the original "Lofty" in *The Good-Natured Man,* and author of several Harlequin pantomimes. He contrasted the state of opera when Rich and then Beard were proprietors, and under Colman's reign. In the earlier years, he maintained:

> there were many plays and operas that generally and respectively brought full houses which Colman by his conduct soon reduced to four in number . . . Love in a Village, Maid of the Mill, Busy Body & Every Man in his Humour, and even each of those Colman hath worn down to the unprofitable state of being scarce able to produce a saving house for often a play in which Powell had been advertis'd to act for some time if it so happened that the Boxes were not well taken or that there was a prospect of an indifferent house that Powell or some other person that he could prevail upon was alleged to have been taken ill the night previously which necessarily changed the play, the public being thus disappointed the exigence was generally supplied by acting at such short notice one of the before mentioned pieces. And it occurred so often that at length they lost their power in drawing audiences; and which falling off in attraction is of great loss not only by destroying a valuable exhibition but also by hurting the minds and sowering the tempers of usefull persons.[11]

When Charles Dibdin testified, he blamed Colman for the poor preparation of operas which hurt their chances for continued public approval.

> [Dibdin] saith that during the getting up of the Opera called Lionel

and Clarissa, sd Geo: Colman paid little or no attention to the Business consequent thereof & permitted the Musicians to treat [Dibdin] with a great deal of contempt [notwithstanding Deponent was] as the composer & compiler of the Music of that piece placed in the Orchestra with them to direct them in their performance & in other Instances suffered them to neglect their duty in practising the Music thereof. And saith that on the Night that Opera was first performed the performers were not so perfect in it as Said performers in the Maid of the Mill were 3 or 4 Rehearsals before that piece was exhibited to the public owing to . . . Colman's bad conduct by which means . . . Lionel & Clarissa . . . did not meet with that success as it would have done if it had been properly got up for Representation & verily believes that by the fate that Piece met with a considerable loss was sustained by the proprietors of Covent Garden Theatre. . . .

Not surprisingly, when Bickerstaff testified, he swore that *Lionel and Clarissa* was his best work, and blamed its relative lack of success on Colman and Ned Shuter. It was, he swore, brought out "in an improper time contrary to Deponent's Desire as the author thereof & the Said Colman suffering Mr. Shuter the Principal Performer to come on the Stage without knowing scarce one word of his Part or a note of the musick to which the songs in it were set. . . ." Had it been brought out "under proper care and management . . . instead of being Performed only Eleven nights [it might] have been performed for thirty nights or more with great profits to the Proprietors. . . ." Even allowing for an author's pride, thirty or more nights in one season would be excessive; the opera was performed for twelve nights, which afforded Bickerstaff three Benefits. From them he realized £428 5s 6d, and his third night was a command performance for George III and his Queen.[12]

After Bickerstaff transferred to Drury Lane, he revised *Lionel and Clarissa,* and in 1770 (8 February) it was produced with the alternate title, *School for Fathers;* the plot remained the same. In both versions Lionel and Clarissa, their parents and their friends all live in the same English country inhabited by the folk from *The Maid of the Mill* and *Love in a Village.* Since nothing surprising happened in the comic opera, *Lionel and Clarissa* relied on the music and a quartet of comic characters for success: Jessamy, Lady Mary Oldboy, Colonel Oldboy, and Jenny the maid. Of these four, only Jessamy was new to Bickerstaff's operas. Colonel Oldboy, a restrained descendant of Fielding's Squire Western, was similar to Justice Woodcock and Sir Harry Sycamore. Lady Mary Oldboy would have known Mrs.

Deborah Woodcock and Lady Sycamore. Jenny resembled Fanny the gypsy and Margery. Had these three wenches visited London they would have enjoyed the company of Priscilla Tomboy; and Lady Mary and Molly Cockney would be friends. The serious characters would also have found no trouble in recognizing affinities with the people in Bickerstaff's other country operas.

If the humor is simple and direct, it is no less effective for being so. A fair example occurs when Jenny is afraid to enter a room because Colonel Oldboy who is there had earlier tried to proposition her. When Lady Mary Oldboy is told this by Jenny she is at first on the servant's side:

> Lady Mary: . . . as the poet says, his sex is all deceit. Read Pamela, child, and resist temptation.
>
> . . . .
>
> Jenny [to Col. Oldboy]: . . . you made me a proffer of money, so you did, whereby I told you, you had a lady of your own, and that though she was old you had no right to despise her.
> Lady Mary: And how dare you. . . .
> Jenny: Why, madam, I only said you was in years. (Etc.)[13]

The major comic incident occurs when Harman tricks Colonel Oldboy into writing a letter to the father of the girl who is eloping with Harman—not knowing that Oldboy himself is the father. Diana shows some spirit, but Clarissa is the romantic heroine, pure and simple. Lionel has no sense of humor, and Harman is a harmless, thin-blooded descendant of a rake, tamed by generations of sentimental ancestors dating from Farquhar's comedies.

But Jessamy is a delight. While the others seem to try to live up to their previously defined characteristics—refined and debilitated in the hundred years since the Restoration—Jessamy adds something to the portrait of the fop or macaroni. His name was a synonym for a kind of gentleman in the mid-eighteenth century as explained by Hawkesworth in *The Adventurer,* no. 100, "Gradation from a Greenhorn to a Blood." There were eight degrees: Greenhorn, Jemmy, Jessamy, Smart, Honest Fellow, Joyous Spirit, Buck, and Blood. A Jessamy was expected to dance and swear tolerably well. He would have a comfortable income, carry an imitation Toledo sword, and wear elegant but not particularly neat clothing. He would be country-bred.[14]

By the early nineteenth century, critics complimented themselves by thinking, "The character of *Jessamy* . . . [is] now obsolete. . . . It is a *thing* of other times . . . a coxcomb without passions. [DeCamp, the actor who was currently playing Jessamy] speaks the French language well, and all the impertinence, *nonchalance,* effrontery, and contempt of reason, which characterized such animals, were efficiently brought into notice."[15] Jessamy might have been a coxcomb, but he was not without his passions, and he is never obsolete. His sexual conquests, which he insisted on admitting to Clarissa, did not affect his passions; those he reserved for inanimate objects:

> That's an exceeding fine china jar your Ladyship has got in the next room; I saw the fellow of it the other day at Williams's, and will send to my agent to purchase it: it is the true matchless old blue and white. Lady Betty Barebones has a couple that she gave an hundred guineas for, on board an Indiaman; but she reckons them at a hundred and twenty-five, on account of half a dozen plates, four Nankeen beakers, and a couple of shaking Mandarins, that the custom-house officers took from under petticoats. (I, iii, pp. 6–7)

Jessamy's character remained unchanged when two years after *Lionel and Clarissa* opened at Covent Garden, the revised version played at Drury Lane. Most of the prose changes occurred while the comic opera was still at Covent Garden and are reflected in the differences between the first and fourth editions, both published in 1768. For instance, Jessamy's speech in which he wondered whether Clarissa had been told about his affairs in Italy was tamed.

> 1st ed: Jessamy: Well! I was afraid they might [have told Clarissa], because, in this rude country—However, my dear creature, you ought to prepare yourself against any little trials of this kind; we are naturally volage; yet, I dare venture to promise you, that my flights will be but short; and, I shall soon return again to my destined mate—But, why silent, on a sudden—don't be afraid to speak. (II, viii)
> 4th ed: Jessamy: Well! I was afraid they might, because, in this rude country—But, why silent, on a sudden—don't be afraid to speak.

In three instances, Bickerstaff eliminated the "fine sentiments"; in II, xi, Clarissa originally warned Lionel that she would not hurt her father:

> I would not give my father a moment's pain, to purchase the empire of the world. That he will never force my inclinations, I am confident; and, while he lives, or, till some favourable accident, now unforeseen, offers to befriend us——

Bickerstaff ended her speech with the first sentence in the fourth edition. When Harman and Diana are about to elope Harman had his chance in the first edition to allegorize extemporarily:

> Diana: Yet, one thing more. My fortune depends almost entirely upon my father's generosity: now, think, with yourself, whether it would not be better to devise some other method.
> Harman: Hang fortune! It is the bane of love; and, therefore, they are both pictur'd blind, to shew, that their coming together can never be premeditated; but, if they do meet, it is by chance, when they jostle, and one generally overturns t'other. (III, i, p. 53)

Harman lost his chance in the fourth edition when Bickerstaff cut both speeches. To introduce Lionel, Clarissa apostrophised in the early version:

> He comes! O Heavens, in this trying instant vouchsafe your aid! A mist seems to gather round me, and I am ready to sink under I know not what oppression. (III, ix, p. 66)

In the revision, Clarissa spoke directly to Lionel without preliminary swoons.

The only change in songs between the first and fourth editions occurs in I, xi. The first time round, Harman told Colonel Oldboy that "It's impossible to describe [Diana] to you"; but he promptly did so in song:

> Yes, she is fair, divinely fair,
> And softer than the balmy air
> That vernal Zephir blows;
> Her cheeks transcend the rose's bloom,
> And sweeter is the rich perfume
> Her ruby lips disclose.
>
> Fly swift, oh Love, and in her ear,
> Whisper soft, her lover's near,
> Full of doubt and full of fear;
> If my rashness should offend,
> Intercede
> My pardon plead,
> Her angry brow unbend.

Harman gave up the attempt altogether to describe Diana in the fourth edition; his song ignored the Colonel with whom he had been talking:

> Indulgent pow'rs, if ever

You mark'd a tender vow,
O bend in kind compassion,
And hear a lover now:

For titles, wealth, and honours,
While others crowd your shrine;
I ask this only blessing,
Let her I love be mine. (I, xi, p. 22)

The song might well have been affecting, but to some of the audience it must also have been familiar because Bickerstaff wrote it for *Love in the City* (I, iii, p. 9).

The major changes between *Lionel and Clarissa* (4th ed.) and *School for Fathers* occur in the songs. As Bickerstaff pointed out in his "Advertisement" to Drury Lane version,

> When Mr. GARRICK thought of performing this piece at Drury-Lane theatre, he had a new singer to bring out [Mrs. Wrighten], and every thing possible for her advantage was to be done; this necessarily occasioned some new songs and airs to be introduced; and other singers, with voices of a different compass from those who originally acted the parts, occasioned still more; by which means the greatest part of the music unavoidably became new. (*School for Fathers,* 1781)

What Bickerstaff could do for a new singer is most obvious in the change of song for Diana in Act III, scene i. Originally content to write a song in the vein of "When lovely woman stoops to folly" for Mrs. Baker, he substituted, for Mrs. Wrighten, a bravura piece:

(Mrs. Baker) Ah! how cruel the reflection,
Woman once to error led;
Ev'ry eye wakes for detection,
Ev'ry tongue the tale to spread.

Vainly is her fault lamented,
By the poor, misguided fair;
That which caution had prevented,
Penitence can ne'er repair (III, i, 53)

(Mrs. Wrighten) How can you, inhuman! persist to distress me?
My danger, my fears, 'tis in vain to disguise:
You know them, yet still to destruction you press me
And force that from passion which prudence denies.

I fain would oppose a perverse inclination;
The visions of fancy, from reason divide;

With fortitude baffle the wiles of temptation,
And let love no longer make folly its guide.
(III, i, 46. 1781 ed.)

The music might have been more ambitious, but the new words for Diana certainly were ghastly.

When *Lionel and Clarissa* was first published, Bickerstaff was far from confident that his opera would succeed; consequently he appended an "Advertisement" which differed in tone from his usual hectoring prefaces.

> Since the printing of this little Piece [Bickerstaff began], it has been intimated to the Author, that he is likely to suffer from some ill Will, occasioned by a very faulty, and very unfortunate, Opera [*Love in the City*] of his represented last Winter; but he begs leave to observe, that it is against the Laws of *England* to try a Man twice for the same Fact; and more so, after Punishment has been inflicted. He thinks it can hardly be necessary to say, that he never, in any of his Writings, intended to give the least Offence: And as his trifling Productions, have more than once, been lucky enough to be honoured with the Approbation of the Public; he flatters himself, should he again be found capable of affording them an innocent Entertainment; that those to whose Justice he most readily subscribes, will not refuse him an Opportunity of appealing to their Candour.

Bickerstaff's abject apology prompted at least one printed reply:

> The author rightly observes [wrote "Civicus"], *it is against the laws of England to try a man twice for the same fact,* but if that fact be repeated, he may be *tried toties quoties, especially after punishment* has been inflicted. Surely he cannot think, that damning Love in the City was an adequate punishment for all the nonsense he shall ever write.[16]

"Civicus'" reply was exceptional, and by the fourth edition, Bickerstaff felt emboldened to omit the first Advertisement, and replace it with a "Preface":

> It is impossible for the author to express his grateful sense of the indulgence with which this little piece has been received by the Public: indeed, he was so sensible of some disadvantages it labour'd under before its appearance, that it was not without the utmost dread and apprehension he submitted it to their judgment; and it was at last done so far against his consent, that nothing but absolute necessity could have oblig'd him to do it.

As are most public pronouncements, Bickerstaff's Preface was considerably simplified. He did not want to give Colman the opera, but when held to his articles, he very much wanted it produced; then, when it was in rehearsal, he was unwilling to have it staged because Shuter was (again) unprepared and the musicians ill-rehearsed.

> However [Bickerstaff continued in his Preface], he gives a new edition of his book, with the confidence of a man, who, in this trifling way, has endeavour'd to do his best; and, if the reader should find here something like character and fable; some moral interest, and a few things to laugh at; he hopes, it will be consider'd, that he has borrowed from no other writer; that an Opera is a species of the drama extremely unfavourable for such a combination; and that there are many faults and absurdities attached to it, which no art can avoid.

Now that passage was the Bickerstaff his readers had grown accustomed to. The important point of his remarks is that Bickerstaff was checking off those aspects of his drama which he assumed his critics would note: character, "fable," "some moral interest," humor, and the—to the English—unavoidability of the absurd in any opera. As for his claim that he had "borrowed from no other writer," it can be allowed as long as it is added that he brought nothing new to the stage.

Despite—or because of—his previous operas, London critics had not changed their minds; as one of them put it, "we think it is a pity the town have given such encouragement to this strange kind of composition, to the great neglect of that rational and more elegant entertainment resulting from the representation of a good play" (*Theatrical Register,* II, 48). Bickerstaff had no support except from audiences after Beard retired and Colman tried to compete with Garrick with non-musical dramas. Bickerstaff himself discouraged any other author from writing comic operas, preferring a besieged monopoly; consequently, when critics publicly vented their spleens against opera they used *Lionel and Clarissa,* or other works by Bickerstaff, as a convenience. For example, the critic in *The Political Register* amused himself and his readers with a gentlemanly disquisition about opera in a review nominally about *Lionel and Clarissa:*

> A Certain person being asked what he thought of those high-strained compositions, which, though not wrote in rhyme, and not even in verse, have, or least seem to have, all the elevation of poetry; and whether they were to be considered as poetry or prose; replied, that they were still prose, but prose run mad. This madness, it is true, is more conspicuous in the serious than in the comic opera.
>
> . . . .
>
> The same absurdity, it must be owned, does not prevail in the comic opera, which indeed differs in nothing from a plain comedy, except that

every scene, but for certain every act, concludes with a song; the actors probably thereby meaning to shew us, that whatever high words may pass between them in the course of the dialogue, they are determined at least to part good friends, and to finish their quarrel with a quaver. As to the opera now before us, it may safely be affirmed (and indeed we think the same may be affirmed of all this author's other operas) that, considered as a play, it is a very poor and paltry performance; and that to examine it according to the rules of the drama would be just as reasonable, as to examine the ravings of a man in liquor by the rules of logic. Of the songs it may be said, that, with a very few exceptions, they are

—*Versus inopes rerum, nugaeque canorae.*

But perhaps it ought to be considered, that, among your sing-song people, it has long been held as a maxim, *that nothing is capable* of being set to music, that is not nonsense.[17]

In contrast to *The Political Register,* the critic for the *Court Miscellany* was convinced that *Lionel and Clarissa* "would make a very agreeable entertainment on the stage, though it had not a single song in the whole composition."

The characters are truly comic [the critic continued]. On the first night the audience seemed a little disappointed in finding humour, where they only expected sentiment and sound. . . . There are among our modern play-goers, a set of little beings, who have taken it into their heads to banish all humour from the stage, and who are always ready to cry out *low* where the poet happens not to be dull.[18]

His opinion received recent confirmation, for when *Lionel and Clarissa* was to be broadcast on the B.B.C. in 1963, it was first planned to play it as a comedy—without music; that the music was included was due to some extent to the efforts of Dr. Roger Fiske who orchestrated and edited it from both the 1768 and 1770 editions.[19]

The longest review of *Lionel and Clarissa* appeared in the *Theatrical Monitor* for Saturday, 5 March 1768 (XV, 1-7). The critic suggested three criteria for deciding whether a work is a successful comedy: first, novelty of characterization; that is, "such as we are frequently conversant with in life, but unnoticed by preceding comic writers." If the characters are old, they must be "supported with superior excellence." Finally, "we must be presented with such an assemblage of peculiarities, that we shall confess we have before us an epitome of many of our most pleasing comedies. . ." (pp. 1-2). Failing Bickerstaff's play on all three counts, the *Monitor* concluded that "without any offense to the author . . . if it is an opera, it is not a *comic* opera, that is, it does not contain that wit and humour, which are essentially necessary to a comedy."

Turning from "literary" considerations, *Monitor* objected to Shuter's performance as Colonel Oldboy; his "impertinence both to the author and audience is insufferable; depending upon the protection of the upper gallery, that receptacle of his congenial souls, he ventures to leave out, put in, or alter every sentence of any length; nay, he speaks when he ought to be dumb, is tardy when he ought to speak, and he sings as if he owed music a grudge, and was determined to be revenged upon its admirers" (p. 3).

After the Spring 1768 season, *Lionel and Clarissa* was but infrequently performed at Covent Garden. Ironically, the first production after 21 April 1768 was for Shuter's Benefit on 16 March 1769. At Drury Lane, however, because Bickerstaff and Dibdin revised it for Mrs. Wrighten, the opera continued to be played. One of the Drury Lane actresses who wished to perform in the new version was Jane Pope. To her Bickerstaff wrote on 18 October 1769:

> Madam, As you cannot think me so blind as to be Ignorant of your great merit as an Actress or so little self interested as not to wish you in every piece of mine where that merit cou'd be conspicuous. It will be needless at present to say anything upon either Subjects. The Musical Farce is not design'd to come out Immediately But the Manager's having Engag'd a very capital woman Singer [Mrs. Wrighten] they are so good as to bring out *Lionel and Clarissa* and give me a Benefit for it. I do assure you that the first Song and the Quintetto in the farce you will never be able to sing with reputation to yourself but the character of Jenny in *Lionel and Clarissa* I think you will make a figure in. I mean in the Songs for as to the acting part in Either I think it is out of Dispute. The airs to be sung are not the same that Mrs. Mattocks sung at Covent Garden theatre but those made by Dibdin for his wife at Richmond whose voice is exactly the same as yours; and you can have no doubt but he made the best he cou'd. The Original Songs were not simple enough, were too long, and of too great a compass. If when the Farce comes out there is any One person in it that is chosen for any thing but as a Singer you may depend upon it the part shall remain with you, but on the contrary if it is brought out merely as a Singing thing I hope you will accept the part of Jenny instead of it as it will shew you that nothing cou'd be farther from my thoughts than disobliging you. I beg your immediate answer and wish for nothing more than an opportunity to shew myself Madam your admirer and most obed^{t} serv^{t}. [PS] We wish to keep the coming out of *Lionel and Clarissa* a profound Secret.[20]

Eleanor Radley, not Miss Pope, played Jenny when the revised

Lionel and Clarissa (*School for Fathers*) was produced. But Bickerstaff's admiration for Miss Pope was not feigned; when *Love in a Village* and *The Maid of the Mill* were first performed at Drury Lane (on 3 April and 31 March 1769 respectively), she played Margery and Fanny. Bickerstaff wrote to Garrick that "King, Pope and Vernon in *Love in a Village* were as well as you can possibly conceive. I disagree with everyone about Pope, who with a little care would sing as well as Thompson [née Poitier], and acts a thousand times better."[21] Miss Pope should have known when she asked Bickerstaff for the role that because of the repertory system, she would not get it; for the same reason Miss Radley would have expected to play Jenny because she had sung Lucinda in *Love in a Village,* and Theodosia in *The Maid of the Mill.* After all, at Covent Garden, Mrs. Mattocks, the original Theodosia and Lucinda, also sang Jenny.

The "profound secret" of the coming out of *School for Fathers* was puffed in the London newspapers:

> The Opera of *Lionel and Clarissa* has been altered by Mr. Bickerstaff, who intends to call it the *School for Fathers;* it will shortly be performed at the Theatre Royal in Drury Lane, and we are assured, a young Gentlewoman will make her first appearance in the principal singing character.

After the Gentlewoman Mrs. Wrighten appeared, a writer for the *Town and Country Magazine* wrote that the new and altered music was "much for the better."

> Though this little piece was very well received at Covent Garden, it appeared to much greater advantage here, owing to the parts, in general, being better cast. The character of Miss Diana Oldboy was performed by Mrs. Wrighten. . . . This lady, whose person is not much in her favour, filled the part with great propriety, being quite free from the awkward embarrassment which young performers are generally subject to. . . . ([February 1770], II, 69.)

During the spring of 1770 Bickerstaff's opera was performed nine times at Drury Lane, three fewer than during its 1768 run at Covent Garden. His promised Benefit came on 19 February when two of his most popular pieces, *The Hypocrite* and *The Padlock,* were performed. In contrast, during the same season in Dublin, the play was received "with that enthusiasm and partiality, which has ever peculiarly distinguished its representation in this kingdom."[22] The opera's popularity was so overwhelming that it left Mossop at the Crow-Street Theatre "exhibiting to orders or empty benches[;] an early overflow marked every night this popular opera was announced" (Hitchcock, p. 178). Despite its being brought out late in the season at the Capel-Street Theatre (2 April 1770), it ran for 26 nights, "and closed a season, that will always be distinguished in the theatrical annals of this kingdom" (Hitchcock, p. 178). Attempting to capitalize on the success of *Lionel and Clarissa,* Mossop brought it out three weeks after it opened at Crow-Street; when it failed, he "cut [it] down into a farce, which compleatly finished it in the opinion of every one" (Hitchcock, pp. 178-179). The comic opera continued to be popular and was performed 241 times in Dublin up to the Victorian period.[23] According to Hughes, *Lionel and Clarissa* was the third most popular comic opera in Dublin, following *The Beggar's Opera* with 460 performances, and *Love in a Village* with 415.

In The United States, *Lionel and Clarissa* was "performed twenty-three times, and was presented in practically all the towns in this country where plays were at this time given" (Macmillan, p. 61). Its first performance was at the Southwark Theatre in Philadelphia, 14 December 1772; its title of *A School for Fathers* reveals which version was produced (Sonneck, p. 47). On 18 January 1828 it was played for the last time—at the Park Theatre in New York. Both versions were performed in Jamaica during the 1770s and '80s.

After Bickerstaff's flight in 1772, neither version of the comic opera was popular in London, but it continued to be performed in the provinces. From the start *Lionel and Clarissa* had been successful outside London, as Bickerstaff testified in the suit against Colman, commenting about "the general applause it hath met with from the country audiences under the most unfavourable representations of different companies of itinerant players. . ." (BM ms. 33218). It remained in the provincial repertories for at least twenty years. At the Theatre Royal in Edinburgh, for instance, it attracted married couples to play Lionel and Clarissa; at least in 1782 Mr. and Mrs. Marshall took the roles (April 22, playbill), and on 17 January 1787 at the same theatre, John Kemble played the non-singing role of Sir John Flowerdale while Mrs. Kemble was Clarissa. Mrs. Jordan's brother played Jessamy on 24 August 1787 in Dundee, improbably enough. Occasionally Jessamy was played by a woman: Miss Sestine in Dublin, Mrs. Achmet in Shrewsbury.

By May 1793 the *Anthologia Hibernica* listed *Lionel and*

Clarissa as one of Bickerstaff's discarded works,[24] but it kept popping up. After a twenty-year absence it was revived on 12 December 1807 at Drury Lane: "The opera is called comic," wrote a critic for *The Monthly Mirror,* "but it has not much of that character, and was always thought rather heavy."[25] One of the reasons for its corpulence was that it "had too many cooks," as Dibdin wrote,[26] and the addition in 1807 of more composers (Reeve and Corri) added to its weight. Dibdin allowed that *Lionel and Clarissa* "had considerable merit," but his charge that there were too many cooks was somewhat unfair because Dibdin "composed nearly two-thirds of the music; and, when that opera was altered [1770] . . . it was almost wholly my composition" (*Life,* I, 57).

> This author [Dibdin wrote in his *History*] measured his scenes as an engraver squares a picture, and thus, though correct, by being always regular, they were always cold. The perpetually going off with a song and teaching the audience, in imitation of the opera, when to expect a bravura song, a comic song, a cavatina, a duett, a quartetto, and a finale, began to grow intolerable tiresome; besides sentiment at this time was only for comedy, and . . . [Bickerstaff] complained that *False Delicacy* had anticipated *Lionel and Clarissa.* (V. 261)

Forty-three years after it was first performed, somebody discovered the "grossness of some of the passages." Although James Plumptre did not actually see the October 1810 production in Cambridge by the Norwich Company, he included a purified version of *Lionel and Clarissa* in his three-volume work which he sent to Kemble. The Drury Lane manager politely thanked the Reverend in a letter, but admitted that he had not yet the time to read *The English Drama Purified.*[27]

In contrast to most reviews, the one in *The Dramatic Censor* following performances on 14 and 16 November 1811 at the Lyceum Theatre in London was so favorable that it seems scarcely possible that *Lionel and Clarissa* was the subject.

> We congratulate the town upon having perceived at this Theatre . . . a partial restoration of Good Sense to her proper and required station upon the Stage; we allude to the spirited manner in which the Manager of this place hath prepared and got up that merit-fraught, natural, didactic, impressive, and moral Drama, called *Lionel and Clarissa;* which contains more point and interest in any one of its acts, than any dozen of our *modern Operas;* provided they were all boiled, hashed, stewed, or condensed together, into that limited space, by the way of analysing their force, spirit, originality, bearing, or fire!

In 1811 the reviewer could uphold *Lionel and Clarissa* as a "strong attempt, on the part of the Managers, to make a stand in behalf of the interests of Nature and Common Sense"—a statement which would have been impossible to make in the 1760s and 1770s. But in 1811, the reviewer was upholding this opera against the *"wooden Daemons* [of "Monk" Lewis], and such puerile trash."

Heavy as it might have been in 1807, *Lionel and Clarissa* continued to gain additional composers during the early part of the nineteenth century, when Sir John Stevenson and Horn were added to Corri and Reeve. Then too, that constant plague of playwrights—the star—insisted upon more songs, whether they were relevant or not; by 1816, when *The Theatrical Inquisitor* reviewed the 5 December Drury Lane production, its critic wrote that the part of Clarissa "has been so choaked and crowded with innovated airs, that it is at the option of a singer to elicit such impressions as may best promote her wishes."[28]

The biggest success for *Lionel and Clarissa* occurred 157 years after its first production, when, beginning on 28 October 1925, it ran for 171 nights at the Lyric, Hammersmith. Alfred Reynolds rearranged the music, and Nigel Playfair produced it and played Colonel Oldboy.

Lionel and Clarissa climaxed Bickerstaff's career at Covent Garden; it was also his last new full-length opera to be produced at either theatre, although he was working on one at the time he fled. When the opera began its original run at Covent Garden, Colman had not released Bickerstaff from his contract; yet only a month later, a new farce by Bickerstaff was being produced at Drury Lane. He had broken his agreement with Colman.

Had it not been for the dispute between Colman and the other managers, Bickerstaff would have been tied to Covent Garden until the expiration of his articles in 1770, but his acquaintance with Harris and his willingness to help embarrass Colman, enabled Bickerstaff to switch to Drury Lane. At the time "the disputes now Subsisting began," Bickerstaff testified, he was "intimately acquainted with the Plaintiff Harris." But Bickerstaff was determined not to "intermeddle" in the dispute, and he spoke about the quarrel only once, when he met Powell (Colman's ally and fellow-manager) at "the Lodgings of Charles Holland late of Drury Lane Theatre," where Bickerstaff had gone "on particular business." It is likely that Bickerstaff's business with Holland concerned the farce *The Absent Man,* which he prepared especially "to serve Mr. Holland at his benefit" on 21 March 1768.[29]

Perhaps Bickerstaff did not "intermeddle," but he was a cooperative witness for his friend Harris, who was 'squiring the actress Jane Lessingham, a neighbor of Bickerstaff in Somerset-yard. It is at least plausible that in return for Bickerstaff's testimony Harris helped the playwright break his articles. Unless Colman agreed to let him go, Bickerstaff could have his new works produced at Drury Lane only if he paid £1000—a fine that he never could have afforded. Bickerstaff claimed that he "deserted his connection" with Covent Garden because Colman fired Dibdin:

> At the time . . . Dibdin was discharged . . . and for some time before, [Bickerstaff] had great reason to be offended and displeased with the conduct and Management of [Colman] in respect to Musical Performances, but [Bickerstaff] had no intention of totally deserting his engagement until said Charles Dibdin was discharged. . . . From that time finding it impossible for him to go on with the Business in which he was then engaged at that Theatre without the assistance of said Charles Dibdin, Bickerstaff deserted his connections with said Theatre under the Penalty of £1,000.

Even had he been forced to pay the fine, Bickerstaff maintained, it would have been worth it to work with Dibdin in a theatre where the musical pieces would be "properly got up." At Covent Garden, on the contrary, "it hath been the design of Colman to discountenance Performances of that nature as much as he could," irrespective of profit.

Dibdin's own account of his leaving Covent Garden appears in a letter by him to Garrick, which though undated, was written shortly after Dibdin's Benefit on 24 May 1768:

> I cannot be easy till I have told you more particularly than I had an opportunity of doing yesterday the circumstances of Mr. Colman's discharging me from Covent Garden Theatre; after a great deal of unnecessary cavilling in order to protract my Benefit as much as he could I was obliged to apply to Mr. Harris for redress.
>
> A few days after I was sent for to the House where in the Green Room Mr. Younger shewed me a letter he had just received from Mr. Colman the contents of which were to this—He desired Mr. Younger to acquaint me that though I had behaved so impudently and impertinently he had settled my Benefit; but that for my wickedness in endeavouring to foment a difference betwixt him and the other Managers I should not be considered as belonging to that Theatre after the expiration of my article.[30]

Bickerstaff testified in enthusiastic support of Dibdin. "Colman's misconduct in the management and direction of the business of said Theatre," and his dismissal of Dibdin had contributed to the "almost total ruin of musical performances" at Covent Garden. In contrast to the present condition, in the past Bickerstaff's operas "had for several years . . . been in a great measure the support" of Covent Garden: "in particular . . . the two operas . . . *Love in a Village* and the *Maid of the Mill,* which besides the great nightly profits they have brought to the former managers . . . from their first representation," Bickerstaff asserted, "greatly helped to raise the price of the patents of that theatre in a few years from 40 to £60,000 owing to the publick reception of them by the Town."

Bickerstaff then listed three ways in which his plays, and the fortunes of Covent Garden, suffered because of Colman: "[he had] lessened the value of these pieces . . . by classing and performing them amongst the most hackneyed and indifferent plays from the time he took on himself the sole management . . . and [secondly] by giving them to the Town without any preparation and merely when he had not any thing else to perform. [Colman assigned parts] with scarce any attention to the capacity of the performers . . . giving them to any . . . who pretended to take them as things of little or no consequence. . . ."

Ironically, Bickerstaff left Covent Garden where he thought his operas were being mistreated, to go to Drury Lane where Garrick had no more respect for "tweedle-dum and tweedle-dee" than did Colman. Garrick wanted Bickerstaff "that he might no longer be that thorn in his side, he had been; for, certainly, *Love in a Village,* and the *Maid of the Mill,* had thinned the treasury at Drury Lane. Not, however, with a view to make [Bickerstaff's] fortune . . . but to have him in his power" (Dibdin, *Life,* I, 69-70).

The Absent Man, a two-act farce by Bickerstaff, preceded him to Drury Lane on 21 March 1768. Bickerstaff dedicated the play to Thomas King who acted the title role and who had played Novel in *The Plain Dealer.*

"This farce was written some years ago," Bickerstaff explained in his Preface, "without being offered to the stage; nor should he have ventured it there at all, but to serve Mr. [Charles] Holland, at his benefit. . . ." Holland had played Manly in *The Plain Dealer,* and when that comedy was printed, Bickerstaff thanked him in his Preface for his good performance.

After the initial success of the farce, Bickerstaff was encouraged "to look over it with greater care than he had before done, and having heightened some places where he thought it most deficient, he now submits it to the public, in a form, in which, he hopes it will not utterly displease" (Preface). The source of *The Absent Man* was named by Bickerstaff in his Prologue before the critics could accuse him of plagiarism:

> Hard set are poor bards for your pleasures to cater,
> And thus one provides for you, from the Spectator;
> From volume the first, page three hundred and nine,
> Number seventy-seven, he takes his design. . . .

When the farce was printed, Bickerstaff also cited Regnard's five-act play *Le Distrait,* but denied that he had used it, saying that the similiarity was due to the common ultimate source, "the Menalcas of La Bruyère's characters . . . the hint of the *Absent Man,* and no more, is taken from the same character of Menalcas, translated in . . . the Spectator" (Preface).

Spectator Number 77, by Eustace Budgell, described the absent-mindedness of Will Honeycomb and absent-mindedness in general, and concluded with a précis of Bruyère's Menalcas. Although there are similiarities between *The Absent Man* and Regnard's *Le Distrait,* one need go no farther than to Budgell's *Spectator* essay. Budgell followed Bruyère and presented a theophrastian character rather than create a dramatic framework for his absent-minded man. Bickerstaff took "the hint . . . and no more," but the transformation illustrates the difference between an essayist and a dramatist. Budgell writes *about* the absent-minded man; Shatterbrain *is* that man.

The farce was performed for the second time on 24 March as an afterpiece to *The Merchant of Venice for* King's Benefit, "And on the second night, it met with marks of favour still more manifest . . ." (Preface); therefore, during Holy Week (27 March-3 April 1768), Bickerstaff made some minor changes, and on 4 April *The Absent Man* was published. The changes occurred in the dialogue throughout the farce rather than to the plot itself. To cite only one example, the following dialogue, included in the Larpent Manuscript, was omitted in the first edition: Doctor Gruel has apologised to Shatterbrain after Flavia and Welldon are married. He dismisses his daughter and her new husband; then for no apparent reason, Shatterbrain remarks:

> Well, certainly Paoli is one of the greatest Generals that ever took the field. [Stage directions:] (they all look at him.)
> Mrs. Junket: Prithee leave Paoli to fight his battles and for once in your life think of what's before you. . . .

When *The Absent Man* was first performed, *The Court Miscellany,* and *The London Magazine,* both for March 1768, favorably reviewed it. In the farce, "a variety of whimsical distresses . . . affords us a constant fund of entertainment, without running into a single circumstance of buffoonry from the opening of the first scene to the termination of the catastrophe" (*The London Magazine,* XXXVII, 124-125). The critic in *The Court Miscellany* commented:

> It is odd how a character so common in life, and that has made such a conspicuous figure in our most celebrated novelist, Fielding, should never before have made its way to the theatre.

He concluded by writing that *The Absent Man* "has met with success, and indeed . . . has deserved the applause it met with" (IV, 140).

The farce enjoyed fair success, being performed ten times in 1768, but not again at Drury Lane until 12 and 16 March 1772. At that time, the *Theatrical Review* termed it "very laughable, notwithstanding its absurdities" (II, 138-139). In The United States it was performed three times, once in New York, then in Portsmouth, New Hampshire; and finally in Boston in 1794 (Macmillan, p. 65). The last performances in London were in 1784 and in 1795 when it was revived at Covent Garden. Dibdin's dismissal of this farce, "It was too flimzy to do any thing material" (*History,* V, 262), is incontestable; yet it would be unjust to leave *The Absent Man* with that remark. Like most farces, it is flimsy, but again like most farces, it depends on comic acting to ensure its success. Captain Slang's coterie, and especially Shatterbrain, constantly allowed their performers opportunities to amuse their audiences. If the work never rose beyond slapstick, it was never meant to.

8

BLACK IS BOUNTIFUL: *THE PADLOCK*

While *The Absent Man* was being performed at Drury Lane during the spring of 1768, Bickerstaff was hard at work writing another musical piece with Charles Dibdin—and trying to escape from Covent Garden, with or without Dibdin. The story he adapted was from one of Cervantes' exemplary novels, *El Celoso Extremeño*. Superficially, it bore no resemblance to any of his earlier operas; but the same kind of characters appeared in both his adaptation and *Thomas and Sally*. In *The Padlock,* as the new piece was to be called, Thomas becomes Leander, Dorcas is now Ursula, the innocent Sally is transformed into the still more innocent Leonora, and the squire—albeit with considerable increase in age—becomes Don Diego. But the most popular figure in the new opera was none of these: it was Don Diego's black servant Mungo.

Bickerstaff need not have gone to the Spanish of Cervantes to read *El Celoso Extremeño;* it was translated as "The Jealous Estremaduran," in *A Select Collection of Novels,* edited by Samuel Croxall in 1720. These novels were reprinted during the century, one of the other tales being a version of the Inkle and Yarico story which Bickerstaff dramatized in 1767.

Like "Inkle and Yarico," which disappeared somewhere between Covent Garden and Drury Lane, *The Padlock* had difficulty making the crossing. Both Bickerstaff and Dibdin, who composed the music, left Covent Garden before *The Padlock* was produced, and during the summer of 1768 it was a case of two dramatists and a play looking for a playhouse. Part of the play surfaced during the summer in the form of one of the most popular songs of that season, one which anticipated Leander's concluding song in *The Padlock*. Sung by Vernon (who was to play Leander) at Vauxhall Gardens, "The English Padlock" contained two lines which echoed Prior's poem of the same name and complemented Bickerstaff's song: "Good-humour's the padlock to keep a wife true," and "For the Fair One is safe if you padlock her mind." The song was praised in *Lloyd's Evening Post,* and printed there on 25 July. Whether or not it was an early version of Leander's song, it nevertheless served as advance publicity for the musical farce. But it was not at Vauxhall that Dibdin and Bickerstaff hoped to bring out *The Padlock*.

"In the summer of 1768 [Dibdin wrote], it was intended to bring out *The Padlock* at the Haymarket." But, considering the quarrels which the two men had with Colman, producing their play might have been a tactless venture until the matters of articles and proprietorship were finally settled. At any rate, Dibdin continued:

> Mrs. Jewel was to have been the original Leonora, and Moody the original Mungo. It went off, I apprehend, owing to [Samuel] Foote's [the Haymarket manager] indolence, and Garrick's activity. It was natural that Colman should consider [Bickerstaff] a formidable rival; and, Garrick had hitherto stood aloof to make a better bargain with him; so that the Haymarket became a kind of forlorn hope to that piece, from which Garrick, with all his affected indifference, determined to rescue it. [*Life,* I, 69]

Before Garrick would stage *The Padlock,* however, he had to be sure of Dibdin's music, and "not pretending to be a competent judge himself of that Branch of Management," he had the music "performed before able judges without any one of them knowing who the composer was. . . ." The judges "greatly approved."[1] Once assured of the worth of *The Padlock* Garrick did his best to guarantee it a good production. There were "new Scenes, Dresses, Music and other Decorations" (Stone, 1356); and despite his ill-health, Garrick saw to it at rehearsals that no one in his company would be as unruly as Ned Shuter. "During rehearsals [Garrick] paced the actor through his role, often acting out the scenes for him—including the female roles—with convincing realism. Helfrich Peter Sturz . . . saw him at work during the preparation of . . . *The Padlock* and marvelled that his delicate health could endure the constant strain which he subjected it to as he turned from one actor and character to another, attempting to kindle a fire where often no spark existed."[2] The production must have been especially polished because it was being readied for a command performance for the visiting King of Denmark, Christian VII, and Bickerstaff had been allowed to dedicate *The Padlock* to him.

As Dibdin noted, the original Mungo was to have been John Moody. Bickerstaff

> had promised Moody that he should perform the part; and, indeed, the part would never have been written as it is but for Moody's suggestions, who had been in the West-Indies, and knew, of course, the dialect of the negroes. I knew, however, that Moody would never perform it, and I knew he never could. Perhaps I had taken some care of this in the composition of the songs. His inability became more and more apparent at every rehearsal; and, at last, he himself gave it up as a task to which his powers were inadequate. I received the part with reluctance and secret indignation. I knew what I could do with it, and I knew I ought to have had it from the beginning. (*Life,* I, 70)

For all of Dibdin's reluctance and secret indignation, he proved to be a brilliant Mungo. Bickerstaff swore that "he hath heard Mr. David Garrick speaking of Dibdin [as Mungo] declare that he could not himself perform any one of his characters better than that was performed by Dibdin, and saith that . . . the great success of . . . The Padlock was in great measure owing to the composition of the music and to the performance of the character of Mungo by . . . Dibdin, and that he [Garrick] hath one way or other by the said Opera received a profit of £700 in the space of 18 months or thereabouts" (BM ms. 33218). Of course, Bickerstaff and Dibdin could scarcely restrain themselves when they testified on behalf of Harris against Colman in 1770. Dibdin asserted that *The Padlock* was so successful that the Drury Lane managers made £3000, and besides, "if it had not been for the Behaviour of Mr. Colman [Bickerstaff and Dibdin] should not have quitted the theatre in Covent Garden, and . . . the Padlock would not have been performed at Drury Lane and is . . . very certain that great loss must have happen'd to the Proprietors of Covent Garden. . . ."

The success of *The Padlock,* was, "in the opinion and belief of [Bickerstaff] and other Judges of things of that nature the means of supporting three very indifferent new plays by the representation of [*The Padlock*]. Without the auxiliary assistance of that opera the managers of Drury Lane must have been considerable losers whereas they on the contrary made a very great profit from the performances thereof. . ." (BM ms. 33218). Such was the success of the farce that Garrick presented Bickerstaff £100 "over and above the usual emoluments resulting to [Bickerstaff] as the author of that opera."

"The usual emoluments," according to Dibdin, earned Bickerstaff a good deal more than £100. His Benefit "yielded two hundred pounds . . . the words must have also been greatly productive, for he kept the copyright—and, in the first eight years, there had been upwards of twenty three thousand copies sold."[3] In his *Life,* Dibdin increased the sale of the words to "twenty-eight thousand copies" by 1773 ("thirty years ago"). Dibdin was especially chagrined that he had sold the music to Bickerstaff for £45—the going rate for such a composition. "But the sale of the music can hardly be conceived . . . in thirteen years, nearly three sets of the *Padlock* had been worn out. I make a set of plates, at this time, to take off about three thousand five hundred impressions; so that an estimate may be easily made of the immense profit it yielded" (*Life,* I, 71). By the time Dibdin finished totting up Bickerstaff's profits, he calculated that Bickerstaff "cleared . . . at least seventeen hundred pounds" (*Life,* I, 71). Even if Dibdin was right, he was figuring the profit over a thirteen-year span, and while £130-plus a year was not inconsiderable in 1768, Bickerstaff was unable to collect it after 1772 when he fled the country. Besides, when Bickerstaff testified in 1770, he claimed that he had "made a profit of £200 by the sale of the music," considerably less than Dibdin's estimate, but admittedly a neat return for the £45 which he paid Dibdin.

Dibdin's chagrin was a result of hindsight, because in 1768 he looked upon the music for *The Padlock* as an investment which might lead to his becoming "composer to the theatre, at which my ambitions were naturally roused" (*Life,* I, 72). When the score and the words were originally published, the friendship between Dibdin and Bickerstaff had increased to the point where Dibdin named his son (born on 27 October 1768) Charles Isaac Mungo Dibdin, in honor of the author and the part that had won him fame (*The Padlock* having opened on 3 October 1768). Bickerstaff praised Dibdin in his Preface to *The Padlock,* while, at the same time, he put the composer in his place:

> The music of this Piece being extremely admired by persons of the first taste and distinction [Bickerstaff wrote], it would be injustice to the extraordinary talents of the young man who assisted me in it, was I

> not to declare, that it is, under my direction, the entire composition of Mr. Dibdin; whose admirable performance in the character of Mungo, does so much credit to himself and me. . . .

Then, Bickerstaff concluded his Preface with a compliment to Garrick at the expense of Colman, "as well as to the gentleman, whose penetration could distinguish neglected genius, and who has taken pleasure in producing it to the public."[4] When the music of *The Padlock* was published, it contained Dibdin's dedication to Mrs. Garrick, a dedication that complimented both Bickerstaff and David Garrick.

> It was with pleasure I found the AUTHOR concur with me in offering this mark of my Respect, it is one among those many obligations to him, which I wish I could as warmly Express as I sensibly feel, for he has not only brought me out of obscurity by allowing me the Great advantage of composing a Piece written by him, But secur'd my Welfare by recommending me to the Notice and Favour of Mr. Garrick.[5]

Judging from a letter by Bickerstaff to Mrs. Garrick, Dibdin had good reason to dedicate the music to her. Counting on a profitable Benefit, Dibdin furnished his house on credit. But he gained only about £17 from the 24 May performance. Bickerstaff petitioned Mrs. Garrick to persuade her husband to give Dibdin £100; presumably she was successful.[6]

After Dibdin was fired by Garrick in 1775, and had time to reflect, he forgot any reasons for liking Bickerstaff and Garrick, and remembered only that they, not he, had made money from *The Padlock*. Everything they had done, they did to keep Dibdin for their own profit: "Had I not been the stupidest of all idiots," he moaned in print, "I might have seen that my being pinned to Drury-Lane upon such easy terms, was a matter concerted between [Garrick and Bickerstaff]. I hate to think of it" (*The Musical Tour of Mr. Dibdin,* 1788). "In short, the whole business was a kind of concerted see-saw between [Bickerstaff] and GARRICK; for the first wanted, of course, to get my music as cheap as possible, and the latter my theatrical exertions" (*Life,* I, 72). As a composer, actor, and singer, Dibdin was "engaged in an article at Drury Lane theatre at an encreased salary of £5 7s per week," Bickerstaff testified in 1770. Although not a lordly sum, it contrasts favorably to what Dibdin received as a singer during his last season (1767-1768) at Covent Garden: 10s *per diem* (Stone, 1270).

The Padlock was so well received that it was produced 54 times at Drury Lane during the 1768-1769 season. Most of the contemporary reviews praised *The Padlock,* although the critic for *The London Magazine* could not resist adding, "However, the opera is a species of composition which we must not examine with too critical an exactness; and indeed it would be a kind of ingratitude not to make some small allowances, where, like the *Padlock,* it affords a very agreeable entertainment" (XXXVII, October, 1768, 510).

Mungo was the major reason for the success of *The Padlock.* Dibdin in blackface was the first to portray what was to become in the nineteenth century the ubiquitous stage comic Negro servant. Before Mungo there had been set-upon servants who hated their masters, but the addition of color and dialect made the part new. Mungo became a staple figure in political cartoons; his name served as part of the title for an anthology of otherwise indifferent prose and verse, *The Padlock Open'd, or Mungo's Medley* (London, 1771). Mungo's words even entered Parliament on 26 January 1769, when Colonel Barré attacked Dyson for being the "adviser and conductor" of the measures under debate. The Colonel "rose in his place, and, after stating his objections . . . he concluded with saying that the Honourable Member called to his mind the words of a song that he heard at Drury-Lane, 'Mungo here, Mungo there, Mungo every where.' "[7] The song occurred in Act I, scene vi:

Dear heart, what a terrible life am I led!
A dog has a better, that's shelter'd and fed:
  Night and day 'tis de same,
  My pain is dere game:
Me wish to de Lord me was dead.

  Whate'er's to be done,
  Poor black must run;
  Mungo here, Mungo dere,
  Mungo every where;
  Above and below,
  Sirrah come, Sirrah go;
  Do so, and do so.
  Oh! Oh!
  Me wish to de Lord me was dead.

Such was the popularity of Mungo's sayings that to the question, "Are you tired?" it was common to answer, "No massa,—me lilly tire" (Boaden, I, xlvi; Mungo's reply, I, vi.). "Mungo here, Mungo there, Mungo every where" was soon heard here, there, and everywhere, and inevitably was turned against Dibdin when in 1772 Sir Nicholas Nipclose (Francis Gentleman) rimed in *The Theatres:*

> DIBDIN, alas! we nearly had forgot,
> Perhaps oblivion were the kindest lot:
> How he *composes,* 'tis not fit, we say,
> But grant kind stars that he may never *play:*
> Nor, to enlarge our wish, may ever sing;
> MUNGO in this, in that, and ev'ry thing. (p. 53)

As popular as *The Padlock* was in England, it failed in its initial run in Ireland. The work "was brought out in January, 1769, with every advantage, after Mr. Mossop's Hamlet, to £80" (Hitchcock, II, 164); by the third night it drew only £41, "after which, it was obliged to be tacked to Mr. Mossop's strongest tragedies." "Indeed," Hitchcock continued, "it is the only instance I ever knew or heard, of its failing" (p. 165). Two months after its failure, Miss Cately, "still in fashion, visited Dublin . . . and, as usual, brought crowded houses to her favourite characters. Her playing Leonora, in the Padlock, at this time, first gave it a reputation which it has ever since maintained" (p. 165). In total number of performances, *The Padlock* was second only to Charles Coffey's *The Devil to Pay,* which, according to Hughes, was produced 181 times in Dublin to *The Padlock's* 163. But Coffey's farce was first performed in Dublin in 1731, 38 years before Bickerstaff's.

In the United States, *The Padlock* was first played at the John Street Theatre in New York on 29 May 1769 (Macmillan, p. 65); Lewis Hallam, the younger, played Mungo. The last performance was also in New York, on 13 March 1837 at the Franklin Theatre. By that time it had been acted at various theatres 81 times.

For a time *The Padlock* was a staple for English-speaking companies. When the American Company of Comedians opened at Montego Bay, Jamaica, they followed up *Jane Shore* with Goldsmith's *She Stoops to Conquer* and *The Padlock.* And at Kingston on 2 September 1780, it was an afterpiece to *Merchant of Venice;* as late as 1813 it was played at Kingston. In India it was performed at Madras where it "was got up with infinite success in February last [1788], at the Theatre in the Governor's Gardens, in this settlement, for the benefit of the Asylum for

Female Orphans, patronized by Lady Campbell. The House was crowded, and the cause seemed to inspire the performers with more than usual animation."[8] Performances have been recorded in Calcutta (1789), Capetown (1815), and Bombay (1820). A touring English company gave it at St. Petersburg in 1771 (Loewenberg, col. 303). At Vienna in 1853, *The Padlock* was performed in English and, on 18 April 1857, in German as *Das Vorhangeschloss*. A French version was translated as *La Cadenas* in 1822 but Loewenberg does not record any performance.

One of the English actors who performed Mungo in the eighteenth century was Edward Cape Everard. In his *Memoirs,* published in 1818, he wrote that for his benefit night when he was playing in Brighton, probably in 1778, he was required "to undertake the part of *King Richard III;* as a kind of *desert* [sic] I had to play *Mungo* in the 'Padlock,' and by way of *bon bouche,* was under the necessity of giving my friends in the gallery a horn-pipe after the play. . . ."[9] It was a night all too typical in the provinces, for the manager's wife refused to play the Queen in *Richard III,* and Mrs. Baddeley saved the comedian's Benefit by reading the part, "and after played Leonora in the 'Padlock.'" Everard's most unusual performance as Mungo, and possibly the most unusual production of the opera, came during May-July 1792 at the Apollo Gardens.[10] Walter Claggett, the proprietor, decided to improve his resort with a fantoccini.

> He had prepared a pretty stage in miniature, his scenes and all corresponding with his two-feet figures which were well made and properly dressed, with experienced persons to work them. . . . I had to speak for my little representative, Mungo; after the first we had no rehearsals. (Everard, p. 144)

Everard would begin around eight in the evening. Between the acts he mingled with the spectators who at that time paid sixpence which entitled them to refreshments. There was music every night, and by nine o'clock the gardens were crowded with many who had first visited other public places. They came to the Apollo for "hot suppers." Claggett "prided himself on 'the superior excellence of the Music and Wines' . . . [and] boasted, moreover, of the patronage of the nobility and gentry" (Wroth, p. 269). But at the same time, the gardens were a "resort of cheats and pickpockets" (p. 269). Everard mentioned the "well-selected and good band of music," describing the gardens as "large, delightfully pleasant, accommodating, well laid out and diversified . . . it was resorted to like a little Ranelagh or Vauxhall. The 'Padlock' was thus represented every evening above seventy times, till at last, I got heartily tired of my friend Mungo, and was not very sorry when the season was over" (Everard, pp. 144-145).

Everard was not the only actor who supplied his voice for a puppet-Mungo. *The Padlock* was performed as a puppet show at The Patagonian Theatre in 1776, as were *The Recruiting Serjeant* by Bickerstaff, and *Thomas and Sally*. The theatre was housed in the Exeter Change, a "large bazaar-like building on the north side of the Strand; the ground floor was taken up by a number of small traders' stalls, and the large room above was let out for all kinds of purposes."[11] The theatre held about twenty persons. At various fairs a puppet *Padlock* was presented by one Flocton who for a performance "obtained the services of two Italian singers" (Speaight, p. 159).

In the nineteenth century, the great Negro actor, Ira Aldridge, kept Mungo and *The Padlock* alive. He was apparently the first Negro—if not the last—to play the part. Although *The Padlock* has been termed an Anti-Slavery drama, and Bickerstaff named as probably the "first to bring upon the stage the realistic Negro who became a minor comic figure,"[12] it should be obvious that Mungo was played for laughs, not abolition. Even Mungo's song, "Dear heart, what a terrible life am I led!" was remembered not for its pathos but for "Mungo here, Mungo there, Mungo every where." Whether the speech is West-Indian, as Dibdin reported, or African, Mungo is no Oroonoko. It is true that "Bickerstaff discards the language of the noble Negro; [Mungo] speaks a mongrel English that has its dramatic effect" (Sypher, p. 235). Bickerstaff might not have intended his audiences to feel sympathy with Mungo as a representative of an oppressed race, but when the role was played by Ira Aldridge, they saw it that way. Playing Mungo in St. Petersburg, in November 1858, in English to his Russian audience, Aldridge conveyed to the playgoers the unjust persecution which blacks suffered from their white masters. As a Russian historian wrote after seeing Aldridge as Mungo:

> deep in the heart of every ecstatic spectator, sacred conscience is heard; no, under the dark skin the same flaming blood is excited, the poor heart beats with the same common human feelings, from the strained breast bursts the same heavy sighs as ours, a black body quivers from the same

From the frontispiece to "A New Edition" of Thomas and Sally *(mid 1760s): a "Musical Entertainment," which anticipated the popular nineteenth-century melodramas.*

Love in a Village, *Act I, scene 6, Shuter, Beard, and Dunstall as Justice Woodcock, Hawthorn, and Hodge. Hawthorn: "Right, neighbour* Woodcock! *health, good humour, and competence is my motto. . . ."*

Love in a Village, *Act I, scene 3, DuBellamy and Mrs. Cargill as Young Meadows and Rossetta. Rossetta: "Pray, let go my hand." In this most popular of eighteenth-century comic operas, there is never a doubt—despite her protest—that love blooms between Meadows and Rossetta.*

Love in a Village, *Act II, scene 12, Mrs. Wrighten as Margery sings "Since Hodge proves ungrateful, no further I'll seek." Having been jilted by Hodge, Madge leaves her virtue in the country to "better my fortune as other girls do" in London.*

Maid of the Mill, *Act II, Scene 14, Mattocks and Miss Harpur as Lord Aimworth and Patty. Patty: "Cease, oh cease, to overwhelm me." In this comic opera version of* Pamela, *Patty beseeches Lord Aimworth to remember the social distance between them.*

Maid of the Mill, *Act I, scene 1, Charles Dibdin as Ralph sings "If that's all You want, who the plague will be sorry?" Ralph quits his father's mill but gains a captaincy from Lord Aimworth. Charles Dibdin began as a dancer in* Thomas and Sally, *played comic roles in later operas, and then collaborated with Bickerstaff before writing his own successes.*

Lionel and Clarissa: *Parsons was the first to play Oldboy at Drury Lane (1770); Shuter played him at Covent Garden.*

Lionel and Clarissa: *Mrs. Baddeley as Drury Lane's Clarissa asks Lionel (III, 9), "Can you forsake me? Have I then given my affections to a man who rejects and disregards them?" Lionel and Clarissa are perfect examples of the sentimental hero and heroine.*

The Padlock: *The first blackface comedian, Dibdin sang, "Me wish to de Lord me was dead" (I, 6). In the same song, his "Mungo here, Mungo dere,/Mungo every where" was for a time a common expression.*

The Hypocrite, *Mrs. Abingdon as Charlotte. Dr. Cantwell (Thomas King) has just named the sum he demands before he will allow Charlotte to marry Darnley (IV, 6).*

Maw-worm: "I'm almost sure I have had a call." II, vi: The Hypocrite *was the third English version of* Tartuffe, *but Maw-worm was Bickerstaff's own, and the character helped keep the comedy on the stage for one hundred years.*

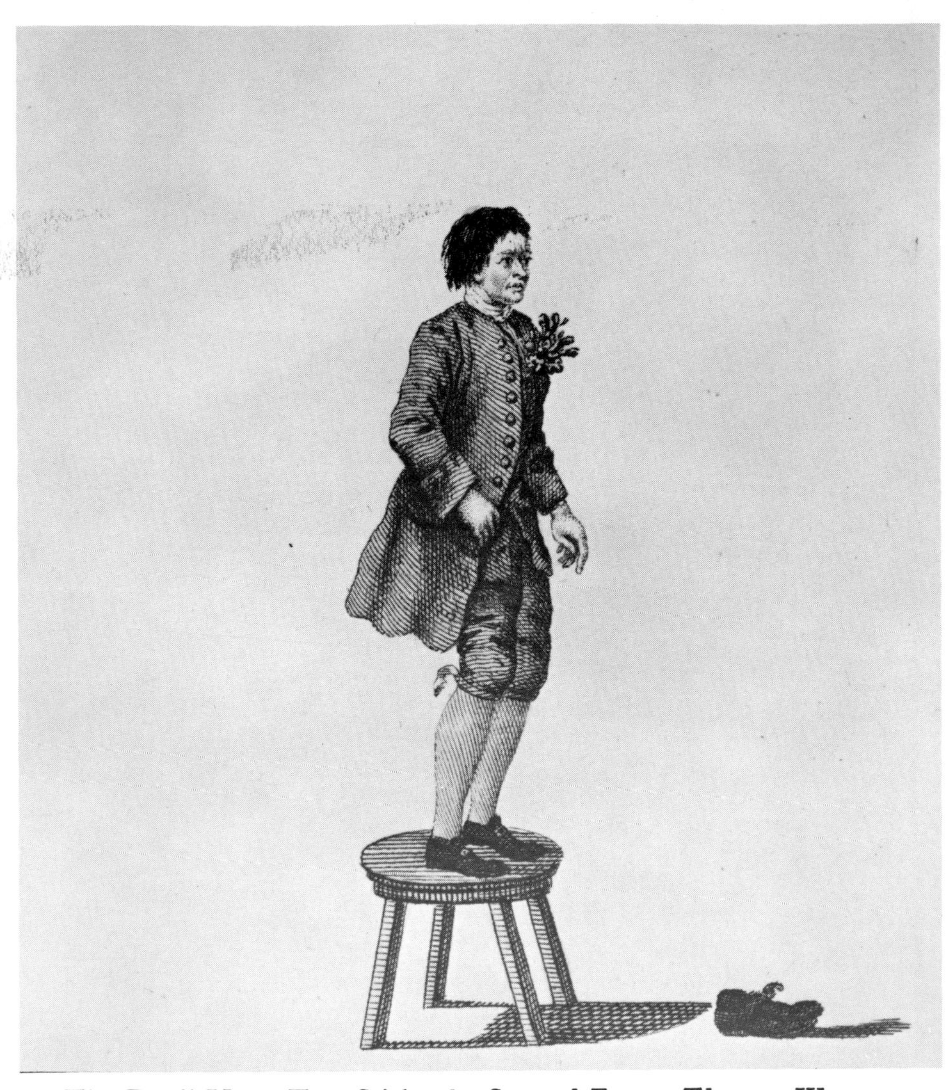

The Devil Upon Two Sticks, *by Samuel Foote. Thomas Weston was so popular as Maw-worm, that Bickerstaff re-created the character as Dr. Last, the word-mangling fool, in* Dr. Last in his Chariot, *the sequel to Foote's play in which Last appeared briefly.*

The Sultan, or, A Peep Into the Seraglio, *Mrs. Abingdon as Roxalana. Although Frances Abingdon caused Garrick to despair, her insistence on changes in this play made her its unrivaled star.*

The Romp, *Mrs. Jordan as the title character sings, "Dear me, how I long to be marry'd." The successor to Mrs. Abingdon in many roles, Dorothy Jordan made Priscilla Tomboy, the "romp," her own for about thirty years—until her daughter played it.*

as the white. . . . What a wonderful spectacle for the friend of goodness to see, when a whole people, black or white, awaken to human life! These are the thoughts that were awakened in me by the acting of the African Negro in . . . the farce, *The Padlock;* when the cruel master raised his stick above the beaten Negro, I saw one thing only—such a quivering movement of his spine, his shoulders, that my very own body was shaking; in my imagination I saw the history of a whole people.[13]

Even if the Russian audience was seeing its own history mirrored in the suffering of Mungo, Aldridge's acting must have been remarkable. Here is the dialogue with which he worked in Act I, scene vi, when Don Diego beats him:

Mungo: La, Massa, how could you have a heart to lick poor Neger man, as you lick me last Thursday?
Diego: If you have not a mind I should chastise you now, hold your tongue.
Mungo: Yes, Massa, if you no lick me again.
Diego: Listen to me, I say.
Mungo: You know, Massa, me very good servant—
Diego: Then you will go on?
Mungo: And ought to be use kine—
Diego: If you utter another syllable—
Mungo: And I'm sure, Massa, you can't deny but I worky worky,—I dress a victuals, and run a errands, and wash a house, and make a beds, and scrub a shoes, and wait a table.
Diego: Take that—Now will you listen to me?
Mungo: La, Massa, if ever I saw—
Diego: I am going abroad. . . . During this night I charge you not to sleep a wink, but be watchful . . . and keep walking up and down the entry. . . .
Mungo: So I must be stay in a cold all night, and have no sleep, and get no tanks neither; then him call me tief, and rogue, and rascal, to tempt me.
Diego: Stay here, perverse animal. . . . (p. 10)

Aldridge, "in his later performances of *The Padlock* . . . interpolated Russian folk songs, which he sang" in Russian; "in particular, *Vo Piru, Vo Besyedushki* ('While Feasting, While Gossiping'), and the audience did not see any incongruity, because they were songs of slaves, black or white" (Marshall and Stock, p. 234). While he performed in Russia he was the only member of the cast who spoke his part in English. Wherever he played, Berlin, or Cracow for instance, he spoke English while the cast spoke German or Polish.

The African Roscius, as Aldridge was billed, first played Mungo sometime after 1827; he would often schedule the farce to follow *Othello*. Whether he toured the provinces, or was in Scotland or London, he invariably received good notices. But by the time Aldridge stopped acting, there was no one else who wanted to play Mungo here, Mungo there, or Mungo anywhere, and no audience eager to see *The Padlock*. Mungo had been replaced by that black-faced song-and-dance man, Jim Crow. With the advent of the minstrel singers, Mungo would have become just another Mr. Bones.

While Mungo held the stage, he became more than merely comic as actor and audience invested him with social and even tragic significance. Without lecturing or moralizing Mungo became a conscience to his white audiences. Emboldened by drink, Mungo ridicules Don Diego in Act II, scene vi, and rebels—and the chemistry of drama, if not of print, transforms the silly black servant into a human being more courageous than Uncle Tom who is too humble to have a temper, or Oroonoko, who is too proud to lose it. Somehow, when Aldridge played him, Mungo became not unworthy to be seen after Othello.

When Bickerstaff dedicated *The Padlock* to the King of Denmark, he wrote that he was the only playwright to have a new play produced while the King was in the country. Actually Bickerstaff was being modest, for he had two new pieces staged, both in honor of Christian VII. At Covent Garden—even though Bickerstaff was no longer there—*The Royal Garland* was produced as an interlude on 10 October 1768 with music by Samuel Arnold.[14] At its conclusion, the King was given a large coronet of flowers. In return, Christian VII gave Covent Garden £40.

This "poetical whipt-syllabub"[15] was performed four times. "The Audience . . . went away extremely well pleased with the performance" (*Lloyd's Evening Post,* XXIII, 11 October 1768, 356); "and the Author of the piece is, no doubt, to be commended, for the compliments he has paid that illustrious and amiable Personage, in honour of whom the Royal Garland was exhibited." The same review appeared in *The London Chronicle* for 11 October. The Danish King, who was neither illustrious nor amiable, was described privately and more accurately as "that woman-like painted puppy" by Sylas Neville in his *Diary,* who also termed him "the Danish tyrant" (Stone, 1354-1355). Unlike *The Padlock, The Royal Garland* caused little comment, and quietly disappeared after its four performances, having served its purpose no doubt prettily enough.

While the Danish King watched Garrick play Sir John Brute

in *The Provoked Wife* on 8 September 1768, William Kenrick was behind the scenes. Despite a contemporary painting that portrays Garrick holding forth in the green room to an attentive audience of actors and actresses, that room must often have been the scene of active politicking by hopeful performers and dramatists whose livelihoods depended upon Garrick's pleasure. Kenrick, who saw himself as a latter-day plain dealer, nevertheless wanted his plays produced at Drury Lane and was not above paying court to Garrick. The sudden move of Bickerstaff from Covent Garden and his ready access to Garrick galled Kenrick—as it did other playwrights. The recollections of Kenrick and Joseph Reed illustrate the tense little world the green room was. Having gratified his curiosity in looking at his Danish majesty, Kenrick wrote,

> I retired into the green-room; for I had frequently seen you play [Sir John] before, and in my life, I think, I never saw you play it so ill. You were yourself sensible of it and extremely out of humour. As almost every body was crowding to the side of the scenes to stare at the king, I was sitting alone in the green-room, when you came in from the stage, with that wretched parasite, sticking to your elbow and slobbering in your ear, "that you never performed so well, by J---s G-d in all your life." The wretch seemed a little disconcerted on turning round and seeing a witness to his meanness; but when I afterwards reproached him for it, he very readily retorted, "Sir, I know he plays damnably to-night as well as you, but don't you see the man's in an ill humour." This, Sir [Garrick], was sufficient to drive me from any place, where I must appear to stand in any degree in the same predicament with such a prostituted being.[16]

That "wretched parasite" and "prostituted being" was Isaac Bickerstaff, and Kenrick sufficiently compromised his principles to work with him two months later on the short-lived *Gentleman's Journal.*

Joseph Reed recalled in his "Theatrical Duplicity" what happened when *he* saw Garrick as Sir John Brute:

> When suspicion hath once taken root in the mind, it is not easily eradicated. Mr. Garrick's looks had of late appear'd more cold, the cause of which I had attributed to his new favourites Messieurs Bickerstaff & [crossed out]. The one was my profess'd enemy, the other had many months been a conceal'd foe under the mask of friendship. They both knew the British Roscius was a Dupe to Flattery, in which science they were considerable proficients, and generally attended behind the scenes whenever that inimitable performer appear'd on the stage. Their praises were often so gross, that I wonder'd they did not disgust instead

> of pleasing a Man of Mr. Garrick's penetration. . . . One evening as he play'd Sir John Brute, I was so convuls'd with laughter that the tears ran down my cheeks, which Mr. Garrick accidentally observ'd while he was on the stage. As he was on his exit receiving the adulation of his two flatterers he said "the House is in high glee tonight. I have certainly play'd the part better than I us'd to!" Bickerstaff exclaimed, "By Jasus! my dear Sir, you never play'd the scene so divinely before!" (pp. 81–82)

The "conceal'd foe" might well have been Kenrick who unbeknownst to Reed wrote verses in *The St. James Chronicle* against his *Dido* in the spring of 1767. Bickerstaff's action in these two accounts is scarcely equal to the writers' reaction; Reed would have gladly traded places. As long as Bickerstaff remained an asset to Garrick, however, he was safe from the grumblings of disappointed playwrights.

9

"AN EXCRESSANCE INTO THE COUNTRY": *THE HYPOCRITE, THE GENTLEMAN'S JOURNAL, AMBROSE GWINNET*

Garrick hired Bickerstaff primarily as an adapter and general factotum. Aside from *Daphne and Amintor* and the altered *Lionel and Clarissa,* Bickerstaff wrote no new musical pieces specifically for Drury Lane up to 1772. As an adapter, however, he wrote one comedy which remained in repertory for over 100 years: *The Hypocrite.*

According to Bickerstaff, it was Garrick's idea to alter Colley Cibber's *Non-Juror,* itself an adaptation of Molière's *Tartuffe.* "Mr. Garrick determin'd to do this about two years ago," Bickerstaff wrote in his Preface to *The Hypocrite* published early in 1769; "but, because the consequence of success wou'd be a benefit easily gotten, he kindly put it into my hands, with some hints for the alteration. He did not think it was necessary to have any thing new, besides a short character for that entertaining comedian, Mr. Weston: Maw-worm therefore in this play is written by me, and scarce any thing more. For the rest, the character of Doctor Cantwell, as it here stands, is almost a verbal translation from Molière, as old Lady Lambert is a counterpart of Madam Pernelle."

Bickerstaff finished his alteration by 27 July 1767 when he wrote to Garrick, "I have put into your brother's hand with this letter the alteration of 'The Non-juror,' and I flatter myself it is not ill done, because I have adhered as strictly as possible to your idea of what it should be; and with the assistance of Molière, I think I have made it a clean, laughable, and (what in my opinion is no small excellence in one) not too long a comedy. . . ." (Boaden, I, 266). That Bickerstaff succeeded in writing "not too long a comedy," is confirmed in Oxberry's 1818 acting edition of *The Hypocrite* where the time for the comedy's representation is given as "one hour and fifty-four minutes."

The Hypocrite depended on three ingredients for its success: the vivacity of Charlotte, the comicality of Maw-worm, and the rascality of Dr. Cantwell. These parts were tailored by Bickerstaff to fit the abilities of Mrs. Abington, Weston and King, and he acknowledged the performances of Mrs. Abington and Thomas King in his Preface:

> Gratitude . . . obliges me to take notice of the great assistance I have receiv'd from Mrs. Abington and Mr King. The former . . . is so excellent, that I cannot conceive it possible for any actress ever to have gone beyond her. There is a natural ease and vivacity in her manner, and, in this part particularly, a fashionable deportment (if I may use the expression) which gives a brilliancy to every thing she says. . . . [King] has shewn that he is capable of assuming characters the most difficult, and at the same time the most opposite; and, by each new effort, to add to the esteem which the public appears to have for him.

Dr. Cantwell was indeed a different role for King who had played Novel in *The Plain Dealer* and Shatterbrain in Bickerstaff's *The Absent Man*. It was neither Cantwell nor Charlotte, however, who assured the hundred-year popularity of the comedy, but Maw-worm. His brief appearance in Act II, and his few lines in the final act alter the tone of the comedy by his unconscious "low" humor. His anticipations of Mrs. Malaprop, and his naive gullibility endeared him to the upper galleries, if not to most critics. But to Hazlitt, the addition of Maw-worm made up for Bickerstaff's botching of Tartuffe: "In his alteration," Hazlitt concluded in his *The Comic Writers of the Last Century* (Lecture VIII), Bickerstaff "has spoiled the Hypocrite, but he has added Maw-worm."[1]

By trade, Maw-worm is a chandler who "deals in grocery, tea, small-beer, charcoal, butter, brick-dust, and the like" (II, vi, 35); but since following Dr. Cantwell's preachings, he has lost most of his customers. Now he "wants to go a preaching" because he is "almost sure" he has "had a call" (p. 35).

I have made several sermons already, I does them extrumpery, because I cann't write: and now the devils in our alley says, as how my head's turned.
Old Lady Lambert: Ay, devils, indeed—but don't you mind them.
Maw-worm: No, I don't—I rebukes them, and preaches to them, whether they will or not. We lets our house in lodgings to single men; and, sometimes, I gets them together, with one or two of the neighbours, and makes them all cry. (pp. 35–36)

Despite discouragement, Maw-worm continues to preach, even on "Kennington Common, the last review day; but the boys threw brick-bats at me, and pinn'd crackers to my tail; and I have been afraid to mount ever since." He tried to placate the boys:

Maw-worm: . . . says I, I does nothing clandecently; I stand here contagious to his Majesty's guards, and, I charges you upon your apparels, not to mislist me.
Old Lady Lambert: And it had no effect?
Maw-worm: No more than if I spoke to so many postesses; but if he [Dr. Cantwell] advises me to go a preaching, and quit my shop, I'll make an excressance farther into the country.
. . . .
I am but a sheep, but my bleatings shall be heard afar off, and that sheep shall become a shepherd; nay, if it be only, as it were, a shepherd's dog, to bark the stray lambs into the fold. (p. 36)

As for Dr. Cantwell, Maw-worm claims, "He's a saint—'till I went after him, I was little better than the devil; my conscience was tann'd with sin, like a piece of neat's leather, and had no more feeling than the soal of my shoe; always a roving after fantastical delights; I us'd to go, every Sunday evenings, to the Three-hats at Islington; it's a public-house; may-hap, your Ladyship may know it: I was a great lover of skittles too, but now I can't bear them; so I sits at home all day, and does nothing but read, and sing hymns, and talk against the world" (p. 37).

Maw-worm's wife has given birth to one baby and is pregnant again—both due, it seems, to Cantwell. Maw-worm, of course, never realizes that he has been cuckolded.

Cantwell: Thus it is madam [That Maw-worm's wife is again pregnant]; I am constantly told, tho' I can hardly believe it, a blessing follows, wherever I come.
Maw-worm: And yet, if you would hear how the neighbors reviles my wife; saying, as how she sets no store by me, because we have words now and then; but, as I says, if such was the case, would ever she have cut me down that there time, as I was melancholy, and she found me

hanging behind the door; I don't believe there's a wife in the parish would have done so by her husband.
Cantwell: I believe, 'tis near dinner time; and Sir John will require my attendance. (p. 38)

As Maw-worm leaves, he says to Old Lady Lambert, "you are a malefactor to all goodness"; to Cantwell, in all innocence he says, "Susy [his wife] desires me to give her kind love and respects to you" (II, vi. p. 38). Maw-worm's innocence continues through the last act, when, still trusting Dr. Cantwell, he denies that the latter could try to seduce Sir John Lambert's wife:

Maw-worm: I say it's unpossible. . . . I say it's unpossible. He has been lock'd up with my wife for hours together, morning, noon and night, and I never found her the worse for him.
Old Lady Lambert; Ah son! son! (V, vi, p. 86)

Those of the audience who did not favor low humor enjoyed Charlotte's teasing of her suitor Darnley. Whether it was Mrs. Oldfield or Mrs. Woffington as Cibber's Maria; or Mrs. Abington or Mrs. Edwin as Charlotte, the role was filled by a star who invariably found it profitable to play one of the most charming coquettes of the century.

Charlotte was not a coquette out of the Restoration drama, however; the "softening process," accelerated by Jeremy Collier, had changed the exciting tease of seventeenth-century comedies into a woman of sense. Charlotte admits to her brother that she enjoys coquetting with her suitor, but the audience knows that she is really a sweet, proper, sensible woman. The process of rationalizing coquetry is apparent in the difference between Cibber's Maria and Charlotte.

By Cibber's time, the popularity of the "gay couple" was low enough, but by the time Bickerstaff wrote his comedies, the Restoration ideal of wit and gaiety between two equal partners in the love game scarcely existed. Not only in *The Hypocrite,* but also in Bickerstaff's comic operas the chance for the game is offered but rejected. To see just how fully the sport had been laid aside, one need only look at a scene in Cibber's *Non-Juror* and compare it with the same one in Bickerstaff's adaptation. Even Cibber's lovers, Heartly and Maria, are anemic copies of earlier models—especially Heartly, who is so love-sick that his only emotions seem to be anguish and jealousy until Maria consents to be his wife. Then, at least, Cibber allows a brief spate of equality in their verbal by-play. Maria admits to being vain:

Heartly: No matter, I love you as you are, I would not have you lose your Pleasantry, *Maria.*
Maria: Well, do, let me be silly sometimes.
Heartly: O! I can play with you, for that Matter.
Maria: Pshah! you'll laugh at me.
Heartly: Not while you are good in Essentials.
Maria: Indeed I'll be very good.
Heartly: O fy! that will be the way to make me so.
Maria: Lord! What signifies Sense, where there is so much Pleasure in Folly?
Heartly: No perfect Passion ever was without it; the Pleasure would subside were we always to be wise in it.[2]

With Heartly's sententious reflection, the light mood passes, and they return to the subject of the canting doctor. For a few moments, Maria and Heartly were sure enough of each other to tease without recrimination, but Cibber had to let Heartly formally conclude the sport. In 1717, when *The Non-Juror* was first performed, audiences had already been conditioned for higher seriousness to replace mere wit. But as harmless as the foregoing passage is, Bickerstaff omitted it and the conversation between the lovers which led up to it. Instead, he began Act V with Charlotte exclaiming, "But really, will you stand to the agreement though, that I have made with the doctor?" (V, i, 76)—the same remark which Maria makes after Heartly has reflected on Sense and Pleasure.

Bickerstaff's Charlotte remained essentially the same as Cibber drew her, but, necessarily, his Doctor Cantwell differed in one respect from Cibber's Wolf. In place of the non-juror, suspected of being Roman Catholic and pro-Pretender, Bickerstaff introduced the Enthusiast, the follower of George Whitfield and the Wesleys. As Bickerstaff wrote in his Preface,

> Cibber's Non-Juror (borrowed from the Tartuffe of Molière) has ever been reckoned an excellent comedy; but being written to expose a party, it was no longer interesting, because the folly and roguery it design'd to ridicule, no longer existed: It was thought, that it might be render'd agreeable to the present times, by once more having recourse to Molière; and, with that view, I have endeavour'd to substitute his celebrated character of Tartuffe, in the room of Doctor Wolf.

The changes Bickerstaff effected concerned topical political allusions, and various shadings in Cantwell's and the others' characters. Cibber's Dr. Wolf, unmasked as a Roman Catholic priest, has no place in *The Hypocrite* because—despite active anti-Roman Catholic bigotry—times had changed: Jacobitism as a political and military force was dead. The '15 and the '45 could still stir up hatred, but it was a hatred of past deeds, not of future threats. The London pleasure gardens heard Scottish ballads sung by their favorite entertainers without reflecting on the punishment "Butcher" Cumberland had inflicted on the Scots. Roman Catholics had served under George II and III in the Seven Years' War, and for the time being Irish politics were quiet. The new threat came from those Protestants who found the Church of England lacking as a spiritual guide, and who had found—or said they had—that missing leadership in their own selves or in others who spoke from pulpits set up outside the portals (literally and figuratively) of the established church. These leaders and their followers, "enthusiasts," were indiscriminately labeled charlatans. Occasionally there were confidence-men who took advantage of the gullible, and it was these men and their gulls—Dr. Cantwell and Maw-worm—whom Bickerstaff satirized. The final speech of the comedy, spoken by Charlotte, made explicit the target of Bickerstaff's play:

> What? because a worthless wretch has imposed upon you, under the fallacious shew of austere grimace, will you needs have it, every body is like him? confound the good with the bad, and conclude, there are no truly religious in the world.—Leave, my dear Sir, such rash consequences to fools and libertines.—Let us be careful to distinguish between virtue and the appearance of it. Guard, if possible, against doing honour to hypocrisy.—But, at the same time, let us allow there is no character in life, greater or more valuable, than that of the truly devout, —nor any thing more noble, or more beautiful, than the fervour of a sincere piety. (V, Scene the last, p. 92)

Although Cantwell masqueraded as an enthusiast, he was able to echo Molière's Tartuffe and Cibber's Dr. Wolf with no sense of incongruity. Parodying Whitfield and other Methodists, Cantwell was always first to proclaim his sinfulness. For instance, to Old Lady Lambert, he confessed:

> Alas, madam, I am not a good man: I am a guilty, wicked sinner, full of iniquity; the greatest villain that ever breathed; every instant of my life is clouded with stains; it is one continued series of crimes and defilements; you do not know what I am capable of; you indeed take me for a good man; but the truth is, I am a worthless creature. (I, iii, 15)

The irony is, of course, that Cantwell was speaking only the truth. It was this kind of humble chest-beating that was popular among the mid-eighteenth-century enthusiasts; but it was also the vocabulary of puritans—French Roman Catholics, or English Protestants—as the original Tartuffe's speech indicates:

> Oui, mon Frère, je suis un méchant, un coupable,
> Un malheureux pécheur, tout plein d'iniquité,
> Le plus grand scélérat qui jamais ait été.
> Chaque instant de ma vie est chargé de souillures,
> Elle n'est qu'un amas de crimes et d'ordures. . . .[3]

Or, as translated by Matthew Medbourne in 1670:

> Yes, Brother, I am Wicked, and a Criminal,
> An unhappy Sinner, full of Impiety;
> The lewdest Villain that was ever bred:
> Each Instant of my Life is full of Stains;
> 'Tis nothing but an Heap of Filth and Sin.[4]

Cantwell, as Bickerstaff pointed out in his Preface, was "almost a verbal translation from Molière." Without the Jansenist tradition of Roman Catholicism and without the Jacobite cause, Bickerstaff had to depend on his contemporaries' recognition of a situation analogous to Lady Huntingdon's making Whitfield one of her domestic chaplains. Selina Hastings was famous in the eighteenth century both as a "Lady Bountiful" and as an enthusiastic adherent of Whitfield and his followers. Bickerstaff discarded Molière's exposition of how Tartuffe insinuated himself into Orgon's confidence; instead, he explained Cantwell's presence in the Lambert household as being there "in quality of chaplain"; he was first introduced by the good old lady that's just gone out [Old Lady Lambert]. You know she has been a long time frequenter of our modern conventicles, where, it seems, she got acquainted with this sanctified pastor. His disciples believe him a saint, and my poor father, who has been for some time tainted with their pernicious principles, has been led into the same snare" (Colonel Lambert, I, vii, 18).

The remaining characters in *The Hypocrite* warrant little attention. Old Lady Lambert was brought in from *Tartuffe* as the excuse for Cantwell's continued presence, but like Maw-worm, she is important for the didactic purpose of *The Hypocrite*. She and Maw-worm represent the kinds of people, according to the satirical view of the eighteenth-century establishment, who form the hard core of enthusiasts. Old Lady Lambert is approaching senility, and however intelligent she once might have been, she is now an eccentric old widow. Maw-worm at the other extreme is an illiterate shopkeeper who, since following Dr. Cantwell, has been cuckolded by the doctor, and has lost most of his customers by his own religious zeal. The message is clearly staged: these are the people who are susceptible to evangelicism; and Maw-worm's pregnant wife and his bankrupt shop are enthusiasm's pernicious consequences.

With the character of Charles Seyward, Dr. Cantwell's servant, Bickerstaff relied on Medbourne and Cibber, rather than on Molière. In *Tartuffe,* Laurence (the equivalent of Charles) never appears and has no importance. But Medbourne brought him onto the stage and made him instrumental in defeating Tartuffe. Both Cibber and Bickerstaff raised him socially from the servant class to that of an improvident gentleman, and eliminated his courtship of the maid Dorina found in Medbourne's comedy. Cibber called him Charles Trueman. Although Bickerstaff named him Seyward, he tells Charlotte in Act II, scene vii, "My father, Madam, was the younger branch of a genteel family in the North, his name Trueman—but dying, while I was yet in my infancy, I was left wholly dependent on my mother" (p. 42). Cibber let Trueman name his uncle as the cause of his involvement with Wolf, but Bickerstaff stressed Cantwell's amorous propensity: the doctor "fatally got acquainted with" Seyward's mother, and became her "bosom counsellor" (p. 42).

Another change between the *Non-Juror* and *The Hypocrite* occurred in Act V when, following Molière, Cibber had Lady John Woodvil hide her husband under a table to hear Dr. Wolf make love to her. Perhaps feeling it a matter of decorum, Bickerstaff let Lady Lambert place *her* husband behind a screen. The subsequent uncovering of Cantwell's hypocrisy influenced Sheridan in his *School for Scandal,* when Joseph Surface's duplicity is also discovered by the use of a falling screen.

Many of the critics who reviewed *The Hypocrite* used the comedy as an excuse to declare their support of the church and their detestation of enthusiasm. Others worried about the possible harm *any* satire about religion might cause. The majority thought Maw-worm to be very funny, but only one defended his presence in the comedy. All critics agreed that Charlotte was one of the finest coquettes on the stage. A disgruntled minority declared that the play was successful because of its acting and despite its adapter. No one had a good word for Methodism.

The first night reaction to the comedy was mostly favorable.

Hopkins noted in his Diary that the comedy "went off very well—some few hisses,—but the play will do" (Stone, III, 1368). In the *London Chronicle* for 24 November 1768 "A.Z." wrote a column-length letter to insist that "*The Hypocrite is* Cibber's Nonjuror; not *taken from it.*"

> The revival, for it is nothing else, of this entertaining Comedy of Cibber's, was received with a moderate share of applause.—Those few, however, of the frequenters of the Theatre, who have a veneration for religion, may very justly be allowed to question the propriety of the character substituted for Dr. Wolf [Cantwell].
>
> . . . .
>
> Surely, irreligion, not enthusiasm is the *ruling passion* of the present age: And the stage, which ought ever to be the school of virtue, should by no means hold forth to ridicule, even a mistaken piety. . . . (XXIV, #1863, p. 504)

Cant, as opposed to piety, mistaken or otherwise, was the proper target of satire, some critics maintained, the *Monthly Review* among them; but others agreed with the review in the *Court Miscellany,* November 1768: "Religious errors have been of an obstinate nature and consequently satire, rather than argument, is their most effectual antidote" (IV, 611). The *Monthly Review* for December insisted that hypocrisy was the proper target for satire:

> We have seen various objections, in the public papers against the introduction of such characters as Dr. Cantwell and Maw-worm on the stage; but we are by no means convinced that hypocrisy, a vice amenable to no laws, is not as fair an object for comic satire to point her shafts at, and expose to the derision and abhorrence of mankind, as any other vice. (XXXIX, 491–492)

In the *London Magazine* for November, a writer observed complacently that the comedy "is changed into a satire against the enthusiasts, who are extremely numerous, and it is to be feared extremely dangerous also in this pious generation" (XXXVII, 563). As for the moral of the play, the same writer found it "Excellent," and described it as "to expose the shameful vice of hypocrisy, and to inspire a universal regard for religion and virtue" (p. 566).

Not everyone was so sure about the moral. Dr. John Hawkesworth,[5] writing in the *Gentleman's Magazine,* admitted that the play was supposed to expose "a modern sect that seems to gain ground among us, the methodists," but he was disappointed in the satirical representation of Dr. Cantwell and his dupes. After all, these characters

> are not calculated to expose any tenets supposed to be hurtful in themselves; to expose atrocious wickedness, or gross folly, by accidentally exhibiting them under any particular sect or denomination, is only inculcating what every one knows, that in all sects and denominations there is atrocious wickedness and gross folly.

It would have been better, Hawkesworth believed, if the comedy satirized good men for their mistaken beliefs than foolish men with misplaced beliefs.

> If the mischiefs that would naturally follow, from acting conscientiously upon [mistaken beliefs] had been humourously exposed, instead of those that arise from implicit confidence in the seeming sanctity of another, this piece might have levelled ridicule at its proper object with success. To represent devotion as hypocrisy, is perhaps rather likely to countenance irreligion than restrain enthusiasm. . . . (XXVIII, Supplement, 1768, 619–620)

"In the closet," as opposed to on the stage, Hawkesworth's reservation was valid; as he noted, Maw-worm "is exposed to mischief not in consequence of false principles of action in himself, but of that hypocrisy in another which might be practiced equally by the Papist and Fanatic, the Faquire and the Bramin." But audiences saw Maw-worm's misfortunes as a result of his enthusiasm, not from the more logical perspective of Hawkesworth.

French reviewers seem to have ignored this off-spring of Molière, but Madame Riccoboni, who was preparing an anthology of English plays, wrote to Garrick on 17 March 1769: *"C'est dommage que la pièce refaite par Mr. Bickerstaff soit toujours un suject pris de Molière; elle est tres-agréable, et je la crois fort bien ecrite, mais je n'en puis faire usage"* (Boaden, II, 557).

The moral reservations of reviewers did not deter audiences from enjoying the comedy fifteen times between its opening on 17 November 1768, and 12 May 1769, its last staging during the spring season. When, on 27 November 1771, Moody played Dr. Cantwell for the first time, the *Theatrical Review* devoted a long article to the comedy. Its position was uncompromisingly against enthusiasm, describing it (as was usual) as "pernicious." The tenets of the sect which Cantwell represents

> are too mysterious for reason and common-sense, when viewed in the

most favourable light, and only tend to propagate superstitious and enthusiastic notions in the minds of the ignorant, to the prejudice of true religion, founded on the most rational principles, and supported on the authority of holy writ. . . . (p. 233)

Bickerstaff's comedy played the provinces as well as London during the eighteenth century, and in 1775 it reached Dublin (Hughes, p. 177). It was first seen in the United States on 10 February 1792 at the Northern Liberties Theatre in Philadelphia. After 22 performances in this country its last production was at the Park Theatre in New York, 15 March 1842 (Macmillan, p. 65). In England, by the end of the eighteenth century, the play had become a stock piece eliciting stock replies from its critics—only the names of the actors had been changed. "After ten years concealment the *Hypocrite* again shows his face," wrote a critic for *The Monthly Mirror* about a production at London's Lyceum Theatre on 23 January 1810; "and he never seems to have appeared more opportunely to do good service" (New Series, VII, February, 1810, 143). Still anti-Methodist, the critic praised the comedy but balked at Mawworm.

The part . . . is short, and what there is of it is trumpery, and altogether unworthy of the comedy. Mr. Mathews did every thing that could be done for it, and his presence was particularly serviceable to the effect of the last scene. . . . The *Hypocrite* was given out for repetition with universal applause. (pp. 143–145)

A year later, *The Dramatic Censor* praised the play and supported the Established Church.

The comedy of the *Hypocrite* [which played at the Lyceum on 18 January 1811] is unquestionably the very best dramatic performance that is exhibited at this Theatre. . . .

. . . .

We are uniformly pleased with the representation of this comedy . . . because the satire which it conveys is not only wholesome, but, in this crisis of fanaticism, indispensable. It is a consideration of a truly melancholy nature to look around in this Empire, and behold so vast a portion of the lower classes, of society gradually renouncing the charities and ethics of Christianity, to embrace opinions which are not only hostile to the main ends of our holy religion, but utterly irreconcileable to the reasoning faculties of the mind; and, in pursuance of this inexplicability, thousands of miserable zealots ponder in thought upon points that are entirely irrational, until the brain becomes diseased, and then sink from despair to madness, into a dark and comfortless grave, where hope hath no influence! (January 1811, cols. 65–66)

Obviously, the reviewer had forgotten completely about *The Hypocrite* in his own zeal, but he remembered it long enough in the paragraph which followed to encourage "all those who are attached in heart and spirit to the furtherance of the doctrines of the Established Church of this country," to "lend their aid in support of every endeavour (whether theatrically expressed or otherwise) that leads to the destruction of those pernicious errors of opinion, that are hourly spreading, like an ulcer, in society, and which threaten the extermination of all charity" (col. 66).

After these Christian sentiments, the critic returned to the comedy to praise it for attacking folly and hypocrisy; but the mention of "that mock-profession of piety" sent the writer back to his pulpit, and he soon was decrying "that hideous monster *Fanaticism,*" which would stand "upon the ashes of reason and the true faith" (col. 66).

Fanaticism, enthusiasm, evangelism, by any name it was attacked through the character of Maw-worm. In the early nineteenth century, although actors like Dowton, Mathews and Oxberry were successful Maw-worms, the comedian who became the favorite of audiences in the role was John Liston who imitated a popular minister. He took advantage of Maw-worm's reference to his "extrumpery" preaching (II, vi) to improvise topical mock sermons partially as a satire of the Scottish minister Edward Irving. Liston preached as Cantwell was led away at the end of the comedy, changing the topic of his sermon as circumstances warranted; Irving's fiery evangelism—which lost him his pulpit at the little Chapel, in Hatton Garden, London, in 1832—helped maintain the popularity of Maw-worm and *The Hypocrite.* The many caricatures of Liston preaching testify to his fame as Maw-worm; but by 1834, Irving had died, and in 1837 Liston retired.

One hundred years after *The Hypocrite* was first produced, *The Times* reviewed the history of the play from Molière to Medbourne to Cibber to Bickerstaff, on the occasion of its being performed at Drury Lane on 1 February 1868. Of Maw-worm, the critic noted, it was "entirely Bickerstaff's own . . . the low pietist, who seems to be a compound of dupe, hypocrite, and fanatic, and whose somewhat broad jokes are sure to excite laughter." The writer credited Liston for originating the mock sermon to caricature Edward Irving. However, "At present Maw-worm's sermon is a mere harmless piece of nonsense, totally unlike the discourse of any religious professor whatsoever. . . ." The 1 February production was in three acts: "The revival . . . is judicious, for it is one of those noted plays which many of the present day can never have seen, and with which everybody who pretends to an acquaintance with the standard English drama ought to be tolerably familiar."[6]

The Illustrated London News also reviewed the 1 February 1868 production, referring to it as "Bickerstaff's famous comedy" when it was actually in the sunset of its career. Edmund Phelps played Dr. Cantwell; "His excellence in the part was tested many seasons ago at Sadler's Wells, and furnished an additional proof of the actor's merit in comedy. . . ."[7] Both the *News* and the *Times* complimented the cast, although it comes as a shock to find Charlotte discussed in the *Times* as "a coquette of the old school."

Five years later, the *Telegraph* reviewed *The Hypocrite* which was being performed at the Gaiety Theatre. The comedy "brought last week the largest audiences ever known at this theatre. . . ."[8] Phelps again played Cantwell. In a Birmingham newspaper of 20 May 1882, *The Hypocrite* was said to have played for the week at the Prince of Wales Theatre in an abridged form. Reminiscing, the writer recalled that "Exactly fifty-five years ago, when Mr. Alfred Bunn was lessee of the Theatre Royal [it] was played at least once a week for a considerable time."[9]

The final performance of *The Hypocrite* in the nineteenth century apparently came on 11 June 1887 at the Strand in London. As a sorry anticlimax from the review in *The Times* of 1868 when it was placed "with the standard English drama," the reviewer called the play "a little known comedy by Isaac Bickerstaff."[10] For a reviewer in *The Telegraph, The Hypocrite* had become obsolete:

> Truth to speak, in spite of its genuiness, the humour of Bickerstaff's comedy is a little out of date. Admitting the eccentricities of Mr. Spurgeon and the extravagances of the Salvation Army, dogma and sect have both been exposed, for some time past . . . an elaborate caricature of cant is something like the flogging of a deceased Horse.[11]

Until 1963, when *The Hypocrite* was produced in Northampton in the courtyard of one of the borough's parks for ten days, with Barry Hillman as its producer, the comedy remained untouched. Nor is it likely—now that in this pious age religious cant has been so long dead—that *The Hypocrite* will experience any more revivals.

1768 was Bickerstaff's most productive year. Besides five produced plays (*Lionel and Clarissa, The Absent Man, The Royal Garland, The Padlock,* and *The Hypocrite*), he helped edit *The Gentleman's Journal,* a short-lived venture published by William Griffin and written by the unlikely combination of Goldsmith, Kenrick and Bickerstaff, with the assistance of Paul Hiffernan and Hugh Kelly.[12] It was to have been published weekly, beginning on Saturday, 19 November, "in Octavo, No. 1. Price 6d." and its full title was *The Gentleman's Journal; or Weekly Register of News, Politics, Literature.*

> Upon these Occasions [the editors advertised], it is usual to offer something by way of Address to the Public, and frequent Experience convinces us, that a great deal may be said in an Advertisement, whatever is done in the Work it is designed to introduce. But though, to perform more than other Publishers of periodical Pamphlets, may be thought no very difficult Task, to promise more is certainly impossible. The Proprietor of *The Gentleman's Journal* therefore begs leave to refer such as may be willing to encourage this Undertaking to his first Number, where they will, at once, be judges of the Design and Execution.
>
> Printed for W. Griffin at Garrick's Head, Catharine Street, Strand.[13]

The Gentleman's Journal, No. 1, was published on 19 November, and in the following week, *The London Chronicle* reprinted a verse fable from it (XXIV, #1864, Thursday, 24 November, 512). On Saturday, 26 November, the second number came out. Again it was advertised in *The London Chronicle,* but this time the public was offered a table of contents, "Containing, among other interesting articles,"

> 1. A Review of New Books. 2. The Life and Extraordinary Adventures of Ambrose Gwinnet, a lame Begger man, literally Fact, and never before printed. 3. A Fable, versified from Æsop, by the Author of the Cuckow Traveller, so universally admired in our last. 4. The present State of Parties, as they subsist in the H—— of C——. 5. Proceedings and Debates in a political Society. 6. The Opinions of the Judges relative to Riots, and calling in the Military to quell them, occasioned by the late affair in St. George's Fields, very curious and never before printed. 7. Remarks upon the Hypocrite, and other Theatrical Matters. 8. List of Plays and Operas, with Observations, &c., &c. (XXIV, #1865, 26–29 November, 519)

From the table of contents, *The Gentleman's Journal* followed a pattern similar to the *London Magazine,* and most of the general journals of the time—except that it was a weekly, not a monthly magazine. The strain after two weeks of publication prompted the editors to advertise in the 1-3 December *London Chronicle:* "The Third Number of the *Gentleman's Journal,* which was to have been published this Day, will not be published till next Saturday; and for the future, this Work will be continued once a Fortnight instead of Weekly" (XXIV, #1867, 534). But neither advertisements nor issues were ever seen again: nor do copies of the first two issues seem to have survived.

The brief account of *The Gentleman's Journal* in the *European Magazine* (September 1793), was generous when it claimed that the journal "failed within six months" (p. 171); it never made it past a fortnight. Of the five writers concerned with it, three of them—Kenrick, Goldsmith and Hifferman—considered themselves doctors. When a friend observed to Goldsmith, "what an extraordinary sudden death" the journal suffered, Goldsmith replied, "Not at all Sir, a very common case; it died of too many doctors" (p. 173). By the end of January 1769, Kenrick was engaged in editing *Critical Memoirs of the Times,* and quarrelling with the rest of London.

Although both "The Cuckow Traveller" and "The Ant and the Grasshopper," the fable which appeared in the second issue and which was reprinted in *The London Chronicle* for 26-29 December (#1856, p. 520), were printed anonymously, Bickerstaff admitted his authorship publicly on 20 November 1771. On that day he published *Proposals for Printing by Subscription, Fables, Philosophical and Moral, in Verse.* William Griffin was to be the publisher. The Fables were not Bickerstaff's only contribution to the *Gentleman's Journal;* another was "The Life and Extraordinary Adventures of Ambrose Gwinnet," whose adventures in print were almost as extraordinary as those of the title figure.

Until now, Bickerstaff's authorship has rested on the hearsay evidence of a note in a copy of the second edition of 1770, which is in the British Museum. In it, the unknown owner of *Ambrose Gwinett* (as it was spelled) stated that Bishop Percy had said that the work was fiction and was by Bickerstaff. On this basis, the work has been "conjecturally attributed" to Bickerstaff by the Museum, and other authorities have followed suit; but there is further, circumstantial evidence which make the identification more sure.

To begin with, the work was published for the first time on

26 November 1768 in *The Gentleman's Journal.* Secondly it was serialized in the *Journal Encyclopédique* on 1 May, 15 May and 1 June 1769. Associated with the *Encyclopédique* were the brothers Castilhon (or Castillon). In 1770, Jean Louis Castilhon (1730-1793), signing himself "M. L. Castilhon," published his lengthened version of *Gwinett;* since Bickerstaff contributed an article in 1765 to the *Journal,* and throughout his career the journal published critiques of his works, Castilhon at least knew of Bickerstaff. The tie between Castilhon and Bickerstaff is explicit on Castilhon's title page: *Le Mendiant boiteux, ou les Aventures d'Ambrose Gwinett, balayeur du pavé de Spring Garden, d'après les notes ecrites de sa main, par M. L. Castilhon, traduit d'Isaac Bickerstaffe,* 2 parties en 1 (Bouillon: Societé typographique, 1770).[14] In his Preface, Castilhon referred to the "incorrect" version in the *Encyclopédique,* and then proceeded to write a greatly expanded version with satirical and literary pretensions, something which the original *Gwinett* sorely lacked.

In brief, the evidence for Bickerstaff's authorship rests on three bases: it was first published in the journal with which Bickerstaff was associated; it was ascribed to him by Bishop Percy; it was translated into French as from Isaac Bickerstaff by Castilhon who either knew, or knew of, him.

Immediately after *Gwinett* appeared in *The Gentleman's Journal,* it was reprinted in two issues of *The Gentleman's Magazine* (Supplement, 1768; January, 1769), which acknowledged its source at the end of the second installment. In the first installment in the *Journal Encyclopédique* (1 May 1769), it was noted in the Preface that *Ambrose Gwinett* had been published *"À Londres,* Chez Gadell [sic]" (III, 457). Presumably, then, the first chapbook edition appeared in the spring of 1769, having been published by Thomas Cadell. In English, *Gwinett* remained in chapbook form, but the French editions were more ambitious. Besides the 1770 *Le Mendiant Boiteux* already cited, there was a two-volume octavo edition in 1770, and in 1771 and 1778 the *Societé Typographique* again published *Gwinett* as a two-part, one volume work. Also in 1771 an edition which was probably pirated appeared "*A Francfort et Leipzig, Aux depens de la Compagnie,*" in two volumes. This edition contained a preface by "L. Castilton [sic]," dated 17 November 1769. It was reprinted in 1781. This edition differed from the other Gwinetts in its title, being called, *Candide Anglois, ou Avantures tragicomique D'Amb. Gwinett avant et dans ses Voyages aux deux Indes,* but the text is the same.[15]

In England, chapbook editions proliferated, but the text remained basically the same. A second edition appeared in 1770, and the first American imprint appeared by 1782 in Boston. It was reprinted in America in 1784 three times, including a German translation printed in Philadelphia as *Die Wunderbare Geschichte Von Ambrose Gwinnett.*[16] As were most chapbooks, *Ambrose Gwinett* was printed for the travelling booksellers, and any town which boasted a printshop could supply the salesmen. *Gwinetts* have turned up with imprints from Shambles (York), Preston, and Newcastle; and in this country, Norwich, Boston, Philadelphia, and New London; during a fifty-year period there were at least twenty editions.

Typical of these editions is the "6th edition" from York with its synopsis immediately below the title:

> *The LIFE, Strange Voyages, and Uncommon Adventures of Ambrose Gwinett,* Containing An Account of his being convicted and hung in Chains, at Deal, in Kent, for the supposed Murder of Mr. Collins; his surprising Recovery after being executed; his Voyage to the West-Indies, his being taken by the Spaniards, where he meets the identical Collins whom he was supposed to have murdered; the Accident that threw Mr. Gwinett into the Hands of Pirates; his extraordinary Adventures with them, and being retaken by the Spaniards, and by them condemned to the Gallies; his being taken and made a Slave of by the Algerines, and after suffering many Hardships, his return to England.

All the foregoing occurred in 25 pages, and could be read for sixpence. In American editions, a moral was attached to the synopsis: "Demonstratively Proving that Condemnations upon Circumstantial Evidence are injurious to innocence, Incompatible with Justice, and Therefore Ought Always to be Discountenanced Especially in Case of Life and Death" (Norwich, 1784). The chapbook was as popular as it was poorly written; but Castilhon, who expanded the work (but kept the plot the same) to some 330 pages was not the only writer to see some hope in *Gwinett.* Douglas Jerrold dramatized it as a melodrama in 1828, *Ambrose Gwinett, or, A Sea-Side Story,* in three Acts.[17] It was crudely done, but at least the play contains a sense of drama, something more than Bickerstaff's *Gwinett* ever did.

When Bishop Percy said that *Ambrose Gwinett* was fiction (even though it was poorly enough written to be true) he was correct. But as usual life belatedly imitated art, and in Ohio in 1842 Marcus Aurelius Bierce named his son Ambrose Gwinett; his life rivalled the adventures of the first Gwinett, and his writings could qualify him as the author of a *Candide Anglois.*

10

"ALL DAVID'S *SWANS* ARE *GEESE!*": *DR. LAST IN HIS CHARIOT*, *THE EPHESIAN MATRON*, *HE WOU'D IF HE COU'D*, *THE RECRUITING SERJEANT*, THE SHAKESPEARE JUBILEE

During the early part of 1769, Bickerstaff helped ready *Maid of the Mill* and *Love in a Village* for their first performances at Drury Lane on 31 March and 3 April. He wrote to Garrick, who was in Bath, of their successes.

> I should immediately have answered the obliging letter with which you honored me last week, but I waited to give you an account of our *Operatical Attempts* at your house which I assure you have had amazing success. The Maid of the Mill was really most admirably performed, and King, Pope and Vernon in Love in a Village were as well as you can possibly conceive.[1]

Turning from business matters, Bickerstaff thanked Garrick for his help on behalf of William Brereton (Bickerstaff's cousin), who was unsuccessfully running for Master of Ceremonies at Bath. This was the second time that Garrick had helped a relative of Bickerstaff; in 1767, it will be recalled, he aided Edward Brereton. These and other favors, plus the money which the manager frequently loaned Bickerstaff, bound him more closely to Drury Lane—and to Garrick—than could any formal contract. Bickerstaff finished his letter by returning to theatre ventures, well aware of how indebted he was to Garrick's generosity:

> I have closed with Foote in the most amicable manner and tomorrow he gets my piece which is immediately to be put in the actors' hands; he likes it very much and will act Ailward himself. I have availed myself as much as possible of your remarks. I have also closed with mad Sir Thomas [Robinson?], he and the other Managers (the others very much like Gentlemen) would have had me fixed my price for the Two [space here in ms.] but I left that to be settle by you and you may be certain I shall willingly submit to your award be it what it will. I think what I give them will be but very poor things.

The "very poor things" probably were the *three* musical entertainments which Bickerstaff and Dibdin wrote for Ranelagh: *The Ephesian Matron, He Wou'd if He Cou'd,* and *The Recruiting Serjeant.* The piece which Bickerstaff gave to Foote was produced at his theatre in the Haymarket on Wednesday, 21 June 1769; Foote acted Ailwou'd in *Dr. Last in his Chariot.* If Bickerstaff's understanding with Garrick was similar to his arrangement at Covent Garden, then he needed the manager's permission to write for any theatre other than Drury Lane or suffer a fine of £1000. Garrick—astute businessman that he was—would never willingly lose any "good things."

In his Preface to *Dr. Last,* Bickerstaff rightly termed himself "the editor"; for *Dr. Last in his Chariot* is both a sequel to Foote's *The Devil on Two Sticks,* and an adaptation of Molière's *Le Malade Imaginaire.* Besides, Garrick suggested some things, and as Bickerstaff noted in his Preface, Foote wrote the consultation-of-physicians scene in Act One, "and some other hints and passages, which, no doubt, the reader will as easily distinguish."[2] All that Bickerstaff was willing to take credit for was the character of Doctor Last—and he had appeared the previous year in *The Devil on Two Sticks.* Weston, who had played the minor role of Dr. Last for Foote, now appeared in the expanded part for Bickerstaff. Realizing the popularity of Weston as Maw-worm, Bickerstaff again employed malapropisms for comic effect. Thus Bickerstaff's play enjoyed the initial advantage of a popular comedian acting a combination of two parts which he had previously made successful. Typical of Dr. Last's verbal misadventures are his description of the Medicean Venus as "Venus the methodist" (I, ix, 36), and his plans for his house and land:

> Next summer I shall make a new reproach to my house, with a fistula that will give us a view of all the gibbets upon the heath [his property is by Hounslow]; then there's a large running ditch that I'll make into a turpentine river. (p. 37)

Bickerstaff successfully adapted *Le Malade Imaginaire* to his shorter comedy. While it has been said that "This free version . . . bears all the marks of hasty composition,"[3] in fact the comedy is an adroit mating of Molière's and Foote's works. Molière's comedy was shortened by eliminating the apothecary, Fleurant, combining the roles of the doctors into Dr. Last, and allowing Ailwou'd's second wife to show her greed without the aid of Molière's notary, Bonnefoi.

Foote's consultation scene, with Drs. Coffin, Skeleton, Bulruddery, and later Dr. Last, was considered the funniest in the comedy by contemporary audiences, and frequently printed in the monthly magazines and newspapers in 1769; it is a natural outgrowth from his *Devil on Two Sticks,* but also owes something to Act II, scene iii of *L'Amour Médicin.* The scene is a healthy reminder that the so-called sacred patient-doctor relationship is a late development.

Anticipating the first night's performance, *The London Chronicle* printed a puffing poem by "O.H." which began, " 'Tis said Doctor Last's coming out in his Chariot," and ended, "I have not for his Chariot the smallest concern,/*The Patentee made it—it can't overturn*" (XXV, #1952, 20 June, 584). Notwithstanding O.H.'s prediction, "The first Night's Audience seemed greatly inclined to overturn *Doctor Last in his Chariot,*" according to Benjamin Victor, "and behaved so refractory, as to oblige Mr. *Foote* to address them in the following manner, 'That the Comedy which they were pleased to treat so severely, was written by a Gentleman who had enjoyed the frequent Pleasure of entertaining the Public with some of their favourite Pieces, and therefore he thought he had a Right to a fair Trial in his Theatre—which, if they would please to permit, the Exceptions they should make, should be struck out, or altered against the next Performance" (III, 195-197). That the comedy was allowed to be finished on the first night was denied by the *Theatrical Register:* "on the first night's representation," its critic wrote, "the murmurs of the audience arose to such a pitch as to prevent conclusion of the last act. . ." (pp. 67-68). Whatever were the offending lines, they were cut for the second performance, and "the whole piece considerably altered" (p. 68).

> I remember going into the House at the second performance [Victor wrote], about the middle of the Play, and found the House not only well filled, but the whole audience in good Humor, and laughing through every Scene of the Comedy. . . . (III, 197)

The *Theatrical Register* also reported that with the changes, *Dr. Last* "was received with more favour" (p. 68). But despite this charitable notice, the farce played only nine nights from 21 June 1769 to 31 August; Bickerstaff received his customary two Benefits, on the third and ninth nights. He was not dissatisfied with Foote's handling of his comedy, but its failure was blamed on Foote in one of the many ephemeral pamphlets which were constantly published at this time.[4] In "A Critical Remonstrance," the author took exception to Foote's prologue spoken at the opening of the Haymarket Theatre in 1770, and printing the Prologue, the anonymous critic commented on every line. For "Blasted the bay on ev'ry classic brow," he asked, "By whom? Who ungenerously sunk Mr. Bickerstaff's piece last year, and was afterwards meanly obliged to have recourse to it?—The secretly repining foe at the merited success of all authors and actors."[5]

Dr. Last was revived sporadically in London, and played in the provinces. It was anthologized in the fifth volume (1786) of *A Collection of the Most Esteemed Farces* (Edinburgh), and in *The Modern British Drama* (London, 1811), volume five; but it was never popular for long on the stage. Dibdin called it "a bad sequel to a good piece" (*History,* V. 262). Genest promoted it to a "pretty good piece—it deserved better success" (V, 251-252).

As an afterpiece to *Dr. Last in his Chariot,* Foote's company presented Bickerstaff's *The Captive,* a two-act comic opera condensed from a sub-plot in Dryden's *Don Sebastian.* In the Advertisement to the first edition, Bickerstaff as usual deprecated his work—to forestall his critics—and explained why it had been presented:

> Mr. Foote's Situation rendering it impossible for him to perform the smaller Pieces of his own Writing as often as the Public would desire them, thought that a Singing Farce, though pretending to no other Merit than that of good Music, would be more acceptable to his Auditors than others destitute of that Ornament, which had been often performed at the Winter Theatres.
>
> The Dialogue of this Trifle is taken, with some Alterations, from a Play of Dryden's: In that Part it is inoffensive; and the Songs, which

have been selected with great care, will, it is hoped, afford Entertainment.[6]

From *Don Sebastian,* Bickerstaff excerpted the comic story of Don Antonio, "A Young Noble amorous Portuguese," and his elopement with Morayma, "Daughter to the Mufti." In Dryden's and Bickerstaff's versions, the Mufti's chief wife, "Johyma," is enamoured of Don Antonio and temporarily complicates matters by falsely crying rape when Antonio ignores her. The Mufti in Dryden's play is actively involved in the plot to overthrow the Emperor of Barbary, and the comic scenes between the Mufti and Antonio are satires against the churchman for meddling in state politics. The political implications are gone from *The Captive,* and in keeping with the comic aspect of the opera, The Cadi (Dryden's Mufti) and his wife escape with Antonio and Zorayda.

To avoid offending his audiences, who deplored coarseness, Bickerstaff pruned most of the enjoyable conversation between Dryden's Antonio and Johyma, and Antonio and Morayma. Where Dryden's young couple speak freely and enjoy each other's sallies, Bickerstaff included fourteen songs to sing away the lack of spoken wit. As poor as it is, *The Captive* could make for an enjoyable summer night's entertainment, and is scarcely worth the effort of being termed "a very poor and much eviscerated coarctation in two acts."[7]

For the music, Bickerstaff drew on eight composers—including Dibdin, who wrote five songs specifically for the opera. The other composers were Gallupi, Cocchi, Vinci, Ciampi, Perez, Vento, and Duny (Table, 1st ed.). One of Zorayda's songs was performed separately by Mrs. Jewell when she appeared at the Haymarket during the Summer 1770 season (Stone, III, 1491; 31 August); she had four plaintive songs from which to choose. Unlike Dryden's Morayma, Zorayda joined Bickerstaff's other sentimental ingenues, and her most popular song—the one she no doubt sang on 31 August—was

Poor panting heart, ah! wilt thou ever
Throb within my troubled breast?
Shall I see the moment never
That is doom'd to give thee rest?

Cruel stars, that thus torment me!
Fortune smooths her front in vain;

Pleasure's self cannot content me,
But is turn'd with me to pain. (I, ii, p. 4)

Deciding that if the song were popular at the Haymarket it deserved to be heard again at Drury Lane, Bickerstaff included it with alterations in the second act of his revised *Lionel and Clarissa* (*School for Fathers*) which opened on 8 February 1770. Dibdin wrote the music which remained the same for both versions. At Drury Lane, Clarissa sang the second stanza—

Cruel stars! that thus torment me,
Still I seek for ease in vain,
All my efforts but present me
With variety of pain. (II, viii)

Besides Zorayda's sentimentalizing, Bickerstaff provided comic songs for Fatima and the Cadi, especially his "In emblem I am like a cat" (I, ii, p. 15), with music by Dibdin. The comic opera ends with Ferdinand and a chorus asking the audience for approval:

And now our scenic task is done,
This comes of course, you know, Sirs,
We drop the mask of every one,
And stand in *statu quo*, Sirs;
Your ancient friends and servants we,
Who humbly wait for your decree,
One gracious smile,
To crown our toil
And happy let us go, Sirs. (II, vi, p. 23)

The Captive did not attract many reviews, and the best of them praised only the music. It is not impossible that *The Captive* prepared the way for one greater than itself, if it can be believed that it was the basis for C. F. Bretzner's libretto for *Belmont und Constanze* (1781), which in turn was adapted with slight alterations by Gottlob Stephanie and Mozart and performed in 1781 as *Die Entführung Aus Dem Serail*. Other plays, including *La Schiava Liberata* and Bickerstaff's *The Sultan* have been suggested as the ultimate source of Mozart's opera.[8] If *The Captive* was the source, it was a long way from what it inspired.

In May 1769, the first of Bickerstaff's "poor things" was produced when on Friday night, 12 May, a Jubilee Ridotto was celebrated at Ranelagh House. The attendance was "exceedingly numerous and brilliant, a great number of whom were in fancied dresses, but none in masks. There were music and illuminations on the canal, the temple, and other parts of the garden, which had a fine effect. Besides the usual entertainments, about nine o'clock a new musical entertainment in the manner of the Italian comic serenata was performed. The company also danced country dances and cotillions."[9]

The Ridotto was a success: "The gardens and the Chinese House were illuminated. 'A large sea-horse stuck full of small lamps floated on the Canal, and had a very agreeable aspect.' The Rotunda and gardens were gradually filled by a brilliant company. The Dukes of York and Cumberland were there, and one of the prettiest characters was a 'rural nymph in rose-coloured sattin, trimmed with silver.' The tickets, which cost a guinea, included the supper. Unfortunately, the wine and sweetmeats were not immediately forthcoming, and some gentlemen broke open the wine cellar and helped themselves. Sir Thomas Robinson, to make things pleasant, thereupon sent a general invitation to the company to sup with him. The dancing began at twelve, and was continued till four, a comparatively early hour at Ranelagh masquerades."[10] Since at Ranelagh, "it was considered as vulgar to listen to music . . . the real effect" of Bickerstaff's "piece was never known" (Dibdin, *History,* V. 262).

The "Comic serenata, after the manner of the Italian," for which Dibdin composed the music, was *The Ephesian Matron.* Bickerstaff's preference for continental musical forms was responsible for the way he dramatized this often-told story.

> Those who are acquainted with Italian musical compositions [Bickerstaff wrote in his Advertisement to *The Ephesian Matron*], must know, that there are among them many short comic dramas (a longer sort of cantatas) where little fables are pursued; such as *La Serva Padrona, Baioco e Serpilla, Lo Maestro di Cappella* &c. It has been suggested to the managers of RANELAGH, by a gentleman . . . that something in the same way would be an improvement upon the detached song and ballads, usually sung in their orchestra. In deference to his judgment, this is an Essay.
>
> It would be useless to observe that the words are to be no farther considered than as they are adapted, and serve to give stile and character to the music. But should the music, when it has been sufficiently heard to render it somewhat familiar, be found pleasing enough to make the entertainment, on the whole, agreeable to the public, other pieces may be written much more pardonable, than what had here, at a short warning, been in great haste put together.[11]

Bickerstaff could have found this tale anywhere from Petronius to George Chapman's comedy, *The Widow's Tears,* or in chapbooks under various guises. He could have chosen to read it in English, Italian, or French,[12] and if he wanted an eighteenth-century dramatic model, he might have seen a manuscript copy of Charles Johnson's unpublished version. For once, however, the source is easy to find: *The Spectator,* No. 11, Tuesday, 13 March 1711; the same number from which Bickerstaff took the story of Inkle and Yarico when he dramatized it in 1768. In that issue, Steele wrote about Will Honeycomb who was talking "upon the old Topick, of Constancy in Love." Will "repeated and murdered the celebrated Story of the *Ephesian* matron." As part of the murder, Will told the fable of the lion and the man, a tale which Bickerstaff versified in *The Ephesian Matron:*

> The Man [Steele wrote] . . . showed him, in the Ostentation of Human superiority, a Sign of a Man killing a Lion. Upon which the Lion said very justly, We Lions are none of us Painters, else we could show a hundred Men killed by Lions, for one Lion killed by a man.

In the vaudeville which concluded Bickerstaff's serenata, the widow's maid sang:

> Says a traveller to a lion,
> Upon yonder sign-post see,
> How a lion like your worship's
> Torn by a man like me.
> Says the lion to the traveller,
> 'Twas a man the daubing drew;
> Had a lion been the painter,
> I had been a-tearing you.

From Ranelagh House, *The Ephesian Matron* moved to the Haymarket Theatre where it was first performed with *Dr. Last in his Chariot* for Bickerstaff's Benefit on 31 August 1769. The serenata, Dibdin supposed, "was performed about thirty times" (*Harmonicon,* p. 88), but he did not specify where or over how long a time.

In all, *The Ephesian Matron* has been rather successful. It played in Dublin in December 1778 (Loewenberg, col. 307), and in this century it was revived in London at the Court Theatre, 3 May 1926, and other theatres up to 1940. Nor should there be any reason why it could not be produced again. It is a cheerful opera on the familiar theme of woman's fickleness, but not even a female chauvinist (assuming that she could have a sense of humor) would take offense. In the concluding vaudeville, each of the characters in his or her own way complimented womanhood. The Maid sang the fable of the lion and the man; the widow's father's verses were more equivocal:

Thus, old wits, in wicked satires,
Formerly the fair malign'd;
Call'd them light, vain, false, affected;
And unsteady as the wind.
If they copy'd after nature,
Bless'd are English dames I trow,
So much alter'd from what ladies
Were two thousand years ago.

Popular though *The Ephesian Matron* was, during the summer of 1769 theatre-goers and curiosity-seekers were looking beyond Ranelagh for their amusement. Garrick was readying his Stratford-Upon-Avon Shakespeare Jubilee, and weather permitting, the event was going to be a showman's dream. Bickerstaff, Dibdin, and others helped by writing masques and songs for the celebration.

The Jubilee ran for three days, beginning on Wednesday, 6 September 1769. Bad accommodations and worse weather doomed the occasion, which could not have been saved by the poetry and music composed for it.[13] It had been designed primarily for spectacle, complete with an outdoor procession of characters from Shakespeare's plays, but the weather ruined the fireworks display and cancelled the procession. The attempts of Garrick and his writers to celebrate the new Town Hall of Stratford, the fame of Shakespeare, and the prowess of Garrick, were gleefully noted in dozens of squibs, epigrams, parodies and satirical accounts which both preceded and followed the Jubilee. Typical of these was the Epigram which appeared in the *London Chronicle* a week after the festival: "On the Modern Poets of Stratford-Upon-Avon":

In honour of the native notes
Of Avon's ever-dying swan
A flight of wild-fowl stretch'd their throats,
To praise their Fav'rite dead and gone!
The Bird, beneath the rushes hid,
Cried, "Peace, ye screech-owls, prithee peace!
Are these my kindred? Heav'n forbid!
These, like all David's *swans* are *geese!*"
(XXVI, Saturday, 16 September, 1769, 271)

On the first morning, Arne's and Bickerstaff's oratorio, *Judith,* was presented at the church, for no relevant reason unless Garrick hoped that it would put his audience in a properly devout mood to appreciate the greatness of Shakespeare. Even Garrick's contemporaries were puzzled about his choice of oratorios, although the practice of including one in "a purely festive occasion" was not unusual.[14] Oratorios—as opposed to operas and standard dramas—were neither "silly" nor "immoral"; in fact, they were so respectable that society attended them more from duty than for pleasure. But why *Judith?* One of Garrick's contemporaries suggested that since there was no oratorio named William, Garrick was determined to honor at least a relation.[15] As for the performance, Joseph Cradock considered that "the airs were all given in the best style, but the choruses were almost as meagre as the appearance of the audience; and I felt much hurt for all that were engaged to perform it. The company of any rank had not half arrived."[16]

While outside on the first evening the rains began to make a marsh out of a meadow, inside the Rotunda built for the occasion a band played, and glees and catches were sung, as paying guests, having spent a guinea to get in, were eating dinner for an additional ten and sixpence. One of the catches was by Bickerstaff.

> *Nym, Pistol* and *Bardolph,* with merry old *Jack,*
> One morning made sport for their pupil, prince *Harry;*
> When Falstaff, cry'd out for a bumper of sack,
> To *Quickly,* his hostess, and bid her not tarry;
> Ah! hah! cry'd the prince, honest boy is it so!
> The wheels of your wit, must be oil'd as they go.[17]

Excepting *Judith,* Dibdin set to music the major musical productions; one of them was Bickerstaff's cantata *Queen Mab,* in which was extolled the power of poetry, and, by name, the greatness of Shakespeare who created Queen Mab and her fairies. Mab became a Fairy Garrick in the cantata, and all her subjects were ordered to hold a Jubilee.

> Recitative:
> Not long ago, 'tis said, a proclamation,
> Was sent abroad through all the *Fairy* nation;
> *Mab* to her loving subjects—A Decree,
> At Shakespeare's tomb to hold a Jubilee.
> Accompanied:

The night was come, and now on *Avon's* side
The pigmy race was seen,
Attended by their queen,
On chafers some, and some on crickets ride.
The queen appear'd from far,
Mounted in a nut shell car;
Six painted lady-birds the carriage drew;
And now the cavalcade,
In order due array'd,
March'd first,
Where erst,
The sacred Mulb'ry grew,
And there their homage paid:
And while
A thousand glow-worms torches glimmer'd round;
Thus *Good Fellow,* the herald of his fame,
Did from the alabaster height proclaim,
The poet's titles and his stile.
Air:
SHAKESPEARE, heaven's most favor'd creature,
Truest copier of Nature,
First of the Parnassian train;
Chiefest fav'rite of the muses,
Which soe'er the poet chooses,
Blest alike in ev'ry strain.
(Etc. *Shakespeare's Garland,* pp. 21-23)

Discretion has veiled the audience's reaction to this early poetic apotheosis of Shakespeare. Even Kenrick chose to pass by *Queen Mab* when he published his attack on Bickerstaff and Garrick in 1772. To be charitable, Bickerstaff did write it for Garrick, who, after all, considered Shakespeare the God of his Idolatry.

The most unlikely combination of friends and enemies of Garrick that the age could produce turned up at the Jubilee where most of them no doubt heard *Queen Mab* and Garrick's "This is the day, a holiday! a holiday!" (*Shakespeare's Garland,* p. 14). With either a singular lack of perception, or a consummate sense of irony, Davies rhapsodised in his *Life of Garrick,* "No company, so various in character, temper, and condition ever formed, at least in appearance, such an agreeable groupe of happy and congenial souls" (II, 222). Some of those souls were Kenrick and Bickerstaff, Murphy and Colman, Garrick and Macklin, Hugh Kelly and Samuel Foote. To make the sanctification proper, Boswell stalked incognito first as a clergyman in disguise, and then as "a Corsican patriot," bearing with him a staff with a carved bird upon the top.

Rained out at Stratford, the elaborate pageant was finally performed at Drury Lane on 16 October 1769 after much careful preparation by Garrick, Messink his stage manager, and the entire company. As part of Garrick's after-piece, *The Jubilee,* it quite overshadowed Colman's own efforts at Covent Garden to satirize the original Jubilee. Garrick's *Jubilee* was so popular that it "created the record run for any piece on the London stage for the whole century, by receiving ninety performances during this one season alone" (Stone, III, 1419). The Chorus for the Pageant, originally planned to be recited at Stratford, was by Bickerstaff:

Hence ye prophane! and only they,
Our pageant grace our pomp survey,
Whom love of sacred genius brings;
Let pride, let flattery decree,
Honors to deck the memory,
Of warriors, senators, and kings—
Not less in glory, and desert,
The poet here receives his part,
A tribute from the feeling heart.

(*Shakespeare's Garland,* p. 17)

Bickerstaff's contributions to the Jubilee were his last acknowledged works for 1769. Presumably he helped Garrick at Drury Lane, and kept on good terms with the London newspapers; no squibs, epigrams, or letters of advice have turned up. Socially he remained on good terms with London's distinguished hacks for he was invited to dinner at Boswell's lodgings in Old Bond Street with Goldsmith, Garrick, Sir Joshua Reynolds, Arthur Murphy, Thomas Davies and Johnson on 16 October. Bickerstaff "observed, as a peculiar circumstance, that Pope's fame was higher when he was alive than now."[18] Johnson singled out "the description of the temple in *The Mourning Bride* [as] the finest poetical passage he had ever read." This was not the first time that Bickerstaff and Johnson had dined together; Murphy, Garrick and Johnson joined Bickerstaff at his house in 1767 to end a quarrel between Murphy and Garrick. Then Bickerstaff had referred to Johnson in a letter to Garrick as "the God of my idolatry" (Boaden, I, 273-274), a not altogether tactful remark since Garrick was less at ease with Johnson than with Shakespeare.

In the spring of 1770, the second of Dibdin's and Bickerstaff's three serenatas was presented at Ranelagh House. *He Wou'd if He Cou'd; or, An Old Fool Worse Than Any* was the title under which the piece was printed, but at Ranelagh it was called *The Maid the Mistress* (28 May). This burletta, as Bickerstaff termed it, was the second English version of Pergolesi's and Frederico's interlude, *La Serva Padrona*. The first had been produced in 1758 at Marylebone Gardens by Stephen Storace the Elder, and J. Trusler. To compete with Bickerstaff's burletta, Samuel Arnold brought out a lengthened version of Storace's translation on 16 June 1770 at Marylebone. Storace had contented himself with the same three characters who were in the original *La Serva Padrona:* Uberto, Serpilla, and the mime Vespone; but Bickerstaff added an Old Lady (played by Dibdin), and allowed Simon (Vespone) to speak. Not to be outdone, Arnold added an Old Lady to *his* version on 31 July 1770. Following Dibdin's lead, Bannister imitated the Old Lady in this production.

By allowing Simon to sing, Bickerstaff lost a fine part for a pantomimist, but Vernon's voice was sufficient excuse to give the servant some songs. As the Old Lady, Dibdin no doubt enjoyed himself, but the serenata failed. It played three times at Ranelagh, 28 May, 28 June, and 3 July. It was just as well that visitors to Ranelagh only casually listened to the music because Bickerstaff took one of Watty Cockney's songs from *Love in the City* and allowed Simon to sing it in Act II, scene II. The song, which does not appear in *The Romp,* celebrates an impending wedding, but in both plays the girl actually marries someone other than the character who sings it.

In the morning, what a dinging,
With the parish bells a ringing,
And the rattling of the drums:
Then be sure the music comes;
Fiddles, bass, and sweet hautboy.
All to wish the bride-folks joy. ["All to wish our honours joy." Watty Cockney, II, iv.]
But plague o'your horn,
'Tis not to be borne;
Oh, silence that ominous sound:
Play, instruments play;
Drums rattle away,
And let it for ever be drown'd.[19]

The serenata was performed once at Drury Lane on 12 April 1771 as *He Wou'd if He Cou'd*, with Vernon as Simon, Mrs. Baddeley as Betty, Dibdin as the Old Lady, and Bannister as

Goosecap (Stone, III, 1539). But whereas *La Serva Padrona* is still performed, *He Wou'd if He Cou'd* was never a success. As Genest wrote, it was "most deservedly damned" (V, 300-301).

For his dual role as singer and composer, Dibdin received £100 for the three serenatas which were performed at Ranelagh House (*Harmonicon,* p. 87); but he did not mention how much Bickerstaff was paid. If *The Maid the Mistress* was admittedly poor stuff, Bickerstaff and Dibdin's third effort, *The Recruiting Serjeant,* must have cheered Sir Thomas at Ranelagh.

Unlike the press-gangs, which were rightfully dreaded by almost every man who lived near English port towns and who even *looked* less than a gentleman, the recruiting bands for the Army inspired no such fear as they travelled through the countryside. Instead of the many stories of hapless young men being kidnapped from their sweethearts to man British warships, there is Farquhar's comedy, *The Recruiting Officer.* A recruiter's life was a happy one, seducing country lasses, and tricking country lads into enlisting.

Perhaps it was not quite so happy as the popular legends made it out to be, but there was no comparison between it and the adventures of a press gang. To see Bickerstaff's *The Recruiting Serjeant* was to see *gemütlichkeit* come home. It was a genuine genre animated painting. The Serjeant sings the praises of army life, and to tease his wife and mother, a countryman pretends to agree with him. The two women plead with the lad to remain at home, and the serjeant keeps praising the army. Finally the lad tells his folks that he was merely teasing, and the musical entertainment ends with a dance in front of the village ale-house. The countryman sings a health to King George and peace; the wife toasts the Queen; the mother pledges her drink to the babies of the nation; the serjeant hopes for success "to his majesty's arms." In between the final verses there is a patriotic chorus of country folk.

After the serenata's first performance at Ranelagh House on 20 July 1770, it was repeated there five times during that season. To bolster Bickerstaff's ailing *'Tis Well it's No Worse,* Garrick produced it at Drury Lane on 7 December 1770 as the afterpiece. At Covent Garden, it was billed as an interlude and produced for the first time on 6 May 1776 between *Amphitryon* and *Midas.* Marylebone produced it on 23 May 1776, with *La Serva Padrona.* It remained in repertory both in London and in the provinces until late into the nineteenth century. In America it was produced in Boston on 15 March 1799 at the Federal Street Theatre, and on 10 May 1800 at New York's Park Street Theatre (Sonneck, Tables *B* and *D*). The BBC broadcast it during the 1950s.

The best song in *The Recruiting Serjeant* was sung by the serjeant himself: "What a Charming Thing's a Battle!" the serjeant's climactic number in his attempt to woo the countryman is a fine satirical paean to war.

What a charming thing's a battle!
Trumpets sounding, drums a beating;
Crack, crick, crack, the cannons rattle.
Ev'ry heart with joy elating.
With what pleasure are we spying,
From the front and from the rear,
Round us in the smoaky air,
Heads, and limbs, and bullets flying!
Then the groans of soldiers dying:
Just like sparrows, as it were,
At each pop,
Hundreds drop;
While the muskets prittle prattle:
Kill'd and wounded,
Lie confounded;
What a charming thing's a battle!
But the pleasant joke of all,
Is when to close attack we fall;
Like mad bulls each other butting,
Shooting, stabbing, maiming, cutting;
Horse and foot,
All go to't,
Kill's the word, both men and cattle;
Then to plunder:
Blood and thunder,
What a charming thing's a battle! (Scene iv, pp. 18–19)

In England *The Recruiting Serjeant* drew no reviews until it was produced at Drury Lane; then nothing but the usual puffs were printed. In France, the *Journal Encyclopédique* dismissed the serenata (II, March, 1771, 301), perhaps because the work has anti-French sentiments.

The three serenatas Bickerstaff and Dibdin prepared for Ranelagh were all cut from the same bolt. They were short musical pieces written for four voices with only recitative between songs. Charles Bannister, who sang in two of them originally, and eventually in all three, was famous for both his bass voice and his falsetto. Dibdin took the tenor role, or falsetto when he played an old woman, and appeared in the three serenatas, as did Mrs. Baddeley. Mrs. Thompson played in two, while Vernon and Legg each appeared in one. The only failure was *The Maid the Mistress,* while the other two have lasted, precariously, to the present. Had Bickerstaff not fled in 1772, the success of his short serenatas, and the availability of tested performers might have encouraged him and Dibdin to try a full-length completely operatic English musical. For this reason, even though Dibdin was a hard man to work with for long—and Bickerstaff not all sweetness and light himself—one must regret the abrupt ending of their collaboration. Without Bickerstaff, Dibdin resorted to adapting French short comic operas, none of them particularly successful, and writing sea-songs, many of which were popular; but compared to what he might have done, they are just so many trips through "Some peaceful Province in Acrostick Land."

11
"BICKERSTAFF, THE SON OF SONG": *'TIS WELL ITS NO WORSE, FABLES, A SELECT COLLECTION OF VOCAL MUSIC*

Having proved an able adapter of two English comedies, *The Plain Dealer,* and Cibber's *The Hypocrite,* Bickerstaff hoped for success with an adaptation of a Spanish comedy of intrigue, Calderon's *El Escondido y la Tapada,* which he entitled *'Tis Well it's No Worse.* If Dibdin's word can be trusted, Garrick "had . . . determined that [Bickerstaff] should not bring out any more operas" (*Life,* I, 81); but it was Bickerstaff himself who recommended the comedy to the Drury Lane manager:

> Nothing could excuse my puting [sic] a play in your hands at this season [Bickerstaff wrote on 31 August] but my at the same time assuring you that when I do so I have no unreasonable views upon your friendship or expectation that (even should you approve it) you will accept it to be acted at a time that will incommode your other business. The plot, which I have partly taken from a Spanish play of Calderon's is uncommon and amazingly complicated by the Spanish poet; and I believe I have contrived to avoid the least obscurity of confusion; which, where all is incident and action, may perhaps have some little merit; and perhaps this will be found to be all its merit. However, I am prepared most cheerfully to abide by your judgment, whom I have always found my best critic and friend, and to whom I shall ever continue the most grateful and affectionate of those who subscribe, Dear Sir, Your most humble and obliged servant.[1]

Like every other author, Bickerstaff convinced himself that the public would applaud his work, despite an ill-omen.

> Some time before his comedy was produced, Bickerstaff invited a few friends, of whom [Paul] Hiffernan was one, to dine with him, and hear him read his play. After dinner, the glass went cheerfully round for about half an hour, when the Author began, and read to the end of the first act, the company making such observations on it as it suggested to their judgments. Hiffernan's only remark all this while was, "Very well, by G–D! very well," till about the middle of the second act, when he began to nod, and in a little time afterwards to snore so loud that the Author could scarcely be heard. Bickerstaff felt a little embarrassed, but raising his voice, went on. Hiffernan's tones, however, increased, till at last Goldsmith could hold no longer, but cried out, "Never mind the brute, Bick; go on—so he would have served Homer if he was here, and reading his own works."
>
> Hiffernan, however, made his best excuse the next day, and which Goldsmith was ready enough to admit as such; for when the latter asked him how he could behave in that manner, the other coolly replied, "It's my usual way—I never can resist sleeping at a *pantomime!*"[2]

Goldsmith's protest did not go unnoticed, however, for in addition to Hiffernan and Hugh Kelly, the ubiquitous William Kenrick was at the party, and Goldsmith's reference to Homer earned him a couplet and a pleasant rhymed epigram in *Love in the Suds:*

> Goldsmith, good-natur'd man, shall next defend
> His foster-brother, countryman, and friend. . . . (5th ed. p. 13)

A "foster-brother," Kenrick explained, "So called from having not long since made one in a poetical triumvirate, which gave occasion to the following verses in imitation of Dryden's famous epigram on Milton; 'Three poets in three distant ages born,' &c."

> Poor Dryden! what a theme hadst thou,
> Compar'd to that which offers now?
> What are your Britons, Romans, Grecians,
> Compar'd with thorough-bred Milesians?
> Step into Griffin's shop, he'll tell ye
> Of Goldsmith, Bickerstaff, and Kelly,
> Three poets of one age and nation,
> Whose more than mortal reputation,
> Mounting in trio to the skies
> O'er Milton's fame and Virgil's flies.
> Nay, take one Irish evidence for t'other,
> Ev'n Homer's self is but their foster-brother. (pp. 13–14)

Undaunted by Hiffernan's snores, Bickerstaff borrowed £100 from Garrick against the profits he expected from his benefits. But after the first performance, he knew that his confidence had been misplaced. Fortunately he had borrowed the £100 on the strength of a bill from the bookseller Griffin. The first night's performance was on Saturday, 24 November; by Monday Griffin was writing to Garrick:

> There is a bill of mine, a good deal over due, for £100, which Mr. Bickerstaff tells me you were kind enough to give him cash for. As it has not been presented for payment, he did intend to pay it out of his benefits, but as they will perhaps not prove so advantageous as he at first hoped, I must beg the favour of you to keep the bill for me till about three weeks or a month after Xmas when I will *most assuredly* take it up.[3]

Griffin's understated remark about the benefits, "they will perhaps not prove so advantageous as [Bickerstaff] at first hoped," sets the tone for comments about *'Tis Well it's No Worse,* a comedy "much hiss'd" on the first night, but "not so much hiss'd as first night" on its second appearance (Stone, 1514, Hopkins's Diary). It was the sort of play that prompted Bickerstaff's friend Victor to write, "tho' this Comedy was not as well approved, and supported, as many Pieces have been from this Author, it was performed Eleven [actually ten] nights" (III, 170-172). In the 1782 *Biographia Dramatica,* Baker grudgingly allowed, "It was not unsuccessfully performed" (#79, p. 373). Other critics were not so nice in their discrimination; but while clearly *'Tis Well it's No Worse* could not have been much worse as a comedy, it did last for ten performances and did give Bickerstaff three Benefits. It lasted that long because Bickerstaff and Garrick lightened the work of some of its deadweight; Garrick shored up the comedy with popular afterpieces; and Mrs. Abington and King starred in it. Had it not been for their acting, Bickerstaff's and Garrick's efforts would have been wasted. In tribute to Mrs. Abington, Bickerstaff dedicated the comedy to her, and praised King in the Dedication. All the contemporary reviews agreed with Bickerstaff's praise of their acting.

Bickerstaff's adaptation was faithful to the Spanish comedy[4]—even if he did adapt it from a literal French translation—perhaps even too faithful, because he retained too much of the sixteenth-century Spanish traditions that first made it popular. Bickerstaff and Garrick were prepared to gamble that this *comedia de capa y espada* would succeed because of its novelty. As Bickerstaff wrote in the preface, Garrick and he agreed "that it [the Intrigue] was a very great curiosity. It must be owned, indeed, in justice to [Garrick's] discernment, that he thought the exhibition of it a hazardous attempt; however, he at the same time declared, that if the Play did not too far clash with the prejudices of the prevailing taste, he thought it had an undoubted right to success."[5] Bickerstaff probably hoped that Garrick would play Don Carlos, and give to the play the same success that Mrs. Centlivre's *The Wonder* had enjoyed with Garrick as Don Felix.

In his own behalf, Bickerstaff discussed Comedies of Character, and Comedies of Intrigue, the two kinds of comedy distinguished by critics.

> Notwithstanding these are undoubtedly the best which are composed of a due portion of both, I never understood, from all I have read about the matter, that Comedy forfeited her name by attaching herself to either, particularly the latter [Comedies of Intrigue]; in which the great difficulty of the dramatic art seems to lie. Nor can I find, tho' it has been of late years the fashion for Comedy to address herself rather to the Heart and Understanding, than the Fancy, that she may not address herself to the Fancy solely, (as in this piece) without calling her title at all in question. (Preface, vii–viii).

For addressing the comedy to Fancy and not to the Heart and Understanding, Bickerstaff and the play were very much questioned in a long, adverse review which appeared in the *Oxford Magazine*. He and the play both were damned: "The bard is damned, and he only leads in the path which his works must follow.—Such be the fate of all poets, who strive to tickle the senses, instead of charming the understanding."[6]

Knowing that for the critics amusement alone would not suffice, Bickerstaff offered them the plot, "in which is preserved a perfect unity of action, at the same time that it is branched into a multitude of incidents."

> These incidents, again, are all naturally prepared; rising one from the other, without confusion, without obscurity; and with less to excuse, on the plea of necessity (a plea which in some cases, a judicious critic will always be ready to admit) than could be easily supposed, in such a tissue of events, drawn from a simple circumstance. Nor . . . will a candid judge, who knows how to rate the merit of invention be very apt to quarrel with such a Play, for a weak Scene, or unguarded Phrase; or for wanting, what in nature it cannot have, laboured Dialogue, and high wrought Character. (Preface, pp. viii–ix)

This bone to the critics was not enough: they demanded

moral instruction; the average spectator, they maintained, did *not* want to be amused; on the contrary, "the greater part of the audience are desirous of carrying home a little shred of morality from the evening's entertainment."[7] Even on Bickerstaff's terms, however, *'Tis Well it's No Worse* fails, mainly because of Don Carlos, Don Ferdinand, Aurora and Marcella. Two less ardent pairs of lovers the stage has rarely seen. They speak in prose to each other as though they were dictating their memoirs. Don Carlos does not love Aurora:

> I used every means possible to make myself really fall in love with Aurora; but my heart refused to be an accomplice in the inconstancy to which my reason advised me. (p. 3)

On Aurora's advice he has come to Madrid to try to gain a pardon.

> And shall I confess, that I am not little flattered with the thought, now I am here, of sometimes accidentally seeing the charming Marcella; and now and then, in an evening paying my homage under her window? (p. 4)

As for Marcella and Don Ferdinand, their match is based on "sincerity," perhaps as befitting their high station in society. At any rate, Don Ferdinand, in his love scene with Marcella, woos her successfully with the following observation:

> The only eloquence to persuade a mind, formed like my Marcella's, is sincerity; and, I always thought, the best way to acquire her esteem, was to convince her that she possessed mine. (Act II, p. 38)

In the last scene, Don Carlos's climactic speech comes in answer to Don Pedro's charge, "The death of a son may be forgiven, but not the ruin of a sister."

> Don Pedro, I never wrong'd you. I honour, I esteem, I admire your sister; and not out of fear of your anger, but in regard to her virtues, and as a debt due to her reputation, brought into danger, by her attention to me, I am willing to make her my wife. (p. 102)

Don Pedro accepts Don Carlos as a brother-in-law, but the audience never hears Aurora's opinion—assuming she still has one. Rightfully, the audience could not care less that this play was an adaptation of a *comedia de capa y espada;* they put up with the noble characters to enjoy King and Mrs. Abington as Muskato and Beatrice.

When *'Tis Well it's No Worse* was produced in 1770, *The Oxford Magazine* accused Garrick of keeping adverse criticism out of the newspapers. While the charge was not new, in this instance at least, there might have been some truth to it.

"It is amusing to observe [wrote the critic for the *Oxford Magazine*], how powerfully self-interest operates through the great circle of society."

> [The writer instanced corrupt senators, lawyers and justices] . . . the *theatrical manager* leads *Printers* by the nose, and locks up the tongues even of the babbling newspapers. It is now several days since the comedy before us was ushered into public view, and (a circumstance, perhaps, never before known in this kingdom) no *real sketch,* no *critical remarks,* no *observations* on the new comedy have yet appeared. The manager nods, and criticism slips her pen: the piece limps on night after night, and the culprit author escapes with all his dulness, and enjoys his third night in peace, while the poppies nod on his brow. On the present occasion, the newspapers, unable to praise, have forborne to blame; they durst not: all candid criticism lies under the broad thumb of the manager. —In a situation so critical, they have done well to smother their feelings: silence, indeed, is the best panegyric. This is real prudence. (V, Dec., 1770, 225)

Two newspaper reviews bear out the *Oxford Magazine.* A writer for *The London Chronicle* gave the cast and summary and concluded: "Tho' some of the scenes were disapproved of by part of the audience, we apprehend, when it has undergone the corrections and alterations which are usually made after a *first* representation, it will, from the merit it possesses, be found deserving the encouragement of the Public" (XXVIII, 24-27 November 1770, 505). In *Bingley's Weekly Journal,* a writer borrowed from *The London Chronicle,* but also mentioned another contribution to the limited success of the comedy: "The managers took all imaginable pains to add to the play, by a variety of new scenery, dresses, and decorations. . ." (#26, Saturday, 1 December 1770). Although it was a lead article, it contained no criticism, but concerned itself with a plot synopsis. From *Bingley's,* the *Chronicle* notice moved up to *The Freeholder's Magazine, or Monthly Chronicle of Liberty* (III, December, 1770, 159-161) which re-published it without adding anything new.

Counting *The Freeholder,* four journals examined the comedy, three of them sympathetically: *The Freeholder's Magazine, The Town and Country Magazine* (II, November, 1770, 594-596), and *The London Magazine* (XXXIX, December, 1770, 603-

604). To make up for what it considered a disgraceful absence of adverse criticism, the December *Oxford Magazine* found *'Tis Well it's No Worse* lacking in its plot, characters, sentiment and moral; and then held forth on comedy in general. After accusing Garrick of rigging criticism about the play, the anonymous *Oxford* critic suggested as a criterion by which to judge the plan of a dramatic piece, that one examine "whether it exhibits the characters of men, and the genuine effects of passions according to the laws of nature" (p. 224). By this Wordsworthian creed, Bickerstaff's plot is "wild, wandering, and improbable":

> The author seems to have caught the true spirit of Centlivre; fearful of lulling the audience into slumber, like his brothers of the modern breed, he has thrown the stage into universal uproar and confusion, and is resolved to keep us awake by the mere dint of noise. (p. 225) [The] confusion encreases as the plot advances . . . and the curtain only relieves [the audience] from doubt, error, and pain. (p. 226)

Only Beatrice was "marked with any stamp of originality." Even this characterization of a flippant chambermaid was a "concatenation . . . [of] all the pert graces of the dramatic Phillis's and Betty's of the present age. . . . The author borrowed a tint from this romp, and that vixen, and finished the picture by adding an uncommon quantity of pertness and forwardness" (p. 226). These qualities, of course, ensured Mrs. Abington's success in the role.

Under "Sentiment," the *Oxford Magazine* critic wrote, "There is but one in the whole piece, and that being trite is not worth repeating." He dismissed the moral—or lack of it—almost as quickly. "Let those who could discover any, declare what it is. We believe there are few who will undertake the task."

> If the greater part of the audience are desirous of carrying home a little shred of morality from the evening's entertainment, the poet in this respect sets them all fairly at defiance.—Indeed, it would cost a man so much trouble to take out a moral from the wild dross of miracles that meets his eye, that we could not be repaid by the acquisition of it. (pp. 226–227)

For a brief moment, the writer allowed some merit to the comedy: "Though envy itself cannot deny, but there are several laughable situations, and truly comic incidents, to extort genuine applause; yet like roses in a desart, there are few, and borrow great lustre from the dark shades that surround them. . . ."

At this point, the critic turned from *'Tis Well it's No Worse* to comment on the state of comedy. "Comic writers," he noted, have been treating "the town with sentiment at the expence of wit and humour."

> What effect this sentimental humour may have upon refined minds, is difficult to say; but we plainly see how it operates on the vulgar, who always imitate their betters. The barber's boy, elbowing through the crowd with his trull under his arm, talks away of sentiment and taste; and the upper gallery displays as much critical quaintness and gusto as the sovereign circle of critics in the pit. Our author, perhaps to chide this peccant humour in the rabble, and to shame sermons divided into five acts out of fashion, was resolved to be even with them on the other side; and drew forth his pantomime against their morality—*Heu! deficit alter*—He stepped too far—intrigue without sentiment is quite as cloying in comedy as sentiment without wit. (p. 227)

Inevitably, in a review of this kind, the critic told his readers "the great charter of the poet is *et prodesse et delectare.*—But what shall we say of [Bickerstaff] who has hardly accomplished the one, and quite forgot the other?"

> Entirely regardless of that artful and delightful pastime of nature and art, which refines the heart by entertaining it—the passions by laughing at them—he has endeavoured to tickle our attention by an improbable jumble of rude mirth and miracles, where humour is stripped of her native smiles, and folly riots over the ruins of simplicity.

The critic turned to painting for comparison: "These wild portraitures in writing are what grotesque is in painting: they are in the true Hogarthian style—they please often by their extravagance." Farce was analogous to Hogarth's caricatures:

> In comedy there is always a certain moderation necessary to be observed in the use of this hyperbole, otherwise it is apt to degenerate into farce; and if the little ambling bards of this age do not take proper care to check their wayward fancies, we shall have comedy and farce run tilt against each other, and it will cost criticism the keenest eyes to distinguish the monster from the man. (p. 227)

The *Oxford Magazine* review represents the mainstream of practical theatrical criticism in the newspapers and magazines of the eighteenth century. It differs only in strenuousness and in its explicit avowal of what the drama was to accomplish. In the same magazine, but for January 1771, "The Censor" surveyed the state of the nation, a country "of great national prosperity and opulence, arising from extensive and profitable commerce." Attendant upon England's prosperity were the vices of "Irreligion, luxury, venality, licentiousness, prodigality and lewdness." The Censor contended that it was the duty of "our *divines* and *legislators*" to check these vices, but they had failed to do so. "When the pulpit has failed," the essayist continued, on occasion the stage has succeeded. This linking together of stage and pulpit forms the bond with which eighteenth-century drama critics worked when they insisted upon their "Fable," "Sentiment," and "Moral"; as such, The Censor's remarks about the stage deserve to be quoted.

> Sometimes, when the pulpit has failed of producing this salutary effect [the eradication of vice], either through the irregularity of the lives of the clergy, or the levity and infidelity of the people—the STAGE has proved an excellent *succedaneum* under the direction of discreet and chaste managers—patronized by virtuous and honest statesmen. In this situation of the THEATRE, the moral tendency of the tragic scene, and the polite, decent, lively humour of the comic muse—kept public virtue, integrity of manners, and good breeding in countenance. But an impartial retrospect on the conduct of our managers, of late years, and a candid inquiry into the present state of our theatrical exhibitions will soon convince us, that the *idol* they worship is *gold;* and that the taste of the town is so vitiated, that such entertainments only give satisfaction, as can neither inform the mind, correct the heart, or mend the manners of the people. ("The Censor," No. viii., 3–5, signed "M.")

Whatever lip-service Bickerstaff, Garrick, and other practicing playwrights paid to the pious platitudes about the role of the theatre, their concern was to provide entertainment for audiences who were only slightly more attentive to critics than to divines. The average viewer of Bickerstaff's comedies equated immorality with social impropriety, and was uninterested in being "informed," "corrected," or "mended" by a play, except, perhaps, in matters of social decorum.

On a more pragmatic level, Francis Gentleman, writing in *The Dramatic Censor,* summarized his opinion of Bickerstaff, after having reviewed several of his plays using the customary heads of "Characters," "Sentiments," "Moral," and the like:

> *Bickerstaff,* this author, with great propriety, we may call the *dramatic cobler* [sic]; for he, figuratively speaking, patches, soles, and heels pieces very well, though he cannot make a new piece of work; he should never attempt any thing out of the Opera stile, as well adapted music may soften many errors; his sentiments are trite, his characters common, and his language most shamefully incorrect; his last piece had an un-

happy title, *'Tis well its no worse;* a critical wag, justly observed that it was a misnomer, for it should have been called, *it cannot be worse*. . . . had Mr. DIBDIN composed [the concluding lines of the comedy], perhaps the harmonical repetitions, for which his inimitable music is so remarkable, might have melted nonsense into captivating sound; what are CONGREVE, FARQUHAR, HANDEL, ARNE, or ARNOLD, to this matchless author, and as matchless composer. (II, 470–471)

Nobody was happy with *'Tis Well it's No Worse.* In France, the *Journal Encyclopédique* adversely reviewed the comedy in February 1771, and dismissed it as a very close translation of Simon Linguet's version, *"cette pièce a été tres exactemente traduite en anglois"* (II, part I, 139).

A speech by the coachman in *'Tis Well it's No Worse* furnished Percival Stockdale with a couplet in his poem, *The Poet* (1773). The coachman drunkenly compared his lot to that of an English coachman:

This it is, to live under an arbitrary government; a man must not speak in his own defence: I wish I had been born in England; a good servant there can bid his master drive his coach himself, if he does not like how he's driven (*hiccups and staggers*). It's no comfort to get drunk in this slavish country. (I. pp. 10–11)

Stockdale scented sedition and rhymed:

Let Spanish coachmen on our laws descant
And in their cups recite the Patriot's rant.[8]

To ensure that his readers caught the allusion, Stockdale footnoted the couplet, "See a late comedy entitled, 'It's Well it's no Worse.' " Earlier in the poem, Stockdale asserted that the true poet "Despises flimsey Bickerstaffes, and Hooles, / Whom scenes, and sing-song gain the herd of fools. . ." (p. 14).

Undaunted by bad notices, the Capel Street Theatre in Dublin produced *'Tis Well it's No Worse* on 7 January 1771 (*Hibernian Magazine,* March 1771), but it does not seem to have been repeated. After its ten London performances, the comedy quietly disappeared until John Kemble, Drury Lane's manager in 1788, realized that the obvious successor to Mrs. Abington was Mrs. Jordan, who had already triumphed in another of the former's parts—Roxalana in Bickerstaff's *The Sultan.* He therefore selected "the most humourous parts of Mr. Bickerstaff's comedy . . ." and made "some trifling additions to connect the scenes."[9] The result was *The Pannel,* named for the entrance to the secret room in Aurora's house, and first produced as a three-act farce afterpiece to *Jane Shore* on 28 November 1788. Kemble sloughed away all the scenes possible where only the fine folk appear to leave the stage clear for Beatrice, Muskato and Lazarillo. According to Kemble, he adapted the comedy "for the purpose of exhibiting the comic powers of Mrs. Jordan [as Beatrice]" (Introduction). Although Kemble adapted the play, the title-page of the first edition shows that *The Pannel* was "Printed by Assignment from Mr. Bickerstaff, for C. Stalkerd, Stationer's Court [etc.]." Did Bickerstaff profit from the belated success of his comedy? Despite one conjectural death date of 1787, Bickerstaff was still alive, possibly in Italy. Although he had never registered *'Tis Well it's No Worse* at Stationer's Hall, as its author he had the right of assigning the copyright to whomever he chose. This right of assignment was set at fourteen years by an Act of Parliament in 1710, which also allowed a second term of fourteen years, if the author should still be living. Since *The Pannel* was published nineteen years (1770-1789) after *'Tis Well it's No Worse,* Bickerstaff was still exercising his proprietory rights. But where? And for how much? The farce was successful, and was in demand at Drury Lanc at least until 1826. In the United States, as *The Recess,* the farce was played twelve times between 27 April 1791 and 7 June 1830 (Macmillan, p. 65).

The Pannel was received with better grace than was its parent comedy. Both the *London Chronicle* for 29 December 1788, and the December issue of the *Universal Magazine of Knowledge and Pleasure* published the same critique, "In the present scarcity of dramatic genius, the manager deserves praise, who, of a bad comedy, makes a tolerable farce" (*Universal Magazine,* LXXXIII [December 1788], 319). *The Times* reported that the farce was presented with "very considerable applause. The plot is Spanish—and abounds with a variety of droll adventures." Bannister and Mrs. Jordan "kept the House in a continual roar" (Saturday, 29 November 1788, #1184).

One review published an epigram which Beatrice recites in Act I, and what it considered the "original" version; both have a nice "Father William" tang:

Beatrice: When first I attempted your pity to move,
You seem'd deaf to my sighs and my prayers:
Perhaps it was right to dissemble your love,
But why did you kick me down stairs? [Act I, scene i]

"G.E. Esq.'s" version: "The Expostulation"

When first I attempted your pity to move,
Why seem'd you so deaf to my pray'rs?
Perhaps it was right to dissemble your love:
But why did you kick me down stairs?[10]

The popularity of *The Pannel* was due directly to the acting of Mrs. Jordan, as was the limited success of *'Tis Well it's No Worse* to Mrs. Abington. Kemble's pruning gave Bickerstaff a belated success for his comedy of intrigue—a success which Bickerstaff needed, wherever he was in 1788.

But in the spring of 1771, Bickerstaff was in London working on the subscription edition of his fables. Fable writing was a favorite pastime of eighteenth-century authors; and they wrote elegant variations and translations of La Fontaine and AEsop, and other standard fabulists, as often as they created new ones. Fables were very much an eighteenth-century genre, as much in evidence as Georgics, odes, and satires whose titles ended in "-iad." As a matter of fact, Bickerstaff was only following his namesake, for in 1709 "Bickerstaff's Fables" was published by William Pittis.

In the 1771 "Proposals," Bickerstaff wrote a Preface about fables and included five of them, the first two from the *Gentleman's Journal*. He also listed five "Conditions," which described the intended book and its price:

I. The greater Part of the FABLES will be New, or such as never appeared before in the English Language, making One Volume in Octavo.
II. Each Fable will be adorned with an elegant Copper-Plate [the one for "The Cuckow Traveller" was printed in the "Proposals"], and the Whole printed on Royal Paper.
III. The Book will be delivered as soon as the Engravings can be ready, which, at farthest, will be in March 1773.
IV. The Engravings alone will amount to the full Value of the Subscription.
V. Price, to Subscribers, One Guinea, to be paid at the time of subscribing.

At the bottom of the "Conditions" page was a receipt form and the signature of "I. Bickerstaff" at "Goodge-Street." On the Title Page there was printed the date, "November 20, 1771."[11]

The work had been some time planning, for on 16 March 1771, Bickerstaff had written apologetically to Garrick:

My Dear Sir, It must not only appear a strange affectation in me, but an instance of great folly, was I to endeavour to hide from you any literary design for my advantage; but at the same time, give me leave to say, the scheme for publishing my Fables is of such a nature as might sufficiently justify some little artifice, or, let me rather call it, decent caution, before I ventured to mention it to you in a manner to desire your assistance: I have troubled you so often with paltry suits, that I really do it now (though in some sort encouraged to it by yourself) with timidity and reluctance.

I have been my own dupe, and the dupe of others; what I have erred in at the instigation of my own folly, I have corrected. Some little success in subscribing my Fables would repair all, and I think I shall err no more. I had no thought farther than Ireland, but Mr. Foote offered to serve me unasked; I knew the warmth of his disposition, however, and made allowances for it, that is, built nothing upon the foundation; but he has, contrary to my expectation, served me in the most ample manner, and I am well assured, done it in a way to deserve my thanks. If you think proper to lend me the Fables you mentioned, I shall be greatly obliged to you. (Boaden, I, 417–418)

As in many of Bickerstaff's letters, he alludes to more than he explains. Obviously he is in debt, but from which form of intemperance? What about Ireland? Was he planning at first to publish his fables only there? What was Foote's role? Did Garrick lend him the requested fables?

On 9 May 1772 *The London Chronicle* seemingly answered one of the questions when it devoted its front page to some fables from a newly published book, *Sentimental Fables,* "Designed Chiefly for the Use of the Ladies," which was "ascribed to I——c B——f." The book had first been published in Belfast, which would make some sense out of Bickerstaff's letter, and in a later issue, the newspaper printed another fable from the same work under the heading, "Bickerstaff's Fables."[12] But years later, in another edition, the author, Thomas Marryat, M.D., revealed his identity and dedicated the fables to Hannah More.[13]

Bickerstaff's flight cut directly across his and Griffin's plans to publish the subscription edition of the "Fables." His flight must have cost Griffin a good deal, because, judging from the copperplate engraving for "The Cuckoo Traveller," the work was to be ambitiously elaborate. For the second time, Griffin was left with "The Cuckoo Traveller," and "The Ant and the Grasshopper"; after all, his *Gentleman's Journal,* which originally printed them (the first as "The Cuckow [sic] Traveller") died after two issues. This time Griffin had at least three other fables by Bickerstaff—the three published with the first two in the prospectus. One of them, "The Brook, and the Torrent," turned up in *The Hibernian Magazine* for September 1772 (p. 504). Fables I and II became the first two fables in Part Three of a now-valuable collection, *Select Fables,* published in 1776, and again in 1784 with engravings by Thomas Bewick. Saint of Newcastle was the publisher. Bickerstaff revised them after they were published in *The Gentleman's Journal* for his "Proposal," and it was the revised version that appeared—with one or two further slight changes—in Bewick's *Fables.*

In his Preface, Bickerstaff gave his opinion about what a fable should be, and what style the "mythologist"—as he called the writer of fables—should adopt. As usual he was positive in his views. Before Bickerstaff's fables,

> "The only Fables which have hitherto appeared in English verse, deserving notice, are those written by the celebrated Gay; and the late ingenious Mr. Edward Moore . . . [his] Fables for the Female Sex; but, however justly these performances may be admired for their polite and well-directed satire; their delicate turns of wit; and their easy versification; they are certainly not only very far removed from the idea of the apologue, as given to us by the most approved ancients; but extremely different from the best examples of that kind of writing to be found among the moderns.

Bickerstaff then gave his criteria for a good fable:

> A Fable should be concise, perspicuous, and in some sort epigramatic [sic]; the conclusion, (if in verse, the concluding stanza) as much as possible, at once, and without the help of any annexed interpretation, giving the moral scope: the incidents should always be natural. Such are the Fables of Æsop. The diction, or perhaps I might say the dialogue (for a Fable is also a kind of short drama)), should be characteristic, sententious, and above all things simple; I mean chiefly that sort of simplicity which the English have no word exactly to express, and the French call *naïveté*. Such are the Fables of La Fontaine.
>
> The truths that Fables may convey are almost innumerable, but they should neither turn on the obvious precepts taught by the nurse, nor the more abstruse maxims inculcated by the philosopher. The mythologist should take the middle way, or, in other words, his truths should be such as strike at the first glance, yet such as are not so apparent, but they require to be pointed out. For the rest, the pleasure derived from Fables, must, like that from other poems, depend upon the ingenuity of the author; upon the liveliness of his imagination, the variety of his expression, and the smoothness of his verse: in short, upon that charm of just composition, which in every work is felt by intelligent minds, as far as it goes; and without which even truth itself is insipid and ineffectual. (Preface, pp. iii–iv)

Bickerstaff's fables were to be, for the most part, new; others "will be paraphrased from AEsop and others. . ." (p. v). Some would have been by Garrick, judging from Bickerstaff's letter; possibly others were to have been by Foote. He concluded his Preface in support of engravings, "too much neglected in books susceptible of it . . . an art, which seems to want nothing but that extensive encouragement, to bring it to the same perfection in England to which it has arrived in some neighbouring countries." With the collapse of the edition, however, it was left to Thomas Bewick to fulfill Bickerstaff's prediction. The five fables which were printed in the "Proposal" are included in Appendix D.

Having proposed his *Fables,* and with *'Tis Well it's No Worse* and the spring season of Drury Lane behind him, Bickerstaff visited the continent where he collected "Flemish and German music, for a new opera, which we hear, he intends bringing out this season at Drury-Lane" (*Bingley's Journal,* Friday, 6 September). *The Town and Country Magazine* heard that "Mr. Bickerstaff is engaged in preparing another new musical piece of three acts, which will very early in the season be brought on Drury-Lane stage" (September, 1771, p. 476).

Sometime late in 1771, Bickerstaff returned to England, presumably laden with the Flemish and German music he had collected, and, if the papers were correct, bringing with him a wife. His marriage to "Miss Dean, of Jermyn-Street, St. James," was announced in five newspapers and the *Gentleman's Magazine* for September; the *Public Ledger's* account was the most circumstantial: "Lately was married at Calais, in France, the celebrated Isaac Bickerstaff Esq., to Miss Dean of Jermyn Street, St. James."[14] It was not until Tuesday, 24 September, that *Bingley's Journal* printed a correction: "Married: A few days since, Donatus O'Callaghan, Esq; (not Isaac Bickerstaff, Esq; as formerly mentioned) to Miss Dean of Jermyn Street" (#69, Saturday, 21 September to Saturday, 28 September 1771).[15]

While no definite trace remains of the three-act musical piece on which Bickerstaff was working in the autumn of 1771, a very rare work of his does exist, *A Select Collection of Vocal Music, Serious and Comic with a Thorough Bass for the Harpsichord.* Edited by Bickerstaff, this collection included music by Ciampi, Galuppi, Perez, and Piccini, with transpositions for the German Flute. Elaborately printed, the book was dedicated to Queen Charlotte, and the royal recognition should have ensured the presence of the handsome oblong folio in many a middle-class music room even if a guest never looked further into it than to the dedication. "Should have," but the flight of Bickerstaff in May, 1772, probably caused the collection to be suppressed to avoid any embarrassment to the Queen.[16]

A Select Collection was the climax of Bickerstaff's efforts to promote continental airs over native ones. Throughout his career, he had insisted upon the superiority of French and Italian music to the English, Scottish, and Irish ballads that were sung at Vauxhall, Ranelagh, and the other gardens, and adapted for ballad operas. His efforts were successful only to the extent that his own operas were enjoyed, and his songs sung along with the Scottish airs—not in place of them. On the contrary, the traditional airs grew more numerous as the century progressed, and the ballad revival flourished. In his Dedication, Bickerstaff explained that his anthology was designed not merely to amuse the amateur musician at home, but to "render an ART, long admired and encouraged in this Country, better understood; and to shew that the English Language, with a little Care, is not less proper for Musical Composition, than the Language of any of our Neighbours." To set off his work from the common run of song books, Bickerstaff wrote a lecturing Preface:

> The Editor of this Collection, flatters himself, that it will not be confounded with those wretched *Compilations,* or, as they have sometimes been mis-titled *Compositions,* which have at different Times, been obtruded on the Public under the Notion of Musical Magazines, &c.
>
> The present Undertaking is expensive, difficult and laborious; and has no less in View, than extending the practical Knowledge of Music, by bringing those, who love and study the Science, acquainted with it, in its ultimate Perfection. The Compositions of the great Masters, whose Works will now, for the first Time (if the Expression may be used) make their Appearance in an English Dress, have been long admired by all Europe for their superior Beauty; nor is this Admiration the meer Effect of Caprice or Fashion; but an undoubted Test of their real Excellency; which is evident from this Circumstance, That the Music of every Country becomes more agreeable to the Natives, and the Professors of it are more encouraged by them, as they learn more closely to imitate the Music of the Italians; so that Italian Music seems not only to be that Mode to which Music would nearly be brought every where, under proper Cultivation; but, in some sort, the Music of Nature itself.

It is no wonder that Dibdin wrote in his *History,* "the fault of this author was that he was bigotted to Italian music" (V. 160). Bickerstaff continued his Preface with a complimentary allusion to his own comic operas:

> It has often been said indeed, that our Language is too hard, and rough to admit of a Union with those graceful and delicate Sounds; but this is a meer Common-place Observation, without any Ground in Reason or Fact; which some late Attempts, to apply English Words to Italian Music on the Stage, have sufficiently destroyed; and the Editor makes no Doubt, the present Work will further prove the Futility of [sic].
>
> It only remains to decide, how far good Music is worth having: They who think it, of no Consequence, will certainly despise this Book; such, on the contrary, as understand, and admire the Art, will probably be glad to have the best Compositions, united to a Language they understand, so as to illustrate both; at a cheaper Rate than they have hitherto purchased the most contemptible Ballads.

Before Bickerstaff presented the music, he explained "such Italian Words as most frequently occur in VOCAL MUSIC BOOKS, Attention to which will be of the greatest Use to Performers." He defined 26 terms, from "Adagio" to "Sotto Voce"; they are standard definitions, typical of which is the explanation of the frequently employed *Da Capo:*

> These Words, at the End of an Air, or their Abreviation [sic] D.C. signify, that the second Part being finished, the first is to be sung over again, beginning the Words, rather without the preluding Symphony, to which the Performer is sometimes guided by the term *al Segno.*

A Select Collection indicates that Bickerstaff knew something about music, and could adapt and edit it even if he did not compose.

In addition to the three-act comic opera Bickerstaff was working on during the autumn and winter of 1771-1772, he had in readiness the *petite* musical piece, "Doctor Ballardo," with music composed by Dibdin.[17] Presumably it was to the three-act opera that Garrick referred when he wrote to John Hoadly on 4 January 1772, "Bickerstaff shew'd me one act of a singing piece, which I have rec'd & approve greatly——" (*Letters,* II, #671, 782). Again, this time on 19 May 1772, Garrick wrote in a letter to Robert Jephson that Bickerstaff "was preparing some pieces that would have been both profitable & creditable—" (II, #688, 801). With the exception of the three-act singing piece, which probably was reduced to two acts and produced in 1775 as *The Sultan,* none of the dramatic works on which Bickerstaff was working at this time reached the stage in traceable form.

During the years that Bickerstaff worked for Covent Garden and Drury Lane, he visited the continent, but nothing indicates how he spent his money. Letters and other evidence prove that he spent a great deal of it. Perhaps the least of it went to rent. From the autumn of 1767 to the end of 1769, Bickerstaff lived in what he called Somerset Yard, but for the tax rates[18] he was listed in Dutchy Lane. The Yard was separated from the Lane by Somerset Stables,[19] where George Garrick lived (*Letters,* II, #614, 719, 15 October 1770). For the two years when Bickerstaff was taxed on Dutchy Lane, he paid £35 rent a year; his tax—which he did not pay for the last quarter in the year 1769, and the first quarter for 1770—was a shilling per pound's rent for a year. After leaving Somerset Yard, Bickerstaff moved to Goodge Street, but there are no records of his tax rate there.

Bickerstaff's income came from three sources: two are known, the third is conjectural. In the first place, he was drawing his half-pay pension of £33. 3s 6d as a second lieutenant in the Marines. Secondly, he had the profits from his produced and printed plays. The third source was from his non-dramatic hack writings.

To examine the second source in more detail: after 1765 he received from Griffin about 50 or 60 guineas for printing a two-act farce, and for a full-length play like *The Plain Dealer,* one hundred guineas.[20] At a Benefit he stood to gain over £100 if the work were popular, and if he had his second and third nights he gained much more.

Both Thomas Arne and Garrick have written on how much an author could hope to make from full-length plays and afterpieces. In 1775, Arne wrote to Garrick asking for £50:

> I think a musician, with regard to theatrical employment, under an unfortunate predicament, if comparatively considered with the author of any little piece, for the following reason. They should both have learning, invention, and a perfect knowledge of effects; but an author of a *petite pièce* can instantaneously write down his thoughts, as they arise, whereas, the poor musician, when he has conceived an air, in every respect suitable to the sense, and emphatically expressed every part, has done but half his business; for he has all the instrumental accompaniments to study and write down; inasmuch as, that in a composition of ten, twelve, or more different parts, when he has written a whole side of music paper, he has the mortification to have composed but one line; all, except the voice part, being requisite to that one line. And yet an author of a farce will frequently make upwards of £100 by his sixth night, besides £50 by the sale of his copy to the printer; while the poor devil of a crotchet-monger is thought well paid with £50 for six times the study and labour. (Boaden, II, 86–87)

Arne's £50 for the crotchet-monger indicates that Dibdin was not so very much underpaid when he received £45 for the music in *The Padlock*.

When Garrick wrote to Suard on 7 March 1776, he explained in detail what a playwright could receive.

> An author who writes a piece of any kind whatever of five acts, is entitled to the third, sixth, and ninth night, and has no other profit from the theatre, but his liberty of the house. We have never had a three-act piece without a petite piece to make up the night's entertainment, and then it is the same thing with a performance of 5 acts; however I should allot 2 benefits and the 3d and 6th night for a 3-act piece; and the author of a farce, or any kind of piece acted *after* the first piece, is entitled to the 6th night. Should a performance have an extraordinary success . . . then the managers will give the author of such a piece a 4th night during the run—but such 4th night cannot be claimed by the author, it is a free gift from the manager. . . . The managers of both theatres have agreed not to perform any of the new pieces which shall be done at either house, till the theatre where any new performance is first acted have enjoy'd it *two* seasons, then it becomes common property. . . . The copyright is his own. The profits, with his copy-money, have sometimes risen to 8 or 9 hundred, and sometimes a thousand pounds. . . . (*Letters*, #983, 1077–79)

As for the third source, the hack writings, Bickerstaff might actually have lost money when he worked on the abortive *Gentleman's Journal,* and only allusions from writers such as Kenrick indicate that Bickerstaff might have been hacking anonymously for some of the London newspapers. In *A Letter to David Garrick Esq.* (London, 1772), Kenrick denounced Bickerstaff, who, "by the assistance of his croney, Griffin, circumvented me in a literary undertaking, which he engaged to conduct for a certain time for twenty guineas, though the proprietors, most of them *honest* booksellers, had actually contracted to pay me a hundred" (p. 32). Kenrick's expression "for a certain time" suggests a periodical, or a "literary undertaking," such as a series of essays. Since he did work with Bickerstaff on the *Gentleman's Journal* Kenrick had some other project in mind. The one non-dramatic work Bickerstaff acknowledged was *A Select Collection of Vocal Music,* but it is impossible to guess what he received.

His income from plays, however much it fluctuated from year to year, should have been considerable. In 1768, a very good year, Bickerstaff earned about £426 from three Benefit performances of *Lionel and Clarissa* during the spring at Covent Garden and perhaps £100 when the opera was printed. In the autumn, at Drury Lane, *The Padlock* and *The Hypocrite* were produced; at Covent Garden, *The Royal Garland.* For *The Padlock,* if Dibdin's word can be trusted, Bickerstaff received about £350 in benefits (*Life,* I, 71). He enjoyed a Benefit for *The Hypocrite*—perhaps £100—and another £100 for its publication. *The Royal Garland* probably brought him very little, £25. But just from his plays, Bickerstaff earned a minimum of £1101 in 1768, about eight times more than he would have earned as a second lieutenant in the Marines.

One year later, 1769, Bickerstaff borrowed £200 on 24 June from Drury Lane.[21] Although he enjoyed two Benefits at the Haymarket Theatre during the summer, he never repaid the debt.

The year 1770 saw *School for Fathers,* Bickerstaff's revision of *Lionel and Clarissa,* performed during the spring, for which he received a Benefit; in the winter, *'Tis Well it's No Worse* earned him three Benefits. At Ranelagh two of his burlettas were played during the summer. For all these works, £600 would seem reasonable—plus his half-pay and whatever he might have made from his non-dramatic writings. With no new plays produced in 1771, and a trip to the continent, Bickerstaff must have relied on income from the projected subscription edition of his fables, perhaps the *Select Collection of Vocal Music,* his pension, miscellaneous writings, and the generosity of David Garrick.

Despite Bickerstaff's varying income, he was in debt in 1768 when he borrowed £100 from Garrick, in 1769 when Drury Lane loaned him £200, and from then on, judging from his letters to Garrick. The only exception to his usual requests for money came on 6 July 1770 when he wrote to Garrick:

> Last night I was tempted to become adventurer at a Raffle, and Fortune favouring me, I won what I send you with this: but why do I lie? Fortune did not favour me but Mrs. Garrick, to whom I made a vow to present it if I was successful; and I earnestly beg that you will be the means of having my vow fulfilled, by prevailing on her to do me the honor to accept it; I wish I was Poet enough to accompany it with a copy of verses.[22]

Usually Bickerstaff's letters illustrate his perpetual insolvency and his attempt to ask for the same thing in a different way. For instance, on a "Wednesday Noon" he wrote to Garrick:

> To ask favours is at any time irksome to a feeling man, but to be so repeatedly troublesome, as I am to you carries such an air of presuming

upon your goodness, that I protest, and the expression is strictly truth, I blush while I write this letter to you.

The inclosed paper will let you know what I want you to do for me, and farther explanation you need not. I consider that I write to Mr. Garrick, whose nature I know is truly good and kind, and who though placed by God above necessities himself can feel for those of others.

I shall only add, Dear Sir, that the inclosed note will be punctually paid, which I can answer for, and that if you should generously consider my request with indulgence, you will if possible make me more truly and strongly than I am already, Your obliged, devoted, and grateful servant.[23]

Garrick responded promptly, for in a letter marked "Wednesday Evening," Bickerstaff wrote:

I beg you will give me leave to return you my most humble and grateful thanks for the exceeding generosity and humanity with which you have been pleased to grant my request. But what signifies my praise and my thanks where they can do you no good; and yet you can have in return but all I have to give. I am, Dear Sir, With the greatest respect and attachment Your most grateful and most humble servant.[24]

On 16 March 1771, in Bickerstaff's letter to Garrick about his fables, Bickerstaff alluded to a debt, "I have been my own dupe, and the dupe of others; what I have erred in at the instigation of my own folly, I have corrected. Some little success in subscribing my Fables would repair all, and I think I shall err no more" (Boaden, I, 417-418). If his erring referred to his debts —however he incurred them—he erred again by 21 May 1771. On that occasion he was Poet enough to rhyme his request for £50, and Garrick sent him the money.

Still, dear Sir, so much good-nature
You have shown to me your creature,
That 'tis now a thing of course,
And you are my first resource,
Fifty times, as I suppose,
I have troubled you in prose;
Let me, if I can, a while
Strive at least to change my style;
Change of style is all my aim,
For my subject is the same;
And in prose or verse a craver,
I must write to beg a favour.

"Well!" cry you with peevish brow,
"What the plague's the matter now?
Teas'd and worried at this rate:

What's inclos'd here—after date?
Promise in six months to pay
Griffin—Ay, this is his way;
Every now and then to send me:
To these Irishmen commend me!
But if in again I'm drawn,
Next he'll send me his brogues to pawn;
And expect me at his need;
Fifty pounds!—not I indeed.
"Hark'e, George, come hither, quick
Give this paper back to Bick;
Tell him that I gladly wou'd
Do him any sort of good;
But demand upon demand
Forces me to stop my hand;
And in short—(but don't be rough)—
Say I *can't*, and that's enough."

Thus, dear Sir, however I
Your good-nature mean to try;
'Tis not but I know in fact
How your judgment ought to act;
And whatever my success,
I am not obliged the less;
But while memory endures
Shall remain for ever yours. (Boaden, I, 423. Endorsed, "Bickerstaff's letter in verse for £50, lent directly.")

Even though "fifty times" is an exaggeration for the number of times Bickerstaff borrowed from Garrick, it is no wonder that according to William Cooke, Bickerstaff "ran away as much for debt as for the crimes imputed to him."[25]

Two years before he fled, a cryptic reference to Bickerstaff appeared in the July issue of the *Town and Country Magazine,* in the first part of "Memoirs of a Sad-Dog" by "Harry Wildfire" (Thomas Chatterton):

> But alas! happiness is of short duration; or, to speak in the language of the high-sounding Ossian, "Behold! thou art happy. . . . The noisy thunders roar; the rapid lightnings gleam; the rainy torrents pour, and the dropping swain flies over the mountain: swift as Bickerstaff, the son of song, when the monster Bumbailiano, keeper of the dark and black cave, pursued him over the hills of death, and the green meadows of dark men." (July, 1770, p. 375)[26]

No doubt, stripped of "high-sounding Ossian," Bickerstaff was avoiding arrest by a bumbailiff, but why? And where did he go?

And where did the money go? Because it costs more to enjoy

vice than virtue, Bickerstaff's finances were exhausted either by general incontinence, or by specialization. Denying the charge of homosexuality—belatedly—a writer for the *Theatrical Inquisitor and Monthly Mirror* declared in 1816, that Bickerstaff "had been conspicuous, for his amorous attachments to the better half of creation, and Dr. Johnson asserts, with a deep knowledge of human nature, that no man is a hypocrite in his pleasures" (IX, December, 1816, 248). No matter which half of creation Bickerstaff loved, his debts were recorded as Notes or I.O.U.'s according to his letters, not as *billets doux.* In any case, when Bickerstaff fled to St. Malo in May 1772, he was not so much worried about insolvency—that was to come—as he was concerned about avoiding a possible death sentence.

12
"THE DEED WITHOUT A NAME"

"Mr. Mervyn Griffith-Jones, prosecuting counsel . . . said: 'It is a perfectly ordinary little case of a man charged with indecency with four or five guardsmen.' " (*New Statesman,* "This England," 20 September 1963)

During the early part of 1772 Bickerstaff was accepted by critics and fellow writers as both a competent playwright and a plagiarist—the two being not incompatible. Though he had not brought out a full-length comic opera since *School for Fathers* in 1770, and his comedy of intrigue, *'Tis Well it's No Worse,* had been withdrawn after ten nights, still his contemporaries expected that Bickerstaff would produce another popular comic opera, if not during the 1771-1772 season then surely in the next.

Typical of the notices he received was the one on 7 January 1772 in which a critic passingly referred to "the *ingenious* Mr. Bickerstaff, who with respect to an Air or an Opera, is as good a plagiarist as any of his Majesty's domains."[1] On the other hand, the anonymous author of *Letters Concerning the Present State of England* concluded his letter on the "Present State of the Theatre," with "a few remarks on the theatrical writers that have made the greatest figure in this age": Colman, Garrick, Hoadley, Murphy, Bickerstaff, Cumberland and Foote:

Bickerstaff has had the honour of introducing a new species of theatric entertainments on the stage, of which the idea is taken from the French Ballats: music is introduced in the most agreeable manner possible; and in the *Maid of the Mill,* it is excellent music; the success that piece has met with, shews, that the mere English audience can relish other compositions than a Scotch ballad, if it is laid before them; but the popularity of those in a vulgar stile, arises from continued efforts to please the gallery.[2]

The popularity of Bickerstaff's operas can be seen on an unusual "Old English Music Handkerchief," 25″ x 27″, which was sold around 1771 with scores and pictures of favorite operas printed on it. Mattocks as the Squire, and DuBellamy as Thomas in *Thomas and Sally,* decorate two corners. Beard appears as Hawthorn from *Love in a Village,* and black-faced Dibdin shows up as Mungo in *The Padlock.* The score from one of Leonora's songs is there, as well as one of Hawthorn's. Only two musical works not by Bickerstaff also appear: *Midas* and *Tom Jones.* In addition there are two unidentified fragments of songs, and four catches.[3]

In March 1772, Bickerstaff, Sir Joshua Reynolds, "and a friend or two more," dined with Goldsmith at Farmer Selby's house "about six miles from [London]" on the Edgeware Road.[4] As at most dinners without Boswell, no one recorded what was said; the incident merely shows that Bickerstaff was enjoying a typical spring. Possibly he discussed his fables with Goldsmith, who wrote children's tales for Newbery. Nothing foreshadows Garrick's comment on 19 May 1772, "My Wife & I have long thought [Bickerstaff] to be out of his Mind—he has hurry'd away in the midst of Conversation, without any apparent reason for it—" (*Letters,* II, #688, 801).

By 19 May, however, Bickerstaff's reputation was gone, and he himself was hiding in France. Plagiarism was counted as the least of his sins, and ignored was his introduction of "a new species of theatric entertainment" to the English stage. The public notices that assassinated his character began innocuously enough, but by the end of the summer, enthusiastic muckrakers had covered Bickerstaff's name with sufficient filth to keep it buried until now.

On Thursday, 30 April, and on Friday, 1 May 1772 there appeared in *The Daily Advertiser* the following advertisement:

Whereas on Tuesday Night last [April 28], between the hours of Eight and Ten, A Gentleman left with a Centinel belonging to Whitehall Guard, a Guinea and a half, and a Metal Watch with two Seals, the one a Cypher, the other a Coat of Arms, a Locket, and a Pistol Hook. The Owner may have it again by applying to the Adjutant of the first Battalion of the first Regiment of Foot-Guards at the Savoy Barracks, and paying for this Advertisement.[5]

The Savoy Barracks ran parallel to Dutchy Lane where Bickerstaff had lived, and were separated from it by the French Church, and some private dwellings including the one in which the printer, Thomas Cadell, lived. At the same time that *The Daily Advertiser* published the foregoing notice, the *St. James Chronicle* and *Lloyd's Evening Post* ran the following explanation of it:

Saturday. London. An Advertisement has appeared giving Notice, that the Gentleman who left his Watch, Seal and Rings, &c. with a Soldier, may have them again, by applying to the Savoy. The History of this Watch, &c. is this: A *Gentleman* grew enamoured, the other Night at Whitehall, with one of the Centinels, and made Love to him; the Soldier being of that rough cast, who would rather act in the Character of *Mars* than a *Venus,* not only rejected the Lover's Suit, but seizing him, threatened to take him immediately to the Guard-Room. The affrighted Enamorato, to avoid the consequences of Exposure, with the greatest Precipitation gave the Soldier his Watch, Rings, and other Valuables, for his Liberty. The Centinel, rejoicing at his good Fortune, soon after tells the Corporal, the Corporal the Serjeant, the Serjeant the Adjutant, and he to the whole Corps of Officers. The Articles of Ransom were examined; one was a Mourning Ring of a Lady who died at Gibraltar; and the Watch had its Maker's Name; he was applied to, and he instantly declared to whom he had sold it, about two months since, a Man of some Fame in the Literary World. Here at present the Incident rests; and there is no Doubt but the honest Soldier will become entitled to the Whole, as it is presumed the owner will scarcely apply for a Return of them.[6]

In a slightly modified form, *The Gentleman's Magazine* for May explained the advertisement in its "Historical Chronicle, Friday, May 1":

An advertisement appeared in the papers, giving notice, that the *Gentleman* who left his watch, seal, and rings, with a soldier, may have them again by applying to the Savoy.—*"Hereto hangth a tale."*—A *Gentleman* became suddenly enamoured of this soldier, who, not liking his manner of address, seized him, and threatened, instead of retiring to a private corner, to carry him instantly before his officer. The gentleman, to procure his release, and to avoid the infamy of being publicly exposed, gave the soldier all that he had valuable about him. The soldier, rejoicing in his good fortune, acquainted his corporal with what had happened, the corporal the serjeant, and so on, till every officer in the corps was apprized of it.—The matter, by means of the watch and seals, has since been traced pretty near home; but as no claim has yet been made, it is thought the soldier will be left in possession of his prize. (XLII, May, 1772. 241.)

With the helpful explanations being printed simultaneously

with the advertisement, no wonder "it is presumed the owner will scarcely apply for a Return" of his belongings! Between the night of 28 April and 1 May, the soldier and his officers found out who owned the watch and other belongings, and deciding to embarrass their owner, wrote the advertisement and "leaked" the story to the other newspapers. Confronted by probable exposure by name whether or not he dared apply for his belongings, and fearing social ostracism and criminal proceedings, Bickerstaff fled the country.

At first the story was known only to a sniggering few. On 9 May, for instance, *The London Chronicle* showed its ignorance by featuring on its front page, *Sentimental Fables* . . . "ascribed to I——c B——f," and on 12-14 May it printed another fable, which it then confidently (but mistakenly) announced was one of "Bickerstaff's Fables" (XXXI, 460). But by 18 May the news had spread out of London: the *Northampton Mercury* reported, "The Literary Character, who has lately absconded in consequence of a detestable attempt in the Park, acknowledges his own guilt in terms of the deepest remorse, and discovers, we hear, a degree of compunction, that sheds a little gleam of merit upon him, even in the midst of so abominable a depravity."[7]

Once the story was released with Bickerstaff's name as the culprit, mere boundaries could not confine it. In Dublin, Robert Jephson heard it early in May, for on 19 May *in reply* to a query from Jephson, Garrick wrote:

> On Eagle's Wings immortal Scandals fly!—So Dryden says, & his Saying is verified by the late Accident, which, I fear, will imbitter the Life of Miserable B——! the affair is reported here just as You seem to have heard it—He is gone, & has written to Mr. Griffin the Bookseller a letter, which shock'd Me beyond imagination—all his friends hang their heads & grieve sincerely at his Misfortune—My Wife & I have long thought him to be out of his Mind—he has hurry'd away in the midst of Conversation, without any apparent reason for it—the Story they tell, if true, is a most unaccountable one; but the Watch, Seal & ring are in the Soldier's hands & B—— would not claim them, but absconded—this business has hurt me greatly, as well as my Wife, the Stage has a great loss, for he was preparing some pieces that would have been both profitable, & creditable— (*Letters,* II, #688, 801.)

To avoid prosecution, Bickerstaff went to France, where from St. Malo, on 24 June he wrote to Garrick in his uncertain French:

> *Mon*[r]. *Si votre coeur a conservé jusqu'a present la moindre trace de cette*

prévention que vous avez autrefois avoué pour un homme qui est aujourdui le plus malhereux qui soit sur la terre; je vous supplie de me le faire connoitre par trois ou quatre mots addressés pour M. Burrows chez M. Vogius Fils Libraire au cotes de cathedral a Saint Malo Bretagn, France.

Penetrer avec une chagrin le plus amer que peut blesser le coeur, soyez persuadé Monsieur que je ne rien de demander de votre bonté que la seul licence de vous ecrire plus au large; si vous n'etes pas dans le sentiment de me permetre, imaginez que cette lettre vien d'un mort, au vivant, jettez la dans le feu, et n'en pensez plus. Je ne pas la moindre doute Mon[r] *que mon chagrin me portera au tombeau, mais par une chemin peutetre, plus long que Je ne le souhaiterai, et cette pensée et une grande augmentation de mes peines car ayant perdu mes amis, mes esperances; tombé, exilé, et livré au desespoir comme je suis, la vie et un fardeau presque insupportable: j'etois loin de soup'zonner, que le dernier fois que J'entré dans votre Librarie, sera Le dernier fois que j'y entrerai de ma vie, et que je ne reverai plus le maitre! mais celle ci est une reflection que je fait le moins souvent que m'est possible.*

Je vous supplie Mon[r]*. de ne dire a personne, que Je vous ai ecrit, et sur tout de gardé silence sur la place de ma retraite, qui est une chose pour moi de la plus grand consequence, comme Je vous ai dit deja, si vous ne me ferai pas la consolation d'une lettre brulez celle-ci et restez comme si elle n'avoit Jamais tombé entre vos mains; si au contraire, votre compassion pour un misserable l'emport, personne* saura *que vous avez eu tant de bonte pour Lui. dieu vous garde mon tres cheri, et tres honoré Monsieur, et comble vous et le votre, avec toute la felicite de cette monde, si y vous rest de demander encore. Je voudrai dire Beaucoup plus, mais je ne sai pas quoi; Je crains fort, que vous aurez de peine d'expliquer mon mauvais Francois.*

Garrick endorsed the letter, "From that poor wretch Bickerstaff. I could not answer it."[8]

With that letter, the most poignant he ever wrote, Bickerstaff retired from a paper war which had scarcely begun. It was fought through the summer months by Kenrick and his allies, against the pro-Garrick forces led by Paul Hiffernan. The issue was Garrick's reputation—for Kenrick had little to lose—and the outcome was a formal surrender by Kenrick and vindication for Garrick. There was also a discreet, and incidental, burial of Bickerstaff's reputation, for Garrick could win only by a thorough disassociation from his erstwhile friend.

None of the printed gossip before 1772 hinted that Bickerstaff might have been homosexual, and even during the printed donnybrook there were only two cryptic allusions to a "masculine dancer," and an even more mysterious line about a letter which Garrick's brother sent. One man loudly said, "I told you so": "when Mr. Bickerstaff's flight confirmed the report of his guilt,

Mr. Thrale said, in answer to Johnson's astonishment, that he had long been a suspected man." Dr. Johnson superbly replied, "By those who look close to the ground, dirt will be seen, Sir. I hope I see things from a greater distance."[9]

As early as 1748 Garrick and Kenrick had been feuding; in that year Kenrick wrote *The Town* (London: R. Griffiths), in which he satirized Garrick, among others. But Garrick's dislike of Kenrick did not prevent him from producing the latter's *Falstaff's Wedding* on 12 April 1766, and his *Widow'd Wife* on 5 December 1767.[10] With the failure of those plays, and the success of others by authors he despised, Kenrick grew increasingly impatient with Garrick and all of the manager's friends. By the spring of 1772, Kenrick's patience was just about used up; if Garrick would not bring out one of his new pieces, would he get up *Falstaff's Wedding* so that Kenrick could have his author's night? He asked for Garrick's decision in writing, having refused to meet with him. Garrick wrote on 14 June, "Be that as it may, as I have something of consequence to both of us to communicate to you, I must again desire to see you—when you have obliged me by naming at what time and place, I shall have the pleasure of seeing you to-morrow morning" (Kenrick, *A Letter,* p. 29). Both men being engaged on Monday, Garrick named Tuesday morning (16 June), and "nine o'clock at the Green-Park coffee-house" as the meeting place. But before then, Kenrick learned from his bookseller, Evans, that Garrick had threatened "to do him [Kenrick] some personal mischief" (*A Letter,* p. 30). On Monday, 15 June, Kenrick wrote a blustering letter to Garrick, in which, among other things, he warned, "You shall not have any reason . . . to complain for the future, of my not being sufficiently your open enemy" (p. 31). On receiving this letter, Garrick immediately wrote a courageous reply . . . which he did not send.[11]

Apparently it was Foote, not Garrick, who was going to attack Kenrick, for in a letter to Captain Edward Thompson on 20 June, Garrick spoke of "the unjust virulence of Foote, who, as he says, had rather be witty than either just or wise; he had been going to beat Dr. Kenrick for his infamy, but the latter 'smok'd ye crab tree,' and wrote a most cowardly letter; Garrick concluded by referring to Bickerstaff's flight . . . —'What a wretch he must be.' "[12]

The 16 June meeting did not take place, but Kenrick's attack on Garrick did. Garrick had wished to see Kenrick to forestall any further circulation of the lampoon, *Love in the Suds,* which suggested that both Bickerstaff *and* Garrick were homosexuals. "About this time," according to Kenrick, "I had written the lampoon . . . of which I had printed a small number, to distribute among my acquaintance, many of whom knew in what manner I had been ill treated both by Roscius and Nyky. . . ." (p. 31).[13] Although Kenrick denied it, the poem had been written to blackmail Garrick into producing Kenrick's play. Not so, wrote Kenrick, "if Roscius had done me the justice I had a right to demand of him, instead of insolently threatening me . . . I might have thought the circulation of the few, I first printed, a sufficient chastisement for his folly, in countenancing Nyky; yet that it was first written with any other view than the liberal one I have before explained, or that I advertised or acquainted Roscius with my design, even in the most indirect or distant manner, *in terrorem,* is an absolute falsehood" (p. 33).

On Monday, 22 June, there appeared in the *St. James Chronicle* (#1769) what seems to have been the first public advertisement for *Love in the Suds:*

> This Day was published,
> (A proper Companion to Love in a Village, and Love in a City,)
> LOVE in the SUDS. A Town Eclogue.
> Being the Lamentations of Roscius for the Loss of his
> —nytry. [sic] With Imitations and Notes.
> By the EDITOR
> Printed for J. Wheble, in Pater-noster-Row.

Kenrick admitted in his *Letter,* "that, by way of mortification, I had advertised my lampoon, not as really published to be sold, but as something in embrio, or contemplation."

> The advertisement, however [Kenrick continued], was too striking, or the consciences of the parties too tender, for them not to take a most terrible alarm. Roscius, with his brother, their retainers, authors, printers, and printer's devils, were in an instant put in motion; orders were dispatched to prevent the advertisement's being inserted in the Public Advertiser, the Gazetteer, the St. James's Chronicle, the London Packet, and every other popular news-paper, in which Roscius was either a sharer, or over which he had any influence. Even the printer of the paper in which it first appeared, refused, though he had been paid for it, to print it a second time. (*Letter*, p. 32)

Because the advertisement was not repeated, and considering that *The Morning Chronicle* was the only newspaper in which both sides warred during the weeks that followed the publication of *Love in the Suds,* Garrick probably did do his best to keep the scandal out of the papers. The London presses were owned by unlikely combinations of writers and booksellers. *The London Packet,* for instance, was a paper in which Garrick, George Colman, Captain Thompson, and Thomas Becket, among others, owned shares (Page, pp. 226-226). Colman also had shares in the *Public Advertiser* and the *St. James Chronicle,*[14] while Garrick held a twentieth share in the latter paper (*Letters,* #280, 349). The *Morning Chronicle* was owned by twenty shareholders including William Kenrick, William Griffin, Thomas Evans, and George Kearsly.[15] Having been denied access to the *St. James Chronicle,* Kenrick advertised in the *Morning Chronicle* on 29 June (#967); again the advertisement announced, "This Day is published . . ." and included for the first time the price, 2s 6d; the original "—nytry" was now "Nyky."

But *Love in the Suds* was not the first widely read attack on Garrick, for on 18 June, the *Public Ledger* published a poem entitled *Leap-Frog,* a nasty work Kenrick consistently denied writing.[16] No copies of the 18 June *Ledger* seem to have survived, but a penned copy of the poem was sent to Garrick; it is all that remains of the letter: the signature is gone, and there is no indication whether the sender was also the author of the poem, an officious friend, or an enemy of Garrick. "Leap-Frog":

As Dapper *Davy* & his favourite Bick
gambol'd from sport to sport from trick to trick
Davy in glee his Sooty Bick ajog.
They'd play'd at length that hateful game *leap frog.*
Poor Bicky fear'd discovery & shame,
But Davy sooth'd him, & *play'd out the game*
Poor Davy sooth'd him [crossed out]
"No eye, tho' e'er so peircing now can *bore* us"
Says the Theatric Caesar to his *Sporus*
"These pleasures licenc'd for the Rich, I prove,
"Illicit rapture, & forbidden Love.
"Let vulgar minds keep *Nature* in their Sight.
"I snatch a joy *beyond the rule of Right*
"Why do I drudge [?] the Monarch of a Stage,
"When sickness presses a declining age?
"What more can [honor?] wish than fame & money [illegible]
"To Tilney the whole Dramatis Personae.
"To Tilney authors Comic—*haud indignum*
"Authors of Farce & Opera—*Ecce signum!"*
"—Bick renews his fears; says crafty Davy,
"Even in *Discovery* my *power* can save you;

"If eyes obtrude, no doubt this sight won't please 'em,
"—But, my dear *Bick—ne times, vehis Caesarem."* [dated] 18th June 1772[17]

Deservedly, the publisher of the *Public Ledger* was taken to court by Garrick for permitting the offensive "Leap Frog" to be printed. On Friday, 19 June, the *Morning Chronicle* lifted its editorial hands in pious indignation:

> To Our Correspondents: The Charge of an abominable crime against a respectable character, shall not appear in the *Morning Chronicle,* imputations of this sort, unsupported by proof, are in the highest degree indefensible and cruel; if a plain positive fact can be proved against any persons so unnaturally depraved, we should join most readily in hunting such members from Society; but we neither should forgive ourselves, nor do we imagine the world would ever shew us a momentary countenance, were we so lost to consideration, humanity and feeling, as to become the willing instruments of fixing a stigma of the blackest and most indelible kind on an innocent person. (#959)

After such a pronouncement, it was only to be expected that the *Morning Chronicle* would not only "join most readily in" the hunt, but also it would be far and away the leader of the pack. Between 19 June and 15 August it published about 130 poetical and prose pieces, the majority siding with Garrick. The *St. James Chronicle,* which first helped publicize the original incident, published a few poems and essays ridiculing Kenrick, and letters which concerned themselves loftily with libel, satire, and the role of a newspaper. The *Middlesex Journal* occasionally ran summaries of articles from the *Morning Chronicle* and published notices generally unfavorable to Kenrick but impatient with the continued prominence of the controversy.

On Tuesday, 30 June, a poem was published in the *London Evening Post* (#6940) which was dated, "St. James's Coffee-House, June 24," and was entitled, "Verses to Dr.******, on his having announced in the newspapers, a Satirical Epistle to Mr. G*****, and afterwards relinquished his design." Calling both Garrick and Kenrick "knaves," the poet concluded:

> A truce prevails! behold a subsidy
> From Av'rice wrung, by Fear and Vanity!
> Resentment's hush'd, Rage sleeps, and Anger's dead!
> Money buys G****** peace, the Doctor, bread.
> The muzzl'd sat'rist sounds a mean *retreat;*
> Doctors tho' stor'd with poetry, *must eat.*

His venom ceases when the money's clutch'd,
Like the *King's evil,* cur'd by being touch'd.

If the poem had been circulated around the coffee houses the week before it was published in the *London Evening Post,* it probably spurred Kenrick to insist that *Love in the Suds* be published in retaliation, to prove that he had not been bought off.

Once *Love in the Suds* was available to the general public—as early as 27 June—and not to the few readers for whom Kenrick claimed he had originally printed it, Garrick had to decide how to reply. He could answer Kenrick directly, by letter or in print. But other men who had been attacked by Kenrick knew that he thrived on controversy; Dr. Johnson, for instance, refused to answer Kenrick's attack on his edition of Shakespeare: "a man whose business it is to be talked of, is much helped by being attacked" (Forster, *Goldsmith,* 492). Still, Garrick had been accused of sodomy, or at least of guilt by association. Perhaps the retort poetical would do:

6

My Morals tho they know & feel,
Cursing & curs'd thro Life I reel;
  The Well known *Brandy Billy*
Yet *grinning with a ghastly Smile*
I can some Soft ones Still beguile,
Cadell, & *Silly Dolly* [publishers. "Dolly" was either
      Charles or his brother, Edward Dilly.]

7

Let honest Blockheads plod for bread
I must with Schemes be better fed
  Produce Each Day new Notions;
I with my Lodgings change my plan,
Shift here & there, cheat all I can
With *my perpetual Motions.* [Kenrick claimed he
      had discovered the secret.]

8

Let Others Sweat to wear ye bays,
I at my leisure Scribble plays;
  So Sceming [sic] is my head:
Nor heed I tho the Grubs have bray'd
That these my Plays are seldom play'd,
And never, never read!

9

While good folks wish & Strive for peace

I would my Country's feuds Encrease,
  A Carrion Crow for blood,
What Genius does I would undo,
And cry with Judas, & his Crew,
  Evil be Thou my good![18]

But the poetical fragment, with Kenrick as speaker, was never published. Instead, Garrick turned to the law. Although libel suits were common at this time, "the law of libel was in rather a confused state. . . ." But on 2 February 1768, Blackstone had given an opinion which greatly facilitated Garrick's action. "A plaintiff only needed to prove the fact of publication, give reasons for supposing the defendant the author, and sign an affidavit that it was generally understood that the libel was intended to point to him, to win his case."[19] Accordingly, Garrick's barristers presented three witnesses who signed affidavits.[20] Harry Burt swore that on 7 July he bought a copy of *Love in the Suds* at Wheble's shop in Paternoster Row, and while there heard from "such Servant or Shopman" that Kenrick was the author. William Parker declared that on having "perused" the letter and poem, he "apprehends that by the word Roscius in the title page the author means . . . David Garrick Esquire, and by the word Nyky . . . one Isaac Bickerstaff a person heretofore occasionally Employed by . . . David Garrick in writing or correcting of writings and productions . . . for David Garrick . . . [at] Drury Lane . . . And this Deponent saith that by common report he hath heard that the said Isaac Bickerstaff hath been lately accused of having made an attempt to commit an unnatural crime with a Grenadier or Soldier in Saint James's Park and hath since on account thereof left this kingdom and gone abroad beyond seas." Parker understood from the poem that it was Kenrick's intention "to raise and propagate a scandalous insinuation against the character of the said David Garrick and if possible to induce the Publick to consider the said David Garrick as a person concerned in sodomitical practices with the said Isaac Bickerstaff." The third witness was John Rees Stokes, clerk to "Messrs Wallis and Parkes," Garrick's solicitors. He swore that on 27 June he bought *Love in the Suds* from Wheble's shop where he heard from a shopman that it had been printed and published there. Stokes heard that Kenrick had written it, and that it reflected adversely on Garrick's character. Thus the three witnesses supplied all the requirements for Garrick to win a libel suit. Kenrick's letter (*A Letter to David Garrick, Esq.,* "Occasioned By his having moved the Court of King's Bench against the Publisher of Love in the Suds. . . .") was added to *Love in the Suds* and both it and the poem were submitted as evidence and dated 27 June. The poem "was read in Court by the Clerk of the Crown, and afforded no small diversion when it came to that part which reflects upon a certain Chief Justice [Mansfield], who was present all the time" (*Morning Chronicle*, #975, 8 July); the hearing was on 7 July. Acting for Garrick, Dunning "made a motion in the Court of King's Bench, for a rule to show cause why an information should not be granted against [Kenrick] . . . the Court was pleased to grant a rule for the first day of next term" (#975, 8 July). In the meantime, Kenrick was to be apprised of the court's decision (PRO, KB 21/40). "Upon reading the same affidavits and Pamphlets annexed the like Rule for John Wheble to shew cause why an Information should not be Exhibited against him for certain Misdemeanors in Printing and publishing a Scandalous libel Upon Notice of this Rule to be given to him in the mean time" (PRO, KB 21/40). Besides Dunning, Wallace [Wallis?], Murphy and Mansfield were engaged to help Garrick (#975, 8 July).

Having "submitted my cause to ye laws of my country," Garrick was content to "abide by their Determination. . ." (*Letters*, II, #711, 821). Garrick saw himself as the injured, law-abiding citizen, and once he allowed the court to prosecute Kenrick, he abstained from personal attacks.

> I most Solemnly protest to You [Garrick wrote to Peter Fountain in January 1773], & give you my Word & honour, y^{t} so far from having any hand in such dirty Work that I would not read a Single paper, nor have I to this Moment—I hinder'd Every friend I had that could write from meddling with the Matter—I had recourse to ye Laws of my Country, & I thought myself bound in honour not, in any way else, to Endeavor my own vindication. . . . (II, #732, 844–845)

Even without Garrick's encouragement, the *Morning Chronicle* was filled with poetic and prose support for him, and because of pressure from him, the other papers for the most part abstained from comment. Garrick's aloofness was pictured in different ways: Kenrick pictured him as the foe to honest satirists, who, with his minions denied Kenrick the freedom of the press while tacitly allowing him to be attacked. Dibdin was convinced that Garrick was relieved to see the last of Bickerstaff, although not at the price of *Love in the Suds:*

> [Garrick] had engaged me, and, probably, had an eye to my being

composer to the house, if the *Padlock* should succeed. . . . (*Life,* I, 69) [Garrick] therefore conceived my whole employ would be to set words of his writing. . . . For this purpose, he was scheming to get rid of Mr. Bickerstaff as fast as he could, and the very particular civilities he just then shewed that pretty gentleman, to cover his intention, probably procured him that . . . poem from Dr. Kenrick. . . . (*Harmonicon,* p. 89)

[Kenrick's attack] might have crushed almost any man but GARRICK, especially such conduct as he adopted, for the steps he took to conquer it were, by no means of the alert kind.

. . . .

He incurred the libel, very probably, by the civilities he shewed BICKERSTAFF at the time he was meditating to get rid of him; and, thus, what was no more than duplicity, was by the machinations of a rascal, construed into infamy. (*Life,* I, 84–86)

To read Garrick's letters, he simply let court action take its course. Kenrick, of course, thought Garrick was as actively engaged in the paper-war as he was, while Dibdin believed that Garrick was altogether too lenient with Kenrick. Bickerstaff heard still a different view.

It is now somewhat more than four years since I was informed, that about that time you not only joined in favour of an ungrateful, perjured, dishonest wretch, who was cutting my throat with my own weapons, to drag a brand of infamy upon me that utterly deprived me of the means of earning bread, but that you also lent your wit upon the occasion; writ letters in newspapers, particularly some in the Morning Post, with an intent to destroy me, as far as the work was still to be done. (Boaden, II, 207–208. Letter dated 18 March, 1777 from Bickerstaff)[21]

Whoever it was who informed Bickerstaff of Garrick's actions, he was no friend of either man. Perhaps, as Dibdin declared, Garrick *was* scheming to get rid of Bickerstaff—although Bickerstaff was preparing musical works for Drury Lane—but it is absurd to think of Garrick joining Kenrick to attack Bickerstaff.

Both Bickerstaff and Kenrick's poem were considered embarrassments to the partisans of each side; they were disposed of early in the war, which became a dogfight with the correspondents nipping at each other's tails. *Love in the Suds; A Town Eclogue, Being the Lamentation of Roscius for the Loss of his Nyky*[22] was the best of the lamentably large number of verse epistles, town eclogues, fables, and juvenilia which filled the papers. It consisted of 340 lines written in doggerel couplets; in them appeared much biographical information about Bickerstaff, ironically not found elsewhere, and references to his run-in with the grenadier. "Roscius" is the speaker, and between his own comments, and the "editor's" notes, Garrick is condemned and Kenrick praised. In the same manner, the newspapers friendly to Garrick are satirized, and those who are "independent" are complimented. Playwrights whose works have been produced while Kenrick's have been ignored are damned, and so the poem goes until some of the best people of the age have been lashed by Kenrick.

Ironically, in the squabble that followed, Kenrick has to be relied on for identification of some of the participants. Kenrick had fewer adherents, or more literary masks, as it appears that he wrote most of his defenses himself. His leading opponent, according to Kenrick, was Paul Hiffernan, who appeared in various guises and was chopped down by Kenrick in each of them. Actually Hiffernan (if it were he) provided the only comic relief from the sordid mess because he never knew when he was beaten, and he was *always* beaten.

As "Mother Shipton," Hiffernan began his attack on Tuesday, 30 June, with "A Monitory Card": "Mother Shipton presents, not her compliments, but hints, to the literary culprit, that she has now under her cognizance a *certain Lucubration,* that shall prove before the tribunal of the publick, his certain *Tenebrification. Billy,* my dear, how foolishly you'll look!" (*Morning Chronicle,* #968). On 7 July, Mother Shipton published a long exegesis of Kenrick's poem; it effectively revealed the weak point of the pro-Garrick clan, for instead of answering Kenrick's charges it ridiculed him and attempted to avoid the subject by pedantically pointing out the inaccuracies (#974). Kenrick's side replied to Mother Shipton's salvo on Wednesday, 8 July (#975):

> *To the pretended* Mother Shipton, *author of the elaborate and learned criticism* on his "Lamentations of Roscius," *inserted in yesterday's paper.*
>
> THOU, *Mother Shipton!*—Thou hast not her nose.
> Some filthy male art thou in woman's clothes:
> No, by the beastly look and brazen brow,
> No simple fortune-telling bawd art thou:
> Thou'rt *gallows-Paul**! I know thee by this light,
> *Roscius's* runner, pimp, and parasite!
>
> *Dr. P[au]l H[ifferna]n, long known by the above appellation among his friends and companions, the Printer's Devils, of whose consequences he is so very tenacious; he is, however, in the opinion of Roscius, one of the first dramatic writers of the age, and is to father the embriobrats of the fugitive Nyky, of which he is accordingly preparing to lie-in next winter.

On Thursday, 9 July, *Love in the Suds* was advertised as being readied for a second edition, "printed in quarto," the first edition having been a folio (#976). In the succeeding issues of the *Morning Chronicle* neither side seriously considered answering the charges of the other. Occasionally a correspondent cried out "a plague on both your houses," or attempted to impose some decorum, but the combatants were having too much fun to worry about the causes of the battle. Every so often somebody remembered Bickerstaff:

> A certain literary character, who lately absconded in Consequence of a detestable Attempt, is, we are told, shut up in a little Retreat on the Sea Coast, where he flies to drinking as a Refuge from Thought, and generally consumes two Quarts of Spirits in the Course of the Day. (*St. James Chronicle,* #1778, 10 July)

Nobody paid any attention. If no one had pity for a repentant alcoholic, perhaps a hanged one might do:

> Conscious that his conduct will not bear examination [Garrick] would wish to suppress all conversation about, or enquiry into it. Hence it is that he hath caused it to be industriously reported that his late friend and favourite has had the virtue to hang himself; and therefore now, *nil nisi bonum de mortuis;* the name of Nyky must be buried in oblivion. But till I am better assured of the fact, neither my tongue nor pen shall be so obsequious to the good pleasure of Roscius.
>
> Forbid my tongue to speak of Nyky!
> I will go find him when he lies asleep,
> And in his ear I'll holla Nyky!
> Nay, I will have a starling taught to speak
> Nothing but Nyky, and give it him
> To keep his anger still in motion. [signed] VERITATIBUS
> (*Morning Chronicle,* 17 July, #983)

In the 25 July *Morning Chronicle,* one of the six pieces involved in the fray alluded to an incident between Kenrick and Foote which presumably took place about the time that Kenrick "smok'd ye crab tree"—about 16 June. In a long allegorical letter by "T. H."—entitled "The last Lesson appointed for this Morning's Chronicle, is the first Chapter of the Acts of Doctor Daedalus"—the writer suggested that Kenrick was envious of Bickerstaff's success:

> 12. And rushing into the theatre [Haymarket] at the time of the morning rehearsal, he [Kenrick] communed with that comic genius [Foote] and spake thus unto him [about slandering Garrick].
> 13. Then Aristophanes, the son of Thalia, took up his parable and said:

> O Daedalus, Doctor newly created! though thou art a Goliath of Gath in thine own eye, yet little David has cracked thy perricranium, which brother Stevens [George Alexander], having dissected, discovered to be an empty void.
>
> . . . .
>
> 16. And it came to pass that Aristophanes being in wrath, lifted up his toe, even the toe of that *Foote* which is composed of cork, and straightway applying it to the posterior front of Daedalus the Doctor, thrust him forth from the theatre. (#990)

In the same issue of the *Morning Chronicle,* "B.T." from Kenrick's side, raised one of those obvious questions which both sides did their best to avoid, and alluded to an earlier indiscretion by Bickerstaff:

> Would ye him, then, defend, Sirs, assert something striking;
> Affirm that foul slander has banish'd his Nykin:
> That the tall grenadier, tho' his head's held so high,
> Has told of poor Bicky an infamous lye.
> Give at once to the world a good mouth-stopping answer;
> Swear he ne'er fell in love with a masculine dancer;
> That G--k ne'er heard, no, nor ever suspected,
> To whom brother George, once a letter directed. (25 July)

On Sunday, 26 July, the champions rested. But on Monday seven challengers rode into print, one of them being Kenrick himself as "Beatrice," replying to Joseph "Benedict" Reed. The matter of that "masculine dancer" was again raised: is it "worse —I bid him answer—/T'assail a soldier than a dancer" (*Morning Chronicle,* #991)? Nobody answered.

By 1 August, Bickerstaff's flight was hardly news, and *Love in the Suds* was over a month old. Besides, an even more splendid scandal had occurred. On 20 July, Captain Robert Jones was sentenced to death for "committing a detestable crime upon Francis Henry Hay, a boy under 13 years of age" (*St. James Chronicle,* #1783). Accounts of this alleged sodomy crowded the older story from the newspapers, especially when the officer eventually received the King's pardon. There was far more circumstantial evidence against Jones than against Bickerstaff, but Jones gained the support of all but one of his fellow officers in a petition to the crown. The accounts of his action were both sensational and ludicrous, providing far better material than the exiled Bickerstaff. The best anyone could say for *him* was that he had died (again).

On Thursday, 30 July, it was reported in the *London Evening*

Post that "Bickerstaff, the compiler of *Love in a Village,* etc., who lately absconded for a detestable crime, died a few days ago in Sussex" (#6953). Not to be out-done, the *St. James Chronicle* announced on 1 August, "A celebrated Dramatick Writer, who lately absconded for a detestable Crime, it is assured, has drowned himself" (#1788). Thus, within a month, Bickerstaff was said to have hanged himself, died in Sussex, and drowned himself. If he escaped those fates, he might still have been "shut up in a little Retreat on the Sea Coast" consuming his "two Quarts of Spirits" every day. The stanzas might change, but the refrain remained the same; he "absconded for a detestable Crime."

Kenrick published his 34-page pamphlet, *A Letter to David Garrick, Esq.* on 8 August, and the *Morning Chronicle* published four long installments from it from Wednesday, 12 August, through Saturday, 15 August. On 15 August, the 5th edition of *Love in a Suds,* with the "poetical altercation between Benedict and Beatrice," was published as well as the 2nd edition of the *Letter.*

At the same time that Kenrick was making money at Garrick's and Bickerstaff's expense, one of Bickerstaff's and Dibdin's musical works was being produced for the first time at Sadler's Wells. On 25 July, the libretto of the *Brickdust-Man and Milk-Maid,* a "Musical Dialogue,"[23] was published in the *St. James Chronicle* (#1784). The *London Evening Post,* #6952, published it on the same day, and both the *London Magazine* (XLI, August 1772, 392-393), and the *Oxford Magazine* reprinted the piece, the latter journal commenting, "The Musick of the following little piece is very happily adapted to the manner and character of it; and as it has had a frequent effect on the muscles of the numbers of good folks who like to 'laugh and grow fat,' and therefore resort nightly to Sadler's Wells, the Summer seat of frolic and whim, we have procured a copy for the entertainment of our readers" (IX, July 1772, 34-35. See Appendix E).

Gradually the tumult and the shouting died away in the *Morning Chronicle,* but when the Michelmas Law Term began, gossipers speculated whether Garrick would even continue his suit, let alone win it. "I am told," Garrick wrote to Peter Fountain, "the Papers Mention my having drop'd my prosecution—I cannot help what they say, it is not so, nor can it be so—" (*Letters,* II, #711, 821). The *Morning Chronicle* for 7 October had reported:

> Mr. Garrick is said to have withdrawn his motion, made in the Court of King's Bench . . . in conformity to Mr. Dunning's opinion. A Gentleman, at the Rolls coffee-house yesterday, on hearing this, declared, he wondered Mr. Dunning should give Mr. Garrick any such advice . . . when an aged, but a very sound, Lawyer present instantly took up the matter, and said . . . there was not the least ground to file an information for a libel, as a matter in question, although poetically poignant, and satirically severe, did not contain the shadow of any charge of a libellous nature. (Quoted in *Letters,* II, 821–822)

Garrick would neither drop the charges nor settle out of court; indeed, "Mr. G. is resolv'd for ye Peace of Mankind in General, his own credit, and, he hopes, to the Confusion of ye most abandon'd Profligate, to have the business thoroughly canvass'd in a Court of Law—Mr G. defies the Malice of ye Devil & ye D^{r} in Conjunction" (*Letters,* II, #712, 822, 31 October). Brave words, but within a month Garrick settled for a public apology from Francis Newbery, the publisher of the *Public Ledger* in which *Leap Frog* had appeared, and from Kenrick.

Newbery's apology appeared on the same day that the *London Evening Post* reported, "Mr. Garrick's information against Mr. Kenrick for *backbiting,* it is thought, will come on the latter end of this week in the Court of King's Bench, where the latter gentleman intends pleading his own cause in *propria persona*" (#6998, 12 November). Newbery published his apology in his newspaper:

> A Copy of Verses, containing the basest and most malignant Reflections upon Mr. GARRICK, having appeared in the Public Ledger on the 18th of June last, the Publisher of that Paper, after solemnly declaring that he has not the least Knowledge of the Author, thinks it his Duty as a Man who wishes to do every Act of Justice in his Power, to express his Concern that he was any Way accessory to so vile and groundless a Calumny. He is most sincerely sorry that the Lines were inserted without his Privity, and takes this public Method of begging Mr. Garrick's Pardon. (Clipping, Harvard Theatre Collection)

Garrick's only recorded comment about this apology was, "I shall not suffer Mr Newberry to pay my Costs—" (*Letters,* II, 826-827, #715). The author remained unknown and unscathed. There still were Wheble and Kenrick to deal with. The course of "The King v. Kenrick & Wheble" can be traced in Garrick's solicitors' account book.[24]

During Trinity Term, 1772, Garrick's solicitors bought "4 Pamphlets by Kenrick," and began the necessary steps "to take against the Author and Printer." When Kenrick finally submitted "to make a public acknowledgement in the news papers," the solicitors attended "the Council to settle the terms &c. &c." Both Mr. Wallace and Mr. Murphy were offered ten guineas each "for their fees in this Business but they refused to take any fee." The cost to Garrick by the time Kenrick apologized was £17 17s 2d.

Autumn 1772, was the season for apologies, real and counterfeited. In addition to Newbery's on 12 November, Kenrick advertised his in the London newspapers between 21 and 24 November. It appeared in the *London Evening Post* on Saturday, 21 November:

> The Author of a Pamphlet entitled LOVE in the SUDS, is much concerned to find it has been conceived that he meant to convey a Charge of a scandalous and detestable Nature against DAVID GARRICK, Esq; who, under that Impression, has had Recourse to the Court of King's Bench for Redress. He thinks it incumbent on him, therefore, as well in Justice to himself as to Mr. Garrick, thus publicly to declare, that he had no Intention whatever to convey or insinuate any such Charge against him; being well convinced there is no Ground for casting an Imputation, or even harbouring a Suspicion of the Kind against his Character. He thinks it also farther incumbent on him to apologize to Mr. Garrick, as a Gentleman, for the Uneasiness he may have unintentionally given him on this Occasion; at the same Time assuring him he will suppress the Sale of the Pamphlet and reprint it no more. [signed] William Kenrick. (#7003, 21 November 1772)

"I did not believe him guilty," Kenrick told Thomas Evans, the bookseller, "but did it to plague the fellow."[25]

Sometime shortly after Kenrick's apology there appeared *The Recantation and Confession of Doctor KENRICK, L.L. D.* (London, 1772), written according to Kenrick,[26] by "that filthy Yahoo, *Paul Hiffernan.*" A prose work, it is divided into the "Introduction" and the Recantation proper. In the "Introduction," which lives up to Kenrick's description of its author, Kenrick is said to have told Wheble on 10 August 1772 that he meant the poem [*Love in the Suds*] "as a pleasant joke" (p. 5); but now, because of the impending libel suit, Kenrick is willing to recant, and "live in peace upon bread and cheese and porter" (p. 7). The "Recantation" supposedly takes place "in the presence of F[rancis] Gentleman, and John Wheeble, Nov. 13, 1772." In it Kenrick rescues some part of Bickerstaff's character:

> Indeed, I was so far from thinking there was any unnatural propensity

in the disposition of Nyky, that (when I came out of the King's Bench, and Mrs. Less[in]gh[a]m was kind enough to take me into her house, in Somerset Yard, where Nyky had a house also) I frequently used to visit him, and have spent many chearful evenings in his company, and always thought him a good-natured harmless man; though I have since declared I always *avoided* his company and hated him, as it were from instinct.

I have asserted that Roscius had sufficient reason to suspect the abominable disposition of Nyky long ago; but I do not believe that either he or any one else had any such reason, as the man had nothing effeminate in his manner; nor did I ever say, or hear any one else say, a word to the prejudice of his character in that way, till he himself had fixed the suspicion by leaving England, and then I was the first to attack him, which I should not have done if he had continued here.

I have been offended with Nyky for applauding Roscius, when the whole audience have done the same thing. A natural failing in me. I have too much envy in my composition to bear the success of any man, let his profession be what it will—I have been of many professions, and have succeeded in none. (pp. 8–10)

Ideally, Kenrick's real apology would have ended the matter, but a war once set in motion tends to remain in motion, and there were still a few writers with left-over poems to publish. The author of *The Kenrickad* ("Ariel"), identified by Kenrick as "that literary trollop, Mrs. *Brokes* [Frances Brooke?],"[27] wrote a sixteen-page allegorical effusion in which Pope's Ariel declared, "Satiric strains now fire my Muse."

Parnassian nymphs attend my strains;
K[enrick] I sing; the pride of swains. . . .[28]

For no good reason, the Reverend Evan Lloyd, a friend of Garrick and Peter Fountain, brought out his *An Epistle to David Garrick, Esq.* early in January 1773. Originally advertised in the *Morning Chronicle* of 25 July 1772, it was not published then at Garrick's request.[29] Lloyd's work took a lofty view of things, observing, for instance, that "Jove" shines down on the Rose and the Thistle alike (p. 6). He ventured into prosaic specific attack on page twenty, and that was relegated to a footnote: "If the whole Poem was not execrably dull, and offensively dirty, the Reader would be desired to peruse the *wretched lines,* together with the *injudicious* and *illiberal* Notes, in *Love in the Suds,* on those eminent Barristers, *John Dunning* and *James Mansfield,* Esqr."

That footnote was all Kenrick needed to squelch "that forgiving and forgetting Christian Divine the Reverend *Evan*

Lloyd, Master of *Arts.*"[30] He republished Evans's poem with his own notes in *A Whipping for the Welch Parson,* "Being a Commentary on the Rev. Evan Lloyd's Epistle to David Garrick Esq. By Scriblerius Flagellarius. To which is super-added The Parson's Text." Kenrick sold his work for 18d, less than the cost of Lloyd's poem. Since that poem was worthless, Kenrick explained, and so were his own notes upon it ("the inanity of nothingness of both"), he was selling both together for less than the original cost of one.

Lloyd's *Epistle* and Kenrick's *Whipping* were the last major attacks, but small sorties continued through the following summer. After everything for and against Garrick had been said and written, after Hiffernan returned to his address, which no one knew, in London; after Kenrick returned to his vituperative writings; after Garrick returned to acting at Drury Lane; what could Bickerstaff return to?

Assuredly not writing for the stage under his own name; his old works continued to be popular, but audiences rioted at the thought that a new play was by him. On 1 February 1773 Garrick brought out Dibdin's comic opera after-piece, *The Wedding Ring:* "The Town fancy'd that [it was] one of Mr. Bickerstaff & call'd out to know who was the author." Garrick's assurances to the contrary did not satisfy the audience, and Dibdin himself was forced to declare himself (Stone, 1690). Maria Macklin wrote to her father that "the house being nothing but confusion, Dibdin was push'd upon the stage ready to drop with fright, and declared that he was the author himself" (Stone, 1690-1691). Or as Dibdin remembered the event, "I was called on the stage, and required to declare the author, which I did without hesitation. . ." (*The Harmonicon,* p. 88).

As long as Bickerstaff's name continued to be used as a convenient symbol of shame and depravity, Bickerstaff was effectively barred from writing for the London stage. In 1773, for instance, William Heard wrote *The Tryal of Dramatic Genius,* a poem in which all of the dramatic authors of the time were brought before Apollo and his court to be judged. Kenrick was turned away because of his spitefulness.[31] But Bickerstaff ("mankind *forget* his name!") inspired the author to moralise:

> Painful the thought! in these degenerate times,
> When men of sense commit atrocious crimes;
> When those, who shou'd example's force convey,
> And virtue in her fairest form display;

In Private life, adopt a different plan,
Degrade their nature, and throw off the man;
No wonder vice in gorgeous pomp array'd,
Shou'd browbeat virtue, meek and artless maid!
When her admirers dare not speak her name,
Lest FASHION blast their int'rest and their fame.
  Next came a *man, mankind forget his name! *a late EXILE
As a dramatist, he put in his claim;
O had he practic'd what his scenes impart,
Had he preserv'd strict rectitude of heart,
His fame would not so soon have been forgot,
Nor on his name be made the fatal blot;
But let *oblivion* bury in each mind
What *now he is*—to all his works be kind.

In contrast to what was usually said and written about Bickerstaff at this time, Heard's poem is merciful, but it was more fun to play at Juvenal than at Portia. The Reverend William "Doctor Viper" Jackson, one of the Duchess of Kingston's creatures, published *Sodom and Onan* in 1776; a nasty attack against—and dedicated to—Samuel Foote, it made *Love in the Suds* positively horatian:

Where is the Author of the Village Love
Sweet Isaac Bickerstaff, who never strove
To wipe away the ignominious strain,
Convinc'd that kicking 'gainst the *Pricks* was vain.
For safety flown to soft Italia's shore,
Where Tilney, B--l, Jones and many more
Of Britain's cast outs, revel uncontroul'd
Who for their bestial lust their country sold. . . .
. . . .

Bick--f, B--l, Bu[gge]rs all,
Jones, S--e; S-v-is shall support the pall;
And as requiem to his burning Soul,
Lamenting Niky'll chaunt the Irish howl.[32]

Despite the Reverend Jackson's poem, and other similar allusions to Bickerstaff, Dibdin was accurate when he summed up the reaction to his friend's attempt on the soldier: "It was, as those things generally are, food for the newspapers and the town for a few days, and then nobody cared three-pence about it" (*Life,* I, 84). For instance, on 16 November 1773, John Hoadly was writing to Garrick, "I was thinking that the very old mock play of 'Gammer Gurton's Needle,' might be reduced to one act with songs, by somebody you can bid do anything, like Bickerstaff" (Boaden, I, 583). But long after the actual incident was forgotten by the general public, the stain on Bickerstaff's reputation remained.

He had committed, as the *Biographia Dramatica* put it, *"the deed without a name."*

By the twentieth century, writers were having difficulty deciding which deed that was. William Freeman suggested in 1951 that Bickerstaff was a murderer.[33] An Oxford scholar contributed to *Cassell's Encyclopaedia of Literature* the following sentence which argues her ignorance or her sense of humor, "A satire published after [Bickerstaff's] disappearance from London society couples him with Garrick."[34]

One curious postscript involves John Hoadly. On 29 December 1771 he wrote to Garrick promising to send him improvements "begun forty years ago" on a pantomime, the subject of which was Baucis and Philemon (possibly the pantomime, *Baucis and Philemon, or, The Wandering Deities,* produced in 1740 at the New Wells, Leman-street, Goodman's Fields). Hoadly sent the work secretly—"I will say nothing of it to the nearest friend I have" (Boaden, I, 448-449). Apparently Garrick gave the material to Bickerstaff who fashioned it into a burletta of two acts (still entitled *Baucis and Philemon*) which was in rehearsal at Drury Lane when the scandal broke. It was not produced, "probably from an apprehension that the ignominy of the author might attach in some measure to the production, and induce a suspicion that a correspondence might be kept up with so despicable a character in his exile" (*The British Drama, a Collection of the Most Esteemed Dramatic Productions, with Biography of the Respective Authors; and a Critique on Each Play,* London, 1817, vol 8, *Love in a Village,* 3–4). The editor (Richard Cumberland) printed the following lines as being "the most perfect that ever came from the pen of [Bickerstaff], both in point of sentiment and versification."

'Tis not the smoke from incense roll'd
Or pomp of ostentatious rights:
Or hecatombs inflam'd with gold
Can reach the empyrean heights.
Would you to heavenly acts aspire,
And wafted be on eagle's wings; [so too, does scandal, see p. 224]
Know that the deed supremely good
Outweighs the sacrifice of kings.

13
WHERE IS MR. BICKERSTAFF?
THE SULTAN, THE SPOIL'D CHILD

Despite occasional rumors that Bickerstaff was writing for Garrick or for Dibdin, his two letters to Garrick, from St. Malo in 1772, and Vienne in 1777, indicate that when Bickerstaff fled he left both England and the London stage behind. Aside from his half-pay pension from the marines, he had no known income, although a friend of Garrick reported dubiously that he was writing for the French stage: "I hear our poor unfortunate acquaintance Bickerstaffe is at Marseilles," wrote Mrs. J. Henrietta Pye on 21 November 1774, "& has brought out a comic Opera there. I own I don't believe it, tho' I had the intelligence from so infallible an authority as my Husband. . . ."[1]

Whether or not Bickerstaff was writing for the Marseilles stage in 1774—and if he did so, he used an untraceable *nom de plume*—in 1775 a new work by him was produced at Drury Lane, *The Sultan; or, A Peep into the Seraglio.*[2] The play did him no good financially, for the lead actress, Frances Abington, who was responsible for its success, owned the copyright and received the profits from the Benefit.[3]

The published version with its two songs is the result of a long shrinking process which probably began in September 1771, when Bickerstaff returned from a summer on the continent. At that time, so the journals puffed, he was preparing a new musical piece of three acts. No such work appeared, but Bickerstaff's relations with Mrs. Abington could explain what happened to it.

As Charlotte in his *The Hypocrite,* she was one of the loveliest coquettes on the stage; and as Beatrice, the comic maid in *'Tis Well It's no Worse,* she was good enough to warrant Bickerstaff's dedicating the comedy to her. In Mrs. Abington, Bickerstaff had an actress whose presence in his play would almost guarantee him a success; it would be plausible, therefore, to assume that he gave her a manuscript version of his three-act musical piece for her approval—and left it with her when he fled the country. But in three acts, the play was too long, so by 14 June 1774 it was cut:

> Dear Sir [wrote Mrs. Abington to Garrick], I take the liberty of sending you the copy of the Intertainment you received last winter [1773–1774] from Wilton House. It is now made into two acts, and has been considerably shortened, which I think removes the two chief objections you made to the Piece in your letters. The author seems to be possesssed of the same degree of partiality for it which all authors have in common for their own productions, whether good or bad; and tho I know he wishes very much that I should perform the principal part, yet I apprehend he may carry the Piece to another Theatre if it should be rejected at yours: This would be a circumstance of real mortification to me, as the author has been pleased Publickly to Declare that it was my stile of acting which first suggested to him the Idea of bringing Roxalina upon the English stage; and my friends are, one and all, particularly anxious to see me in the character.[4]

Roxalana—or "Roxalina" as Mrs. Abington would have it—was the lead role in *The Sultan.* Mrs. Abington's remarks set the pattern for the following year and a half of bluff and bickering between her and Garrick: the author was never named—nor the original source—and except when she needed a favor, Mrs. Abington stayed consistently on the offensive. Then she became sweet reason itself:

> But permit me, Sir [she continued in her 14 June 1774 letter], to return to the business—when you spoke to me of the Farce you observed that it wanted here and there some little alterations to make it quite theatrical. Why may I not, Dear Sir, Intreat of you to take it under your protection, and give it but a touch of that Promethean heat with which you have for so many years past animated the clay of every successful modern Play-wright; this you know, Sir, most unexceptionably intitles you to receive the Piece upon your own terms as it will then be so much *yours;* and you may either begin the season with it, or bring it out at what time you yourself think proper.

Garrick agreed, but insisted that he be given a free hand and that Mrs. Abington perform in the play when requested to.[5]

Professional that he was, Garrick put up with Mrs. Abington's sulks, pouts, huffs, and peeves for the sake of the play. She for her part still needed his help, "I am very certain that a few of your nice touches, with a little of your fine polish, will give it that stamp of merit as must secure it a reception with the public, equal to the warmest of my expectations" (Boaden, II, 29. dated 29 June 1775). Even on 7 December 1775, five days before *The Sultan* premiered, Mrs. Abington was still worried, and Garrick eliminated her one song. Finally, on 12 December, as an after-piece to *Richard III, The Sultan; or, a Peep into the Seraglio,* with settings by de Loutherbourg, and music by Bach and Giordani, was produced. There were five songs in the opening night's performance, but three of them were dropped by the second night, and other changes were made to suit the taste of the town.

The Larpent manuscript version of *The Sultan* reveals that even in two acts, the play is a very close adaptation of *Soliman II* by Charles Simon Favart, who, in turn, based his play on a story from Marmontel's *Contes Moraux.* The plot always remained the same: Roxalana, the pert new slave girl, becomes Solyman's favorite, and despite the opposition of some of the other harem girls, and Osmyn the eunuch, she converts him to her ideas of freedom; the sultan frees his harem and marries Roxalana. First produced in Paris on 9 April 1761,[6] Favart's comedy might well have been seen there by Bickerstaff. And Garrick, as an acquaintance of Favart, should have recognized the piece as a plagiarism; but except for Mrs. Abington's phrase, "bringing Roxalina upon the English stage," in her 14 June 1774 letter, and Garrick's "ye Author or translator of ye piece" in his reply of 18 June, *The Sultan* was treated as an original work.

Bickerstaff has been blamed by modern critics[7] for departing from (or disgracing) the French original, whereas the responsibility belonged to Mrs. Abington, Garrick and the audience who found "an indelicacy in the subject not to be pardoned" (*The Gazetteer and New Daily Advertiser,* 15 December 1775). Heeding the will of his public, Garrick purged the play of offensive passages after the first night; and "On the second representation, it having undergone some judicious alterations, the auditors gave stronger tokens of approbation, and it may probably turn out a good Christmas mince pye to the managers"

(*Town and Country Magazine,* December, 1772, p. 627).

The Larpent manuscript shows that Bickerstaff had originally planned for Osmyn, chief of the Eunuchs, to be a blackamoor,[8] probably to be played by Dibdin, considering his success in black-face as Mungo in *The Padlock*. By the time the play was produced, however, Dibdin was no longer at Drury Lane, and the blackamoor allusion in Roxalana's opening soliloquy in Act II had been removed.

The Sultan proved a successful vehicle for Mrs. Abington, who, as the copyright holder, received £60. 7s 6d profit from the author's Benefit night. She kept the play in her repertory until 1787; then "A new candidate for fame" undertook the "very agreeable and lively part"[9] of Roxalana. Mrs. Jordan replaced Mrs. Abington at Drury Lane on 15 February 1787, and the latter played Roxalana at Covent Garden (9 February 1787). Once Mrs. Jordan appeared as Roxalana, Covent Garden stopped producing *The Sultan*. It was produced at Drury Lane as late as 2 June 1817.

The farce turned up in New York on 3 May 1794 as *The American Captive* by Hodgkinson at the John Street Theatre (Macmillan, p. 65), and continued to be performed for a total of 22 times between 1794 and 14 February 1840 in various theatres. As *The Sublime and the Beautiful,* by Thomas Morton, it reappeared at Covent Garden on 5 December 1828 (Kinne, p. 139). Although greatly changed, it was curtly dismissed, "An alteration of Bickerstaff's obsolete and stupid farce . . . which the acting of a Jordan could scarcely render tolerable, has been produced here. . . . We shall only say, The name of *Morton* honours this corruption, / And chastisement doth therefore hide its head."[10]

The best compliment that anyone has paid *The Sultan* is that it was partially responsible for the plot of Mozart's *Die Entführung Aus Dem Serail.*[11]

Between 1774, when Mrs. Pye's husband heard that Bickerstaff brought out a comic opera for the Marseilles stage, and 1777, when Bickerstaff wrote to Garrick, he was reported dead by Garrick's friend Peter Sturz. "If the Philosopher Wilson lives [Sturz wrote to Garrick on 26 August 1776] pray my benedictions to him as also to everybody who remembers me. Sir John Pringle[,] Doctor Hunter [,] Mrs. Colman—Poor Bickerstaff is dead I hear" (Forster Collection. The letter was written in "Oldenburgh near Bremen"). But he was not dead, just suffering:

> Sir [Bickerstaff wrote to Garrick], So little do I know of the world in the remote nook in which I breathe, that it is but very lately I accidentally heard of your having quitted the stage; whenever that event happened, it was my intention to write to you,—not to beg, but to complain.
>
> It is now somewhat more than four years since I was informed, that about that time you not only joined in favour of an ungrateful, perjured, dishonest wretch, who was cutting my throat with my own weapons, to drag a brand of infamy upon me that utterly deprived me of the means of earning bread, but that you also lent your wit upon the occasion; writ letters in newspapers, particularly some in the Morning Post [*Chronicle*?], with an intent to destroy me, as far as the work was still to be done. As I never in my life offended you either in word or deed, but, on the contrary, by every means possible endeavoured to recommend myself to you, as I was highly in your good graces, and really deserved to be so, as far as the most devoted attachment can be termed desert; you may imagine this account could not reach me without causing me the most bitter anguish, and in a manner utterly depriving me of both head and heart. In a word, Sir, you have shown implacable, unprovoked resentment against the most unhappy of men; while you thought proper to pardon the vilest miscreant that ever dishonoured a pretension to literature, and for whom there should be a whip in the hand of every honest man to lash him out of human society. I need not say who this monster it, nor shall I dwell upon matters that overwhelm me with passion and indignation. I will come at once to the purport of this letter.
>
> I have already said, that when I first designed to write to you, it was not to beg but to complain; but necessity changes all things. I am in the greatest distress, so great that words cannot express it. I remember, that during the interval of my small prosperity, I presented you at different times with some trifles; their value, I believe, might be about ten pounds; these would now feed and clothe me. I need not say more; what must be the circumstances capable of wringing from me so much! If this letter should produce in your mind the goodness and compassion natural to you, and you should not afterwards reason yourself out of them, any thing sent to Mr. Cartony, opposite Somerset House, will come safe to my hands without his knowing who sent it. If, on the contrary, this letter produces no effect, you will still remember there is something due to the unfortunate as to the dead, and that as it is addressed solely to your own breast, and designed for your own eye, it ought not to be exposed. On this instance of your justice and generosity I rely, and am Sir, your obedient servant, I. B. . . . . . ff (Boaden, II, 207–208)

Robert Cartony, who lived "opposite Somerset House," in the Strand, was listed in the Rates Books for the Parish of Mary le Strand in 1772-1773 as paying £60 rent per year; he was the executor of William Griffin's estate after the bookseller died in 1776, and described himself as a "friend" of Mrs. Griffin.[12] Aside from these isolated facts, nothing is known about him. Nothing indicates that Garrick sent Bickerstaff anything.

The remote nook of Vienne was not so very much removed from the world in 1777, for Englishmen choosing to go overland to the south of France usually travelled by way of Paris and thence to Lyon and down the Rhone. Vienne had been a stopping-off place from Roman times onward, and boasted of a pyramidical monument which supposedly marked the grave of Pontius Pilate. Rhone wine was inexpensive and good, and so was the food. In Vienne there was a theatre of sorts; three actors from Grenoble obtained permission in September 1775 to utilize *la grande salle* of the hotel de ville. With Bickerstaff's training in practical theatre work, possibly he was associated with the Grenoble troupe.[13] By 1783, however, Bickerstaff was no longer living in Vienne, despite the following item in a London newspaper on 2 October 1783: Bickerstaff, "who formerly wrote for the stage, is not dead, as was reported, but is now living in great distress in an obscure Baillage in the South of France." The information was out of date: "A correspondent says we were misinformed respecting Mr. Bickerstaff, he being at present at Milan, in Italy, where he goes by the name of Mr. Commandoni" (3 October 1783). Three years later another flotsam of gossip surfaced:

> A paragraph in yesterday's papers, observes that "Bickerstaff, after a long residence in Italy, cannot acquire any proficiency in the language."—In reply to this, it may be said, that he was a finished *Italian* before he absconded from this [end of clipping][14]

Even after Bickerstaff left England, and until March 1786, the military cash books show him drawing his half-pay every six months, £33. 3s. 6d per year. The cash books for 1787 to 1797 are missing, but his name was carried in the published Army Lists through 1808.[15]

The 1777 letter from Bickerstaff is the last direct proof that he was alive, except for his pension; but so many different years after 1777 have been cited as the year of his death that they stand in lieu of other proof that he still lived.

The strongest indication that he was alive in 1790 is a note in John Kemble's Memoranda books for Monday, 22 March:

"Mrs. Jordan's Benefit. Belle's Stratagem. Spoil'd Child. The Farce is written by Mr. Bickerstaffe. it was hissed, but I think it will do yet.—Mrs. Jordan played well in the Farce, ill in the Play."[16] *The World* noted briefly on 29 April 1790, "*The Spoil'd Child* was sent to Mrs. Jordan from *Bickerstaffe,* in Italy, where her fame had reached. The divine manner in which she sings the two songs, redeem the piece from censure" (#1036, p. 3). When the farce was first played in Liverpool on 2 August 1790, the playbills advertised it as "Written by the Author of *The Maid of the Mill, Love in a Village,* &c." There is some doubt about the accuracy of *The World's* account because *The Spoil'd Child* was reported to have been performed at Ulverstone on 16 October 1787 with Harriet Mellon (who later married the banker Thomas Coutts and became the Duchess of St. Albans) as the comic lead, Little Pickle.[17] From another note in Kemble's Memoranda Book, it seems probable that Bickerstaff had the same sort of arrangement with Mrs. Jordan as he had with Mrs. Abington and *The Sultan:* "The play to-night [8 May 1790] was to have been *The Confederacy* . . . with *The Spoil'd Child* for Mrs. Jordan's Benefit, to whom the Authour of the Farce gave his Profits" (BM, add. ms. 31,972). By a curious quirk of logic, the fact that *The Spoil'd Child* was advertised as by Bickerstaff was enough to convince the *Edinburgh Dramatic Review* that the author was still unknown: "When it was performed at Liverpool in 1790, it was repeatedly advertised as the work of Bickerstaff, which only goes to prove that the real author was unknown."[18] Whatever the critic knew to the contrary, he was not telling anyone in print. The *Edinburgh Dramatic Review* notwithstanding, none of the notices about Bickerstaff's alleged authorship denied him that doubtful credit on the grounds that he was dead. Even those who favored Prince Hoare, Mr. Ford, or even Mrs. Jordan as its author never suggested that Bickerstaff had died before the play was written.

Like their opposites, bad works of art are bad, not just for their own age but for all times. As it now reads, no one would wish to claim credit for writing *The Spoil'd Child.* It seems a much-abridged version of a lost comedy, but unlike *The Romp, The Pannel* or *The Sultan,* it has no merits of its own. It was damned by nearly all the critics wherever it was performed, but stayed in the repertory at first because of the acting of Mrs. Jordan, and later, of other actresses who thought it fun to play Little Pickle. As late as 1873 in America *The Spoil'd Child* was being performed. Seventy-one performances have been recorded by Macmillan in this country up to 1852, but there is an acting copy in the Widener Library marked and signed by Augustin Daly, and dated by him, 1873. His version cuts a good number of speeches from an already short farce.

At the same time that *The Spoil'd Child* was first playing at Drury Lane, Dibdin was still denying that he plagiarized from Bickerstaff to write his own comic operas. By 1792, the charge had become so insistent that "On Sunday, 18 March, 1792, Dibdin wrote a letter to the *Diary,* promising to sue the very next person who made such a statement, and the same day, the *Observer* published 'an unqualified libel . . . upon the old infamous subject which the reader may remember I had so completely quashed two-and-twenty years before.' "[19]

> I am at length under an indispensable necessity of publicly noticing those reports [Dibdin wrote to the *Diary*], which, with so much industry, have lately been propagated against me: implying, that Mr. BICKERSTAFF is the author of my songs, and hinting at a slander so infamous as to dishonour the age and country in which we live; yet such a slander as the noble indignation of a generous public, wounded through me, shall I trust, avenge on the heads of those who have had the wanton and wicked audacity to promulgate it. (*Life,* III, 221–222)

The slander was of the same sort that Kenrick had perpetrated against Garrick. Bickerstaff, it was implied, "was hiding behind the curtain of the Sans Souci, engaging in 'disgusting relations' with Dibdin."[20] At the trial, " 'several performers' attested that the implication was unfounded inasmuch as Bickerstaff had left the country several years earlier . . . and had not returned" (Werkmeister, p. 317). Wherever Bickerstaff was in 1792, nobody at the trial claimed he was dead.

Dibdin's insistence on the originality of his lyrics became something of a joke to his contemporaries. In *The Children of Apollo,* for instance, an anonymous poem published in 1794, the author pretended to consider the charge of plagiarism, and then dismissed it by declaring that Bickerstaff would not write as badly as Dibdin did in a work such as *Harvest Home.*

> Since busy fame, that lying saucy jade,
> With sly invectives publishes abroad
> They are not his, the works which we applaud;
> Nay, dares insinuate that one, who late
> Rais'd humble op'ra from a sinking state;
> Now lends a helping pen, but this to hide,

His *Padlock* has to his friend's mouth applied. (p. 42)
. . . .
. . . is it likely that a man of note,
Who the best operas in English wrote,
Would scribbler of meer ballad acts become,
And write such flimsy trash as *Harvest Home;*
Consider this and do not then make less,
That little which my client may possess,
For I insist that DIBDIN has display'd,
His ballad-pieces without any aid; . . . (p. 45)

Even if it was at Dibdin's expense, somebody was once again praising Bickerstaff as an opera writer, one who, to judge from the poet's tense, was presumed to be still alive. But though his reputation as a writer might have been rising again, his own character continued to be painted black. Perhaps the most sternly moral account of him appeared in *Anthologia Hibernica* I (Dublin, 1793), May, 366-367.

> Of this man little is known, and that little unhappily is not good.
> . . . .
> We find him also an officer of marines, but he left the service with imputed infamy, from practices at which humanity shudders, and decency hides the head.
>
> It hurts us to pursue the narrative—an irreclaimable depravation of appetite rendered him an exile from his country; in some foreign sink of debauchery and wretchedness, he perhaps even yet lingers, a striking monument of the absurdity of that maxim, which teaches, that an author's life may be best known in his works.
>
> The writings of Bickerstaff are uniformly marked with much purity and simplicity.—Had he *lived* as he *wrote* this little book were perfect.

With what negative joy the anonymous author wrote! His prose stinks of curdled virtue.

In 1816, however, somebody finally had a kind word for Bickerstaff. In fact an effort was made to exonerate him from the charge of homosexuality and restore him to respectability. In *The Theatrical Inquisitor, and Monthly Mirror,* IX (December 1816), the reviewer made the following plea:

> We should feel indebted to any of our readers who may be enabled to furnish some information about Bickerstaffe . . . who absconded in 1772, upon a charge of the most heinous nature, and was reported in the public prints of that time to have drowned himself in exile soon after. The circumstances of this case were hardly examined, from the repulsive accusation with which they were disgraced. In returning to his lodgings at a late hour, through Whitehall, Bickerstaffe attempted

> the imputed offence against a common soldier, who taxed him with the horrid crime, and upon reflection, we are inclined to argue, unjustly. He had been conspicuous for his amorous attachments to the better half of creation, and Dr. Johnson asserts, with a deep knowledge of human nature, that no man is a hypocrite to his pleasures. We have questioned a very old and honourable actor upon this subject, who enjoyed a near intimacy with Bickerstaffe, and still professes an utter disbelief of the atrocious calumny, which must have originated, he asserts, in a shameful practise of the soldier upon the inebriety of his unfortunate friend, who shrunk from the dreadful stigma he was unprepared to obliterate, and fled, in a moment of despondency, from the only means of establishing his innocence. This respectable person also informed us, that he met Bickerstaffe about eight years ago, near Charing-cross, and accosted him in terms of familiarity, but has not seen him since, having left London immediately after, for the place in which he has since continued to reside. It would be gratifying to have this testimony verified, and the slander reversed which has so long degraded a name of such literary eminence. (pp. 428–429)

But the testimony was never verified, nor was the "old and honourable actor" identified.

Two years later, the *History of the City of Dublin,* an ambitious two-volume work by John Warburton, Reverend James Whitelaw, and Reverend Robert Walsh, included Bickerstaff among its roll of Irish writers. Although the account was one of the few which did not depend upon the *Biographia Dramatica,* it nevertheless repeated the false statement that Bickerstaff "left [the marines] in disgrace in consequence of being suspected of a most disgraceful crime"; unlike other biographies, it defended Bickerstaff:

> If the robust nerves of Samuel Foote were unable to sustain a similar charge, made at the instigation of an infamous woman . . . —how much less could one of Bickerstaff's refined sensibilities (if one might judge by his writings) support it? It is now generally believed, at least in Ireland, that the accusation was alike malicious and unfounded. . . .

The biographer then noted casually, "He was known to be living in London in 1811, but there are later reports of his death, which it is supposed took place two years ago [1816]." The persistent rumors that Bickerstaff secretly wrote under an assumed name (Charles Dibdin) were accepted by Warburton and the others, "The Deserter; The Waterman; The Spoiled Child, and other pieces are said to have been written by him, though published under other names."[21] The death date of 1816 has the virtue of being the latest year put forth, but the authors gave no more reason for that year than did another historian when he gave 1787 as the year of Bickerstaff's death.[22]

In addition to the December 1816 *Theatrical Inquisitor,* there was one other reference to Bickerstaff. He was listed in *A Biographical Dictionary of the Living Authors of Great Britain and Ireland,* an anonymous compilation published in 1816. Unfortunately the work cited the 1812 *Biographia Dramatica* to assert that Bickerstaff still lived (p. 26). In 1819, the first volume of Richard Ryan's *Biographia Hibernica* stated that Bickerstaff in 1811 "was known to be living in obscurity in London and is supposed to have died towards the close of 1816" (p. 99). It is likely that Ryan copied his account from the *History of Dublin,* although he gave no sources.

The most important of the reports about Bickerstaff published from 1816 to 1819 was that in the *Theatrical Inquisitor* because of its reference to the actor who saw Bickerstaff "about eight years ago [1808]." If he were correct, then some credence can be given to the 1808 *List of the General and Field Officers* which numbered Isaac Bickerstaff as still on half-pay as of 1 January 1808 (p. 619), the last year it did so. Because Bickerstaff would not voluntarily give up his only known income, 1808 seems a plausible death date, later reports of his being alive notwithstanding.

Thus, after a 36-year (or more) anticlimax, Bickerstaff's life ended without even the dignity of a positive death date to finish his biography, or a tombstone to mark his grave.

Appendix A

DATES AND CASTS OF FIRST-NIGHT AND OTHER PERFORMANCES

Unless otherwise noted, the dates and casts have been drawn from The London Stage.

Thomas and Sally, 28 November 1760, Covent Garden
The 'Squire Mattocks
Thomas Beard
Sally Miss Brent
Dorcas Mrs. Vernon (the former Jane Poitier; later, Mrs. Thompson?)
A Covent Garden playbill for 23 April 1761 listed the 'Squire to be sung by Mattocks, and Thomas by Beard for the first time.

Judith, 27 March 1761, Drury Lane
Ozias Mrs. Corneli
Charmis Tenducci
Holofernes Champness
Judith Miss Elizabeth Young
Abra Fawcett
Miss Brent [no part assigned]
Chorus of Israelites. Chorus of Assyrians. *Judith* (London, 1761).
Judith follows the Old Testament story of Judith and Holofernes in which Judith saved Israel from the Assyrian invaders by seducing their leader, Holofernes, and beheading him.
Last Performed: 19 February 1950, Town Hall, Oxford, by the Oxford Harmonic Society.

Love in a Village,	8 December 1762, Covent Garden	3 April 1769, Drury Lane

Justice Woodcock	Shuter	Hartry
Hawthorn	Beard	Vernon
Young Meadows	Mattocks	Dodd
Hodge	Dunstall	King
Eustace	Dyer	Fawcett
Sir William Meadows	Collins	Parsons
Rossetta	Miss Brent	Mrs. Baddeley
Deborah Woodcock	Mrs. Walker	Mrs. Love
Margery	Miss Davies	Miss Pope
Lucinda	Miss Hallam*	Miss Radley

* Afterwards Mrs. Mattocks

Jamaica, 9 October 1779, Montego Bay, the American Company of Comedians

Justice Woodcock	David Douglass
Hawthorn	Mr. Woolls
Young Meadows	Mr. Wall
Eustace	Mr. Allyn
Hodge	Mr. Hallam
Sir William Meadows	Mr. Morris
Rossetta	Miss Wainwright*
Lucinda	Miss Hallam**
Mrs. Deborah Woodcock	Mrs. Douglass
Margery	Mrs. Harman***

[Wright, *Revels in Jamaica,* 1682–1838, p. 97.]

*Miss Wainwright first appeared at Covent Garden on 12 December 1764 in Arne's *The Guardian Out-witted.*
**Related to the Miss Hallam who played Lucinda originally at Covent Garden, but not the same one.
***Grand-daughter of Colley Cibber.

8 July 1763, Crow-Street Theatre, Dublin.

Justice Woodcock	Shuter
Hawthorn	Wilder
Young Meadows	Mahon
Hodge	Glover
Eustace	Dyer
Sir William Meadows	Morris*
Rossetta	Mrs. Lessingham
Deborah Woodcock	Miss Mason
Margery (Madge)	Miss Willis
Lucinda	Mrs. Mahon

[Hitchcock, p. 113]

*Migrated to America after 1765 and joined Douglass' American Company of Comedians.

Other performances of *Love in a Village:*

- 10 May 1923, Guildhall School of Music, London
- 21 December 1923, Everyman Theatre, London
- 27 March 1926, Leeds

19 April 1928, Lyric, Hammersmith [Loewenberg, *Annals,* cols. 266–267]
1952, revised by Arthur Oldham for the Aldeburgh Festival
October, 1954, English Opera Group produced Oldham's version at Sadler's Wells.

The Maid of the Mill,	31 January 1765, Covent Garden.	31 March 1769, Drury Lane
Lord Aimworth	Mattocks	Reddish
Sir Harry Sycamore	Shuter	Parsons [first night only; thereafter: Baddeley.]
Mervin	Baker	Fawcett
Fairfield	Gibson	Jefferson
Giles	Beard	Bannister
Ralph	Dibdin	Dibdin
Lady Sycamore	Mrs. Pitt	Mrs. Bradshaw
Theodosia	Miss Hallam	Miss Radley
Patty	Miss Brent	Mrs. Baddeley
Fanny	Miss Poitier	Miss Pope

25 March 1765, Crow–Street, Dublin.		23 [26?] March 1765 Smock Alley, Dublin
Lord Aimworth	Barry	Ryder
Sir Harry Sycamore	Mahon	Collins
Fairfield	Glover	Dawson
Ralph	Hamilton	Waker
Mervin	Palmer	Jagger
Giles	Morris	Wilder
Fanny	Mrs. Glover	Signora Spiletta [Giordani's wife]
Lady Sycamore	Mrs. Kennedy	Mrs. Kelf
Theodosia	Mrs. Mahon	Mrs. Wilder
Patty	Mrs. Dancer	Miss Catley [Hitchcock, II, 138

Daphne and Amintor, 8 October 1765, Drury Lane.

Amintor	Vernon
Daphne	Miss Elizabeth Wright [Married Michael Arne in 1766]
Mindora	Miss Young

The Plain Dealer, 7 December 1765, Drury Lane.

Manly	Holland
Freeman	Palmer
Lord Plausible	Dodd
Novel	King
Vernish	Lee
Major Oldfox	Love
Jerry Blackacre	Yates
Counsellor Quillit	Baddeley

Oakam	Moody
A Boy	Master Burton
Olivia	Miss Pope
Fidelia	Mrs. Yates
Mrs. Blackacre	Mrs. Clive
Eliza	Miss Plym
Lettice	Mrs. Hippisley

Love in the City, 21 February 1767, Covent Garden.

Barnacle (guardian to Priscilla)	Dunstall
Wagg (an attorney's clerk)	Shuter
Spruce (a mercer)	Mattocks
Sightly (a military officer)	DuBellamy
Old Cockney (a grocer)	Gibson
Young Watt Cockney	Dibdin
Priscilla Tomboy (a West Indian)	Mrs. Mattocks (former Miss Hallam)
Miss Molly Cockney (an old maid)	Mrs. Green
Penelope (daughter to Old Cockney)	Miss Brickler [first appearance]
Miss La Blond (a milliner)	Miss Poitier

[Stone, 1222. *Love in the City,* 2nd ed., 1767]

The Romp, 23 March 1774, Crow–Street Theatre, Dublin

Watty Cockney	Mr. O'Keeffe [probably John O'Keeffe the playwright]
Old Cockney	Mr. Jackson
Cap't Slightly [sic]	Mr. Glenville
Barnacle	Mr. Wilder
Penelope	Miss Shewcraft
The Romp	Mrs. Sparks (former Miss Ashmore, married Richard Sparks, the son of actor Isaac Sparks)

[Dublin newspaper clipping, Wednesday, 23 March 1774]

	Lionel and Clarissa, 25 February 1768. Covent Garden	*School for Fathers,* 8 February 1770. Drury Lane
Sir John Flowerdale	Gibson	Aikin
Colonel Oldboy	Shuter	Parsons
Mr. Jessamy	Dyer	Dodd
Lionel	Mattocks	Vernon
Harman	Mahoon	Fawcett
Jenkins	Dunstall	Bannister
Diana	Mrs. Baker	Mrs. Wrighten [née Matthews, first appearance]
Clarissa	Miss Macklin	Mrs. Baddeley
Lady Mary Oldboy	Mrs. Green	Mrs. Bradshaw
Jenny	Mrs. Mattocks	Miss Radley

School for Fathers, 14 December 1772, Southwark Theatre, Philadelphia

Sir John Flowerdale	Douglass

Colonel Oldboy	Goodman	
Mr. Jessamy	Wall	
Harman	Henry	
Lionel	Woolls	
Jenkins	Parker	
Clarissa	Miss Storer	
Lady Mary Oldboy	Mrs. Harman [sic]	
Jenny	Mrs. Henry	
Diana Oldboy	Miss Hallam	[Sonneck, p. 47]

The Absent Man, 21 March 1768, Drury Lane

Doctor Gruel	Hurst
Shatterbrain	King
Welldon	Cautherly
Captain Slang	J. Palmer
Coxcomb	Fawcett
Frank	Palmer
Robin	J. Burton
Mrs. Junket	Mrs. Hopkins [4 April: Mrs. Johnston]
Miss Frolick	Mrs. Jeffries [4 April: Miss Reynolds]
Flavia Gruel	Mrs. Barry
Landlady	Mrs. Bradshaw [Stone, 1319, 1320; 1st ed. *Absent Man*]

The Padlock,	3 October 1768, Drury Lane.	January, 1769, Smock Alley
Don Diego	Bannister	Vernel
Leander	Vernon	J. Bannister, from Drury Lane
Leonora	Mrs. Arne	Mrs. Hudson
Mungo	Dibdin	Wilder
Ursula	Mrs. Dorman	Mrs. Saunders [Hitchcock, II, 165]
Scholars	Fawcett, J. Burton	

26 February 1770, Capel Street Theatre (opened after being closed for several years)

Don Diego	Glenville	
Leander	Wilkes	
Leonora	Miss Ashmore	
Mungo	Mahon	
Ursula	Mrs. Hoskins	[Hitchcock, II, 172]

25 March 1833, Edinburgh

Don Diego	Webster	
Leander	Edmunds ("Who will introduce a favourite Song.")	
Leonora	Miss Byfeld	
Mungo	The African Roscius [Ira Aldridge]	
Ursula	Mrs. Nicol	[playbill]

The Royal Garland, "A New Occasional Interlude in Honour of His Danish Majesty,"

10 October 1768, Covent Garden

Genius of England	Mahoon
Old Shepherd	Barnshaw
Young Shepherd	DuBellamy
Calliope	Mrs. Baker
Young Shepherdess	Mrs. Mattocks

Choruses of Shepherds and Shepherdesses. Dancers. [1st edition]

The Hypocrite,	17 November, 1768, Drury Lane.	11 June 1887, Strand, London.
Dr. Cantwell	King	William Farren
Sir John Lambert	Packer	Henry Crisp
Colonel Lambert	Jefferson	H. B. Conway
Darnley	Reddish	Reeves Conway
Charles Seyward	Cautherly	John Tresahar
Maw-worm	Weston	Edward Righton
Tipstaff	Strange	
Servant	Watkins	
Old Lady Lambert	Mrs. Bradshaw	Miss Fanny Coleman
Lady J. Lambert	Mrs. W. Barry	Miss Alma Stanley
Betty	Mrs. Smith	Miss Mary Burton
Charlotte	Mrs. Abington	Miss Amy Roselle
[Stone, 1368; 1st ed.]	[Final 19th century performance. Newspaper clipping, Harvard Theatre Collection]	

The Ephesian Matron

	12 May 1769, Ranelagh House.	31 August 1769, Haymarket.	8 May 1771, Drury Lane.
Centurion	Charles Dibdin	Dibdin	Bannister [?]
Father	Jonathan Legg	Bannister	Davies [?]
Maid	Mrs. Thompson	Mrs. Thompson	Mrs. Dorman [?]
Matron	Mrs Sophia Baddeley	Mrs. Baddeley	Mrs. Wrighten [?]

[Sands, pp. 102–103]

Stone is not sure which parts the actors took.

Other performances: During the summer of 1772 *The Ephesian Matron* was performed at Williams's Grotto-Gardens in St. George's Fields. As the Centurion, Aitkin sang "in character the favourite song *That my Wife Wo'd drink Hooley and Fairly*" (Stone, 1649). The serenata was performed eight times that summer at the Grotto, according to advertisements in *The Morning Chronicle.*

Dr. Last in His Chariot, 21 June 1769, Haymarket.

Ailwou'd	Foote
Dr. Last	Weston
Friendly	Sowdon
Hargrave	Davis
Wag	Bannister
Dr. Balruddery	Sparks
Dr. Coffin	Sharpless

Dr. Skeleton	Arthur
Mrs. Ailwou'd	Mrs. Jeffries
Nancy Ailwou'd	Miss Ogilvie
Polly	Miss Rose [First Appearance]
Prudence	Mrs. Gardiner [*London Magazine,* XXXVIII (June, 1769), 283–284]

The Captive, 21 June 1769, Haymarket, with Dryden's characters from *Don Sebastian*

The Cadi	Bannister	[The Mufti]
Ferdinand	DuBellamy	[Don Antonio]
Fatima	Mrs. Arthur	[Johyama]
Zorayda	Mrs. Jewel	[Morayma]

The Maid the Mistress; or as it was printed, *He Wou'd if He Cou'd; or, An Old Fool Worse Than Any.*

28 May 1770, Ranelagh House. Cast not known. Other performances here were on 28 June and 3 July 1770

12 April 1771, Drury Lane.

Simon	Vernon
Goosecap	Bannister
Old Lady	Dibdin
Betty	Mrs. Baddeley

The Recruiting Serjeant. 20 July 1770, Ranelagh House.		7 December 1770, Drury Lane.
Serjeant	Charles Bannister	Charles Bannister
Countryman	Charles Dibdin	Charles Dibdin
Wife	Mrs. Thompson	Mrs. Wrighten
Mother	Mrs. Baddeley	Mrs. Dorman

[Sands, p. 105]

'Tis Well It's No Worse, 24 November 1770, Drury Lane.

Don Guzman de Ribbera (Don Ferdinand's uncle, Marcella's father)	Parsons
Don Carlos de Pimentel (Loves Marcella, woos Aurora, killed Don Alonzo)	Reddish
Don Pedro Pacheco (Aurora's brother)	Davis
Don Ferdinand (Don Guzman's nephew, Don Alonzo's cousin, Marcella's cousin and suitor)	Brereton
Muskato (servant of Don Carlos)	King
Lazarillo (Don Ferdinand's servant)	Baddeley
Marcella (daughter of Don Guzman, sister of Don Alonzo who loved Aurora)	Mrs. Jefferies
Aurora (Don Pedro's sister, loves Don Carlos)	Mrs. Baddeley
Leonarda (Aurora's maid)	Mrs. Love
Beatrice (Marcella's maid)	Mrs. Abington
An Old Nun [dropped after second performance]	Mrs. Dorman

Servants, lawyers, soldiers: J. Aickin, W. Palmer, Wrighten, Keen, Castle, Booth, J. Burton.

The Sultan; or, A Peep into the Seraglio, 12 December 1775, Drury Lane.

Solyman the Great, Emperor of the Turks	Palmer
Osmyn, chief of the Eunuchs	Bannister
Elmira	Mrs. King
Ismena	Mrs. Wrighten
Roxalana	Mrs. Abington

Dancing by Fontaine, Como, Giorgi, etc; Sga Crespi, Mrs. Sutton etc.

	9 February 1787, Covent Garden.	15 February 1787, Drury Lane.
Solyman	Davies	Barrymore
Osmyn	Fearon	Dignum
Elmira	Mrs. Inchbald	Mrs. Cuyler
Ismena	Mrs. Martyr	Miss Romanzini
Roxalana	Mrs. Abington	Mrs. Jordan [1787 edition]

The Spoil'd Child,	16 October 1787, Theatre Ulverstone.*	22 March 1790, Drury Lane.**
Old Pickle	Mr. Farquharson	Suett
Tag [or Tagg]	Mr. Bibby [manager of the company]	R. Palmer
Miss Pickle	Mrs. Blanchard	Mrs. Hopkins
Maria	Miss Valois [former singer at CG]	Miss Heard
Little Pickle	Miss Mellon [her first performance]	Mrs. Jordan
Margery		Mrs. Booth
Susan		Mrs. Edwards
John		Burton

*Mrs. Cornwell Barron-Wilson [Margaret Harries], *Memoirs of Miss Mellon Afterwards Duchess of St. Albans,* new edition (London, 1886), I. 78. The playbill that she quotes for the 16 October 1787 production named the day as Wednesday, but the 16th fell on a Tuesday.
***The European Magazine,* XVII (London, April, 1790), 307.

The only time a male played Little Pickle on the stage seems to be at the New Theatre in Baltimore, 21 October 1794, the first performance of this farce in The United States. Mr. Marshall was Little Pickle. *Baltimore Gazette and Daily Advertiser,* XXI (Tuesday, 21 October 1794).

Appendix B
THE REPERTORY SYSTEM

The following table illustrates the importance of the repertory system at Covent Garden during the time when Bickerstaff was employed there. It lists the actors and actresses who appeared in the original and early productions of the plays that Bickerstaff wrote for Covent Garden.

Because Bickerstaff wrote only one full-length comic opera for Drury Lane (the revised Lionel and Clarissa*), there is little point in tabulating the performers and Bickerstaff's plays for that theatre. The same system was employed, however, and Mrs. Baddeley appeared in four of his works, and the actor Parsons, five. But many of the parts were originally either written for Covent Garden performers, or were adaptations, like Lord Plausible in* The Plain Dealer *or Beatrice in* 'Tis Well It's no Worse.

In miniature, the best example of the writer working for the repertory company is that of Bickerstaff and Dibdin writing serenatas for Ranelagh, but there Bickerstaff had only four performers to worry about; at Covent Garden he was writing for a full company. In each of his four full-length comic operas he drew upon the company to fill ten roles; it might be as accurate to say that the make-up of Covent Garden required Bickerstaff to create ten roles. Having found the successful formula in Love in a Village, *he repeated it with variations in his next three operas so that instead of casting a total of 40 performers for his four dramas, Bickerstaff (and Beard of course) needed only 21.*

Actors and Actresses	*Thomas and Sally* 28/11/60	*Love in a Village* 8/12/62	*Maid of the Mill* 31/1/65	*Love in the City* 21/2/67	*Lionel and Clarissa* 25/2/68	*The Royal Garland* 10/10/68
Beard 23/4/61:	Thomas Squire	Hawthorn	Giles			
Mattocks 23/4/61:	Squire Thomas	Young Meadows	Lord Aimworth	Spruce	Lionel	
Miss Brent (Mrs. Pinto)	Sally	Rossetta	Patty			
Mrs. Vernon (Miss Poitier)	Dorcas		Fanny	Miss LaBlond		
Shuter		Justice Woodcock	Sir Harry Sycamore	Wagg	Colonel Oldboy	
Dyer		Eustace	Mervin (25/2/66)		Jessamy	
Collins		Sir William Meadows				
Dunstall		Hodge	[Ralph: intended]	Barnacle	Jenkins	
Miss Davies		Margery				
Mrs. Walker		Deborah Woodcock				
Miss Hallam (Mrs. Mattocks)	Sally 18/3/65	Lucinda Rossetta (18/10/66)	Theodosia Patty (19/2/65)	Priscilla	Jenny	Young Shepherdess
Gibson			Fairfield	Old Cockney	Sir John Flowerdale	
Dibdin			Ralph	Young Cockney		
Baker			Mervin			

Mrs. Pitt			Lady Sycamore			
DuBellamy	Thomas (20/5/67)	Young Meadows (11/11/66)		Sightly		Young Shepherd
Mrs. Green				Molly Cockney	Lady Mary Oldboy	
Miss Brickler				Penelope		
Mahoon					Harman	Genius of England
Miss Macklin					Clarissa	
Mrs. Baker	Sally (29/4/65)	Margery (18/10/66)	Theodosia (19/2/65)		Diana	Calliope
Barnshaw						Old Shepherd

Appendix C
COMPOSERS AND BICKERSTAFF'S COMIC OPERAS

While Bickerstaff always maintained that his words were subservient to the music in his comic operas, with three exceptions, the composers were relegated to the "Table of Songs" when one was printed with the play. When the scores were published, the composers were recognized, but music books rarely achieved the circulation that the printed plays received, and often the music was attributed to the wrong composer.

Of the 42 composers listed in the following table, only 17 were in London during the time that Bickerstaff wrote his comic operas. At least seven had died before Bickerstaff began to write, and the rest were on the continent. It seems doubtful that Bickerstaff or his compiler bothered about possible copyright infringements. On the other hand, none of the 17 composers in London seems to have complained publicly that his music had been unfairly appropriated.

The three composers who were associated with Bickerstaff—Thomas Arne, Samuel Arnold, and Charles Dibdin—were reimbursed for their work—no more than £50 an opera if Arne's and Dibdin's accounts are correct. But their contributions were recognized to the extent that later musicologists have referred to their *operas rather than to Bickerstaff's. In addition to these three composers, four others knew that their music would appear in comic operas by Bickerstaff: Karl Abel, who wrote the overture for* Love in a Village; *Samuel Howard, who wrote two songs for* Love in a Village; *Thomas Alexander Erskine, Earl of Kelly (or Kellie), who wrote the overture for* Maid of the Mill; *J. C. Bach, who composed two songs for* Maid of the Mill, and one for *The Sultan. The following six operas for which Arne, Arnold and Dibdin wrote all the music will not be included in the table:* Thomas and Sally *(Arne);* The Royal Garland *(Arnold);* The Padlock, The Recruiting Serjeant, *and* He Wou'd if He Cou'd *(these last by Dibdin).*

The Table will show approximately how the airs in seven of Bickerstaff's operas were divided among 42 composers. Traditional airs of course are excluded, and no attempt has been made to reconcile discrepancies among various music editions of the same operas.

Explanation of abbreviations:
LIV: *Love in a Village,* first produced 8 December 1762
MOM: *Maid of the Mill,* 31 January 1765
DA: *Daphne and Amintor,* 8 October, 1765
LIC: *Love in the City,* 21 February 1767
LAC: *Lionel and Clarissa (School for Fathers),* 8 February 1770
CAP: *The Captive,* 21 June 1769
SUL: *The Sultan,* 12 December 1775

A number under each comic opera and on line with the composer's name signifies the number of airs by that composer in the opera.
* An asterisk indicates that the composer was in London when the opera was first performed.
X: No complete score of *Love in the City* has been found. As for *Daphne and Amintor,* an *X* signifies that the composer has at least one tune in the work.

Composers	LIV	MOM	DA	LIC	LAC	CAP	SUL
Abel, Karl F. * 1725–1787	over-ture						
Abos, Geronimo ?1708–?1786	1	1					
Agus, Joseph*[?]	1						
Arne, Thomas* 1710–1778	18				1		
Arnold, Samuel* 1740–1802		4					
Bach, J. C.* 1735–1782		2					1
Baildon, Joseph* ?1727–1774	1						
Barnard, John? 17th century	1						

Composers	LIV	MOM	DA	LIC	LAC	CAP	SUL
Barthelemon, Francois* 1741–1808				X			
Boyce, William* 1710–1779	1						
Carey, Henry ?1690–1743	1						
Chalon, Jan* [?]			2				
Ciampi, Legrenzio V. 1719–? [London, 1748–?]		1			2	1	
Cocchi, Gioacchino* before 1720–1804?		3	X	X		2	
Dibdin, Charles* 1745–1814 d. London, 1765				X	21	6	3
Duni, Egidio R. 1709–1775		4				1	
Festing, Michael C. d. 1752	1						
Galuppi, Baldassare 1706–1785	2	2		X	1		
Geminiani, Francesco 1680–1762	2	1					
Giardini, Felice De* 1716–1796	2	1					1
Handel, George F. 1685–1759	2						
Hasse, Johann Adolph 1699–1783		2					
Howard, Samuel* 1710–1782	2						
Jommelli, Niccolo 1714–1774		1		X			
Laschi?		1					
Monsigny, Pierre A. 1729–1817		3	X				
Earl of Kelly* 1732–1781		over- ture					
Paradies, Pietro D.* 1710–1792	1						
Perez, David 1711–1778						1	
Pergolesi, Giovanni B. 1710–1736		3		X			
Philidor, Francois 1726–1795		2					
Piccinni, Niccolo 1728–1800		1	X				
Rinaldo di Capua [?]		1					

Composers	LIV	MOM	DA	LIC	LAC	CAP	SUL
Scarlatti, Giuseppe 1712–1777		1					
Scolari, Giuseppe d. 1769					2		
Vento, Mattia* ?1736–1777?			X		2	1	
Vinci, Leonardo 1690–1730		1			1	1	
Weldon, John	1						

Two other composers have been listed in the music of *The Maid of the Mill:* "The late Elector of Saxony" (1 air); Martini (1 air). "Potenza" is mentioned as a composer in *Lionel and Clarissa;* and finally, James Oswald* might have contributed to *Love in a Village.*

Appendix D
PROPOSALS FOR PRINTING, BY SUBSCRIPTION, FABLES, PHILOSOPHICAL AND MORAL, IN VERSE

(London: William Griffin, 20 November 1771).

The first two fables appeared originally in the Gentleman's Journal *with the changes noted below.*

Fable I. "The Cuckoo Traveller."

Proposals	*Gentleman's Journal,* 19 November 1768
	Once, says the fable, a cuckow—
A Cuckoo, once, as cuckoos use,	Lords, Knights, and 'Squires, the tale's for you—
Went out upon a winter's cruize.	
Return'd, with the returning spring,	A cuckow once, as cuckows use,
Some hundred brothers of the wing,	
Curious to hear from foreign realms,	
Got round him in a tuft of elms.	The birds about him form a ring;
He shook his pinions, struck his beak,	While, puff'd with pride and self-conceit,
Attempted twice or thrice to speak;	High on an elm he takes his seat, Harranguing thus the num'rous band:
At length, up-rising on his stand,	
"Old England! Well, the land's a land!	
"But rat me, gentlemen, says he,	
"We passage fowl that cross the sea,	

"Have vast advantages o'er you,
"Whose native woods are all you view.
"The season past, I took a jaunt,
"Among the isles of the Levant;
"Where, by the way, I stuff'd my guts,
"With almonds and pistachio nuts.
" 'Twas then my whim some weeks to be,
"In that choice garden, Italy:
"But, underneath the sky's expanse,
"No climate like the south of France!
"You've often heard, I durst to swear,
"How plenty ortolans are there;
" 'Tis true, and more delicious meat,
"Upon my soul, I never eat;
"The eggs are good; it was ill luck,
"The day I had not ten to suck;
"Yet, notwithstanding, to my goût
"The bird's the sweeter of the two."

He went on, talking pert and loud,
When an old raven, 'mongst the crowd,
Stopp'd short his insolent career—
"Why, what a monst'rous bustle's here!
"You travell'd Sir, I speak to you,
"Who pass so many countries thro';
"Say, to what purpose is't you roam,
"And what improvements bring you home?
"Has Italy, on which you doat,
"Supply'd you with another note?
"Or France, which you extol so high,
"Taught you with better grace to fly?
"I cannot see that both together,
"Have alter'd you a single feather:
"Then tell not us of where you've been,

"Of what you've done, or what you've seen;	
"While you, and all your rambling pack,	For you and all your rambling pack
"Cuckoos go out, cuckoos come back.	Cuckows go out, cuckows come back."

Fable II. "The Ant and the Grasshopper." *Gentleman's Journal,* 26 November 1768

'Twas that bleak season of the year,	
In which no smiles, no charms appear;	
Bare were the trees; the rivers froze;	The ice-bound stream forgot to flow,
The hills, and mountains, capt with snows;	The hills around were capt with snow;
When lodgings scarce, and victuals scant,	
A grasshopper address'd an ant;	
And, in a supplicating tone,	
Begg'd he would make her case his own.	
"It was, indeed, a bitter task,	
"To those who were unus'd to ask;	To those who were oblig'd to ask;
"Yet she was forc'd the truth to say,	
"She had not broke her fast that day;	
"His worship, tho' with plenty bless'd,	
"Knew how to pity the distress'd;	
"A grain of corn to her was gold,	
"And Heav'n would yield him fifty-fold.	
The ant beheld her wretched plight	
Nor seem'd unfeeling to the sight;	
Yet, still inquisitive to know,	
How she became reduc'd so low;	
He ask'd her, (we'll suppose in rhime)	
What she did all the summer time?	
"In summer-time, good Sir, said she,	
"Ah! these were merry months with me!	
"I thought of nothing but delight,	

"And sung, Lord help me! day and night:
"Through yonder meadows did you pass,
"You must have heard me in the grass.

"Ay! cry'd the ant, and knit his brow—
"But 'tis enough I hear you now;
"And, Madam songstress, to be plain,
"You seek my charity in vain:
"What, shall th' industrious yield his due,
"To thriftless vagabonds like you!
"Some corn I have, but none to spare;
"Next summer learn to take more care;
"And in your frolic moods remember,
"July is follow'd by December.

To idle vagabonds like you!

Hence, seek assistance, morrice, prance,
In summer sing, in winter dance."
[end]

Fable III. "The Brook, and the Torrent" (reprinted in *Hibernian Magazine,* September, 1772).

Two silver springs, as rumour goes,
Among the Alpine mountains rose;
One, near the lofty summits plac'd,
Soft o'er the crags its passage trac'd;
The other, in a gentle flow,
Meander'd through a vale below.

However, all things, late or soon,
Must change, that lye beneath the moon:
The snow dissolves, the rain descends,
The upper brook augments, extends,
Its head above its channel lifts,
And furious tumbles down the clifts; [sic]
Where soon a mighty torrent grown,
The former stream's no longer known:

Onward it rushes, loud and strong,
And, while it carries all along,
Thus, from afar, begins to hail,
The humble current of the vale.
"Brother, look here, observe, and
see,
"How vast a change is wrought in
me:
"Tho' late so shallow, weak, and
small,
"My waters now a cat'ract fall;
"And driving ev'ry thing before,
"Shake rocks and mountains with
their roar:
"While you, unless appearance
lies,
"Unalter'd in your state or size,
"A petty streamlet yet distil,
"Scarce half enough to turn a mill.

The brook, with modesty,
reply'd,
"The fact is not to be deny'd:
"I am but petty, I confess,
"And, by comparison, seem less;
"But if your waters are enlarg'd,
"With foulness too I see them
charg'd;
"Turbid, and turbulent, no more
"They shine, and smile as
heretofore:
"Unenvy'd then pursue your course;
"Increase in tumult, bulk, and
force:
"I seek no greatness, bought so
dear,
"Let me be little still, and clear.

Fable IV. "The Painted Goose."

An arch designing knave, as e'er
Impos'd on clowns at country fair;
Pockets distrest, and credit low,
Resolv'd to rise upon a show.
He takes a goose, of portly size,
And paints it in a thousand dyes:
The neck was shining green, the
head
Glow'd to the sight a fiery red;

The wings display'd a mingled hue
Of burnish'd yellow, mixed with blue:
In short, the whole was of a piece;
Gaudy, and well contrived to fleece:
And, when he saw his work was dry,
He brought it to a village nigh;
And cry'd, with trumpet, up and down,
A Phoenix to be seen in town.

A phoenix! that must be a sight!
Folks are agog, and all goes right.
The bird, as ev'ry one agreed,
Was a CUROSITY indeed;
A charming, most delightful creature;
Nay, 'twas a prodigy in nature.

At length, among the shoals that came,
A lout (no matter for his name)
Pay'd at the door, nor fool, nor dunce,
Entered, and saw the thing at once.
"A phoenix this! (cry'd he in heat)
"Zounds! 'tis a damn'd confounded cheat;
"Why, comrade, (to a bumkin near)
"What is the marv'lous matter here?
"Have people got their senses loose?
" 'Tis nothing but a painted goose.

"Hush, (whisper'd t'other) make no fuss;
"Tis true, but what is that to us:
"E'en let the folly have its run,
"As sure to end, as it begun.
"Those colours, now so bright and sleek,
"Will all be faded in a week;
"The town will its own error see,
"And smoke the goose as well as we.

Fable V. "The Painter, The Connoiseur [sic], and the Coxcomb."

An artist of th' Athenian school,
Led by an academic rule,
Expos'd a picture to the crowd,
And bad the judges speak aloud.
The subject was from hist'ry ta'en,
Perseus had just Medusa slain;
And rais'd aloft, 'twixt earth and sky,
Appear'd on Pegasus to fly.

A critic came, and shook his head;
"What is amiss? the painter said.
"Those figures all betray constraint;
"That shade's too strong, that light's too faint;
"Your stile, in fact, I scarce should know;
"And though, perhaps, some strokes may show
"A master's pencil here and there,
"Upon the whole, the merit's bare.

Thus spoke the critic; but in vain:
The painter bid him look again;
Examine closer; he was sure,
The thing must please a connoisseur;
And if his art he understood,
He never finish'd ought so good.

A coxcomb presently drew nigh,
And o'er the canvas glanc'd his eye;
"Gods! in an ecstacy cries he,
"Was ever such a prodigy!
"Ay, here, indeed, we have a piece,
"The wonder and the pride of Greece;
"Where art and nature seem to strive;
"Perseus and Pegasus alive:
"And Gorgon's head, so much her own,
"I fear 'twill turn me into stone.

The painter heard, stretch'd forth his hand,
And snatch'd the picture from its stand;
Then turn'd, and as beneath his cloke
He put it, to the critic spoke:
"I now perceive, and own I must
"With shame, your censure was too just:
"When men of sense and taste find fault,
" 'Tis more than odds a work is naught;
"But if a coxcomb can admire,
"At once condemn it to the fire.

Appendix E
THE BRICKDUST-MAN AND MILK-MAID, "A MUSICAL DIALOGUE"

The Man driving an Ass laden with Brickdust, the Woman carrying her Pail.

AIR

Man. I am a lad, by fortune's spite,
Condemn'd to trudge from morn till night;
Thro' streets, and lanes, and squares I pass,
My riches all on one poor ass.
Gee ho then, Jack for on thou must,
Come maids, and buy, brickdust! brickdust!
O, if my hopes you now should bilk,
Buy brickdust, brickdust, hoa!

Woman. ——— ——— ——— milk, milk.

RECITATIVE

Woman. Good morrow, John!
Man. Good morrow, Moll!
Woman. Is that all?
Man. Is that all?

AIR

Man. O, Molly, I'm charm'd when you come in my sight,
Your breasts than your milk are more soft and more white,
And the pails that you carry, tho' both made of tin,
Are less bright than your eyes, and less smooth than your skin.
Both your trade and mine in your person I see,
Your lips, and your cheeks, with my brickdust agree;
So red is their colour—but, oh! to my smart,
No brickbat was ever so hard as your heart.

RECITATIVE

Woman. Think not, base Monkey to cajole me so,
When, at St. Giles's Church, full well you know,
We were out-AXED, above three months ago,
And if so be as how
We are not married now,
That it was my fault can you say?
(Willing as the flowers in May)
What bought I this brass ring for, pray?
You came dress'd out upon the day!
I too was dress'd—a silly toad!
But frighten'd at the man in black,
At the church door you turn'd your back,
And run away down Tyburn–road.

AIR

Woman. Get you gone, you nasty fellow,
You could hear me scream and bellow,
Yet return not to my cries.
You could leave me to the slanders,
Taunts and slurs of the bye-standers.
O, I could tear out your eyes.

RECITATIVE

Man. Moll, here's my hand—lay hold on't if you dare!
And now I will expose this here affair.

AIR

Man. In short, dearest Moll, you alone were in fault,
Ill tongues put it into my head you were naught:
With Darby O'Shannon I heard you were seen
At the Three Jolly Topers on Bedleum Green;
And could I in honour accept of a heart,
Where a great Irish chairman laid claim to a part?

Woman. Nay, John, as for that, you have no right to talk.
With Betty M'Gregor you oft sought a walk,
And at the Blue Postes you did not much think
To treat her with Hot-pot as long as she'd drink.
You may coax me, and turn the thing off with a laugh,
But I'll give her the whole, since the hussey has half.

Man. One day, having gotten a sup in my eye,)
I frolick'd with Betty, I cannot deny;)
But again if I kiss her, I wish I may die!)

Woman. And if with O'Shannon I went—put the case,)
I was o'er persuaded; in the very next place)
I meet him, I'll give him a slap in the face.)

Man and Woman. Then let us agree,
I with you, you with me,
Too long from our pleasure we've tarry'd,
To church let's once more, hear the service read o'er
Nor repent again till we are marry'd.

[*The London Magazine, or Gentleman's Monthly Intelligencer,* XLI (August 1772), 392–393.]

NOTES

Chapter 1

1. *The London Stage,* 1660–1800, Part 4, ed. George Winchester Stone, Jr., 1747–1776 (Carbondale, Illinois, 1962), I, 435. Statistics about the London theatres will be found in this fine work unless otherwise noted. For the comparison between Covent Garden, 1755, and 1765, see Stone, 460–491, 495–518, 1090–1145.

2. David Erskine Baker and Isaac Reed, eds. I, 28. In the 1812 edition the same biography appeared in I, part 1, 40.

3. Genealogical information supplied by Irish Genealogical Society. The playwright spelled his last name *without* a final *e.* It is a Lancashire name, and Bickerstaff's ancestors migrated to Ireland, County Antrim, during Cromwell's time.

4. Information supplied by R. J. Hayes, Director of the National Library of Ireland, from the *Gentleman's and Citizen's Almanack* [nd] of Dublin.

5. *Liber Munerum Publicorum Hiberniae.* Report by Rowley Lascelles (London, 1852), Part II, 93.

6. Constantia Maxwell, *Dublin Under the Georges 1714–1830,* revised ed. (London, 1956), pp. 124–125. Also passim 121–125. *Grove's Dictionary of Music and Musicians,* ed. J. A. Fuller Maitland (Philadelphia, 1915), V, 154.

7. Hubert Langley, *Doctor Arne* (Cambridge, 1938), pp. 55–56. W. H. Grattan Flood, "Dr. Arne's Visits to Dublin," *The Musical Antiquary,* I (July 1910), 215–233.

8. H. M. Walker, *A History of the Northumberland Fusiliers* 1674–1902 (London, 1919), p. 65. Public Record Office, London, Army Index 5436.

9. Walker, p. 64.

10. *The Letters of Philip Dormer Stanhope,* ed. Bonamy Dobree (London, 1932), IV (1748-1751), 1743.

11. Public Records Office, Dublin. Sir William Betham's Abstracts from Prerogative Wills. Deed 173 159 115763. *The Registry of Deeds,* Dublin, dated 10 January 1755. Bickerstaff's mother (the former Jane Brereton) died in 1744, his father in 1751. In addition to his sister Catherine, he had a brother Robert who died sometime before 1755.

12. *Army List* 5438.

13. Information about the Marine Corps furnished by the Royal Marine Historian, Captain G. H. Hennessy. See *Army Lists* under Marine reduced Second Lieutenants for Bickerstaff's name.

14. *Journal Encyclopédique,* "Love in a Village," III, 3d Part (1 May 1763), 113: *"L'Auteur donnera dans un autre genre de Comique. Il est jeune, & veut se livrer tout entier à la carrière du théâtre; & pour s'y former, il s'est rendu à Paris, òu il étudie les bons modèles du Théâtre François.* The 1 May 1763 date was the formal date for reduction in Marine Corps strength, according to Colonel J. T. Hall. In fact, Bickerstaff would have returned to civil life perhaps by January, 1763.

15. William Cooke, *Memoirs of Samuel Foote* (London, 1805), II, 123.

Chapter 2

1. Stone, 467, 472.

2. Isaac Bickerstaff, *Leucothoë* (London, 1756), "To the Reader," pp. v-vii. Garrick was popularly supposed to be the author-adaptor of both *The Fairies* and *The Tempest.* He denied his authorship in a letter to James Murphy French: Jesse Foot, *Life of Arthur Murphy* (London, 1811), p. 100.

3. *A Select Collection of Vocal Music,* ed. Isaac Bickerstaff (London, nd [1771?]), from the Preface (no pagination).

4. Benjamin Christie Nangle, *Indexes to The Monthly Review, First Series, 1749–1789* (London: Oxford, 1934), p. 146. Entry 2548. *Leucothoë,* XV, p. 153, identified as by Ralph Griffiths. See *The Monthly Review, or Literary Journal,* XV (September 1756), 153–162.

5. *Journal Encyclopédique, "Leucothoë,"* A Dramatique Piece. *Leucothoë Pièce Dramatique.* A Londres, 1756, vii (A Liège, 15 October 1756), 114–116. Quotations from p. 114.

6. *The Letters of David Garrick,* ed. David M. Little and George M. Kahrl (Cambridge, Mass., 1963), III, 1266, 1224. The letter is undated but must have been written after July, 1759, when Arne received his D. Mus. at Oxford.

7. "The Monthly Catalogue," *The London Magazine,* XXIX (December, 1760), 672.

8. *The Theatrical Register: or a Complete List of Every Performance at the Different Theatres for the Year 1769,* 2 parts (London [1769?]), II, 51.

9. *The Theatrical Review; or, New Companion to the Play-House,* 2 vols. (London, 1772), I, 15. The reviews, which originally appeared in *The Public Ledger,* were written "By a Society of Gentlemen, Independent of Managerial Influence," according to its title page. John Potter and Hugh Kelly probably wrote the majority, if not all, of the articles. See Charles Harold Gray, *Theatrical Criticism in London to 1795* (New York, 1931), p. 194.

10. *The Theatrical Review,* I, 271–272.

11. *Annals of Opera 1597–1940,* Compiled by Alfred Loewenberg, 2nd ed. (Geneva, 1955), col. 249.

12. Rev. S. C. Hughes, *The Pre-Victorian Drama in Dublin* (Dublin, 1904), p. 104. The Reverend Hughes totalled the number of performances for each of the many plays he catalogued, but he neglected to give a cutoff date for a last performance. From the title one can conclude that he traced the plays to the 1830s if they lasted that long.

13. Ethel Macmillan, "The Plays of Isaac Bickerstaff in America," *Philological Quarterly,* V (January 1926), 60. She gives 10 February 1767 as the earliest date

of the opera's performance at the Southwark Theatre, while *Annals* gives the earlier date.

14. Richardson Wright, *Revels in Jamaica 1682–1838* (New York, 1937), pp. 97, 201.

15. Benjamin Victor, *The History of the Theatres of London, From the Year 1760 to the Present Time* (London, 1771), III, 15.

16. Stone, 827, gives the first-night cast with Beard singing Thomas, and Mattocks, the 'Squire. See also Rev. John Genest, *Some Account of the English Stage, from the Restoration in 1660 to 1830* (Bath, 1832), IV, 622–623.

17. In "A New Edition" printed for W. Griffin and others, the casts for both Covent Garden and Drury Lane performances are given. Thomas was sung by DuBellamy at Covent Garden, a role he first assumed on 20 May 1767; thus this edition was printed sometime after that date.

18. John Aikin, *Essays on Song-Writing:* "With a Collection of such English Songs as are most Eminent for Poetical Merit," (London, 1772), p. iv.

19. *The Works of the Reverend John Wesley, A.M.*, ed. John Emory, 3d ed. (New York, 1856), IV, 168.

20. Winton Dean, *Handel's Dramatic Oratorios and Masques* (London, 1959), p. 113.

21. Charles Burney, *A General History of Music From the Earliest Ages to the Present (1789)*, ed. Frank Mercer (New York, 1957, from the edition of 1935), II, 1015–1016.

22. W. R. Anderson, "Round About Radio," *The Musical Times,* XCI (September, 1950), 346–347.

23. *The Private Correspondence of David Garrick with the Most Celebrated Persons of His Time,* ed. James Boaden (London, 1832), II, 87. In spite of Boaden's emendations, this is an invaluable work.

Chapter 3

1. John Burgoyne, *The Lord of the Manor* (London, 1781).

2. Charles Dibdin, *The By-Stander; or Universal Weekly Expositor* (London, 1790), pp. 301–302.

3. William J. Lawrence, "Early Irish Ballad Opera and Comic Opera," *The Musical Quarterly,* VIII (July, 1922), 398–399.

4. Lawrence, p. 399. Both Lawrence and I have necessarily generalized. His closing remarks could be made even more specific, for outside Covent Garden in the early 1760s there was no theatre prepared to stage full-length comic operas as part of its repertory. Drury Lane could not compete for most of the decade.

5. Boaden, I, 262. Letter from Joseph Reed to Garrick, 16 June 1767.

6. Playbills for *Love in a Village* advertised only twelve composers: Abos, Agus, Arne, Baildon, Boyce, Festing, Galluppi, Geminiani, Giardini, Handel, Howard, and Paradies; "with a New *Overture* by Abel." But from the third edition (1763) on, a "Table of the Songs" listed fifteen composers without adding any songs to those found in the original editions. The three additional were Barnard, Cary, and Weldon.

7. *Love in a Village;* a Comic Opera, 2nd ed. (London, 1763), The Advertisement appears in all the early editions. It follows the Dedication.

8. Charles Dibdin, *Complete History of the Stage* (London, 1800), V, 160. Hereafter cited as *History.*

9. Willard Austin Kinne, *Revivals and Importations of French Comedies in*

England, 1749–1800 (New York, 1939), pp. 86–87. Kinne also points out that "Justice Woodcock's amorous pursuit can be paralleled by that of Lisimon in Destouches's *Le Glorieux.*"

10. *The Theatrical Review; or, Annals of the Drama,* (London, 1763), I, January 1, 1763, 28.

11. Charles Johnson, *The Village Opera* (London, 1729).

12. Tate Wilkinson, *The Wandering Patentee; or, A History of the Yorkshire Theatres, From 1770 to the Present Time* (York, 1795), I, 112. No doubt every evangelist is reported sooner or later to have said something similar. The Salvation Army's General Booth allegedly made the same remark.

13. When Incledon played Hawthorn for the first time, William Hazlitt declared: "He makes a very loud and agreeable noise without any meaning. At present he both speaks and sings as if he had a lozenge or a slice of marmalade in his mouth. If he could go to America and leave his voice behind him, it would be a great benefit—to the parent country." *The Complete Works of William Hazlitt,* ed. P. P. Howe after the edition of A. R. Waller and Arnold Glover (London, 1933), XVIII, 328–329.

14. *The St. James Chronicle,* 1655, Tuesday, 1 October 1771. The letter is dated 27 September.

15. W. Chappell, FSA, *Popular Music of the Olden Time,* 1st ed. (London, nd), II, 667. A budge, according to Chappell, who quoted from Grose's Dictionary, "is a thief who slips into houses in the dark, to steal cloaks and other clothes." A pair of recent scholars have not been able to find out more about the words, which they assume were traditional: *The Oxford Dictionary of Nursery Rhymes,* ed. Iona and Peter Opie (Oxford, 1962), pp. 308–309.

16. Francis Gentleman, *The Dramatic Censor; or, Critical Companion* (London, 1770), I, 160. The most persistent purifier of English drama was James Plumptre, B.D., whose *The English Drama Purified* (Cambridge, 1812) cleaned up all those plays not utterly beyond redemption (*The Beggar's Opera* was beyond the pale).

17. Anon. [Hugh Kelly], *The Babler* (London, 1767), II, 23–27. *The Babler* was "a Careful Selection from those . . . Essays . . . under that title [published] during a course of Four Years, in *Owen's Weekly Chronicle.*" No. 70, Saturday, May 29 [1762] contained the essay on the drama.

18. Hazlitt, XVIII, 391–392. The review had appeared in *The Examiner,* 27 April 1828.

19. 9 December 1762, reprinted in *London Magazine* (December, 1762), p. 674.

20. #844, 8 to 10 December, 1762, p. 554.

21. *London Chronicle,* XXIII, 1775, Saturday, 30 April–Tuesday 3 May, 1768, p. 424.

22. Stationer's Hall records, p. 232. "Then Enter'd for their Copy. Love in a Village, a Comic Opera as it is performed at the Theatre Royal in Covent Garden. By Isaac Bickerstaff Esqr. Received Nine Copies for the Proprietors [signed] Charles Marshall." The four proprietors, each with a ¼ share were listed.

23. *Journal Encyclopédique* (1 May 1763, à Bouillon), III, part 3, 106–113.

"In London, as in France, audiences required nothing of a comic opera save wit and plenty of gaiety: the Author has perfectly satisfied these two requirements: it may even be that had he wished to endow the piece with greater verisimilitude, he would have been forced to sacrifice enjoyment to regularity. Besides, ought one to judge according to the rules, works belonging to a genre which is itself outside the rules, and which has nonetheless afforded much pleasure for the past several years? we fear only lest it please a little too greatly, and that by amusing, it may in the end elevate the taste for frivolity above the love of the beautiful, the good and the useful."

"One must see this work as a happy omen for the success of the pieces which the Author will give us in this new kind of comedy. He is young, and wishes to devote himself entirely to a career in the theatre; and to further his training, he has come to Paris, where he is studying the fine models of French Theatre, not only by reading them, but also by seeing them performed. We have moreover heard him sing some airs from his play, those which pleased best in London; but what a difference from those are the successes achieved by our modern plays in this genre[!]"

24. *The Diary of John Baker,* ed. Philip C. Yorke (London, 1931), p. 174.

25. Gentleman judged plays by their moral or lack of it. He himself explained that a critic must "enquire for the moral, without which no dramatic piece can have intrinsic worth" (I, 9).

26. Oscar G. Sonneck, *Early Opera in America* (New York, 1915), p. 34.

27. Macmillan, p. 63.

28. Hughes, p. 136. Hughes gives no cutoff date, but 1836 seems reasonable.

29. Henry Grattan, Esq., M.P., *Memoirs of the Life and Times of the Rt. Hon. Henry Grattan,* (London, 1849), III, Appendix VII, 509.

30. Aloys R. Mooser, *Operas, Intermezzos, Ballets Cantates, Oratorios Joués En Russie Durant Le XVIII Siecle,* 2nd ed. (Geneva-Monaco, 1955), pp. 78–79. Mooser cited the *Sankt Peterbourgskya Viedomosti* as his source.

31. Pp. 452–453, not to be confused with Gentleman's *Dramatic Censor* of some forty years earlier.

32. Newspaper clipping (Y.d. 23. Winston Papers), Folger Library.

33. Colley Cibber, *The Dramatic Works of Colley Cibber* (London, 1754), III, Preface, iii–iv.

34. Newspaper clipping dated 20 October 1816. Clipping from Genest's *Ana,* a scrapbook of theatrical cuttings, 1815–1818, Harvard Theatre Collection. The correspondent spelled *Rossetta* with one "s," a practice very common.

35. *The London Chronicle; or, Universal Evening Post,* XII, 931, Friday, 10 December 1762, 561–562.

36. Hazlitt, XVIII, 391–392.

37. Hazlitt, VI, 163.

38. Cuthbert Shaw, *The Race,* 2nd ed. (London, 1766), pp. 27–28. Shaw used the pseudonym, "Mercurius Spur, Esq."

39. Thomas Davies, *Memoirs of the Life of David Garrick, Esq.,* 3rd ed. (London, 1781), II, 64.

40. Davies, II, 87. The operas were *The Royal Shepherd,* by Richard Rolt and music by Rush; *Almena,* by Rolt and music by Michael Arne and Battishall; and *Pharnaces,* by Thomas Hull with music by Bates. This last opera was produced in 1765.

41. Manuscript in the Larpent Collection, Huntington Library, "Music Alamode, or Bays in Chromatics," author unknown. Lacy wrote to the censor, "Sir, If this Farce . . . meet the approbation of the Lord-Chamberlain, we intend to have it perform'd at the Theatre Royal in Drury Lane 29 March 1764."

42. *Memoirs of John Bannister, Comedian,* ed. John Adolphus (London, 1838), I, 232–233.

Chapter 4

1. Isaac Bickerstaff, *The Maid of the Mill.* A Comic Opera. As it is Performed at the Theatre Royal in Covent Garden. The Music Compiled, and the Words written by the Author of *Love in a Village,* (London, 1765), Title page. For the repertory system with which Bickerstaff worked, see Appendix B.

2. Henry Saxe Wyndham, *The Annals of Covent Garden Theatre from 1732 to 1897* (London, 1906), I, 156. Wyndham's source was Busby's *History of Music,* (London, 1819), II, 468. Thomas Busby collaborated with Arnold in 1786 on a *Musical Dictionary,* so his word can be accepted when he writes that Arnold told him the details of the financial arrangements.

3. Isaac Bickerstaff, *The Maid of the Mill* (London: John Bell, 1781). The music was published and sold by R. Bremner, at the Harp and Hautboy Opposite Somerset House in the Strand, no date.

4. Charles Dibdin, *The Professional Life of Mr. Dibdin* (London, 1803), I, 46.

5. Stone, I, xxvii. His source was the British Museum Add. MSS. 38,730, fol. 104b which contains many transactions of this sort. It is the source for the sale on 16 November when Becket and others bought the ⅛ share.

6. Beaumont and Rowley, "The Maid in the Mill," *The Works of Beaumont and Fletcher,* ed. Rev. Alexander Dyce (London, 1845), IX, 199–294.

7. Review of the opera, *Gentleman's Magazine,* XXXV, (February, 1765), 77–78. He was called a "graceless booby" in "Theatrical Intelligence," *The Gentleman's and London Magazine,* XXXV (February, 1765), 68–70. This Dublin-published magazine combined reviews, added an original comment or two, and published them as its own.

8. Quoted in *The St. James Chronicle,* 611, Thursday, 31 January–Saturday, 2 February 1765.

9. *The London Chronicle,* XVII (Friday, 1 February 1765), 1267, 116–117.

10. Wednesday, 30 January—Friday, 1 February 1765, 1180, 111.

11. Francis Gentleman, *Dramatic Censor,* II, 114.

12. 31 January–2 February 1765. In the same review, Bickerstaff's lyrics were thought "not without Merit," but would have been better "if the Author's Attention had not necessarily been too much engaged in reconciling the Words to the Music he had chosen."

13. Quoted in Charles Sanford Terry, *John Christian Bach* (London, 1929), I, 97. *The Public Advertiser* for 7 May 1765.

14. Letter to the *Morning Herald,* 11 November 1815, by Hugh Prankland. Harvard Theatre Collection, clipping.

15. XXXV (February, 1765), "The Maid of the Mill," a new ballad opera, 77–78.

16. February, 1765, pp. 55–56. After reviewing *The Maid of the Mill,* the writer discussed the superiority of Covent Garden to Drury Lane. His article began with a condemnation of *Pharnaces,* which was playing at DL. Another journal, *The Monthly Review,* XXXII (February 1765), "Monthly Catalogue," 155–156, cautioned Bickerstaff about the morality of his work, and asked his pardon "if we take the liberty of recommending to him, in respect of his future productions, to be more attentive to one capital circumstance—their TENDENCY— . . . . To encourage young people of family and fortune to marry so very disproportionately, as, in the present instance . . . is even worse than the story of Mr. B. and Pamela: . . . and very little better than Lady —'s running away with her footman.—Ought such gross indiscretions to be *countenanced* on the public stage?"

17. III (May 1765), 121–127.
18. III, 68–69.
19. I (London, 1772), 107–109.
20. "Postscript. Dramatic Strictures," 14 November 1772.
21. Charles Dibdin, *The By-Stander; or Universal Weekly Expositor* (August 15 1789–February 6, 1790), published as one volume (London, 1790), p. 170.
22. Terry, *Bach,* I, 97. Terry termed this air and the other which Bach contributed, "Simple ditties with a right English flavour. . . ."
23. *Anthologia Hibernica,* I (Dublin: May, 1793), 366–367. When *The Maid of the Mill* was performed at the Theatre-Royal, Edinburgh, on Monday, 25 April 1825, it was reviewed by *The Edinburgh Dramatic Review,* III (Monday, 25 April 1825), 529–530. In the review, the anonymous critic quoted the fears of the *Anthologia Hibernica,* and replied: "This is a piece of most precious cant. When, we should wish to know, was the *proper subordination of society* ever destroyed in this country; and by such delusions as novels and operas? So far as we understand the novel of *Pamela,* its tendency is not to inspire ambitious thoughts in females of a humble rank, but to strengthen their virtue against the temptation of wealth; and so far from teaching them disdain of all around them, *Pamela,* after her elevation, is made to set an example of the most grovelling humility. The opera is a very fine one . . ." (528).
24. Newspaper clipping, Harvard Theatre Collection.
25. Robert Hitchcock, *An Historical View of the Irish Stage; From the Earliest Period Down to the Close of the Season in 1788* (Dublin, Vol. II, 1794), II, 137–138.
26. Mooser lists the 5 May performance in St. Petersburg, while Loewenberg gave the 16 May date. Both Loewenberg and Wright (Richardson Wright, *Revels in Jamaica,* 1682–1838, New York, 1937) give 13 November 1779 for the Kingston performance.
27. *'Tis Well It's No Worse* (London, 1770), Preface, viii.
28. James Winston manuscript papers, Folger Library, T.a.66, "From Arthur Murphy's papers lent me by Mr. Upcott. 11 June 1823." A copy of the articles of agreement.

Chapter 5

1. Genest, V, 128.
2. See Stone, 1126–1132.
3. Isaac Bickerstaff, *Daphne and Amintor* (London, 1765). The first edition was published for William Griffin, Newbery, etc. Stone (1133) wrote that the comic opera was first published on Saturday, 12 October 1765. After the comic opera opened, there appeared an advertisement in *The London Chronicle* which hinted at what happened to such works when they were performed in the provinces. "To prevent this Opera from being performed in the Country in an imperfect Manner, which has been the Fate of others. Such companies as intend to bring it on the Stage, may be supplied by the Publisher with a complete score on reasonable terms" (XVIII, 7–10 November, 1765, 554). Books of the opera were available at the theatre on opening night, 8 October (Stone, 1132). *Daphne and Amintor* went through six editions within a year.
4. M. De Saint-Foix, "L'Oracle," *Oeuvres Complettes* (*A Paris,* 1778), I, 1–36.
5. VIII (November 1765), 140–141.
6. *The Universal Museum and Complete Magazine,* I (October 1765), 504–505.
7. XVII, 1314, 9 December 1765. For Dibdin, see *History,* V, 160.

8. *Catalogue of Opera Librettos Printed before 1800 in the Library of Congress,* ed. Oscar Sonneck, (Washington, D.C., 1914), I, 349.

9. *Biographisch-Bibliographisches Quellen-Lexikon der Musiker und Musikgelehrten,* ed. Robert Eitner (Leipzig, 1900), II, Chalon, Jan, 401.

10. *The London Magazine,* XXXIV (October 1765), 592, "Prologue to *Daphne and Amintor.*"

11. Thursday, 10 October–Saturday, 12 October 1765.

12. Frances Brooke, *The Excursion,* II (London, 1777), Book V, Chapter vii, 27.

13. *Lloyd's Evening Post,* XVII (Monday, 7 October–Wednesday, 9 October 1765), 1285, 350–351. *The Public Ledger,* VI (Thursday, 10 October), #1799.

14. XVIII, 1380, 397.

15. This letter owes its immediate genesis to "The Occasional Prologue" spoken by Thomas King at the opening of Drury Lane.

16. (London, 1767), p. 5.

17. Jesse Foot, *The Life of Arthur Murphy, Esq.* (London, 1811), p. 205.

18. Anon. [Isaac Bickerstaff], *The Plain Dealer* (London, 1766), IV, x, pp. 78–79. It was published "With Alterations from Wycherly." (Title page)

19. Samuel Johnson, *A Dictionary of the English Language,* 10th ed. (London, 1810), II, "symmetry."

20. *History,* V, 260.

21. Foot, p. 345. Foot published an excerpt of Murphy's brief for the case of Miller against Taylor which dealt with copyright protection. The booksellers of Bickerstaff's adaptation were Griffin, T. Lowndes, Nicoll, and Becket and DeHondt: the usual vendors of Bickerstaff's plays. Reference to this sitting at Guildhall will be referred to again when Bickerstaff's income is discussed.

22. *Love in the Suds; a Town Eclogue. Being the Lamentation of Roscius for the Loss of his Nyky,* anon., 5th ed. (London, 1772), footnote 24.

23. Newspaper clipping, James Winston Collection, Folger Library, Y.d. 25 (2).

24. ALS, John Hoadly to David Garrick, 4 December 1766, in the Forster Collection, Victoria and Albert Museum, F.48.F.38, Ms 11 and 12. Manly might not have been castrated, but he certainly was the worse for wear.

25. I (London, 1772), 98–102: The critic wrote, "the task of altering a Play written by a first-rate Genius, may be compared to that, of re-touching an excellent Picture, painted by an eminent Artist, which should never be attempted but by a very able Hand" (p. 99).

26. Arthur Murphy, *The Life of David Garrick, Esq.* (Dublin, 1801), 268–269. Considering Murphy's own career as a dramatist, his advice was a matter of a rival calling a plagiarist dishonorable.

27. John Philip Kemble, *Wycherley's Comedy of the Plain Dealer, with Alterations* (London, 1796), Reprinted in *Kemble's Select British Theatre* (London, 1815).

28. Stone, p. 1141, 6 December 1765. The work was advertised as a "New Musical Comedy in 3 Acts." Lawrence, "Early Irish Ballad Opera and Comic Opera," p. 399, states that this was the first time that the term "musical comedy" was employed.

29. *Memoirs of Richard Cumberland* (London, 1806), p. 186.

30. Sir Nicholas Nipclose, Baronet [Francis Gentleman], *The Theatres.* A Poetical Dissection (London, 1772), p. 12. The poem was dedicated to Mrs. Abington in November, 1771, but it is dated as 1772; John Bell was the printer. That Gentleman meant Bickerstaff for the "gross, ignorant, sycophant" is evinced by his poetic description of Bickerstaff which will be quoted later.

31. Kalman A. Burnim, *David Garrick, Director* (Pittsburgh, 1961), p. 14.

Burnim gives no date, but Cumberland's last play for Covent Garden was *The Brothers,* December 1769, and his first for Drury Lane was *The West Indian,* 19 January 1771. It is logical to assume that Cumberland began work for Garrick in 1770.

32. Stone, I, cviii.

33. Whitefoord Papers, 36,595, #68. Also #36 and #84 for related material and the epigrams.

34. Richard Cumberland, *The Choleric Man* (London, 1793), p. xi. The first edition was published on 12 January 1775; see Garrick's *Letters,* III, Ltr. 888, footnote 2.

35. Garrick's *Letters,* III, Ltr. 888, 985. Date is conjectural.

Chapter 6

1. Probably the review referred to by the Garrick *Letters* editors of *The Clandestine Marriage: Journal Encyclopédique,* IV, part 2 (1 June 1766) 110–118. The "review" was merely a summary.

2. Newspaper clipping, James Winston Collection, Folger Library. *Y*.d.25 (2).

3. Isaac Bickerstaff, *Love in the City;* a Comic Opera, 2nd ed. (London: W. Griffin, 1767), Preface, pp. i–ii. The comic opera was first published in April; see *The London Magazine,* XXXVI (April, 1767), 206. There were only two editions.

4. James J. Lynch, *Box Pit and Gallery* (Berkeley, 1953), p. 204.

5. Anon., *The Theatrical Campaign* (London, 1767), p. 40.

6. George Colman, *The English Merchant* (London, 1767), Prologue.

7. Charles Dibdin, *Life,* I, 53.

8. This version of the anecdote is a combination of two versions by Dibdin, one in his *History,* V, 261; the other in his *Life,* I, 57. The comic opera was performed only four nights.

9. "Account of Love in the City," *The London Magazine,* XXXVI (February 1767), 90–91. The review was reprinted from *The London Chronicle,* XXI, 1589, Tuesday, 24 February 1767, 192.

10. "From *The Rosciad," Lloyd's Evening Post and British Chronicle,* XX, 1503, 23 February 1767, 186.

11. "Monthly Catalogue," XXIII (London, February, 1767), 139.

12. Attributed to Langhorne by Nangle, p. 235.

13. "Monthly Catalogue," XXXVI (London, February 1767), 164.

14. III, part 1 (April 1767), 145.

15. (London, 1767), pp. 85–89.

16. *Biographia Dramatica,* (London, 1782), I, 199, #130.

17. In his translation of "L'Ecole des Femmes," Henri Van Laun wrote that Bickerstaff "has partly imitated" Act II, scene vi in his Act III, scene ii. *The Dramatic Works of Molière,* (Edinburgh, 1875), II, Appendix H, 223–225. But if he did, the imitation is too general to place Bickerstaff in Molière's debt this time. Kinne doesn't even mention *Love in the City* in his *Revivals and Importations of French Comedies in England.*

18. "The Clandestine Marriage," in *The Dramatick Works of George Colman* (London, 1777), I, 151–292.

19. It follows p. 292 in *The Dramatick Works of Colman,* I.

20. Thomas Gilliland, *The Dramatic Mirror* (London, 1808), I, 268. *"Love in the City,* opera, 1767, reduced to an after-piece called The Romp, 1767." The earliest notices so far found of *The Romp* appeared in *Faulkner's Journal* for

19/22 January 1771, and in *The Hibernian Magazine, or, Compendium of Entertaining Knowledge* (Dublin: March 1771), "Theatre Chronicle," pp. 85–87. Both papers listed a performance of the farce at the Capel-Street Theatre for 23 January 1771 with *The Lying Valet* as afterpiece. This production was not billed as a new play. Hitchcock also refers to *The Romp* during the 1770–1771 Dublin season (II, 185). A playbill for the New Theatre in Lancaster for Monday 25 August 1777 advertised for Mrs. Bogle's Benefit that day, a "Comic Opera of Three Acts (never performed here) *The Romp;* Or, *A Cure for the Spleen*" (Playbill, Harvard Theatre Collection).

21. *Diary and Letters of Madame D'Arblay* (1778–1840), ed. by Charlotte Barret (London, 1905), III, 386–387.

22. The first edition of *The Romp* was printed with the following title-page: "*The Romp.* / A Musical Entertainment. / In Two Acts. / Altered from *Love in the City,* / By Mr. BICKERSTAFF, / As it has been acted at / The Theatres Royal in Dublin and York, / and now Performed at . . . Drury Lane." The ambiguous placing of Bickerstaff's name allows him to be author of both plays, or either one of them. *The Biographia Dramatica* assigned authorship to "—Lloyd. An actor in the York company" (I, part 2, 457).

23. For Bickerstaff's possible contribution to anti-slavery literature, see Wylie Sypher, *Guineas's Captive Kings: British Anti-Slavery Literature of the XVIIIth Century* (Chapel Hill, 1942), p. 235. Sypher's work will be referred to again in the chapter on *The Padlock.*

24. Hazlitt, XVIII, 229–230; from *The Times,* 23 May 1817.

25. Actually Garrick hired Bickerstaff to prevent Covent Garden from giving its audiences what they wanted; he did not encourage Bickerstaff to continue writing comic operas. Garrick's opinion of opera is epitomized in his comment to Arne, "music is at best but pickle to my roast beef." (George Hogarth, *Memoirs of the Opera,* A New Edition of the *Musical Drama* [London, 1851], II, 59.)

26. Pp. 555–558.

27. ALS, "Bickerstaff to Garrick," Harvard Theatre Collection; copy in Forster Collection, Victoria and Albert Museum. On the original letter someone has pencilled in "1768" after 14 July; but in July 1768, Bickerstaff was a neighbor of George Garrick in Somerset-Yard.

28. Joseph Reed, "Theatrical Duplicity; or a Genuine Narrative of the Conduct of David Garrick Esq. to Joseph Reed on his Tragedy of 'Dido,' Containing all the Letters, and Several Conversations, which passed between the Manager, Author, and others on that Subject." Ms. in Harvard Theatre Collection. Page 62. Referred to hereafter as Reed.

29. *European Magazine,* XXIV (December, 1793), 422. Bickerstaff of course knew about Kelly's play before 1 September 1767 according to Kelly's letter. When Goldsmith was asked "about Kelly's writing a comedy, he said, 'He knew nothing at all about it—he had *heard* there was a *man of that name* about the town who wrote in Newspapers, but of his talents for comedy, or even the work he was engaged in, he could not judge.'"

30. Murphy had been annoyed with Garrick because he thought the manager had staged *The Country Girl,* an adaptation of Wycherley's *The Country Wife,* purposely to anticipate his own adaptation, *The School for Guardians,* which he had written for Ann Elliott, a young actress with whom he was involved. Bickerstaff prevailed upon Murphy to leave with him his tragedy "The Conquest of Peru," which Bickerstaff then recommended to Garrick.

31. ALS, Bickerstaff to Garrick, Donald F. Hyde Collection, Somerville, New Jersey. Copy in the Forster Collection, Victoria and Albert Museum. The letter is dated only "Battersea August 18th," but the only time that Bickerstaff lived in Battersea was in 1767; he moved to Somerset-Yard by November, 1767.

32. Anthony J. Camp, Director of Research, Society of Genealogists, London; letter to the author. For William Brereton, see Chapter 10.

Chapter 7

1. Letter, "Isaac Bickerstaff to unnamed correspondent," Hyde Collection. Punctuation added. It might have been to George Colman or to John Nourse, a printer to Paul Vaillant. Vaillant's shop, at this time, was in the Strand near Somerset Yard where Bickerstaff lived. A note at the Folger Library (W.b. 475, op. p. 221) by Bickerstaff to John Nourse, dated 20 November, shows that Nourse has been giving him money: "Sir please to pay the bearer three Guineas which place to account of Sir your most Obed. Servt. Isaac Bickerstaff." Under the address are the following transactions but with no dates:

"rec'd——10——10——0
6 6
3 3
3 3"

Bickerstaff sent another note to Nourse on 23 December 1767, this time for two guineas (Osborn Collection, Yale University Library).

2. ALS, "Bickerstaff to Colman, undated," Harvard Library.

3. *Catalogue of the Valuable Library and Collections of . . . William Wright, Esq.,* (London, 1899), 6, item 1087, ALS 1 p. 4to, to George Colman Sr., dated 30 November 1767; and copy of Colman's answer on back of letter. The sale was 12 June 1889 at Sotheby.

4. ALS, "Bickerstaff to Younger," 9 December 1767, Bodleian Library, Oxford. MS. Montagu d. 11. Younger's reply is written beneath Bickerstaff's letter.

5. John Forster, *The Life and Adventures of Oliver Goldsmith* (Boston, nd), III, 94. Other references are to the first edition (London, 1848).

6. Als, "Bickerstaff to Colman," in *David Garrick, A Memorial Illustrative of His Life . . . .* Collected by Henry Irving (London, nd), III, #206. Garrick Club, London.

7. *The Theatrical Monitor,* No. XIV (27 February 1768), p. 10. Stone, p. 1313 notes, "Hardly possible for '500 orders' to have filled the house which took in £233 19s."

8. Eugene R. Page, *George Colman the Elder* (New York, 1935), p. 150.

9. For details of the feud and its outcome, see Page, pp. 150–185.

10. Except when otherwise noted, the testimony of Garrick, Lacy, Bickerstaff and Dibdin has been taken from British Museum Manuscript 33218, the notes of Harris's attorneys (possibly by Arthur Murphy) which set forth the attack they used, what they wished to prove, and the depositions of their witnesses.

11. Harry William Pedicord, *The Theatrical Public in the Time of Garrick* (New York, 1954), pp. 120–121. His source is a copy of the "Winston Ms. Relative to Covent Garden Theatre," Records of a court action (or several) involving Covent Garden, Folger Library.

12. Stone, 1314, 1316, 1317.

13. *Lionel and Clarissa* (London: W. Griffin, 1768), III, iii, p. 57.

14. *The British Essayists,* xxi (Boston, 1885), Saturday, 20 October 1753, 57–66.

15. *The Dramatic Censor:* or, Critical and Biographical Illustrations of the British Stage. For the Year 1811, ed. J. M. Williams, L.L.D. (London, 1812), November, column 441.

16. And much more. *The Theatrical Monitor,* No. XV, Saturday, 5 March 1768, pp. 6–7.

17. *The Political Register, and Impartial Review of New Books, For MDCCLXVIII* (London, April 1768), II, 318–319.

18. London, March 1768, IV, 139–140.

19. Conversation with Dr. Fiske. It was broadcast on 25 August 1963.

20. ALS, "Bickerstaff to Jane Pope," 18 October 1769, Bodleian Library, Oxford, MS. Toynbee Vol. 1. The farce has not been identified.

21. Copy of a letter from Bickerstaff to Garrick, Forster Collection, Victoria and Albert Museum. The copyist misdated the letter as 1767 (April 5), but the references prove it to be 1769.

22. Hitchcock, II, 177. Presumably this was the first version, because Hitchcock refers to its success at Covent Garden, p. 176.

23. Hughes, p. 136. The usual problem of dating occurs.

24. I, 366–367.

25. New Series II, 434–435.

26. *History,* V, 261.

27. Plumptre had a curious adverse criticism of this opera: "The Airs in this Opera are by no means what I could wish them to be. Few of them will stand independent of the dialogue with which they are connected; and many of them have the fault . . . of arising out of the incident of the moment" (p. 10). Kemble's reply, see ALS, "Kemble to Plumptre," University Library, Cambridge.

28. IX, December, 426.

29. Isaac Bickerstaff, *The Absent Man* (London: William Griffin, 1768), Preface, no pagination.

30. Copy of a letter from Dibdin to Garrick, Forster Collection, Victoria and Albert. Dibdin's Benefit had been scheduled for 13 May, but it was postponed until the 24th because the theatres closed in deference to a death in the royal family.

Chapter 8

1. British Museum Ms. 33218.

2. Kalman A. Burnim, *David Garrick Director* (Pittsburgh, 1961), p. 50.

3. Charles Dibdin, *The Musical Tour of Mr. Dibdin,* (Sheffield, 1788), pp. 285–299. This section of Dibdin's work was reprinted in a slightly abridged form in *The Harmonicon, A Journal of Music,* I, part I (London, 1824), No. XVII, May, 1824, 87, and quotations will be drawn from the journal.

4. His original Preface, written in Larpent Manuscript LA 285, has no mention of Dibdin, and concluded with Bickerstaff writing, "Was the author conscious of any further obligations, he would not fail to acknowledge them."

5. Charles Dibdin, *The Padlock* [music] (London: John Johnston, [1768]). Diblin's concluding paragraph agrees with Bickerstaff's statement that Dibdin had worked for Bickerstaff:

> I am indeed told there are some who affect not only to doubt my having set the MUSICK of the PADLOCK but even to name the composer as some Italian master (God knows who) that I stole it from: but if any such composer exists, my enemies would do well to produce his works for I declare I am not conscious

of having receiv'd any assistance in what I here do myself the Honour to present to you [Mrs. Garrick], but from the Author of the Opera, and my Obligations to his Taste and Judgment, I am very ready to Acknowledge.

6. ALS, "Bickerstaff to Mrs. Garrick," Folger Shakespeare Library, W.b. 492. (Copy in Victoria and Albert Museum).

7. Horace Walpole, *Memoirs of the Reign of King George the Third,* ed. Sir Denis D. Le Marchant, reedited by G. F. Russell Barker (London, 1894), III, 211. And Arthur Murphy, *Life of David Garrick* (Dubin, 1801), p. 293.

8. *The European Magazine* (London, August, 1788), XIV, 103–104.

9. *Memoirs of an Unfortunate Son of Thespis; Being a Sketch of the Life of Edward Everard,* Comedian (Edinburgh, 1818), pp. 62–63.

10. Warwick Wroth, *The London Pleasure Gardens of the Eighteenth Century* (London, 1896), p. 269. Everard described the fantoccini, and Wroth dated it.

11. George Speaight, *The History of the English Puppet Theatre* (London, 1955), pp. 117, 123, Appendix B, pp. 330–334.

12. Wylie Sypher, *Guinea's Captive Kings,* pp. 235–238.

13. Herbert Marshall and Mildred Stock, *Ira Aldridge The Negro Tragedian* (London: Rockliff, Salisbury Square, 1958), p. 233. Translated from *Life and Works of M. P. Pogodin (Zhizn i Trudy M. P. Pogodin)* (St. Petersburg, 1902), XVI, 192–196.

14. Isaac Bickerstaff, *The Royal Garland,* a New Occasional Interlude, in Honour of His Danish Majesty. Set to music by Mr. Arnold (London: T. Becket and P. A. De Hondt, 1768), Cast of Characters.

15. *London Magazine,* XXXVII (October 1768), 556.

16. William Kenrick, *A Letter to David Garrick, Esq.* (London, 1772), p. 23.

Chapter 9

1. Hazlitt, VI, 163.

2. *The Dramatic Works of Colley Cibber, Esq.,* "The Non-Juror" (London: Henry Lintot, 1753), III, Act V, scene i, 76.

3. Monsieur De Molière, "Tartuffe, ou L'Imposteur" (London: John Watts, 1732), V, in *Select Comedies of Mr. Molière,* In French and English, trans. by John Watts, Act III, scene vi, p. 100.

4. *Tartuffe: or, The French Puritan,* "Rendered into English, with much Addition and Advantage" by Matthew Medbourne (London, 1707), III, vi, p. 34. Dudley H. Miles, "The Original of *The Non-Juror,*" PMLA, XXIII, 1915, 195-214, wrote (p. 197) that the 1707 edition is the same as that of 1670 except there is more capitalization than in the first. Miles concluded that Cibber used Medbourne's *Tartuffe,* not Molière's.

5. Identified by Charles Harold Gray, *Theatrical Criticism in London to 1795* (New York, 1931), pp. 171–175.

6. 3 February 1868, p. 12.

7. 8 February 1868, LII, 146.

8. Newspaper clipping, Harvard Theatre Collection, no other dating except 24 December 1873, no pagination.

9. Newspaper clipping, Harvard Theatre Collection.

10. *The Times* (London, 13 June 1887), p. 12.

11. Newspaper clipping, Harvard Theatre Collection; no date, but the clipping gives the cast for the 11 June 1887 production.

12. *European Magazine,* XXIV (September, 1793), 171. Forster, *Goldsmith*

(London, 1848), p. 492. "Goldsmith yielded to Griffin's solicitation . . . and consented to take part in the editing of a new *Gentleman's Journal* in which Kenrick was a leading writer, and for which Hiffernan, Kelly, and some others were engaged."

13. Advertisement in *The London Chronicle,* XXIV (Saturday, 12 November 1768), 463. Repeated on Tuesday, 15 November, p. 471; Wednesday, 16 November, p. 476.

14. Listed in *Bibliography of French Translations of English Works 1700–1800,* ed. Charles Alfred Rochedieu, Introduction by Donald F. Bond (Chicago, 1948), p. 24.

15. Castilhon (or Castillon) is listed as the author of *Le Mendiant Boiteux* in *Manuel Bibliographique de la Littérature Française Moderne,* Nouvelle Edition (Paris: Librairie Hachette, 1921), p. 821, #11349. Castilhon's *Gwinett* was reviewed favorably in the *Journal Encylopédique,* III, part 3 (15 March 1770), 478–479, with no mention of Bickerstaff.

16. *American Bibliography,* ed. Charles Evans (New York, 1910), VI, 1779–1785; VII (1912); X (1929); XII (1934); XIII, ed. Clifford K. Shipton (1955).

17. No. 67 in Cumberland's *Minor Theatre* (London, [1828]). In America it was published as part of Turner's *American Stage* (Philadelphia, 1833).

Chapter 10

1. Copy of a letter from Bickerstaff to Garrick, dated 5 April 1767, but which obviously should be 1769. Forster Collection, Victoria and Albert Museum.

2. Isaac Bickerstaff, *Dr. Last in His Chariot,* A Comedy (London: W. Griffin, 1769). The Prologue was by Garrick and the Epilogue by Bickerstaff.

3. Kinne, p. 76.

4. *Foote's Prologue Detected; with a Miniature Prose Epilogue of his Manner in Speaking it,* by Philo-Technicus Miso-mimides (London, 1770).

5. As above, p. 23. In the prologue itself, Foote lamented the decay of drama and taste. It is unlikely that Philo-Technicus-Miso-mimides was referring to *The Captive,* Bickerstaff's companion-piece to *Dr. Last.*

6. Isaac Bickerstaff, *The Captive* (London: W. Griffin, 1769). The scenes which Bickerstaff adapted from *Don Sebastian* were Act II, ii; Act III, ii; Act IV, i.

7. Montague Summers, ed. *Dryden The Dramatic Works* (London, 1932), VI, "Don Sebastian," 15.

8. Edward J. Dent, *Mozart's Operas,* A Critical Study, 2nd ed. (London, 1947), p. 71. See also Loewenberg's *Annals of Opera* under Andre, *Belmont und Constanze.*

9. *The London Chronicle,* XXV (Saturday, 13 May 1769), #1936, 450.

10. Wroth, p. 212. See also, Mollie Sands, *Invitation to Ranelagh,* 1742–1803 (London, 1946), p. 102. Sands silently follows Wroth in her details. Both write that it was ten o'clock when Bickerstaff's serenata was performed, while the *Chronicle* said nine o'clock. Loewenberg, who saw none of these accounts, wrote "the date is given here for the first time" when he dated the work, *Annals,* col. 307.

11. Isaac Bickerstaff, *The Ephesian Matron,* A Comic Serenata, After the Manner of the Italian (London: W. Griffin, 1769), Advertisement, pp. 5–6. See also Sands, p. 102, who quoted the same passages, but credited Dibdin with their composition.

12. For a partial history, see *Come Pervenne e Rimase in Italia, La Matrona D'Efeso,* Studio di Augusto Cesari (Bologna, 1890).

13. Christian Deelman, *The Great Shakespeare Jubilee* (New York, 1964), and Martha Windburn England, *Garrick's Jubilee* (Ohio State University Press, 1964),

give the best accounts of the Jubilee.

14. England, p. 45. See Winton Dean's *Handel's Dramatic Oratorios and Masques* for a fine study of eighteenth-century attitudes toward the oratorio.

15. Deelman, p. 192. He is paraphrasing from a short play, *Garrick's Vagary.*

16. Carola Oman, *David Garrick* (London, 1958), pp. 293–294.

17. *Shakespeare's Garland. Being a Collection of New Songs . . . Performed at the Jubilee. . . .* (London: T. Becket, 1769), p. 18. Also, *The London Chronicle,* XXVI (7–9 September 1769), #1987. Bickerstaff is named as one of the song writers, along with "Mr. GARRICK and others."

18. James Boswell, *Boswell in Search of a Wife 1766–1769,* ed. Frank Brady and Frederick Pottle (New York, 1956), pp. 317–318. The reference is taken from the manuscript of Boswell's *Life of Johnson.*

19. Isaac Bickerstaff, *He Wou'd if he Cou'd, or An Old Fool Worse Than Any* (London: Griffin, 1771), p. 16.

Chapter 11

1. ALS, "Bickerstaff to unnamed correspondent," Garrick Club. *David Garrick, A Memorial Illustrative of His Life. . . .* Collected by Henry Irving (London, nd), III, #207. The recipient was Garrick; see Bickerstaff's Preface where he echoes the opening of this letter, "When this Comedy was put into Mr. Garrick's hands. . . ." Although someone has pencilled "1768" on this letter, 1770 is a more logical date. Bickerstaff made use of a French translation of the comedy by Linguet to whom he referred in his Preface. Linguet's translation was dated as 1769 by Bickerstaff and the *Journal Encyclopédique* (in its review of *'Tis Well it's No Worse,* February, 1771). I have seen only a 1770 edition: Théâtre Espagnol, Tome II, La Cloison (À Paris: Chez De Hansy, le jeune, Libraire, 1770). 1769 is unlikely as a date; what with Garrick preparing for the Shakespeare Jubilee the timing would be pretty awkward. The similarity of language in the letter and the Preface argues a short time between the two.

2. *The European Magazine, and London Review,* XXV (March, 1794), "Table Talk: Paul Hiffernan," 184. Forster quotes the story and Kenrick's verses in his *Goldsmith,* and attributes the magazine article to William Cooke. It also appears with variations in Cooke's *Foote,* and Richard Ryan's *Poetry and Poets,* 1826.

3. ALS, "Griffin to Garrick," Forster Collection (F. 48. F. 43. ms #9).

4. With the exception of the Old Nun, who was dropped after the second performance, and the changes in name, Bickerstaff's characters correspond to Calderon's:

Bickerstaff:	*Calderon:*
Don Guzman	Don Diego
Don Carlos	Don Cesar
Don Pedro	Don Felix
Don Ferdinand	Don Juan
Lazarillo	Castaño
Muskato	Mosquito
Octavio	Octavio
Marcella	Lisarda
Aurora	Celia
Leonarda	Inez
Beatrice	Beatriz

See *Select Plays of Calderon,* ed. Norman Maccoll, M.A. (London, 1888), *El Escondido y la Tapada* (pp. 389–497).

5. Isaac Bickerstaff, *'Tis Well it's No Worse* (London: W. Griffin, 1770), Preface.

6. *Oxford Magazine,* V (December, 1770), 226. Of its kind, superb, this review will be quoted at length.

7. As above, p. 227.

8. Percivale Stockdale, *The Poet* (London, 1773), p. 16. In the second edition, Stockdale identified himself as the poet.

9. John P. Kemble, *The Pannel* (London, 1789), Preface.

10. *The Analytical Review, or History of Literature,* IV (May–August, 1789), May, Article IX, 37. The "Expostulation" was written before 1786 because it appears in a commonplace book compiled by John Baynes (d. 1787) at that date (Osborn Collection, Box 77 #15).

11. Isaac Bickerstaff, *Proposals for Printing, By Subscription, Fables, Philosophical and Moral, In Verse* (London: William Griffin, 1771, "Where Subscriptions are taken in"). The only known copies are two in the Bodleian Library.

12. *The London Chronicle,* "Bickerstaff's Fables," XXXI (27–30 June), 620. The first excerpt appeared in XXXI (9–12 May 1772), 449–450. Two fables actually by Bickerstaff, *The Cuckow Traveler* and *The Ant and the Grasshopper,* were reprinted respectively by the *Universal Magazine of Knowledge and Pleasure,* XLIII (December 1768), 323; and *The Scots* Magazine, XXXI (February 1769), 100.

13. Marryat's authorship was confirmed in an "Account of the Author's Life," in Thomas Marryat, *Therapeutics* (Bristol, 1805); and in *The Poets of Ireland,* ed. David J. O'Donoghue (London, 1892–1893), p. 20. O'Donoghue also wrote an article on Bickerstaff as part of a series of articles on Irish literature which appeared in the *Evening Telegraph* (date unknown), and which is included as Vol. II of three volumes which were presented to Harvard Library in 1919. The series was called *Irish Humorists. Sentimental Fables* carried Marryat's name on the 3rd edition (Bristol, 1791).

14. XII, #3655, Friday, 13 September 1771. The other newspapers were *The St. James Chronicle, Middlesex Journal, General Evening Post,* and *Bingley's Journal.*

15. Any relation to the Donat O'Callaghan, the elderly Irishman who was associated with Isabella Jones, the "older woman" in Keats's life?

16. The date on which J. Johnston printed Bickerstaff's *A Select Collection* is not known; the British Museum suggested 1770 as a convenient date because, according to H. E. Crossman of the Museum, Johnston had his music shop on York Street, Covent Garden, from the end of 1768 until August 1772; since the collection was printed there, it must have been done between 1768 and 1772. But the Winter 1771–1772 or Spring 1772 seems more plausible than other dates; in the first place, Bickerstaff had spent the summer of 1771 on the continent collecting music; secondly, because he had no new play on the boards during the Autumn 1771 season, he might well have wished to earn some money. Finally, considering the elaborateness of the work, only a calamity would have prevented it from being widely circulated. Bickerstaff's "crime" was such a calamity. Had the work been published earlier than the Winter 1771–1772, then some mention of it would appear in Bickerstaff's correspondence or in the newspapers; there is no mention. For these reasons, the most likely dates are Winter 1771–1772, or Spring 1772.

17. E. R. Dibdin, *A Charles Dibdin Bibliography* (Liverpool, 1937), p. 17. "Doctor Ballardo. A piece altered from Molière, by Isaac Bickerstaff in this year (1770). It was not produced or printed however. Charles Dibdin composed the music." *The London Magazine,* XXXIX (December 1770), 603–604, also refers to

this piece, as did Charles Dibdin, *Life,* I, 81. Dibdin received a bond for £50 for the music.

18. "Poor Rate of the Parish of St. Mary le Strand for the 4th Quarter in the year 1769 and the first quarter for the year 1770." Duchy of Lancaster, Parish of Mary le Strand: Dutchy Lane.

19. *A Plan of . . . the Savoy in the Strand,* James Wood and William Pond (London, November 1770), a map showing the residents, houses and grounds as of 15 November 1770, PRO, London.

20. Foot, p. 345. Bickerstaff's payment for *The Plain Dealer* has already been mentioned.

21. Forster Collection, F.48. F.30 #26, "Account for June 18, 1776: 'Mr. Bickerstaff owes on his Note dated 24 June 1769 £200.'"

22. Forster Collection, Copy, ALS, Bickerstaff to Garrick.

23. ALS, Bickerstaff to Garrick, Folger Library (W.b. 492), undated except for "Wednesday Noon." Copy in Forster Collection.

24. Copy of a letter, undated except for "Wednesday evening". Forster Collection.

25. *Memoirs of Samuel Foote* (London, 1805), II, 123.

26. Reprinted in *Miscellanies in Prose and Verse,* Thomas Chatterton (London, 1778), *Memoirs of a Sad-Dog,* pp. 184–208.

Chapter 12

1. Stanley Thomas Williams, *Richard Cumberland, His Life and Works* (New Haven, 1917), p. 41, quoting from *The Whitehall Evening Post,* 7 January 1772.

2. Anon., *Letters Concerning the Present State of England* (London: J. Almon, 1772), p. 317.

3. William Lawrence, "An Old English Music Handkerchief," *Musical Quarterly,* III (October 1917), #4, 503–508.

4. *The Collected Letters of Oliver Goldsmith,* ed. Katharine C. Balderston (Cambridge, 1928), pp. 110–111.

5. The *Daily Advertiser,* 12902, Thursday, April 30; 12903, Friday, 1 May 1772.

6. *St. James Chronicle,* 1747, Thursday, 30 April to Saturday, 2 May 1772. *Lloyd's Evening Post,* 2315, 2 May 1772.

7. Quoted in a letter to this writer by Barry Hillman.

8. Original letter in Forster Collection, Victoria and Albert Museum. The French mistakes are Bickerstaff's. Corrected copy in Boaden, I, 472–473. A translation:

> "Sir, if your heart still preserves the slightest trace of that regard which you have formerly avowed for one who is today the most wretched man on earth; I implore you to make this known to me by two or three words addressed to Mr. Burrows, in care of Mr. Vogius the Younger, Bookseller, beside the Cathedral in Saint Malo, Brittany, France.
>
> "Pierced by the bitterest grief which can afflict the heart, please believe Sir that I have no demand to make upon your goodness except only your permission to write to you at greater length; if you are not disposed to grant me this, imagine that this letter comes from a dead man, to a living, toss it in the fire, and think no more of it. I have not the least doubt, Sir, that my sorrow will carry me to the grave, but by a road, perhaps longer than I could wish, and that reflection is a great addition to my troubles—for, having lost my friends, my hopes; fallen, exiled, and abandoned to despair as I am, life is an almost insupportable burden: I was far from imagining that the last time I entered your study, would be the last time in my life that I should enter it, and that I should never again see its Master! but this is a reflection which I avoid as much as possible.
>
> I beg you, Sir, to tell no one that I have written to you, and above all to

> remain silent about the whereabouts of my retreat, which is a matter of the greatest importance to me. As I have said already, if you will not grant me the consolation of a letter burn this one and remain as though it had never fallen into your hands; if on the other hand your compassion for a miserable creature prevails, no one will know that you have shown him such kindness. God keep you, my very dear, and very honored sir, and crown you and yours with all the happiness in the world, if indeed you could have any more to wish for. I should like to say much more, but I know not what; I am very much afraid that you will have trouble deciphering my bad French.

The St. Malo archives were destroyed in World War II. A search in Rennes has uncovered a bookseller in St. Malo in 1772 named Louis Hovius, and a printer named Valais to whom Hovius referred in a letter—but no Vogius, and no Bickerstaff/Burrows. Weighed against Garrick's refusal to answer this letter must be the many instances of his generosity to Bickerstaff, but indeed how much more expensive than money is humanity?

9. Hesther Lynch Piozzi, *Anecdotes of Samuel Johnson,* ed. S. C. Roberts (Cambridge, 1932), p. 110.

10. This account is a summary of William Kenrick's *A Letter to David Garrick, Esq.* (London, 1772). This 24-page letter is Kenrick's version of the events which led up to *Love in the Suds.* Containing letters from Garrick and from Kenrick, it is the fullest account of the Kenrick-Garrick feud available. Biased though it is, one can accept Kenrick's word on many factual items. In an odd sort of way, Kenrick followed his own rules in all of his many squabbles; he enjoyed a good fight, and though his premises were false, he kept logically true to them.

11. See Boaden, II, 341, and *Letters,* II, #694, 807.

12. Index card by David M. Little, one of the first editors of Garrick's *Letters,* Harvard Theatre Collection. In the published *Letters,* it is referred to in II, 807, where Puttick & Simpson, Catalogue, 1862, is cited as the source of the summary. It was a letter of three pages, quarto. The *Letters* editors believe that Garrick, not Foote, was going to beat Kenrick. Grammatically this is quite possible, but in an article to be quoted later in the *Morning Chronicle* for 25 July 1772, Foote—somewhat allusively—is credited with kicking Kenrick. On the basis that one good kick deserves another, we've given the nod to Foote (for wishing to give the boot to Kenrick).

13. Nyky—or Nickin, Nikey or Nizey; "A soft simple fellow; also a diminutive of Isaac." Captain Francis Grose, *A Classical Dictionary of the Vulgar Tongue,* ed. by Eric Partridge (New York, 1963), p. 243.

14. Lucyle Werkmeister, *The London Daily Press* 1772–1792 (Lincoln, Nebraska, 1963), p. 95.

15. Charles Mackay, *Through the Long Day* (London, 1887), I, 66.

16. In *A Whipping for the Welch Parson* (London, 1773), p. 2, Kenrick named the author as "—Shirley." Possibly William Shirley? Kenrick did not write the poem: he had already written *Love in the Suds* by 18 June, and the poem is too poor to be Kenrick's. The Reverend William Jackson edited the *Public Ledger* at this time (Werkmeister, p. 409); he was morally capable of writing the poem; see below, #17.

17. Forster Collection, Volume 9, #9. Lord Tilney, according to contemporary gossip, was homosexual: Anon. *Garrick's Jests, or Genius in High Glee* (London, nd), contains an anecdote at Tilney's expense. See *Sodom and Onan* (London, 1776) written by the disgusting Reverend William Jackson.

18. Photo-copy of two pages in Garrick's hand which were sold at Sotheby's, 17 December 1935. Harvard Theatre Collection has the copy, the original has

not been found. The fragment has not been previously published, nor have the first five verses been found.

19. Cecil J. L. Price, *"A Man of Genius, and a Welch Man"* (Swansea, 1963), p. 19. Prof. Price cites as his source, BM, Add. MS. 33230, ff. 34–36.

20. Public Record Office, London: KB 21/40. Affidavits from King's Court Bench (Trinity, 1772), "Yet Tuesday next after Three Weeks from the day of Holy Trinity in the twelfth year of King George the Third." Affidavits, 1772–1774, No. 19.

21. The original, in the Forster Collection, is postmarked from Vienne, and will be quoted in full in Chapter Thirteen. The *Morning Post* was not begun until 2 November 1772 (Werkmeister, p. 409); Bickerstaff probably meant the *Morning Chronicle*.

22. References are to the 5th edition (London: J. Wheble, 1772), "With Annotations and an Appendix" which included correspondence first printed in the *Morning Chronicle* and the poetic duel between Benedict (Joseph Reed) and Beatrice (Kenrick). "In the suds; in trouble, in a disagreeable situation, or involved in some difficulty" (Grose, ed. Partridge, p. 330).

23. Dibdin named Bickerstaff as the writer of *The Brickdust-man,* in his *Musical Tour,* reprinted in the *Harmonicon,* I, part 1, No. XVII, May, 1824, 88. Brickdust was an abrasive used by housewives for scouring.

24. Copy in Folger Library.

25. Forster, *Goldsmith* (London, 1848), p. 491.

26. Kenrick, *A Whipping for the Welch Parson* (London, 1773), p. 20.

27. Kenrick, as above, p. 20.

28. "Ariel," *The Kenrickad* (London: W. Griffin, 1772).

29. *Letters,* II, 732, 844–845, To Peter Fountain, Friday [January 8? 1773]. When Garrick heard about the poem "last summer . . . I sent to him to beg that he would print Nothing relative to my quarrel with Dr. K—— he did so, & I hop'd that I had put a Stop to it. . . . I beg that You will convince our good Friend Mr. Lloyd that I have not, nor will I concern Myself in any dirty business of that kind——."

30. Kenrick, *A Whipping,* p. 20.

31. William Heard, *The Tryal of Dramatic Genius* (London, 1773), pp. 15–17.

32. William Jackson, *Sodom and Onan* (London, 1776), p. 20. The reverend published under the name of Humphrey Nettle.

33. William Freeman, *Oliver Goldsmith* (London, 1951), p. 205.

34. *Cassell's Encyclopaedia of Literature,* ed. by S. H. Steinberg (London, 1953), I, 681, "R. M. H." identified in the list of contributors as Ruby Margaret Hobling, B.A. Oxon.

Chapter 13

1. ALS, 21 November 1774, from Paris, "Mrs. J. Henrietta Pye to David Garrick," Folger Library. A search by Prof. H. Isnard, *Université D'Aix-Marseille,* has found no play ascribed to Bickerstaff. A search by this writer at the *Bibliotheque* d'Arsenal has proved equally fruitless.

2. Isaac Bickerstaff, *The Sultan; or a Peep into the Seraglio* (London: C. Dilly, 1787). This edition was registered at Stationer's Hall on 17 February 1787, "Property of C. Dilly (for editor) . . . A Farce, in two Acts. By Isaac Bickerstaffe." The first edition was published in 1780 by M. Mills, Dublin.

3. *The Monthly Mirror,* IV, 2nd ed. (London, 1797), November, 261–262.

4. Extra-Illustrated edition of *Actors and Actresses,* ed. Brander Matthews and Laurence Dutton, Vol. I, no. 7 (Foote, Sheridan, Mossop, Abington), Harvard Theatre Collection. Letter dated from "Halfmoon Street, June 14, 1774." The way Mrs. Abington wrote about "the author," one could believe that someone other than Bickerstaff wrote *The Sultan;* but considering the lingering odor around Bickerstaff's reputation, why would anyone jeopardize the success of *The Sultan* by allowing the public to be deceived about its author? When it was publicly suggested that Hugh Kelly wrote it, Mrs. Abington denied it, but refused to name the real author.

5. *Letters,* III, #847, 942–943, 18 June 1774.

6. *Théâtre De M. Favart* (Paris, 1763), IV, *"Soliman Sécond," Comédie en trois Actes, en Vers; Representée pour la première fois par les Comédiens Ordinaires du Roi, le 9 Avril 1761.*

7. Alfred Iacuzzi, *The European Vogue of Favart* (New York, 1932), pp. 94–95. Willard Austin Kinne, *Revivals and Importations of French Comedies in England, 1749–1800* (New York, 1939), p. 139. Rene Guiet, "An English Imitator of Favart: Isaac Bickerstaffe. Plagiarism in *The Sultan,"* MLN, XXXVIII (January, 1923), 54–56.

8. Larpent ms: LA 397, p. 28.

9. Advertisement to the 1787 edition of *The Sultan.*

10. *The Literary Gazette; and Journal of Belles Lettres, Arts, Sciences, &c.* (London, Saturday, 13 December 1828), #621, p. 796.

11. Edward J. Dent, *Mozart's Operas,* 2nd ed. (London, 1947), p. 71.

12. Werkmeister, p. 29.

13. Information graciously supplied by Jean Lecutiez, at the Bibliotheque de la Ville de Vienne

14. Unidentified newspaper clippings, James Winston Collection, Y.d.25(2), Folger Library. Research in Milan has not come up with a Mr. Burrows, a Mr. Bickerstaff or a Mr. Commandoni.

15. PRO, London. "Half-Pay Cash Books," Adm. 96/88. There is no record of Bickerstaff drawing his pension in "Half-Pay Cash Books—Royal Marines," 1799–1808, Adm. 96/90–91. According to M. Godfrey at the PRO, "It is thought that when an Officer failed to collect his half-pay, and no other news of him was received, his name would continue to appear in the *Army Lists* for a certain period, possibly 7–10 years, when the name was then removed, without explanation" (Letter, 30 November 1962). But the *Army Lists* carried Bickerstaff's name for 21 years (1787–1808) after his last recorded payment. He was reported alive in London in 1808.

16. British Museum, Add ms. 31,972.

17. Mrs. Cornwell Barron-Wilson [Margaret Harries], *Memoirs of Miss Mellon Afterwards Duchess of St. Albans,* new edition (London, 1886), I, 78–79.

18. New Series, Vol. I (15 November 1824 to 17 January 1825), Friday, 10 December 1824, 81. Review of the 9 December performance in Edinburgh.

19. Werkmeister, p. 216. (In her *The London Daily Press 1772–1792.*)

20. Lucyle Werkmeister, *A Newspaper History of England, 1792–1793* (Lincoln, Nebraska, 1967), p. 317.

21. John Warburton, Reverend James J. Whitelaw, Reverend Robert Walsh, *History of the City of Dublin . . . To Which are Added Biographical Notices* of Eminent Men. . . . (London, 1818), II, 1203–1204.

22. W. Davenport Adams, *A Dictionary of the Drama,* A–G (Philadelphia, 1904), I, 157.

BIBLIOGRAPHY

Adams, W. Davenport. *A Dictionary of the Drama, A–G.* Philadelphia, 1904.

Addenda to Catalogues of Old English Plays. London, n.d. [1909].

Addison, Joseph, Richard Steele, and others. *The Spectator,* ed. G. Gregory Smith. 8 vols. New York, 1897.

Aikin, John. *Essays on Song-Writing: With a Collection of Such English Songs as are Most Eminent for Poetical Merit.* London, 1772.

Analytical Review, or History of Literature, IV. London, 1789.

Anderson, W. R. "Round about Radio," *The Musical Times,* XCI (September, 1950), 346–347.

Anthologia Hibernica, I. Dublin, May, 1793.

"Ariel," *The Kenrickad.* A Poem. London, 1772.

Austen, Jane. *Jane Austen's Letters to Her Sister Cassandra and Others,* Collected and ed. R. W. Chapman. 2nd ed. London, 1952.

Baker, David E. *Biographia Dramatica; or, A Companion to the Playhouse.* A new edition. 2 vols. London, 1782.

———, Isaac Reed, and Stephen Jones. *Biographia Dramatica. . . .* 3 vols. London, 1812.

Baker, John. *The Diary of John Baker,* ed. Philip C. Yorke. London, 1931.

Baltimore Gazette and Daily Advertiser. Baltimore, Maryland, 1794. [Recorded first performance of *The Spoil'd Child* in the United States.]

Bannister, John. *Memoirs of John Bannister, Comedian,* ed. John Adolphus. 2 vols in one. London, 1838.

Barbeau, A. *Life and Letters at Bath in the XVIIIth Century.* London, 1904.

Barron-Wilson, Mrs. Cornwell. *Memoirs of Miss Mellon Afterwards Duchess of St. Albans.* New edition. 2 vols. London, 1886.

———. *Our Actresses; or Glances at Stage Favourites, Past and Present.* 2 vols. London, 1844.

The Bath Contest. Bath, 1769.

Beaumont, Francis. *The Works of Beaumont and Fletcher,* ed. Rev. Alexander Dyce. 11 vols. London, 1845.

Berger, Arthur V. "The Beggar's Opera, The Burlesque, and Italian Opera," *Music and Letters,* XVII (April 1936), #2. 93–105.

Bewick's Select Fables of Æsop's and Others. Preface by Edwin Pearson. London, n.d.

Bickerstaff, Isaac. *The Absent Man.* London, 1768.

———. "Brickdust-Man and Milkmaid," *London Magazine,* XLI (August 1772), 392–393.

———. *The Captive.* London, 1769.

———. *Daphne and Amintor.* London, 1765.

———. *Doctor Last in His Chariot.* London, 1769.

———. *The Ephesian Matron.* London, 1769.

———. *He Wou'd if He Cou'd; or, An Old Fool Worse than Any.* London, 1771.

———. *The Hypocrite.* London, 1769.

———. *Judith,* A Sacred Drama. 1st ed. London, 1761. 2nd ed. nd [1764].

———. *Leucothoë,* a Dramatic Poem. London, 1756.

———. *Life, Strange Voyages and Uncommon Adventures of Ambrose Gwinett . . . the lame beggar who for a long time swept the way at the Mews-Gate, Charing Cross.* 4th ed. London, nd.

———. *Lionel and Clarissa.* London, 1768.

———. *Love in a Village.* 2nd ed. London, 1763.

———. *Love in a Village.* The Music. I. Walsh, nd [1709].

———. *Love in the City.* 2nd ed. London, 1767.

———. *Maid of the Mill.* London, 1765.

———. *The Padlock.* London, 1768.

———. *The Pannel,* ed. John Kemble. London, 1789.

———. *The Plain Dealer* (Wycherley), ed. Isaac Bickerstaff. London, 1766.

———. *Proposals for Printing . . . Fables.* London, 1771.

———. *The Recruiting Serjeant.* London, 1770.

———. *The Romp,* ed. Lloyd [?]. London, 1786.

———. *The Royal Garland.* London, 1768.

———. *School for Fathers.* London, 1781.

———. *A Select Collection of Vocal Music Serious and Comic . . .,* ed. Isaac Bickerstaff. London, nd [1771–1772?]

———. *The Spoil'd Child.* Dublin, 1792.

———. *Thomas and Sally.* London, 1761.

———. *'Tis Well It's No Worse.* London, 1770.

Bingley's Weekly Journal: or, The Universal Gazette. London, 1770–1771.

A Biographical Dictionary of the Living Authors of Great Britain and Ireland. London, 1816.

Boaden, James. *The Life of Mrs. Dorothy Jordan.* 2 vols. London, 1831.

Boas, Frederick S. *An Introduction to Eighteenth Century Drama, 1700–1800.* London, 1953.

Boswell, James. *Boswell in Search of a Wife 1766–1769,* ed. Frank Brady and Frederick A. Pottle. New York, 1956.

Brooke, Mrs. Frances. *The Excursion.* 2 vols. London, 1777.

Burgoyne, John. *The Lord of the Manor.* London, 1781.

Burney, Charles. *A General History of Music from the Earliest Ages to the Present Period* (1789), ed. Frank Mercer. 2 vols. New York, 1957.

Burney, Fanny. *Diary and Letters of Madame D'Arblay* (1778–1840), ed. Charlotte Barrett. 6 vols. London, 1905.

Burnim, Kalman. *David Garrick Director.* Pittsburgh, 1961.

Busby, Thomas. *History of Music.* 2 vols. London, 1819.

Calderon, Pedro de la Barca. *Select Plays,* ed. Norman Maccoll. London, 1888.

Caledonian Mercury. Edinburgh, 1782 ff.

Campbell, Archibald. *The Sale of Authors.* London, 1767.

Castilhon, Jean Louis. *Candide Anglois, ou, Avantures tragi-comiques D'Amb. Gwinett avant et dans ses voyages aux deux Indes.* 2 vols. Francfort et Leipzig, 1771.

Catalogue of the Valuable Library and Collection of . . . William Wright, Esq. London, 1899.

Cesari, Augusto. *Come Pervenne E. Rimase in Italia La Matrona D'Efeso.* Bologna, 1890.

Chappell, W. *Popular Music of the Olden Time.* 2 vols. London, nd.

Chatterton, Thomas. *Miscellanies in Prose and Verse.* London, 1778.

Children of Apollo. London, 1794.

Churchill, Charles. *Poems,* ed. James Laver. 2 vols. London, 1933.

Cibber, Colley, Esq. *The Dramatic Works.* 5 vols. London, 1736–1754.

Collection of Songs, Chiefly Such as are Eminent for Poetical Merit. London, 1782.

Colman, George, *The Dramatick Works of George Colman.* 4 vols. London, 1777.

[Combe, William]. *Sanitas, Daughter of Aesculapius.* London, 1772.

Cooke, William. *Memoirs of Samuel Foote.* 2 vols. London, 1805.

Court Miscellany, or Gentleman & Lady's New Magazine, IV. London, 1768.

"Covent Garden Theatre," British Museum Add. ms. 33,218. "Depositions for the Plaintiffs in Harris vs. Colman, 1770."

Critical Review. London, 1767ff.

Croxall, Samuel, ed. *A Select Collection of Novels.* London, 1720.

Cumberland, Richard. *The Choleric Man.* London, 1793.

———. ed. *London Review.* London, 1809.

———. *Memoirs of Richard Cumberland.* 2 vols. London, 1806.
———. *Summer's Tale.* London, 1765.

Daily Advertiser. London, 1772.
Davies, Thomas. *Memoirs of the Life of David Garrick, Esq.* 2 vols, 3rd. ed. London, 1781. 4th ed. London, 1784.
Dean, Winton. "Review of Love in a Village," *Opera,* III (August 1952). #9, 466–469.
———. *Handel's Dramatic Oratorios and Masques.* London, 1959.
Deelman, Christian. *The Great Shakespeare Jubilee.* New York, 1964.
Dent, Edward J. *Mozart's Operas.* 2nd ed. London, 1947.
Dibdin, Charles. "An Account of Mr. Charles Dibdin's Theatrical Pieces," *The Harmonicon, A Journal of Music,* I, Part 1 (May 1824), 87–90.
———. *The By-Stander; or Universal Weekly Expositor.* London, 1790.
———. *Complete History of the Stage.* 5 vols. London, nd [1800].
———. *The Musical Tour of Mr. Dibdin.* Sheffield, 1788.
———. *The Padlock* [Music]. London, 1768.
———. *Professional Life of Mr. Dibdin.* 4 vols. London, 1803.
Dibdin, Edward Rimbault. *A Charles Dibdin Bibliography.* Liverpool, 1937.
Dibdin, Thomas. *The Reminiscences of Thomas Dibdin.* 2 vols. London, 1827.
Dickens, Charles. *The Plays and Poems,* ed. Richard Herne Shepherd. 2 vols. London, 1885.
Diprose, John. *Some Account of the Parish of Saint Clement Danes (Westminster) Past and Present.* 2 vols. I, London, 1868. II, London, 1876.
Dryden, John. *Dryden, The Dramatic Works,* ed. Montague Summers. 6 vols. London, 1932.
Dunbar, Howard Hunter. *The Dramatic Career of Arthur Murphy.* New York, 1946.

Edinburgh Dramatic Review, III. Edinburgh, 1825.
England, Martha Winburn. *Garrick's Jubilee.* Ohio State University Press, 1964.
Eitner, Robert, ed. *Biographisch-Bibliographisches Quellen-Lexikon der Musiker und Musikgelehrten. . . .* 10 vols. Leipzig, 1900–1904.
Emery, John Pike. *Arthur Murphy.* Philadelphia, 1946.
Essay on the Pre-Eminence of Comic Genius, An: with Observations on the Several Characters Mrs. Jordan has Appeared in. London, 1786.
The European Magazine, and London Review. Vols. XIV–XXV. London, 1788–1795.
Evans, Charles, and Clifford K. Shipton. *American Bibliography.* New York, 1910–1955.
Everard, Edward Cape. *Memoirs of an Unfortunate Son of Thespis.* Edinburgh, 1818.

Faulkner's Journal. Dublin, 1771.

Favart, C. M. *Théâtre de M. Favart.* Vol. IV. Paris, 1763.

Flood, W. H. Grattan. "Dr. Arne's Visits to Dublin," *The Musical Antiquary,* I (July, 1910), 215–233.

———. "Letter," *The Musical Times,* LXI (August 1920), 559.

Foot, Jesse. *The Life of Arthur Murphy, Esq.* London, 1811.

Foote's Prologue Detected; With a Miniature Prose Epilogue of His Manner in Speaking it, by Philo-Technicus Miso-mimides. London, 1770.

Forster, John. *Life and Adventures of Oliver Goldsmith.* London, 1848.

The Freeholder's Magazine, or Monthly Chronicle of Liberty. II–III, London, 1770.

Freeman, William. *Oliver Goldsmith.* London, 1951.

Fuller-Maitland, J. A. ed. *Grove's Dictionary of Music and Musicians.* 5 vols. Philadelphia, 1916.

Gagey, Edmond McAdoo. *Ballad Opera.* New York, 1937.

Garrick, David. "The Garrick Manuscripts," Forster Collection, Victoria and Albert Museum, London. (41 vols. of original correspondence).

———. *Letters of David Garrick.* ed. David M. Little, George M. Kahrl. Associate ed. Phoebe deK. Wilson. 3 vols. Cambridge, Mass., 1963.

———. *The Private Correspondence of David Garrick with the most celebrated persons of his time.* ed. James Boaden. 2 vols. London, 1832.

Garrick's Jests or Genius in High Glee. London, nd.

Gay, John. *The Beggar's Opera, The Plays of John Gay.* 2 vols. London, nd.

———. *The Poetical Works.* 2 vols. Boston, nd.

General Evening Post. London, 1772.

General Magazine and Impartial Review. I, 1787 ff.

Genest, Reverend John. *Some Account of the English Stage, From the Restoration in 1660 to 1830.* 10 vols. Bath, 1832.

Gentleman, Francis. *The Dramatic Censor; or, Critical Companion.* 2 vols. London, 1770.

———. ["Nicholas Nipclose"]. *The Theatres. A Poetical Dissection.* London, 1772.

Gentleman's and London Magazine, XXXV. Dublin, 1765.

Gentleman's Magazine. 1762 ff.

Gilliland, Thomas. *The Dramatic Mirror.* 2 vols. London, 1808.

Goldsmith, Oliver. *The Collected Letters,* ed. Katharine C. Balderston. Cambridge, 1928.

Gordon, Pryse L. *Personal Memoirs.* London, 1830.

Grattan, Henry. *Memoirs of the Life and Times of the Rt. Hon. Henry Grattan,* ed. Henry Grattan, Esq., MP. 5 vols. new ed. London, 1849.

Gray, Charles Harold. *Theatrical Criticism in London to 1795.* New York, 1931.

Grose, Captain Francis. *A Classical Dictionary of the Vulgar Tongue,* ed. Eric Partridge. New York, 1963.

Guiet, Rene. "An English Imitator of Favart: Isaac Bickerstaff. Plagiarism in *The Sultan,*" Modern Language Notes, XXXVIII (January, 1923), 54–56.

Hawkesworth, John, ed. *The Adventurer,* in *The British Essayist,* XXI. Boston, 1855.

Hazlitt, William. Prefatory Remarks, *The New English Drama,* I, *The Hypocrite.* London, 1818.

———. *The Complete Works of William Hazlitt,* ed. P. P. Howe. 18 vols. London, 1933.

[Heard, William]. *The Tryal of Dramatic Genius.* A Poem. London, 1773.

The Hibernian Magazine, or, Compendium of Entertaining Knowledge. Dublin, 1771–1772.

Hitchcock, Robert. *An Historical View of the Irish Stage; From the Earliest Period Down to the Close of the Season, 1788.* 2 vols. Dublin, vol. I, 1788; vol. II, 1794.

Hogarth, George. *Memoirs of the Opera in Italy, France, Germany & England.* A new edition of the *Musical Drama.* 2 vols. London, 1851.

Holcroft, Thomas. *The Life of Thomas Holcroft,* ed. William Hazlitt, newly edited with introduction and notes by Elbridge Colby. 2 vols. London, 1925.

Hughes, Rev. S. C. *The Pre-Victorian Drama in Dublin.* Dublin, 1904.

Iacuzzi, Alfred. *The European Vogue of Favart.* New York, 1932.

Illustrated London News. London, 1868.

Irving, Henry. *David Garrick. A Memorial Illustrative of his Life.* The Garrick Club, London.

[Jackson, William]. "Humphrey Nettle." *Sodom and Onan.* London, 1776.

Jerrold, Clare. *The Story of Dorothy Jordan.* London, 1914.

Jerrold, Douglas. *Ambrose Gwinett,* a seaside Story. Cumberland's Minor Theatre, #67. London, nd.

Johnson, Allen, ed. *Dictionary of American Biography.* Vol. II. New York, 1929.

Johnson, Charles. *The Village Opera.* London, 1729.

Johnson, Samuel. *A Dictionary of the English Language.* 10th ed. 2 vols. London, 1810.

Journal Encyclopédique, 1756–1770. Liège et Bouillon.

Kavanagh, Peter. *The Irish Theatre.* Tralee, 1946.

Kelly, Hugh. *The Babler.* 2 vols. London, 1767.

———. *Thespis.* Book the Second. London, 1767.

Kemble, John P. *The Plain Dealer,* with Alterations. London, 1796, 1815.

———. "Private Memoranda Books [ms]." British Museum, Add. ms. 31,972.

Kenrick, William. *A Letter to David Garrick.* London, 1772.

———. *Love in the Suds;* a Town Eclogue. 5th ed. With Annotations and Appendix, including A Letter to David Garrick, Esq. occasioned by his having moved the Court of King's Bench. . . . London, 1772.

[———]. *The Spleen: or, The Offspring of Folly.* "John Rubrick." London, 1776.

[———]. *A Whipping for the Welch Parson.* "Scriblerius Flagellarius." London, 1773.

Kinne, Willard Austin. *Revivals and Importations of French Comedies in England, 1749–1800.* New York, 1939.

Knight, Joseph. *David Garrick.* London, 1894.

Lamb, Charles. *The Dramatic Essays,* ed. Brander Matthews. New York, 1891.

Langley, Hubert. *Doctor Arne.* Cambridge, 1938.

Lawrence, William J. "An Old English Music Handkerchief," *Musical Quarterly,* III (October, 1917), 503–508.

———. "Early Irish Ballad Opera and Comic Opera," *Musical Quarterly,* VIII (July 1922), 398–399.

———. "The Early Career of Mrs. Jordan," *New York Dramatic Mirror* (9 December 1905) included in Harvard Theatre Collection Extra-Illustrated ed. *Actors and Actresses,* ed. Brander Matthews and Laurence Hutton, II, #6, nd.

Lee, Nathaniel. *Theodosius; or, The Force of Love.* London, 1793.

Letters Concerning the Present State of England. London, 1772.

Liber Munerum Publicorum Hiberniae, or The Establishments of Ireland. The Report of Rowley Lascelles of the Middle Temple. London, 1852.

Linguet, Simon Nicolas Henri (translator). *La Cloison, Théâtre Espagnol,* II. Paris, 1770.

List of the General and Field Officers as they Rank in the Army. . . . London, 1754–1809.

The Literary Gazette [*London*]*; and Journal of Belles Lettres, Arts, Sciences. . . .* London, 1828.

Lloyd, Evan, M.A. *An Epistle to David Garrick, Esq.* London, 1773.

Lloyd's Evening Post, and British Chronicle. London, 1761 ff.

Lodge, John. *The Peerage of Ireland.* 4 vols. London, 1754.

———. *The Peerage of Ireland, or, A Genealogical History of the Present Nobility of that Kingdom.* Enlarged by Mervyn Archdall. 7 vols. Dublin, 1789.

Loewenberg, Alfred. *Annals of Opera 1597–1940.* 2nd ed., revised and corrected. 2 vols. Geneva, 1955.

London Chronicle, or Universal Evening Post. 1760 ff.

London Magazine. 1760 ff.

Lowe, Robert W. *A Bibliographical Account of English Theatre Literature.* London, 1888.

Lynch, James J. *Box Pit and Gallery, Stage and Society in Johnson's London.* Berkeley, 1953.

Mackay, Dr. Charles. *Through the Long Day, or, Memorials of a Literary Life During Half a Century.* 2 vols. London, 1887.

MacMillan, Dougald. *Catalogue of the Larpent Plays in the Huntington Library.* San Marino, California, 1939.

———. *Drury Lane Calendar* 1747–1776. London, 1938.

Macmillan, Ethel. "The Plays of Isaac Bickerstaff in America," *PQ,* V (January, 1926), 58–70.

Macqueen-Pope, W. *Pillars of Drury Lane.* London, 1955.

Malcolm, James Peller, FSA. *Anecdotes of the Manners and Customs of London During the Eighteenth Century.* London, 1808.

Manuel Bibliographique de la Littérature Française Moderne. Nouvelle ed. Paris, 1921.

Marryat, Thomas, MD. *Sentimental Fables, Designed Chiefly for the Use of the Ladies.* 1st ed. Belfast, 1771. 2nd ed. London, 1772. 3rd ed. Bristol, 1791.

Marshall, Herbert, and Mildred Stock. *Ira Aldridge, The Negro Tragedian.* London, 1958.

Matthews, Brander, and Laurence Dutton. *Actors and Actresses, Extra-Illustrated ed.* I, #7 (Foote, Sheridan, Mossop, Abington), Harvard Theatre Collection.

Maxwell, Constantia. *Dublin Under the Georges 1714–1830.* 2nd ed. revised. London, 1956.

Middlesex Journal; or, Chronicle of Liberty [sub-titled *Universal English Post* in 1772]. London, 1771–1772.

Miles, Dudley H. "The Original of *The Non-Juror,*" PMLA, XXIII (1915), 195–214.

Medbourne, Matthew. Tartuffe: or, *The French Puritan.* Rendered into English, with much Addition and Advantage. London, 1707.

Memoirs of the Bedford Coffee-House. By a Genius. 2nd ed., with many corrections. London, 1763.

Molière, J. B. Poquelin de. *Select Comedies of Mr. De Molière.* In French and English. Vols. 4, 5, 8. London, 1732.

———. *The Dramatic Works of Molière*, ed. Henri Van Laun. 6 vols. Edinburgh, 1875.

The Monthly Mirror; Reflecting Men and Manners. London, 1796–1797.

The Monthly Review. "A New Series." London, 1807.

The Monthly Review, or Literary Journal, ed. Ralph Griffiths. London, 1756 ff.

Mooser, A. R. *Operas, Intermezzos, Gallets Cantates, Oratorios Joués En Russie Durant Le XVIIIe Siècle.* 2nd ed. Geneva-Monaco, 1955.

Morning Chronicle. London, 1772–1775.

Morning Herald. London, 1815.

Morning Post, and Daily Advertiser. London, 1775.

Murphy, Arthur. *The Life of David Garrick, Esq.* Dublin, 1801.

"Music Alamode or Bays in Chromatics," Larpent Collection, Huntington Library.

Nangle, Benjamin Christie. *The Monthly Review, First Series, 1749–1789.* London, 1934.

O'Donoghue, David J. *The Poets of Ireland.* London, 1892–1893.

———. "Irish Humorists," A Series of articles which appeared in the *Evening Telegraph,* pasted into three volumes and presented to Harvard University in 1919. Vol. II. Article V. "Derrick and Bickerstaff."

O'Keeffe, John. *Recollections of the Life of John O'Keeffe.* 2 vols. London, 1826.

Oman, Carola. *David Garrick.* London, 1958.

Opie, Peter, and Iona Opie. *Oxford Dictionary of Nursery Rhymes.* London, 1962.

Oxford Magazine. London, 1770 ff.

Page, E. R. *George Colman, the Elder.* New York, 1935.

Pasquin, Anthony. *Poems.* 2 vols. London, 1795.

Peake, Richard Brinsley. *Memoirs of the Colman Family. . . .* 2 vols. London, 1841.

Pedicord, Harry William. *The Theatrical Public in the Time of Garrick.* New York, 1954.

Piozzi, Hesther Lynch. *Anecdotes of Samuel Johnson,* ed. S. C. Roberts. Cambridge, 1932.

Plumptre, James, B.D. *The English Drama Purified.* 3 vols. Cambridge, 1812.

The Poetical Review. A Poem. 3rd ed. with additions. London, nd [1778].

The Political Register. London, 1768.

"Poor Rates of the Parish of St. Mary le Strand . . . 1769–1772." London Public Library, Buckingham Palace Road.

Price, Cecil J. L. *"A Man of Genius, and a Welch Man."* Swansea, Wales, 1963.

Public Advertiser. London, 1766.

Public Ledger, or the Daily Register of Commerce and Intelligence. London, 1767–1772.

Rae, Fraser W. *Sheridan.* 2 vols. London, 1896.

Recantation and Confession of Doctor Kenrick. London, 1772.

Reed, Joseph. "Theatrical Duplicity; or, A Genuine Narrative of the Conduct of David Garrick, Esq. to Joseph Reed on his Tragedy of *Dido.*" Harvard Theatre Collection ms: TS 1253,84.

Registry of Deeds, Dublin, 1755.

Rochedieu, Charles Alfred. *Bibliography of French Translations of English Works, 1700–1800.* Chicago, 1948.

Ryan, Richard. *Poetry and Poets. . . .* London, 1826.

———. *Biographia Hibernica.* 2 vols. London, 1819–1821.

St. Foix, Germain François Poullain de. *Oeûvres Complettes de M. Saint-Foix.* Paris, 1778.

St. James's Chronicle, or The British Evening Post. London, 1762 ff.

Sands, Mollie. *Invitation to Ranelagh 1742–1803.* London, 1946.

Schultz, William Eben. *Gay's Beggar's Opera Its Content History & Influence.* New Haven, 1928.

Shakespeare's Garland. London, 1769.

Shaw, Cuthbert. *The Race.* "Mercurius Spur, Esq; with notes by Faustinus Scriblerus." 2nd ed. London, 1766.

Sichel, Walter. *Sheridan.* 2 vols. London, 1909.

Silburn, Muriel. "An Old English Opera," *The Musical Times,* LXI (August 1920), 485–486.

Smith, Dane Farnsworth. *The Critics in the Audience of the London Theatres.* Albuquerque, New Mexico, 1953.

Smith, John Harrington. *The Gay Couple in Restoration Comedy.* Cambridge, Mass., 1948.

Sonneck, Oscar. *Catalogue of Opera Librettos Printed before 1800.* Library of Congress. 2 vols. Washington, D.C., 1914.

———. *Early Opera in America.* New York, 1915.

Speaight, George. *The History of the English Puppet Theatre.* London, 1955.

Squallini, Seignior. *Man of the Mill.* A New Burlesque Tragic Opera. London, 1765.

Stanhope, Philip Dormer, 4th Earl of Chesterfield. *The Letters of Philip Dormer Stanhope,* ed. Bonamy Dobree. 6 vols. London, 1932.

Steinberg, S. H., ed. *Cassell's Encyclopaedia of Literature.* 2 vols. London, 1953.

Stockdale, Percival. *The Memoirs of the Life and Writings of Percival Stockdale.* London, 1809.

———. *The Poet.* London, 1773.

Stone, George W. Jr. *The London Stage 1660–1800.* Part 4, 1747–1776. Carbondale, Illinois, 1962.

Sturz, Helfrich Peter. *Vermischte Schriften.* Starber am See, 1946.

Sypher, Wylie. *Guinea's Captive Kings: British Anti-Slavery Literature of the XVIIIth Century.* Chapel Hill, North Carolina, 1942.

Terry, Charles Sanford. *John Christian Bach.* 2 vols. London, 1929.

Theatrical Campaign, The, for MDCCLXVI. and MDCCLXVII. London, 1767.

Theatrical Inquisitor, and Monthly Mirror. London, 1816.

Theatrical Monitor. London, 1768.

Theatrical Portraits, Epigramatically Delineated. . . . London, 1775.

Theatrical Register, The: or, A Complete List of Every Performance . . . for . . . 1769. 2 parts. London, 1769.

Theatrical Review; or, Annals of the Drama. London, 1763.

Theatrical Review; or, New Companion to the Play-House. 2 vols. London, 1772.

Thespian Dictionary, or the Dramatic Biography of the Eighteenth Century. London, 1802. 2nd ed. London, 1805.

The Times. London, 1788, 1868, 1887, 1925.

Tobin, J. E. *Eighteenth Century English Literature & its Cultural Background.* New York, 1939.

Toms, Edward (translator). *The Accomplish'd Maid.* London, 1781.

Town and Country Magazine, or Universal Repository. II, London. 1770 ff.

Universal Magazine of Knowledge and Pleasure, The. LXXIV. London, 1784.

Universal Museum, and Complete Magazine. London, 1767 ff.

Victor, Benjamin. *The History of the Theatres of London, From the Year 1760 to the Present Time.* Vol. III. London, 1771.

Walker, H. M. *A History of the Northumberland Fusiliers 1674–1902.* London, 1919.

Walpole, Horace. *Memoirs of the Reign of King George the Third,* ed. Sir Denis D. LeMarchant, re-edited by G. F. Russell Barker. Vol. III. London, 1894.

Warburton, Rev. John, James J. Whitelaw, Rev. Robert Walsh. *History of the City of Dublin . . . To Which are Added Biographical Notices of Eminent Men. . . .* 2 vols. London, 1818.

Werkmeister, Lucyle. *The London Daily Press. 1772–1792.* Lincoln, Nebraska, 1963.

———. *A Newspaper History of England, 1792–1793.* Lincoln, Nebraska, 1967.

Wesley, John, A. M. *The Works,* ed. John Emory. 3d ed. 7 vols. New York, 1856.

Whitefoord, Caleb. Manuscript Papers, British Museum Add. ms. 36,595–596.

Wilkinson, Tate. *The Wandering Patentee.* 4 vols. York, 1795.

Williams, J. M., ed. *The Dramatic Censor; or, Critical and Biographical Illustrations of the British Stage.* For the Year 1811. London, 1812.

Williams, Stanley. *Richard Cumberland.* New Haven, 1917.

Winston, James. Manuscript, Folger Library. T.a. 66.

The World. London, 1790.

Wright, Richardson. *Revels in Jamaica 1682–1838.* New York, 1937.

Wroth, Warwick. *The London Pleasure Gardens of the Eighteenth Century.* London, 1896.

Wyndham, Henry Saxe. *The Annals of Covent Garden Theatre from 1732 to 1897.* 2 vols. London, 1906.

INDEX